THE CAMPAIGNS OF

ALEXANDER

ARRIAN

THE CAMPAIGNS OF

ALEXANDER

TRANSLATED BY
AUBREY DE SÉLINCOURT

*Revised, with a new introduction
and notes by J. R. Hamilton*

DORSET PRESS
New York

This translation first published as
Arrian: The Life of Alexander the Great, 1958
Revised and enlarged edition published 1971

Copyright © the Estate of Aubrey de Sélincourt, 1958
Introduction and Notes copyright © J. R. Hamilton, 1971
All rights reserved

This edition published by Dorset Press,
a division of Marboro Books Corporation,
by arrangement with Penguin Books Ltd.
1986 Dorset Press

Distributed in the United Kingdom by Bibliophile Editions

ISBN 0-88029-079-X
(Formerly ISBN 0-14-044-253-7)

The paper used in this book meets
the minimum requirements of the
American National Standard for
Permanence of Paper for Printed
Library Materials Z39.48 — 1948.

Printed in the United States of America
M 9 8 7 6 5 4 3 2

Contents

From the Translator's Preface

After the end of the Alexandrian age, from early in the second century before Christ, Greek literature rapidly declined, and during the hundred years – say from 50 B.C. to A.D. 50 – when Latin literature was at its height, it had almost petered out. It had had a long run, having been one of the glories of the world for not much less than a thousand years. However, it was not yet finished, and the second century of our era had hardly begun when there was a renaissance of the Greek spirit, and Greek began once again to be used as a literary language – it had, of course, never ceased to be spoken over great tracts of the eastern Roman empire, and educated Romans were as familiar with it as educated Englishmen are with French today. The beginning of no literary movement can be precisely fixed in time, and there were eminent Greek writers, of whom Plutarch was one, in the first century of the Christian era; but it is convenient to date the beginning of the Greek renaissance from the accession of Hadrian to the Imperial throne in A.D. 117. Much of its force and vigour was, indeed, due to this remarkable man, himself something of a poet and steeped in the literature of the ancient world. The patronage he gave to the Greek sophists of the day was responsible for their great and increasing influence, and that influence, in its turn, acted as a spur to the revival of Greek letters. The Emperor Marcus Aurelius, it will be remembered, wrote his famous little book in Greek.

Arrian was very much in the movement, which included such other contemporary writers as Appian, the Greek historian of Rome; Pausanias, whose *Tour of Greece* is a mine of antiquarian information; Galen the writer on medicine; and – in many ways the most readable of them all – the shallow but brilliantly amusing Lucian.

All these writers were employing an idiom very different from the Greek speech current at the time. They were deliberately *archaizing*, consciously imitating, or trying to imitate, the literary language and style of three or four hundred years ago. This could not but affect the quality of their work. All art is largely artifice, and there is no such thing as a 'natural' style, nevertheless we have come to believe, especially of late, that the best literary style is that which best achieves the effect of naturalness, and employs all the power of artifice to subdue the current spoken idiom to its purpose. The Greek writers of the second century thought otherwise; for them, the best literary style had been fixed by the great writers of the classical age, four or five hundred years before their time, and the only way to achieve distinction was to copy their idiom as closely as they could. The only two books we possess of which the language approaches the *koiné*, or contemporary spoken Greek of Syria and Asia Minor, are the New Testament and the records taken by Arrian of the lectures of Epictetus. For centuries scholarship and pedantry, too often the same thing, supposed that the Greek of the New Testament was barbarous and debased – Nietzsche's notorious jibe about God having learnt Greek, and having learnt it so badly, is a case in point. But today most of us are wiser, and the beauty of New Testament Greek and its power of expressing what its users wanted it to express make us wish that the professional literary men, too, of that epoch had taken their language warm from contemporary lips instead of seeking it in the written pages of the past. An instance of the lengths to which this artificiality could go is provided by Arrian himself. In one of his books – the *Indica*, a short piece in which he wrote up Nearchus' account of his voyage from the Indus to the Persian Gulf – he uses, apparently for a change, or simply to show that he could manage it, the Ionic dialect of Herodotus.

This strange convention imposes an almost intolerable burden upon the writers of the period. Lucian alone of them manages to carry it gracefully; the rest, including Arrian, show inevitable signs of strain, as might a modern Englishman who, admiring the coloured, supple, and racy idiom of Elizabethan prose, elected to write historical portraits in the style of Sir Thomas North.

From the point of view of style, therefore, Arrian is not a writer of the first rank. In some ways this is an advantage to his translator; for a translator of the great Greek classics is perpetually humbled by a sense of inadequacy, while a translator of Arrian is warmed from time to time by a flush of self-satisfaction, almost pardonable, as it is borne in upon him that, instead of flattening and dimming his author by what even Shelley, speaking of his beautiful version of Plato's *Symposium*, called 'the grey veil of his own words', he may, here and there, even have improved him. However, Arrian is, in the main, clear and easy to understand; and that is a virtue.

Abbreviations

AJP: American Journal of Philology.

CQ: Classical Quarterly.

Ehrenberg Studies: Ancient Society and Institutions.
                Studies presented to Victor Ehrenberg,
                edited by E. Badian (Oxford, 1966).

Fuller: Major-General J. F. C. Fuller, The General-
                ship of Alexander the Great (London, 1958).

JHS: Journal of Hellenic Studies.

Tarn, Alexander: Sir William Tarn, Alexander the Great,
                2 Vols. (Cambridge, 1948).

Tod: M. N. Tod, A Selection of Greek Historical
                Inscriptions, vol. 2 (Oxford, 1948).

Wilcken, Alexander: Ulrich Wilcken, Alexander the
                Great, translated by G. C. Richards (Lon-
                don, 1932); reprinted with an introduc-
                tion to Alexander studies, notes, and a
                bibliography by Eugene N. Borza (New
                York, 1967).

INTRODUCTION

ARRIAN is remembered today only as the author of *The Campaigns of Alexander* and as the pupil of the philosopher Epictetus who preserved his master's teachings from oblivion. Yet he was a famous man in his own time. *The Campaigns of Alexander* was only one of a number of substantial historical works, while he held the chief magistracies at Rome and Athens and governed for a lengthy period an important frontier province of the Roman empire.

Life of Arrian

Flavius Arrianus Xenophon, to give him his full name,[1] was a Greek, born at Nicomedia, the capital of the Roman province of Bithynia, probably a few years before A.D. 90.[2] His family was well-to-do, and Arrian himself tells us that he held the priesthood of Demeter and Kore in the city. Like other wealthy Greeks, Arrian's father had received the Roman citizenship, evidently from one of the Flavian emperors, most probably Vespasian. Hence Arrian became at birth a Roman citizen with the prospect, if he wished it and possessed the requisite ability, of a career in the imperial service.

1. Philip A. Stadter (*Greek, Roman and Byzantine Studies* 8, 1967, 155ff) has shown that Xenophon was not merely a nickname, but part of the historian's name.

2. Arrian was suffect consul in 129 or 130 A.D., and in his day it was usual for a man to hold the consulship at about the age of 42; see *JRS* 55 (1965), p. 142 n. 30.

Arrian's boyhood and youth were spent in his native city, where he presumably received the customary upper-class Greek education in literature and rhetoric. Then, like many other young Greeks of similar social standing who planned a career in the imperial service, Arrian decided to complete his education by studying philosophy. He went about the year 108 to Nicopolis in Epirus, where the Stoic philosopher Epictetus had founded a school after the general expulsion of philosophers from Rome by Domitian in A.D. 92/3.[3] This remarkable man, a former slave, concerned himself mainly with ethics, and his teachings with their emphasis on the need for the individual to concern himself with his soul and their contempt for wealth and luxury had certain affinities with Christianity. Indeed, they have sometimes been thought, though wrongly, to have been influenced by the new religion. Like Socrates, Epictetus wrote nothing for publication, but fortunately he made such an impression on the young Arrian that he took down his master's words in short-hand and later published them in eight books of *Discourses*.[4] Four of these still survive to give us a vivid portrait of a striking personality. Also extant is the *Manual* or

3. We do not know why Arrian chose to study under Epictetus rather than, as we should have expected, at Athens. In an important article on Arrian's governorship in the *English Historical Review* 1896 (reprinted in his *Essays*, ed. F. Haverfield, Oxford, 1906), Professor H. F. Pelham has suggested that Arrian was probably influenced by the traditions of his mother's family, the 'gens' Arria, famous in the history of Roman Stoicism. He conjectures that the *cognomen* Arrianus indicates the family of the historian's mother, as *cognomina* often did in the first and second centuries A.D.

4. In a letter to a Lucius Gellius Arrian gives his reasons for publishing them. We now know that this Gellius was an eminent citizen of Corinth, L. Gellius Menander, who with his son, L. Gellius Iustus, set up an inscription in honour of Arrian at Corinth; see G. W. Bowersock in *Greek, Roman and Byzantine Studies* 8 (1967), 279-80.

Handbook (*Encheiridion*) in which, for the benefit of the general public, Arrian combined the essentials of Epictetus' teaching. In the Middle Ages it enjoyed great popularity as a guide of monastic life. It is clearly from Epictetus that Arrian derived the high moral standards by which he judges Alexander. Epictetus, too, warmly commends repentance after wrongdoing, an attitude which finds an echo in Arrian's praise for Alexander's conduct after the murder of Cleitus. Since Epictetus drew on his experience of life in Rome under Domitian to illustrate his teachings, it is possible that Arrian's comments on 'the bane of monarchs', the courtier, have their origin in the same source.

Of Arrian's career in the imperial service until he reached the consulship in 129 or 130 we know only that he served on the Danube frontier and possibly in Gaul and Numidia. Arrian's career may have been forwarded by the phil-hellenism of Hadrian, the 'Greekling' as he was nicknamed, who succeeded Trajan as emperor in A.D. 117. But his appointment, in the year following his consulship, to the governorship of Cappadocia, it is safe to say, recognised his military and administrative abilities; for there is no evidence that Hadrian allowed sentiment to imperil the security of the empire. At this time the large and important frontier province of Cappadocia extended northwards to the Black Sea and along its eastern coast from Trapezus as far as Dioscurias, and Arrian commanded two Roman legions and a large body of auxiliary troops, a rare, perhaps unexampled, command for a Greek at this period. It was an unsettled time 'produced by Trajan's momentary conquests beyond the Euphrates, and by Hadrian's prompt return to a defensive policy.'[5] In 134

5. The quotation is taken from page 218 of Pelham's article mentioned in n. 3.

the Alans from across the Caucasus threatened to invade Cappadocia and although they did not cross the frontier Arrian is recorded to have driven the invaders out of Armenia. The extant work of Arrian, *The Formation against the Alans*, describes the composition of his force, with its order of march and the tactics to be followed. Two other works dating from the period of his governorship are extant, the *Circumnavigation of the Black Sea* (*Periplus Ponti Euxini*) and a *Tactical Manual*, the latter dated precisely to 136/7 A.D. It is concerned only with cavalry tactics; for Arrian tells us he had already written a work on infantry tactics. The *Circumnavigation* is an account, based on the official report (in Latin) which he, as governor, submitted to the emperor, of a voyage from Trapezus to Dioscurias combined with two other passages to form an account of the whole Black Sea coast. This voyage took place at the beginning of his office – he mentions hearing of the death of king Cotys in 131/2 in the course of it – in order to inspect the defences of his area.

Arrian is attested as governor of Cappadocia in 137, but he retired or was recalled before the death of Hadrian in June 138. He seems not to have held any further office, for reasons we can only guess at, but to have taken up residence at Athens and to have devoted the remainder of his life to writing. He became an Athenian citizen and in 145/6 held the chief magistracy, the archonship. We last hear of him in 172/3 as a member of the Council, and in 180 the satirist Lucian refers to him in terms which reveal that he was already dead.

The writings of Arrian's Athenian period are numerous and varied. The order in which they were composed cannot be determined with certainty, but we may with confidence place early in his stay his biographies of Dion of Syracuse and Timoleon of Corinth, and possibly a life of

Tilliborus, a notorious bandit who plagued Asia Minor. Of these no trace remains. In his writings he frequently refers in a spirit of rivalry to his namesake, the Athenian Xenophon, and a short work on hunting forms a supplement to the older writer's book on the same topic. By choosing the same title, *On the Chase* (*Cynegeticus*), Arrian stresses the connexion and challenges comparison. Indeed, he writes that he had from his youth onwards the same interests as the Athenian Xenophon – hunting, tactics, and philosophy. His major historical works came later. Apart from *The Campaigns of Alexander* (*Anabasis Alexandri*), whose title and division into seven books are clearly modelled on Xenophon's *Anabasis*, he wrote the still extant *Indica*, an account of the voyage of Alexander's fleet from India to the Persian Gulf (based on Nearchus' book) prefaced by a description of India and its people. Of his *Events after Alexander* in ten books we have virtually only the narrative of the first two years. The rest has perished – undoubtedly the greatest loss among the works of Arrian. We possess only fragments of his other works, a *Parthian History* dealing with Trajan's campaigns in seventeen books, and a *History of Bithynia* which traced the story of his native land from mythical times down to 74 B.C., when the last king, Nicomedes IV, bequeathed his kingdom to Rome.

The Campaigns of Alexander

This book was intended to be Arrian's masterpiece, his lasting claim to fame. How important it was to him, his own words (I.12) make clear:

I need not declare my name – though it is by no means unheard of in the world; I need not specify my country and family, or any official position I may have held. Rather let me say this: that this book is, and has been since my youth, more precious than country and kin and public advancement – indeed, for me it *is* these things.

He had, he felt, a splendid subject, and a splendid opportunity. No one had had more written about him than Alexander, yet no one, poet or prose-writer, had done him justice. The real Alexander was hidden behind a mass of contradictory statements, while the works of earlier writers contained downright error. They could not even get right the location of the decisive battle against Darius; they did not know which men had saved Alexander's life in India. Not to speak of Achilles' good fortune in having Homer relate his exploits, lesser men, such as the Sicilian tyrants, had fared better than Alexander. Arrian's book was intended to end this state of affairs. Such is the importance of Alexander that he will not hesitate to challenge the great historians of Greece.

For this task Arrian possessed substantial advantages. We cannot say with any certainty when he began his book, but a date before the middle of the second century would seem highly unlikely. Arrian, therefore, was probably in his sixties; he had read widely in the Alexander-literature and was thoroughly familiar with the classical historians, Herodotus, Thucydides, and Xenophon; he had written a considerable amount, although perhaps nothing as ambitious as this; he had at least some philosophical training and considerable military and administrative experience; finally, and not least important, he possessed, it is evident, a good deal of common sense.

But he faced formidable difficulties, difficulties he shared with the other extant writers on Alexander. Of these the earliest is the Sicilian Greek Diodorus, who almost exactly three hundred years after Alexander's death, devoted the 17th Book of his *Universal History* to his reign.

The Latin writer Quintus Curtius wrote his *History of Alexander* in the first century A.D., while early in the next century the Greek biographer Plutarch wrote a *Life of Alexander* which provides a useful supplement to Arrian. The *Philippic Histories* of the Romanised Gaul Pompeius Trogus, who wrote a little earlier than Diodorus, is extant only in the wretched summary of Justin (3rd cent. A.D.).[6] All these authors were faced with the problem of choosing from a multiplicity of conflicting sources. For Arrian does not exaggerate the mass of material that confronted the historian of Alexander. Much of this has perished almost without trace, but enough remains, in the shape of 'fragments' embedded in extant writers, to confirm his statement that many lies were told about Alexander and many contradictory versions of his actions existed.

Many of those who accompanied Alexander wrote of the expedition and its leader from their particular standpoint.[7] Callisthenes, Aristotle's nephew, acting as Alexander's 'press-agent' composed for Greek consumption – for Alexander's allies were by no means enthusiastic – an account of the expedition in which the king, who surely 'vetted' Callisthenes' narrative, bore a distinct resemblance to the 'heroes' of legend. This official version was necessarily broken off when its author was arrested, and later executed, on suspicion of treason. The last event

6. Diodorus' 17th Book is translated (with useful notes) by C. Bradford Welles in the Loeb Classical Library, Curtius by J. C. Rolfe in the same series, and Justin (with Cornelius Nepos and Eutropius) in Bohn's Library. Plutarch's *Alexander* has been frequently translated (usually with a number of other Lives), most recently by Ian Scott-Kilvert in *The Age of Alexander* (Penguin Books).

7. These authors are the subject of detailed study by Lionel Pearson, *The Lost Histories of Alexander the Great* (New York, 1960).

certainly dealt with was the battle of Gaugamela. Chares, the royal chamberlain, wrote a book of anecdotes, valuable when he is dealing with events at court, otherwise useless, while Onesicritus, Alexander's chief pilot, who had been a pupil of Diogenes, created a dangerous blend of truth and falsehood with a Cynic flavour. For him Alexander was the 'philosopher in arms', a man with a mission. Nearchus, who commanded Alexander's fleet on its voyage from India to the Persian Gulf, followed with a more sober account, beginning, unfortunately, only with the start of his voyage. Lastly, to mention only the most important of the contemporary accounts, we have the histories of Ptolemy, who after Alexander's death became ruler and later king of Egypt, and of Aristobulus, apparently an engineer or architect. With these I shall deal later. But the history of Alexander which enjoyed the greatest popularity in succeeding centuries – Caelius, the friend of Cicero, read it – was written by a man who was not a member of the expedition, Cleitarchus, who wrote at Alexandria at the end of the fourth century, or perhaps even later. He portrayed Alexander as 'heroic', as Callisthenes had done, and (somewhat incongruously) as the possessor of the typical virtues of a Hellenistic king. But the main attraction of his book was almost certainly the vivid descriptions and the sensational incidents it contained – the Greek courtesan Thais leading Alexander, the worse for drink, in a Bacchic revel to set fire to the palace at Persepolis, Alexander's wholesale adoption of Persian luxury and practices, including a harem of 365 concubines, the week-long revel in Carmania, the poisoning of Alexander – to mention but a few.

All or much of this Arrian will have read. He will doubtless have been familiar, too, with the criticisms of the philosophical schools, particularly the Stoics, and the rhetoricians.[8] These found a congenial theme in Alexander's drunkenness, his conceit, his lack of self-control erupting into murderous violence, and his divine aspirations.

Faced with this mass of evidence Arrian decided, very sensibly, to use the histories of Ptolemy and Aristobulus as the basis of his narrative. Where their versions tallied, he tells us, he accepted their consensus as true. Where they differed, he sometimes gives both versions; more often, one suspects, he followed Ptolemy. Certainly for military matters Ptolemy is his principal source. His reasons for his choice, admittedly, do not inspire confidence. Since Alexander was dead when they wrote, neither, he claims, had anything to gain by not telling the truth, while it would be disgraceful for a king, as Ptolemy was when he wrote, to tell lies. It is not difficult to think of reasons why Aristobulus and, especially, Ptolemy might not care to tell the truth, at least the whole truth. But it would seem reasonable to suppose that Arrian had come to the conclusion, after long study of the available material, that these authors provided the most honest and most reliable accounts of Alexander. To supplement their works Arrian includes the 'stories' of other writers, such as Callisthenes and Chares, where these appeared 'worth relating and reasonably reliable'.

So far as we can judge, Arrian's choice of Ptolemy as his main source was fully justified, particularly as he concerned himself largely with military matters. For Ptolemy was an experienced soldier who had taken a part, although not at first a prominent one, in many of the operations he describes. His accounts of Alexander's major battles, as we see them through Arrian's eyes, are by no means free

8. On these see my *Plutarch* Alexander: *A Commentary* (Oxford, 1969), lx–lxii.

from problems, perhaps because of the difficulty a partici-
pant has in obtaining an overall view of the fighting. We
should remember too that Ptolemy was not promoted to
'the Staff' until late in 330. The other military operations,
particularly those in which Ptolemy took part, are reported with admirable clarity, although Ptolemy's tendency
to exaggerate his personal contribution seems well established.[9] This is understandable, and unimportant. Less
excusable is the apparently systematic denigration of Perdiccas, his bitter enemy in the struggle for power after
Alexander's death.[10] The main fault of his book, it seems,
lies elsewhere, in his reticence about some of the more
controversial, and perhaps discreditable, episodes in
Alexander's career. Arrian does not cite him as a source
for his narrative of the murder of Cleitus, although it is
difficult to believe that Ptolemy did not mention the
tragedy, while neither he nor Aristobulus is the basis of
Arrian's account of Alexander's attempt to introduce the
ceremony of prostration (*proskynesis*). It would seem that
Ptolemy said no more than he had to about these incidents.
The same is probably true of the 'plot' of Philotas and the
conspiracy of the Pages, although he asserted the guilt of
Philotas and Callisthenes.

9. See the convincing analysis by C. B. Welles, 'The reliability of
Ptolemy as an historian', in *Miscellanea . . . A. Rostagni* (Turin 1963)
101ff. Curtius, who had the advantage of reading Ptolemy's book,
presumably refers to this aspect of Ptolemy's writing when he describes him (9.5.21) as a man 'who was certainly not inclined to
depreciate his own glory'.

10. R. M. Errington, 'Bias in Ptolemy's History of Alexander',
in *CQ* 1969, 233ff., gives several instances of misrepresentation by
Ptolemy. He considers that Aristonous was deprived of the credit
for helping to save Alexander's life, but he contests the usual view
that Antigonus' hard-fought victories over the survivors of Issus
were ignored by Ptolemy, because of his rivalry with Antigonus
in the years following 314.

Aristobulus' book provided a useful supplement to Ptolemy, since he was, it seems, more interested in geography and natural history. Most of the geographical and topographical detail in the *Campaigns* comes from Aristobulus and it was he who described Alexander's measures to improve the canal system of Babylonia and the navigation of the River Tigris. Aristobulus was ordered by the king to restore the tomb of Cyrus near Pasargadae which had been plundered by robbers, and it is to him that we are indebted for the description of the tomb before and after it was robbed, a description that modern archaeology has confirmed. It is probable that the vivid narrative of the march through the Gedrosian desert with its valuable botanical observations comes from the same source. It is Aristobulus too who related the exploration of the coasts of Arabia and the plans which Alexander had made for its conquest. One of Alexander's motives for the expedition, Aristobulus tells us – we learn this from Strabo, for Arrian does not mention the name of his source – was the expectation that the Arabians would recognize him as a god.

But it is on the personal side that Aristobulus' account is open to question. Whereas Ptolemy had been content to pass over the less pleasant aspects of Alexander's character, Aristobulus' book seems to have had a distinctly 'apologetic' character which earned him in antiquity the soubriquet of 'flatterer' (*kolax*). He justifiably stressed the generosity of the king towards the captured Persian royal family, and put forward the tenable view that Cleitus asked for trouble, but although he asserted the guilt of Philotas and Callisthenes he was apparently as reticent as Ptolemy about the reasons for his judgement. Then his statement that the king was not a heavy drinker, but remained long at banquets only for the sake of the conversation, must provoke a smile. The murder of

Cleitus alone disproves it. In fact, it represents an excessive reaction from the quite indefensible view that Alexander was habitually drunk. Many writers depicted the king towards the end of his life as a prey to superstitious fear. According to them Alexander, on the advice of his seers, put to death the sailor who had worn the royal diadem and the man who had sat upon the royal throne. Aristobulus, however, stated that the sailor was merely flogged and then let go and that the second man was tortured to reveal his motive, implying, it would seem, that he suffered nothing worse. But, as the man was a scapegoat, this seems doubtful. On the other hand, Aristobulus relates that he learned from the seer Peithagoras himself that Alexander had treated him with great favour because he had told the king the truth, namely that his sacrifices had disclosed impending disaster for him.

Arrian brought to his task patience, common sense, and a shrewd knowledge of human affairs, as well as considerable military and administrative experience. In military matters his adherence to Ptolemy produced good results. Here he followed a first-rate source well up in the inner circle of the Macedonians, whom he seems almost always to have understood. We might be tempted to depreciate Arrian by saying that he did little more than summarize Ptolemy's narrative. To do so would be unfair. We have only to compare his account of Issus or of Gaugamela with that of Quintus Curtius, who certainly had access to Ptolemy's book at first or second hand, to see his achievement. This is not to say that his account of military operations is everywhere satisfactory or that he tells us all we would like to know about the Macedonian army. We do not know, for example, what the soldiers in the various units were paid, and, more important, we hear almost nothing of the logistics of the army. Again, at Gaugamela

Arrian fails to explain how a messenger from Parmenio could reach Alexander after he had begun the pursuit of Darius. Only occasionally does he appear to misunderstand Ptolemy, for it is unlikely that the Macedonian supposed that Alexander, after crossing the Hydaspes, rode ahead with his cavalry in the expectation that he could defeat Porus' entire army with it alone. On the other hand he offers sensible criticism of Aristobulus' statement that Porus' son was sent with only 60 chariots to oppose Alexander's crossing of the R. Hydaspes, and rightly commends Alexander for refusing to risk attacking the Persians by night at Gaugamela, as Parmenio advised. Moreover, Arrian nearly always uses technical terms correctly, an immense help to the student of military history, and takes care to name the commanders of the various units. His use of *taxis* ('unit') as a utility word and of 'Companions' (*Hetairoi*) to refer either to the Companion cavalry or to Alexander's 'Peers' does give rise to difficulties, but for this Arrian can hardly be held responsible. The same painstaking attention to detail is evident in administrative matters. Appointments of governors are duly mentioned, and throughout his book Arrian is careful to give the father's name in the case of Macedonians, e.g. Ptolemy son of Lagus, and in the case of Greeks their city of origin. One can imagine the confusion that would have resulted had he not done so, in view of the shortage of Macedonian proper names and the resultant abundance of Ptolemys and Philips.

We must regret, however, that Arrian has interpreted his subject in a somewhat narrow fashion, perhaps because his model, Xenophon, had concentrated on *his* expedition. Unlike Polybius, he does not discuss *why* Alexander invaded Asia – he might, however, have said that this was a matter for the historian of Philip and that

Alexander never thought of not continuing an operation already begun – nor does he mention previous operations in Asia or the existence of a Macedonian force in Asia in 334. His account of the events of 336, which determined Alexander's relations with the Greek states, formally at least, are dealt with so summarily as to be barely intelligible. Consequently the reader, I suspect, is in the dark when, without having heard of the League of Corinth, he is told of 'the resolutions of the Greeks'. In fact, Alexander's relations with the Greek states and events in Greece during the expedition are almost entirely neglected. This is to some extent understandable and justifiable, although Persian hopes of transferring the war to Greece in 333 are not fully intelligible without the background of Greek discontent. Indeed, Arrian's preoccupation with Alexander leads him to treat this important, though admittedly abortive, episode in the war very sketchily. Again, the reader must be curious, one would think, to learn what happened to King Agis of Sparta who vanishes from the pages of Arrian after receiving 30 talents and 10 ships from the Persians, even if we regard the Spartan revolt in 331, as Alexander is said to have regarded it, as 'an affair of mice'.

Arrian clearly made no attempt to give a comprehensive account of the war, or of its antecedents. We hear only incidentally of the troubles in the Persian empire that preceded Darius' accession in 336, and every reader must have asked himself the question: 'Why did the Persians allow Alexander's forces to cross into Asia unopposed?' Even after the start of the expedition we hear what the Persians have been planning and doing only when they come into contact with Alexander. It is only on the eve of Issus in November 333 that we are told of Darius' plans in the preceding months. Arrian deliberately chose to disregard the Persian background, as Professor Brunt has proved.[11] He was not ignorant of Persian matters; but his method 'was to follow the movements and describe the activities of Alexander himself'.

Arrian's portrait of Alexander is in general more open to criticism than his narrative of military operations, partly through his reliance on Ptolemy and Aristobulus. Yet Arrian's portrait is more than the sum of his sources; for he possesses a distinct personality of his own which we can detect most clearly in his attitude to religion and morals. Many of the characteristics of his Alexander are undeniably true. We can see clearly the qualities which enabled Alexander to maintain for so many years his hold upon his men, the dashing leadership which was expected of a general in his day – although Arrian does not conceal the fact that his officers thought that the king sometimes went too far in hazarding his life – the confidence (seldom disappointed) of success, with which he inspired his troops, and his care for their welfare. We remember how after the victory at the Granicus Alexander 'showed much concern about the wounded, visiting each, examining their wounds, asking how they were received, and encouraging each to relate, and even boast of, his exploits'. We recall his determination and persistence in many sieges, notably in the face of the desperate resistance by the Tyrians for seven long months, and his courage in adversity, exemplified by his 'noblest deed', the refusal to drink the helmetful of water, too little for his troops to share, in the burning heat of the Gedrosian desert – a proof, as Arrian remarks, of his endurance and his generalship. Arrian, too, rightly praises his generous treatment of the defeated Indian rajah Porus – although this was not altogether disinterested –

11. See his 'Persian Accounts of Alexander's Campaigns' in *CQ* 1962, 141ff. The quotation which follows is taken from p. 141.

and his compassion for the captured Persian royal family. There are many instances of Alexander's affection for his friends, particularly his *alter ego* Hephaestion, and his trust in them is portrayed in the celebrated scene with his doctor Philip, while Arrian warmly commends his repentance after his murder of Cleitus.

It is when Arrian's imagination is kindled by incidents such as these that he raises the pitch of his narrative and achieves eloquence. For the most part he is content to let the story speak for itself. Certainly he deliberately avoided sensationalism and he explicitly denied the truth of such favourite stories as the visit of the Amazon queen or the week-long revel through Carmania. Perhaps no passage better illustrates Arrian's admiration for his hero and the heightened tone of his narrative than that in which he describes the king's return to his army after his recovery from the wound which so nearly caused his death. I quote the end of the passage:

Near his tent he dismounted, and the men saw him walk; they crowded round him, touching his hands, his knees, his clothing; some, content with a sight of him standing near, turned away with a blessing on their lips. Wreaths were flung upon him and such flowers as were then in bloom.

But Arrian's evident admiration for Alexander and his achievements did not prevent him from criticizing his hero where he failed to reach the high standard which, as a Stoic, Arrian felt a king ought to attain. In particular, Alexander is censured several times for his excessive ambition. Arrian does not know, and commendably will not speculate about, Alexander's future plans, but he is convinced that he would never have rested content with his conquests. The Indian wise men are expressly commended for their view that 'each man possesses just so much of the earth as he stands on', and Alexander, despite his applause of this sentiment, is said to have acted always in a way completely opposed to it. It is clear that for Arrian Alexander's conquests are merely an expression of Alexander's insatiable appetite for fame. There is some truth in this, but it is not the whole story. It is, however, entirely to Arrian's credit that he wholeheartedly condemns Alexander's letter to Cleomenes, the governor of Egypt (7.23.6–7), in which the king offers to pardon him for his past misdeeds and to give him a free hand in the future if he erects temples in Egypt for the dead Hephaestion. The historian's understanding and humanity is apparent in his attitude to the murderer of Cleitus. Alexander's act excites in him pity for the man who has given way to two grave vices, passion and drunkenness. The king has failed to achieve that self-mastery which, as Arrian has remarked a little earlier, is necessary before one can be happy. A similar sentiment occurs in the speech of Coenus at the River Hyphasis when he says to Alexander 'when things go well with us, the spirit of self-restraint is a noble thing' – surely Arrian's own view, whether or not it was shared by Coenus.

The main weaknesses in Arrian's portrait of Alexander seem to me two-fold – a tendency, which he derives from his sources, to gloss over the less attractive side of the king's character, and a failure to appreciate Alexander's intentions, especially with regard to the Persians.

The first of these is apparent before the expedition gets under way. The slaughter of the Thebans, perhaps rightly, and the destruction of the city and the enslavement of the survivors is blamed on the Greek allies of Alexander. Nothing is said of his responsibility for permitting them, as in fact he did, to pass this sentence. Yet even Plutarch, whom no one could accuse of hostility to Alexander, implicitly holds him responsible; as he saw, Alexander's intention was to terrify the other Greek states into submission. At the battle of the Granicus Arrian relates without comment the massacre of the Greek mercenaries, nearly 18,000 according to his own account; he does not remark on the cruelty or the inadvisability of the massacre. In the same way at Massaga in India the massacre of 7,000 Indians passes without comment. Nor should we guess from Arrian that some writers had doubts about the involvement of Philotas in a plot against the king. He is content to accept Ptolemy's statement, although the 'manifest proofs' of his guilt adduced by him do not amount to much. Again, the burning of the palace at Persepolis is very briefly referred to with no mention of the alternative tradition that it was set on fire during a drunken revel. On the other hand, Arrian gives a much more balanced account of the murder of Cleitus than Aristobulus seems to have done, and he is obviously reluctant to accept the statements of Ptolemy and Aristobulus that Callisthenes was involved in the conspiracy of the Pages.

What the modern reader misses in Arrian's book is an appreciation of the larger issues. Alexander emerges as a great leader, a great conqueror possessed of boundless ambition, a man who reached the height of human prosperity and who, if he committed great crimes, had the magnanimity to repent of them. Certainly the conquest of the Persian Empire was his most lasting achievement, but what we want to know is whether he was more than the supreme conqueror. What plans did he have for his empire? What part did he intend the conquered peoples to play in it? Amid a great deal that is obscure about Alexander, one thing is certain, that he was very much in earnest about what modern writers have called his 'policy of fusion'. The clearest expression of this policy is his prayer at Opis – a prayer that Arrian records without comment – that Macedonians and Persians might live in harmony and jointly rule the empire. This was a revolutionary idea, not shared by his Macedonians, nor, we can be sure, by many Greeks either. For the most distinguished of Alexander's many teachers, the eminent philosopher Aristotle, who inspired him with a love of Greek literature and particularly of Homer, is said by Plutarch to have written to Alexander advising the young king to behave towards the Greeks as a leader but towards the 'barbarians' as a master. This contemptuous attitude towards 'barbarians' was no doubt widespread. But Alexander, who may have felt doubts about it even before the expedition – Artabazus and other leading Persians lived as exiles at Philip's court when Alexander was a boy – soon came to reject it. After Gaugamela we find him appointing Persians as governors, certainly not through a lack of suitable Macedonians.

Arrian clearly shared Aristotle's prejudice against 'barbarians' and had no conception of Alexander's vision of a partnership between the two peoples. In the characterisation of Alexander at the end of his book he sees Alexander's adoption of Persian dress and his introduction of Persian troops into the Macedonian army as a mere 'device', designed to render him less alien to his Persian subjects. Indeed, Arrian has earlier (4.7) condemned his adoption of oriental dress as a 'barbaric' act not so different from his 'barbaric' punishment of the pretender Bessus. Both acts, in Arrian's view, indicate a deterioration of Alexander's character. Even in the case of Bessus Arrian does not see that the punishment was a Persian punishment inflicted on him by Alexander in his position as 'Great King'. Elsewhere, he refers to Alexander 'going some way towards "barbarian" extravagance', and his comment on the king's marriage to Roxane, the Bactrian princess, is illuminating. 'I approve', he writes, 'rather than blame'. This 'policy of fusion' with the adoption of Persian dress and Persian court ceremonial was bitterly resented by the Macedonians, as Arrian is well aware. Drink led Cleitus to give utterance to grievances which were deeply felt and widely shared, while the extent of the Pages' conspiracy leads one to think that their motives were not so much personal as political. Yet Arrian does not ask himself whether Alexander would have persisted in a policy so universally detested if it were nothing more than a 'device' to win Persian favour.

Plutarch, perhaps exaggerating, puts the number of cities founded by Alexander at seventy. In his *Campaigns* Arrian mentions fewer than a dozen foundations; not a cause for complaint, for he was not compiling a catalogue. But we are not told what Alexander's motives were, military or economic or, as some scholars believe, part of his mission to spread Greek culture throughout Asia. It is from the *Indica* that we learn that cities were established among the conquered Cossaeans to encourage them to forsake their nomadic habits and become a settled people.

Alexander took his religious duties very seriously indeed, as the account of his last days makes plain. Arrian frequently records that the king offered sacrifice or made drink-offerings, and the prophecies made by his seers, notably Aristander, are faithfully reported. Only once, before the siege of Tyre, is he provoked to sarcasm; 'The plain fact', he writes, 'is that anyone could see that the siege of Tyre would be a great undertaking'. But Arrian's hostile or sceptical attitude to the ruler cult of his day – an attitude he shares with Plutarch and the historian Appian – prevents him from doing justice to Alexander's divine aspirations. That Alexander believed himself to be the son of Ammon-Zeus, as his ancestor Hercules was son of Zeus, is very probable, although admittedly not susceptible of proof. Arrian will have none of this. Alexander set out for Siwah 'hoping to learn about himself more accurately, or at least *to say that he had so learnt*'. For him Alexander's claim was merely another 'device', to impress his subjects. He displays the same sceptical attitude towards Alexander's divinity. In 324 the Greek states, probably in response to a 'request' from the king himself, sent *theoroi* (envoys sent on sacred missions) to crown him with a golden crown at Babylon. That the envoys were *theoroi* admits of no doubt; the fact that they themselves wore crowns proves it. If Arrian writes that 'they came as *theoroi* forsooth', using a Greek particle implying disbelief or sarcasm, he is suggesting that Alexander, as a mortal, could never be a god. Gods were immortal, men were not, and 'after all', as Arrian drily comments, 'Alexander's death was near'.

Arrian set out to produce the best and most reliable account of Alexander's expedition, avoiding the exaggerations of his predecessors and correcting their errors. That he succeeded few will dispute. The histories of Diodorus and Curtius and, particularly, the biography of Plutarch throw light (and sometimes darkness) on the character of Alexander and occasionally even on his military exploits, but Arrian's book is the basis of our knowledge. It impresses one as the work of an honest man who has made a serious and painstaking attempt to discover the truth about Alexander – a task perhaps impossible by his time – and who has judged with humanity the weaknesses of a man exposed to the temptations of those who exercise supreme power. We need not deny the limitations of the work, but it is proper to remember that Alexander's idea of an empire in whose rule conquering Macedonians and conquered Persians were to share perished with him. To spare the conquered was one thing, to associate them with one in government was another, an idea that was not to reach fulfilment until long after Alexander's death.

Alexander's Army[12]

In the spring of 334 Alexander set out from Macedonia, leaving Antipater with 12,000 infantry and 1,500 cavalry to defend the homeland and to keep watch on the Greek states. The size of the army with which he crossed the Hellespont has been variously reported, totals ranging from 30,000 to 43,000 for infantry and 4,000 to 5,500 for cavalry. But the detailed figures given by Diodorus (17. 17), 32,000 infantry and 5,100 cavalry, agree essentially with the totals in Arrian (Ptolemy), and may be taken as substantially correct. The size and composition of the force holding the bridgehead at Abydos – there surely must have been some troops there in 334 – is not known, but the likelihood is that it was small and consisted mainly of mercenary infantry.

The backbone of the infantry was the Macedonian heavy infantry, the 'Foot Companions', organized on a territorial basis in six battalions (*taxeis*) of about 1,500 men each. In place of the nine-foot spear carried by the Greek hoplite, the Macedonian infantryman was armed with a pike or *sarissa* about 13 or 14 feet long, which required both hands to wield it. The light circular shield

12. For details of Alexander's troops see especially Major-General J. F. C. Fuller, *The Generalship of Alexander the Great* (London, 1958); E. W. Marsden, *The Campaign of Gaugamela* (Liverpool, 1964), Appendices I and II; A. R. Burn, 'The Generalship of Alexander', in *Greece and Rome* 1965, 140–54.

was slung on the left shoulder, and was smaller than that
carried by the Greek hoplite which demanded the use of
the left arm. Both Greek and Macedonian infantry wore
greaves and a helmet, but it is possible that the Macedonians did not wear a breastplate.[13] The *phalanx* (a
convenient term for the sum total of the Macedonian
heavy infantry), like all the Macedonian troops, had been
brought by Philip to a remarkable standard of training
and discipline. Unlike the phalanx which the Romans encountered over a century later, Alexander's phalanx was
capable of rapid movement and was highly manoeuvrable,
as one can see from a reading of the first half-dozen chapters of Arrian's book.

In battle the right flank of the phalanx was guarded by
the *Hypaspists* or 'Guards'. These were an élite corps,
consisting of a Royal battalion (*agema*) and two other
battalions, each of approximately 1,000 men. Alexander
used them frequently on rapid marches and other mobile
operations, often in conjunction with cavalry and light-
armed troops. This suggests, although it does not prove,
that they were more lightly armed than the heavy infantry; but if they were less heavily armed, we do not know
where the difference lay.

The member states of the Corinthian League contributed 7,000 heavy infantry, while 5,000 Greeks served as
mercenaries. The remainder of Alexander's infantry consisted of 7,000 Thracian and Illyrian light troops armed
with javelins and two bodies of archers from Crete and
Macedonia respectively. The outstanding unit among the
light troops was the Agrianians, 1,000 strong, who have
been well compared in their relation to Macedon and in
their quality to the Gurkhas of the Indian army. Alone of

13. See G. T. Griffith, *Proceedings of the Cambridge Philological Association*, 4 (1956/7), pp. 3ff.

the allies they served throughout the campaign and
Arrian mentions them almost fifty times. With the archers
and the Guards they took part in all the reconnaisances and
skirmishes as well as fighting superbly in the set pieces.

Pride of place among the cavalry was held by the Macedonian 'Royal Companions', originally 1,800 troopers
divided into 8 squadrons or *Ilai*, all under the command
of Parmenio's son, Philotas. Among them the Royal
Squadron, consisting of perhaps 300 men, was Alexander's own bodyguard, which spearheaded the devastating
cavalry charge in the major battles. Their position was on
the immediate right of the Guards, who had the task of
maintaining contact between the Companions and the
phalanx. The counterpart of the Companions on the left
of the phalanx was the Thessalian cavalry, also 1,800
strong at the start of the expedition. Under the general
command of Parmenio, they had the difficult task at Issus
and Gaugamela of holding much superior forces of Persian cavalry while Alexander delivered the decisive blow
on the right. The Greek allies furnished 600 horsemen,
and the remaining 900 were made up of Thracians,
Paeonians, and 'Scouts' (*Prodromoi*) who were also called
'Lancers' (*Sarissophoroi*) since they were armed with the
sarissa, presumably shorter than those carried by the infantry which required the use of both hands. Whether
these light cavalry were Macedonians or Thracians is not
clear; certainly they were distinct from 'the Thracians'.
Finally, although Diodorus does not mention mercenary
cavalry in his list of forces, Alexander may have had some
from the beginning. By Gaugamela at least he had perhaps 1,000 of these.[14]

14. P. A. Brunt, 'Alexander's Macedonian Cavalry', in *JHS* 83
(1963), 27–46 discusses the many problems concerning Alexander's
cavalry.

Despite the need for garrisons in Asia Minor and Egypt, Alexander's army at Gaugamela numbered 40,000 infantry and 7,000 cavalry. The only substantial reinforcements of Macedonian and allied troops recorded by Arrian reached Gordium early in 333, and there is no good reason to suppose that Alexander received any worthwhile number of Macedonians or allies apart from these before Gaugamela. For Quintus Curtius, who after 331 records the arrival of many reinforcements not mentioned by Arrian, mentions reinforcements only of mercenaries in this period. Indeed, it is clear that the increase in the number of Alexander's troops was due principally to the recruitment of mercenaries from Greece and to the enlistment of mercenaries who had fought for Persia. Alexander had begun by treating the latter as traitors, but finding that this merely encouraged desperate resistance decided within a few months to change this unsuccessful policy. Many of the garrisons doubtless consisted in large part of mercenaries.

Soon after Gaugamela Alexander received strong reinforcements of Macedonian troops, no fewer than 6,000 infantry and 500 cavalry. This enabled him to create a seventh battalion of infantry, which was certainly operating early in 330.[15] The other battalions must have remained over strength for some time. This is the last draft of Macedonians he is known to have received until he returned to the west after his Indian campaign, and there is no compelling reason to think that he received any others. In 330 the allied troops from the Greek states and from Thessaly were discharged at Ecbatana. Many, we are told, chose to re-enlist as mercenaries. Increasing use was made of Greek mercenaries, and the garrisons of the many cities

15. As R. D. Milns has demonstrated in *Greek, Roman and Byzantine Studies* 7 (1966), 159–166.

founded by Alexander in the eastern satrapies consisted of them together with the native inhabitants and some unfit Macedonians. Presumably few of the 10,000 infantry and 3,500 cavalry left behind to protect Bactria in 327 were Macedonians.

After Gaugamela the pattern of warfare changed. In Bactria and Sogdiana Alexander found himself faced with a national resistance which, under the leadership of Bessus and then of Spitamenes, wisely avoided major conflicts and concentrated on widespread guerrilla activity. It was probably to cope with this altered mode of fighting that in 329 Alexander made an important change in the organization of his Companion cavalry. We no longer hear of eight *squadrons* (*Ilai*), but of (at least) eight *regiments* (*Hipparchiai*), each consisting of two, or perhaps more, squadrons. Some of these squadrons, it seems likely, now included or consisted of the excellent Persian cavalry.[16] Certainly Alexander made use of Persian cavalry outside the Companions. As early as 330 we hear of a unit of Persian mounted javelin-men (3.24), and at the battle of the River Hydaspes in 326 he had in his army a body of Daae, mounted archers, as well as horsemen from Bactria, Sogdiana, Scythia, Arachotia, and the Parapamisus, or Hindu Kush, region.

At Massaga in India Alexander is said to have attempted to enlist Indian mercenaries in his army, but when they attempted to desert to have massacred them. No further recruitment of Indian mercenaries is recorded, and the only Indian troops that we hear of in his army are those provided by the rajahs Taxiles and Porus and the city of Nysa, some 11,000 in all. However, if Nearchus is correct in saying (*Indica* 19.5) that at the start of the voyage down the River Hydaspes Alexander had 120,000 fighting men

16. On the Hipparchies see Appendix A.

with him (a figure given by Curtius (8.5.4) for the army at the start of the Indian campaign and by Plutarch (Alexander 66.4) for the (Infantry) force with which Alexander left India), Alexander must have had a great many Indian troops in his army. But their presence was only temporary, since there is no indication that any Indians returned to the west with him.

Among the grievances of the Macedonians in 324 Arrian (7.6.4) mentions the (recent) creation of a fifth cavalry regiment consisting, if we accept Professor Badian's emendation of Arrian's text,[17] almost entirely of Iranians. This means that the division of the Companion cavalry into eight regiments had been abandoned and that for a brief period after the return from India there were only four. It is sometimes said that the change reflects the losses sustained in the march through the Gedrosian desert. This need not be the case. Hephaestion's command is described (7.14.10) as a 'Chiliarchy', a group of 1,000 men, and, although it is true that he was 'Chiliarch' or 'Vizier', it is not self-evident that the preservation of his *name* required that his unit be called 'the chiliarchy of Hephaestion' rather than 'the regiment of Hephaestion'. It is probable, it seems to me, that the new regiments were (nominally) 1,000 strong. If this is so, the change will have been a change in organization, a consolidation of the cavalry into fewer and stronger units.

In 324 the 30,000 young Persians (the 'Successors'), who had been undergoing training in Macedonian fashion for the last three years, joined Alexander at Susa. Later in the same year, after the mutiny at Opis, Alexander sent home those Macedonians who were unfit or past the age for service, about 10,000 infantry and perhaps 1,500 cavalry, probably the bulk of his Macedonian forces. In

17. E. Badian in *JHS* 85 (1965), 161.

323 strong reinforcements reached Babylon. Philoxenus brought an army from Caria and Menander one from Lycia; while Menidas came with the cavalry under his command. It is likely that, as Brunt suggests,[18] these were fresh drafts from Macedon to replace the veterans now on their way home; Alexander had not drawn on the manpower of the homeland since 331 and it is not likely that he wished the Macedonian element in his army to be reduced to negligible proportions. In addition, Peucestas brought 20,000 Persian archers and slingers, as well as a considerable force of Cossaean and Tapurian troops, presumably infantry. Alexander now carried out his last reform. The Persians were integrated into Macedonian units in such a way that each platoon consisted of 4 Macedonian NCOs and 12 Persians, each armed in their national fashion.

For the future, then, or at least for the immediate future, the army in Asia was to consist predominantly of Iranian troops. The only indication of the size of the Macedonian component is given in a speech in Quintus Curtius purporting to have been delivered by Alexander but certainly the historian's own composition. There (10.2.8) the king mentions an army of 13,000 infantry and 2,000 cavalry, surely all Macedonians, excluding the garrisons already in being.

18. *JHS* 83 (1963), 39.

BOOK ONE

WHEREVER Ptolemy and Aristobulus in their histories of Alexander, the son of Philip, have given the same account, I have followed it on the assumption of its accuracy; where their facts differ I have chosen what I feel to be the more probable and interesting.[1] There are other accounts of Alexander's life – more of them, indeed, and more mutually conflicting than of any other historical character; it seems to me, however, that Ptolemy and Aristobulus are the most trustworthy writers on this subject, because the latter shared Alexander's campaigns, and the former – Ptolemy – in addition to this advantage, was himself a King, and it is more disgraceful for a King to tell lies than for anyone else. Moreover, Alexander was dead when these men wrote; so there was no sort of pressure upon either of them, and they could not profit from falsification of the facts. Certain statements by other writers upon Alexander may be taken to represent popular tradition: some of these, which are interesting in themselves and may well be true, I have included in my work.

If anyone should wonder why I should have wished to write this history when so many other men have done the same, I would ask him to reserve judgement until he has first read my predecessors' work and then become acquainted with my own.

Philip of Macedon died when Pythodelus was archon at Athens.[2] He was succeeded by his son Alexander, then

---

1. On Ptolemy and Aristobulus see the Introduction, pp. 21ff.

2. Philip was stabbed to death in the summer of 336. His assassin was a young nobleman named Pausanias, who some years before

about twenty years of age.[3] The story goes that Alexander, upon his succession to the throne, went into the Peloponnese, where he assembled all the Greeks in that part of the country and asked them for the command of the campaign against Persia, which they had previously granted to Philip. The only people to refuse his request were the Lacedaemonians, who declared that the tradition of their country forbade them to serve under a foreign commander; it was their prerogative to lead others. At Athens, too, there was a certain amount of trouble; but resistance collapsed the moment Alexander approached, and he was granted even greater honours than his father Philip before him.[4] This settled, he returned to Macedonia and prepared for his Asian campaign.

The following spring he marched towards Thrace, having learned that the Triballi and Illyrians were up to

had been grossly outraged by Attalus, whose daughter Philip had recently married. He is said to have resented Philip's failure to take action against Attalus. Alexander and his mother, Olympias, now estranged from Philip, were suspected of being implicated, although the brothers of Alexander of Lyncestis were executed for alleged complicity (p. 92 below), and later King Alexander accused the Persian King of boasting that he had bribed Pausanias (p. 127 below). For the circumstances see Diodorus 16.93–4; Aristotle *Politics* 1311b2. E. Badian, *Phoenix* 17 (1963) 244ff., provides the best recent discussion. See, however, A. B. Bosworth, *CQ* 1971, 93ff.

3. Plutarch *Alexander* (3.5) dates Alexander's birth to about 20 July 356.

4. Arrian's summary is so brief as to be misleading. From Diodorus' account (17.3–4) it appears that Alexander, faced with widespread unrest in Greece, secured recognition of his position as 'Leader' of the League of Corinth from the Thessalian League and the Amphictyonic League at Delphi, as well from the individual states both inside and outside the Peloponnese. Finally, he summoned a meeting of representatives to Corinth and was appointed 'Captain-General' of the League.

mischief.[5] The territories of these two peoples bordered upon Macedonia, and since his expedition would take him so far from home he did not think it wise to leave them in his rear, unless they were first thoroughly crushed. Starting from Amphipolis he entered the territory of what are known as the free Thracians, leaving Philippi and Mount Orbelus on his left; then, crossing the Nestus, he reached Mount Haemus, according to all accounts in ten days. Here, where the lower slopes of the mountain rise through a narrow defile, he was met by a large force of natives[6] under arms and the free Thracians, who had occupied the high ground which he would have to pass, with every intention of stopping his advance. They had collected a number of carts, which they intended to use, if they were hard pressed, as a sort of defensive palisade, with the further idea of sending them crashing down upon the Macedonian phalanx as the men were climbing the steepest part of the slope; their hope was that the impact of the vehicles would cause damage to the enemy troops in proportion to the closeness of their order.

Alexander had now to consider how to cross the ridge with least loss, for cross it he must, as there was no way round. His orders were that those sections of the heavy infantry which had room enough were to break formation when the carts came tearing down the slope, and so let them through; any sections, on the other hand, which were caught in the narrow pass were to form in the closest possible order, such men as were able lying prone on the ground with shields locked together above their bodies, so as to give the heavy wagons, as they careered down the

5. For an account of this campaign see Fuller 219ff. The Triballians lived south of the Danube in the modern province of Pleven.

6. As the manuscripts read 'traders', Alexander may have met an armed caravan.

hill, a chance to bounce over the top of them without doing any harm. Alexander accordingly gave his orders, and the result was what he expected: those who had room left a space between their ranks, and as for the rest, the carts passed harmlessly over their locked shields. There were no casualties. The wagons had been the most serious cause of apprehension; so, when they proved ineffectual, the Macedonian troops plucked up their courage, raised a cheer, and charged. Alexander brought his archers across from the right wing to a more convenient position in front of the main body of his troops, and instructed them to meet with a volley any attack the Thracians might make; he himself took charge of his personal Guard and the other Guards' regiments together with the Agrianes, and moved across to the left. Then the archers checked the Thracian attacks, and the infantry battalions, moving up to close quarters, had no difficulty in dislodging the inadequately armed and equipped enemy. Indeed, even before the troops under Alexander on the left wing came into contact with them, they flung down their arms and fled in a *sauve-qui-peut* down the mountain side. Some 1,500 were killed, but only a few captured; for most of them were too quick, and knew the country too well, to fall into their enemies' hands. The women, however, who had followed the fighting men were all taken, together with the children and all the gear and stores.

The booty was sent back to the coastal towns, with orders to Lysanias and Philotas[7] to dispose of it, and Alexander crossed the ridge. He then proceeded across the Haemus range to the Triballians, and arrived at the river Lyginus, three days' march, on this route, from the Danube. His movements had been known for some time

7. Not Philotas, son of Parmenio, commander of the Companion cavalry. He is mentioned below.

to Syrmus, the King of the Triballians, who had taken steps accordingly, sending the women and children on to the Danube with orders to cross over to an island in the river called the Pine Tree. The neighbouring Thracians had also taken refuge on this island upon Alexander's approach, together with Syrmus himself and his personal entourage, though the majority of the Triballians hurriedly retreated to the river from which Alexander had started the previous day.

The moment the news of the Triballians' move reached him, Alexander set off to engage them. He turned in his tracks, retraced his steps, and found them already occupied in pitching camp. The tribesmen, caught napping, prepared to fight in the shelter of the wood by the river, and Alexander, forming his infantry in column, advanced against them, with orders to the archers and slingers to proceed in front at the double and discharge their missiles, in the hope of drawing the enemy from the shelter of the wood into open ground. The tribesmen, once they felt the effect of the missiles, came surging forward to get to'grips with the lightly armed Macedonian archers, whereupon Alexander, having succeeded in drawing them out of cover, ordered Philotas to attack their right wing, which was well ahead of the rest of them, with the cavalry from upper Macedonia. At the same time he instructed Heracleides and Sopolis to advance against the enemies' left with the cavalry from Bottiaea and Amphipolis. The main body of infantry, preceded by the rest of his cavalry, he led against the enemy centre.

The Triballians held their own while the fighting was at long range; but once they had felt the weight and drive of the Macedonian infantry in close order, and the cavalry, instead of shooting at them, had begun actually to ride them down in a fierce assault all over the field, they broke

and ran, in an endeavour to make their escape through
the wood to the river. Three thousand were killed. Only
a few of these too were taken alive, because the wood
along the river-bank was very thick, and there was not
enough daylight left for the Macedonians to finish the job
properly. According to Ptolemy, the Macedonian losses
were eleven men from the cavalry and about forty from
the infantry.

Three days after the battle Alexander reached the
Danube. This river is the largest in Europe; it drains a
greater tract of country than any other, and forms the
frontier to the territories of some very warlike tribes.
Most of them are of Celtic stock – indeed, the source of
the river is in Celtic territory – the most remote being the
Quadi and the Marcomanni; then, flowing east, it passes
through the country of the Iazyges, a branch of the Sauromatae, of the Getae ('the immortals'), of the Sauromatae
themselves, and finally of the Scythians, where it reaches
the end of its course and debouches through five mouths
into the Black Sea.[8] On the river Alexander found warships awaiting him: they had come up across the Black
Sea from Byzantium.[9] He manned them with heavy infantry and archers, and, sailing for the island to which the
Triballians and Thracians had fled for refuge, attempted

8. Arrian describes (from west to east) the tribes living along the
north bank of the Danube in the second century A.D., not in
Alexander's day. He had served on the Danube frontier (*Indica*
4.15).

The Getae were the Thracian people whom the Romans called
Dacians. They were finally subdued by Trajan early in the second
century A.D., and their territory was annexed as the province of
Dacia. Herodotus (4.94) relates that they believed that the dead did
not perish but went to join the god Salmoxis.

9. Alexander clearly planned not a mere punitive expedition but
the establishment of the Danube as his northern frontier.

to force a landing. Circumstances, however, were against him: the ships met with resistance at every point where they tried to run ashore; they were few in number and not strongly manned; in most places the island shore was too steep for a landing, and the current, sweeping past it through the narrows, was strong and very awkward to deal with. Alexander accordingly withdrew the ships, and determined instead to cross the river and attack the Getae who lived on the further side. A large force of them – some 4,000 cavalry and more than 10,000 on foot – was already assembled on the river-bank, evidently prepared to resist a crossing, and the sight of them was one reason for his change of plan. Another was the fact that the idea of landing on the further side of the Danube suddenly seemed attractive.[10] He joined the fleet in person, having left instructions for the tents under which the men bivouacked to be filled with hay, and for all available dug-outs to be collected. There were a great many of these boats in the neighbourhood, for they are used by the natives for fishing, and for visiting neighbouring tribes up the river, and – fairly generally – for plundering expeditions. As many as possible of them were collected, and the troops, or as large a part of them as was practicable with this sort of transport, were ferried across. Actually, the number which crossed with Alexander was about 1,500 cavalry and 4,000 infantrymen.

The crossing took place at night, and the landing on the river-bank was more or less concealed by a tract of land

10. This is the first occurrence in Arrian of the word *pothos*, 'longing, yearning', which he and other Alexander-historians use to describe the desire to penetrate into the unknown and investigate the mysterious. Victor Ehrenberg, *Alexander and the Greeks* 52ff., argues that the word was used by Alexander himself. The present passage, however, he regards as an exception.

in which the grain stood high. Just before dawn Alexander moved forward through the grain-field, having given orders that the infantrymen should lead the way to the open ground, clear of crops, beyond, carrying their spears parallel with the ground and obliquely to their line of march, to flatten the grain as they advanced. The mounted troops followed the infantry through the cornfield, but once they were out in clear ground Alexander took charge of them and led them over to the right wing, at the same time ordering Nicanor to proceed with the infantry in close formation on an extended front.

The very first cavalry charge was too much for the Getae; the crossing of the Danube, greatest of rivers, so easily accomplished by Alexander in a single night, without even a bridge, was an act of daring which had shaken them profoundly; and added to this there was the violence of the attack itself, and the fearful sight of the phalanx advancing upon them in a solid mass. They turned and fled to their town, which was about four miles from the river; but as soon as they saw that Alexander, with his mounted troops ahead, was pressing on along the river-bank to avoid ambush or encirclement, they abandoned the town, which had few defences, and, taking with them as many women and children as their horses could carry, continued their flight into uninhabited country, as far from the river as they could go. Alexander took the town, together with anything of value which the Getae had left behind. This material was removed to the base by Meleager and Philip, after which the town was razed to the ground, and Alexander offered sacrifice on the banks of the Danube to Zeus the Saviour and Heracles,[11] not omitting the River himself, for allowing the passage.

11. From whom the kings of Macedon believed themselves to be descended.

The same day he led his whole force back to camp, safe and sound.

At this point Alexander was visited by envoys from Syrmus, the King of the Triballians, and from the various other independent tribes along the Danube. The Celts from the Adriatic Sea also sent representatives – men of haughty demeanour and tall in proportion. All professed a desire for Alexander's friendship, and mutual pledges were given and received. Alexander asked the Celtic envoys what they were most afraid of in this world, hoping that the power of his own name had got as far as their country, or even further, and that they would answer, 'You, my lord.' However, he was disappointed; for the Celts, who lived a long way off in country not easy to penetrate, and could see that Alexander's expedition was directed elsewhere, replied that their worst fear was that the sky might fall on their heads. None the less, he concluded an alliance of friendship with them and sent them home, merely remarking under his breath that the Celts thought too much of themselves.[12]

He then made for the territory of the Agrianes and Paeones, where a message reached him that Cleitus, the son of Bardylis, was in revolt, and had been joined by Glaucias, the prince of the Taulantians, and further, that the Autariates intended to attack him on the march.[13] For these reasons Alexander thought fit to get on the move without delay.

Langaros, King of the Agrianes, who had made no

12. It was nearly 50 years before the Celts invaded Macedonia and Greece.

13. Cleitus had been subdued by Philip in 349. The Taulantians and the Autariates were Illyrian tribes, the former living near Epidamnus (Durazzo), the latter further north on the borders of Paeonia.

secret of his respect for Alexander even in Philip's life-
time, had already been on an embassy to him in person,
and on the present occasion attended him with his bodyguard, the finest and best-equipped troops he possessed.
Hearing that Alexander wanted to know who the Autariates were and what their strength was, he advised him
to think no more about them, as they were the least warlike tribe in that part of the country. He offered to keep
them occupied by invading their territory himself, and,
with Alexander's consent, actually did so, causing severe
losses. For these services Langaros received from Alexander every mark of honour, including such presents as
are considered in the Macedonian court to be of the highest value. Alexander also promised that if Langaros visited
him at Pella, he would give him his sister Cyna in marriage.[14] Langaros, however, after his return home, fell ill
and died.

Alexander now proceeded along the river Erigon on
his way to Pelium, a town which had been occupied by
Cleitus as the most defensible in the district.[15] Arriving
there, he halted by the river Eordaicus with the intention
of making his assault the following day. The town was
ringed with commanding heights, thickly wooded, which
were held by Cleitus' troops, who were thus enabled, in
the event of an assault, to attack the Macedonian forces
from every side. Glaucias, the King of the Taulantians,
had not yet come upon the scene. Alexander, however,
lost no time, and the enemy, on his approach to the town,

14. Cyna was the half-sister of Alexander, the daughter of Philip
and an Illyrian woman named Audata. For Philip's numerous wives
see Athenaeus 13.557c.

15. The Erigon was a tributary of the Axius (Vardar), now the
Tzerna. Pelium was a Macedonian border fortress situated south of
Lake Lychnitis.

having sacrificed three boys, three girls, and three black rams, made a movement as if with the intention of engaging the Macedonians at close quarters; but no sooner had the latter come within striking distance than they abandoned their defensive positions, strong though they were. The bodies of the victims they had sacrificed were found still lying where they fell.

Alexander now shut them up in the town, and taking up a position close to the walls, proposed to establish a blockade; but on the following day Glaucias appeared with a large force. As a result of this Alexander abandoned his project of taking the town; for his own force was comparatively small, many fine fighting men had withdrawn within the walls, and many more, under Glaucias' command, would be ready to attack him should he make an attempt upon the defences. Accordingly he dispatched Philotas on a foraging expedition with the baggage animals and a small squadron of mounted troops to act as guard. The movement did not escape Glaucias; he went forward to the attack, and seized the high ground which ringed the stretch of country where Philotas and his men intended to collect their forage. The danger which threatened both the mounted troops and the pack-animals should they be overtaken by darkness was reported to Alexander, who at once marched to their rescue with a force composed of the Agrianes, the archers, and the Guards, and a squadron of cavalry 400 strong. His remaining troops he left near the town; for had he withdrawn his entire force the enemy who were shut up within it might well have broken out and joined Glaucias. Glaucias, however, abandoned his position on the high ground as soon as he saw Alexander coming, and Philotas' party returned to camp in safety.

Nevertheless it still seemed that the forces under Glaucias

and Cleitus had caught Alexander in an awkward
position. They held the commanding heights strongly,
both with mounted troops and with other detachments
armed with javelins and slings, in addition to a considerable force of heavy infantry; those at present confined
within the town were all ready to attack the moment
Alexander withdrew; and the country through which the
withdrawal would have to be made was in the nature of a
narrow wooded pass, with the river on one side and a
lofty range with precipitous foothills on the other, so that
it would hardly be practicable for his army to get through
even four abreast. Such being the situation, Alexander
drew up the main body of his infantry in mass formation
120 deep, posting on either wing 200 cavalrymen with
instructions to make no noise, and to obey orders smartly.
Then he gave the order for the heavy infantry first to
erect their spears, and afterwards, at the word of command, to lower the massed points as for attack, swinging
them, again at the word of command, now to the right,
now to the left. The whole phalanx he then moved smartly
forward, and, wheeling it this way and that, caused it to
execute various intricate movements. Having thus put his
troops with great rapidity through a number of different
formations, he ordered his left to form a wedge and
advanced to the attack.

The enemy, already shaken by the smartness and discipline of these manoeuvres, abandoned their position on
the lower slopes of the hills without waiting for the Macedonians to come to grips with them. Thereupon Alexander called on his men to raise the war-cry and clash
their spears upon their shields, with the result that the din
was altogether too much for the Taulantians, who hastily
withdrew to the town.

A small party of enemy troops were still in possession

of a hill by which Alexander would have to pass; he gave orders, accordingly, to the Companions and the men of his personal guard to prepare for action and ride to the attack. Their instructions were that if the enemy who had occupied the hill should hold their ground, half their number should dismount and fight on foot in close support of their mounted comrades. The hill, however, was not held; the enemy, as a result of this movement of Alexander's, abandoned it and went off at a tangent towards the mountains. Alexander with the Companions then occupied the hill, sent for the Agrianes and archers – a force of some 2,000 men – and ordered the Guards to cross the river, followed by the other Macedonian units, and, on reaching the further side, to form up towards the left in order to present a solid front to the enemy immediately they were across the river. Meanwhile he kept a careful watch from the hill upon any movement the enemy might make.

Seeing the Macedonian troops crossing the river, the natives moved down from the high ground with the intention of falling upon Alexander's party which would form the rear of the army as it withdrew; and Alexander countered by a rapid sally of his own, while the main body of his infantry, coming to the attack through the river, raised the war-cry. The enemy, under the combined onslaught, broke and fled, and Alexander ordered the Agrianes and archers to advance at the double to the river. He himself was the first across, and, setting up his artillery on the river-bank, he gave orders for every sort of missile it would take to be discharged at long range against the enemy, whom he could see pressing hard upon those of his own troops who were bringing up the rear. The archers, too, who were already part-way over, were ordered to shoot from mid stream. Glaucias' men refused to venture within range, and the Macedonians got across safely, without a single casualty during the process of withdrawal.

Three days later information came in that the troops under Cleitus and Glaucias were encamped without adequate precautions: no regular sentries had been posted, and no palisade or trench constructed for their protection; their line, moreover, was perilously extended. Alexander at once took advantage of this carelessness – which was due, presumably, to the assumption that he had retreated in panic. Under cover of darkness he took the Guards, the Agrianes, the archers, and the troops of Perdiccas and Coenus back across the river, with orders to the rest of the army to follow. The moment was ripe for attack; so, without waiting for the entire force to concentrate, he sent into action the Agrianes and the archers, who made a surprise assault on a narrow front – a formation likely to fall with greatest effect upon the enemy at his weakest point. Some they killed in their beds, others they took without difficulty as they tried to escape. Many were caught and killed on the spot, many more as they fled in panic and disorder. Not a few were captured alive. The pursuit was pressed as far as the mountains in Taulantian territory. None escaped except at the cost of throwing away their weapons. Cleitus' first move was to the town; later he set fire to it and made his way to the Taulantians, where he sought refuge with Glaucias.

Meanwhile events were taking place in Thebes.[16] Certain persons, with a view to overthrowing the government, had invited a number of political exiles to return; these men, having slipped into the city during the night, had seized and murdered Amyntas and Timolaus, two of

16. Diodorus (17.8–14) gives a more detailed account of events at Thebes, considerably less favourable to Alexander.

the men who were holding the Cadmeia and had no suspicion of any danger outside.[17] They then presented themselves in the Assembly and incited the Thebans to rebel
against Alexander, making great play with the grand old
words 'liberty' and 'autonomy',[18] and urging them at
long last to throw off the burden of the Macedonian yoke.
They made their appeal more attractive to the Thebans in
general by insisting that Alexander had died in Illyria –
which was, as it happened, a common rumour at the time
and fairly widely disseminated, because he had been long
absent without communicating with them.[19] In these
circumstances they did what most of us do, and, being
ignorant of the truth, persuaded themselves into believing
what they wished to believe.

The news of these events caused Alexander considerable concern. For a long time past he had had doubts
about Athens, and now had come this attempt from
Thebes. He could not but take it seriously, for the danger
clearly was that the spirit of disaffection might spread to
the Lacedaemonians, who already, in any case, silently
resented Macedonian control, and to other states in the
Peloponnese, and even to the Aetolians, who were by no

17. Since 338 the Cadmeia, the citadel of Thebes, had been occupied by a Macedonian garrison. Timolaus was a leading partisan of
Macedon (Demosthenes, *On the Crown* 295). For Amyntas we should
perhaps read Anemoitas, whom Demosthenes mentions with Timolaus as a Theban traitor.

18. The words 'and autonomy' do not occur in the manuscripts,
but a second noun is clearly required. 'Freedom of speech' has been
suggested (but 'autonomy' appears preferable). 'Freedom' and
'autonomy' are very frequently coupled, and the Greek states were
explicitly guaranteed these rights in the 'Charter' of the Corinthian
League (see Pseudo–Demosthenes 17.8).

19. Demosthenes is reported to have produced at Athens a soldier
who asserted that Alexander was killed in the same battle in which
he himself had been wounded.

means to be trusted. He therefore decided to act, and, proceeding by way of Eordaea and Elimiotis and the mountain ranges of Stymphaea and Paravaea, arrived within seven days at Pelinna in Thessaly. Six days later he entered Boeotia, and the news that he had passed the Gates did not reach the Thebans until his whole force was at Onchestus.[20] Even then the organizers of the revolt continued to maintain that Alexander was dead: an army under Antipater, they declared, had arrived from Macedonia, and anyone who reported that Alexander himself was in command they met with an angry denial – if it was Alexander at all, they insisted, it was another Alexander, Aeropus' son.

The following day Alexander left Onchestus and marched to Thebes. He halted by the enclosure of Iolaus, waiting there in order to give the Thebans time to think things over, in case they should change their minds and decide to treat with him. Nothing, however, was further from their thoughts than coming to terms or yielding a single inch; on the contrary, their mounted troops and a considerable force of light infantry made a rapid sortie and attacked the outposts of the Macedonian army with missile weapons at long range, and not altogether without effect. Alexander ordered out parties of light infantry and archers to check them, which they did without difficulty, though they had already advanced almost within striking distance of his main position. Next day he moved round with his entire force to the gates which lead to Eleutherae and Attica. Here, still refraining from an assault upon the city's defences, he took up a position not far from the

20. Onchestus lies on the shore of L. Copais, some 6 miles north-west of Thebes. The distance from Pelium to Onchestus is not less than 250 miles. By 'the Gates' Arrian means The pass of Thermo-pylæ.

Cadmeia, to provide support for the Macedonians who were holding it. The Thebans had ringed it with a double palisade and were watching it closely, so that no outside help could reach the besieged garrison, or any sudden attack from within interfere with their own operations against their enemies elsewhere. Alexander, however, made no move, but continued to wait; for he still hoped to remain on terms with the Thebans and to avoid action against them.[21]

In these circumstances all who had their city's interest most at heart were anxious to approach Alexander and gain from him a general pardon for the revolt; but the exiles and the party responsible for their recall, especially as some of them were officers of the Boeotian Confederacy, refused to recognize the possibility of humane treatment by Alexander, and urged war by every means in their power. But still Alexander waited and did not attack.

Ptolemy, the son of Lagus, states in his account of these operations that Perdiccas, who, as officer in charge of the guard, was posted with his own battalion not far from the enemies' palisade, began the assault on his own initiative and without waiting for the word of command from Alexander.[22] Forcing a breach in the palisade, he burst in upon the Theban advanced troops, followed by Amyntas, the son of Andromenes, who with his own troops, which formed a part of the same contingent, moved forward immediately he saw that Perdiccas had got inside. It was to prevent them from being cut off and being placed at the mercy of the Thebans that Alexander ordered a

21. Alexander's delay before Thebes is confirmed by Diodorus and Plutarch. The latter relates (*Alexander* 11.7) that he requested the surrender of the anti-Macedonian leaders, Phoenix and Prothytes, promising to pardon those who surrendered, but that he received an insulting reply.

22. In Diodorus (17.12.3) Perdiccas acts on Alexander's orders.

general advance, sending his archers and the Agrianes through the breach in the palisade, but still keeping his personal guard and the remainder of the Guards outside.

Perdiccas was wounded while he was trying to break through the second palisade; he was carried back to the base, but the wound was serious and it was only with difficulty that his life was saved. His men, joined by Alexander's archers, boxed the Thebans up in the sunken road which runs down by the Heracleum, pressing on them hard so long as they retreated towards that temple; but the moment came when they turned to face their pursuers with a yell of rage, and then it was the Macedonians who gave ground. About seventy of the archers were killed, together with their commander, Eurybotas the Cretan; the rest hurriedly sought the protection of Alexander's Guard and the remainder of the Guards.

The sight of his men in full retreat, with the Thebans straggled out in chase of them, soon brought a counter-blow from Alexander, who launched an infantry attack in close order, and drove the enemy inside the city gates. The rout became a panic – so much so, indeed, that they failed to shut the gates behind them in time. The result was that the men of the Macedonian army closest on their heels passed with them, in the general scramble, inside the fortifications, which the need for so many advanced posts had left undefended. One party, joining up with the garrison of the Cadmeia, passed thence by way of the Ampheum into the actual town, while the troops by the walls, which were already held by the men who had got in during the rout, swarmed over the top and made at the double for the market square.

For a short time the Theban armed forces stood firm by the Ampheum, until, attacked from every side by the

Macedonians, with Alexander himself apparently ubiquitous in the field, they broke. Their mounted troops, forcing a way through the streets, fled to the open country,
and the infantry endeavoured to save their skins as best
they could. In what followed it was not so much the Macedonians as the Phocians, Plataeans, and men from other
Boeotian towns who, in the lust of battle, indiscriminately
slaughtered the Thebans, who no longer put up any organized resistance. They burst into houses and killed the
occupants; others they cut down as they attempted to
show fight; others, again, even as they clung to temple
altars, sparing neither women nor children.[23]

The violence of the action, the size and importance of
the fallen city, above all, perhaps, the unexpectedness of
the event both to victors and vanquished, all made the
horror of this disaster to men of Grecian blood hardly less
shattering for the rest of Greece, than for those who were
actually involved. The Sicilian expedition, measured
merely by the number of dead, brought a comparable
disaster to Athens; but that, it must be remembered, took
place far from home: the army which perished was not a
native army, but consisted largely of troops from allied
states; Athens herself remained untouched, still able to
hold out for a number of years against Persia and the
Lacedaemonian confederacy; and for all these reasons her
defeat in Sicily did not bring to Athens the same sense of
overwhelming calamity, or to the rest of Greece a comparable thrill of horror.[24] Again, the defeat at Aegospotami was at sea, and though Athens by that defeat suffered

23. Over 6,000 Thebans were killed and more than 30,000 taken
prisoner. The sale of the captives realised 440 talents (Diodorus
17.14; Plutarch, *Alexander* 11.12).
24. The Athenian losses in the Sicilian expedition (415–13) cannot be precisely calculated, since we do not know how many of the

humiliation in the destruction of her Long Walls, the
surrender of the greater part of her navy, and the loss of
her empire, she nevertheless retained her hereditary form
of government and quickly recovered her former strength;
indeed, the Long Walls were rebuilt, her sea-power was
regained, and she was actually able subsequently to reverse
the position and save from great danger those very Lacedaemonians who had once been so formidable and had
come so near to destroying her.[25] The Lacedaemonians
themselves, after the defeats at Leuctra and Mantinea,
were shaken rather by the unexpectedness of the disaster
than by the magnitude of their losses; and it was the
strangeness of the sight when the Boeotians and Arcadians under Epaminondas launched their attack upon
Sparta, much more than the immediacy of the danger, that
struck terror into them and their allies.[26] Again, the capture of Plataea cannot be considered a major disaster; for

---

crews of over 200 triremes, over 40,000 men, were Athenians. But
at least 4,000 Athenian cavalrymen, hoplites, and light-armed were
lost. For the forces employed in Sicily see the passages from
Thucydides cited by N. G. L. Hammond, *History of Greece* 390, n. 1.
Persia entered the war in 412 and Athens held out until the spring
of 404.

25. The defeat at Aegospotami (August 405) made Athens' surrender inevitable. The terms of surrender were 'demolition of the
Long Walls and the Peiraeus fortifications, surrender of the fleet
save 12 vessels, evacuation of the empire, recall of exiles, and
obedience to Sparta in all matters of foreign policy'. (Hammond,
op. cit., 418). The recovery of Athenian sea-power may be said to
date from August 394 when Conon defeated the Spartan fleet at
Cnidus. The rebuilding of the Long Walls, begun shortly before this,
was completed about 391. Both owed much to Persian subsidies.

26. The Boeotian League under Theban leadership defeated
Sparta at Leuctra in 371 and at Mantinea in 362. The invasion of
Sparta took place in 369. See Xenophon, *History of Greece* 6.4.4–15;
7.5.18–27; and 7.1.15–22 respectively.

the town was a small one, and, as most of its people had
already fled to Athens for refuge, very few were taken
when it fell; and, lastly, the capture of Melos and Scione
was hardly more important: they were merely island
communities, and their destruction, though a disgrace to
its perpetrators, could scarcely be called a severe shock to
Greece as a whole.[27]

With Thebes, on the contrary, it was a different matter:
the lack of planning, the rapid movement of events which
led to the revolt, the suddenness and ease with which the
city fell, the slaughter, so appalling and so inevitable
where men of kindred stock are paying off old scores, the
complete enslavement of a city pre-eminent in Greece for
power and military prestige, were, not unnaturally, all put
down to the wrath of God. People felt that Thebes, at
long last, had been punished for her treachery – she had
paid the penalty for her betrayal of Greece in the Persian
war, her capture of Plataea during the truce, the merciless
enslavement of its population, and the massacre, for which
she alone was responsible, of men who had surrendered
not to her, but to Sparta, and the devastation of a country-
side in which the united armies of Greece had driven back
the Persian invader, and, lastly, for the murderous malig-
nancy she showed towards Athens when she voted in
favour of the suggestion, put forward by the Lacedaemonian confederacy, that the people of Athens should
be sold into slavery.[28] Everyone now declared that the

27. All three towns were forced to surrender during the Peloponnesian War after lengthy sieges, Plataea to Sparta in 427, Melos and
Scione to Athens in 415 and 421 respectively. In each case the adult
males were put to death and the women and children enslaved.

28. A Theban force had surprised Plataea in March 431, but had
been forced to evacuate the town. It was near Plataea that in 479 the
Greeks had defeated the Persians under Mardonius and compelled
them to withdraw from Greece. Thebes had been used as the

calamity had been preceded by many warning signs from heaven – signs ignored at the moment, but remembered now, long afterwards, and clearly proved by the event to have been prophetic of the coming doom.[29]

The allied troops who took part in the fighting were entrusted by Alexander with the final settlement of the fate of Thebes. They decided to garrison the Cadmeia, but to raze the city itself to the ground.[30] All its territory but the places hallowed by religious associations was to be divided among the allies; the women, the children, and all the men who survived were to be sold into slavery – the only exceptions being priests or priestesses and such as had either personal ties with Alexander or Philip or official connexions with Macedon. It is generally believed that Alexander's reverence for Pindar induced him to spare the poet's house and all his living descendants. In addition to this, the allies determined to rebuild and fortify Orchomenus and Plataea.[31]

Persian base and a Theban contingent had fought on the Persian side.

At the end of the Peloponnesian War the Theban Erianthus moved that Athens should be destroyed and her citizens put to death or enslaved. Sparta, to her credit, resisted the proposal.

29. Diodorus (17.10) mentions a variety of portents.

30. The moral responsibility lay with Alexander, although he was doubtless formally correct in submitting the decision to his allies. The revolt constituted a breach of the Common Peace and Alexander (as *Hegemon*) will have called out the League troops although only Thebes' neighbours – the Plataeans, Phocians, Thespians, and Orchomenians are mentioned – can have sent them. But Alexander cannot have failed to realise what the sentence of those states ,bitter enemies of Thebes with many scores to settle, would be. He surely wished the fate of Thebes to be a dreadful warning to any other state which might contemplate revolt.

31. After Chaeroneia Philip had proposed to rebuild Plataea and Orchomenus, destroyed by Thebes in 373 (for the second time) and in 364 respectively, but apparently nothing had yet been done.

When the news of the Theban *débâcle* became generally known, the Arcadians who had started out in order to assist in the rising condemned to death those of their compatriots who had urged them to do so; the Eleans granted a pardon to their political exiles, simply because they were on good terms with Alexander; the various branches of the Aetolians all sent representatives to beg forgiveness on the ground that they had supported the revolt only because of the news from Thebes. In Athens the arrival of Theban refugees straight from the fighting coincided with the celebration of the Great Mysteries; the shock of the news induced the Athenians to cut short the ceremony and begin at once to get all movable property into the city from the surrounding country.[32] The Assembly was convened, and on the motion of Demades ten men, all known to be on particularly friendly terms with Alexander, were sent to him to represent the city's attitude and to assure him, somewhat unseasonably, that the Athenian people rejoiced to see him safely returned from Illyria and the Triballians, and thoroughly approved his punishment of the Thebans for their revolt. Alexander's reply to these representations was in general friendly enough; he did, however, demand, in a letter to the Athenians, the surrender of Demosthenes and Lycurgus, and, in addition, of Hypereides, Polyeuctus, Chares, Charidemus, Ephialtes, Diotimus, and Moerocles, all of whom he held responsible for the defeat at Chaeronea and for certain errors in policy, detrimental to Philip's interest and his own, subsequently committed upon Philip's death.[33] He declared moreover

32. The Great Mysteries of Demeter were celebrated at Eleusis from the 15th to the 23rd of the Attic month Boedromion, corresponding to September/October.

33. According to Plutarch (*Demosthenes* 23.3) the most reliable writers gave eight names, although others mentioned ten. The

that these men were as responsible for the rebellion as were the Thebans themselves, who had actually carried it out.[34] The Athenians, instead of giving the men up, sent again to Alexander and begged him to relent – which he did, perhaps out of regard for Athens, perhaps simply because he was in a hurry to proceed with his Asian campaign and unwilling to leave behind him in Greece any cause for mistrust. He did, however, give orders that one of the men whose surrender he had unsuccessfully demanded – Charidemus – should be exiled. The sentence was carried out, and Charidemus took refuge in Asia at the court of Darius.[35]

Alexander now went north again to Macedonia, and offered to Olympian Zeus the form of ceremonial thanksgiving which had been in use since the time of Archelaus.[36] He also celebrated the Olympian games at Aegae, and, according to some accounts, held games in honour of the Muses. During the ceremonies a report came from Pieria that the statue of Orpheus, son of Oeagrus of Thrace, had been constantly sweating, a phenomenon which was variously interpreted by the seers; one of them,

---

names preserved vary. Those mentioned by Arrian are all orators except the generals Chares, Charidemus, and Ephialtes. Arrian is perhaps thinking of the dedication by Demosthenes of a shrine to Pausanias, Philip's murderer (Aeschines 3.160), and of his correspondence with the Macedonian General, Attalus, who with Parmenio had opened the campaign against Persia early in 336.

34. Demosthenes had supplied the Thebans with arms and the Athenians had voted to support them but had taken no action.

35. Others too left Athens. Chares met Alexander at Sigeum in 334 (p. 67 below), while Ephialtes and Thrasybulus (whose name some think has fallen out of Arrian's list) fought on the Persian side at Halicarnassus (Diodorus 17.25.6).

36. King of Macedonia from 413 to 399. He was renowned as a patron of art and literature, and it was at his court that Euripides spent his last years during which he wrote the *Bacchae*.

however – Aristander of Telmissus – told Alexander that he had no cause for alarm: it merely signified that the writers of odes and the epic and melic poets had hard work coming to celebrate Alexander and his exploits in verse and song.[37]

At the start of the next campaigning season Alexander left Antipater in charge of affairs in Macedonia and Greece, and made for the Hellespont with a force composed of not much more than 30,000 infantry, including light troops and archers, and over 5,000 cavalry.[38] His route lay past lake Cercinitis, in the direction of Amphipolis and the mouth of the Strymon, which he crossed, and proceeded by way of Mount Pangaeum towards Abdera and Maroneia, two Greek settlements on the coast; continuing from there to the Hebrus, which he also crossed without difficulty, he marched through Paetica and across the river Melas to Sestus, which he reached twenty days after leaving home. At Elaeus he offered sacrifice upon the tomb of

37. This phenomenon, caused by the condensation of moisture, is frequently mentioned in classical literature. It is said to have occurred at the moment of Alexander's arrival at Thebes. Aristander was Alexander's (and perhaps Philip's) chief seer, who is frequently recorded in Arrian to have made correct prophecies. The inhabitants of Telmissus in Caria were noted as early as the middle of the sixth century for their skill in divination (Herodotus 1.78; cf. p. 104 below).

38. Antipater was left with 12,000 infantry and 1,500 cavalry. Arrian's figures are confirmed by Diodorus who (17.17) gives a list of Alexander's forces after the crossing into Asia totalling 32,000 infantry and 5,100 cavalry. The higher figures for infantry (43,000; 40,000) given by other writers may include the 10,000 troops who were in Asia in 335, although the majority of these may well have been withdrawn by this time. No satisfactory explanation has been found for their lower figures for cavalry. See, most recently, P. A. Brunt, *JHS* 1963, 33ff., and E. W. Marsden, *The Campaign of Gaugamela* (Liverpool, 1964), 24ff.

Protesilaus, who was supposed to have been the first man of Agamemnon's army to set foot upon the soil of Asia when the Greeks sailed against Troy. His purpose in performing the ceremony was to ensure better luck for himself than Protesilaus had.[39]

The task of getting the mounted troops and most of the infantry across the Hellespont from Sestus to Abydos was entrusted to Parmenio, and the crossing was carried out in 160 triremes and a large number of merchant vessels. It is generally believed that Alexander sailed from Elaeus to the Achaean harbour,[40] himself at the helm of the admiral's ship, and that half way over he slaughtered a bull as an offering to Poseidon and poured wine from a golden cup into the sea to propitiate the Nereïds. There is a further tradition that, fully armed, he was the first to leave the ship and set foot upon the soil of Asia, and that he built an altar on the spot where he left the shore of Europe and another where he landed on the other side of the strait, both of them dedicated to Zeus, the Lord of safe landings, Athena, and Heracles.[41] Once ashore, he travelled inland to Troy and offered sacrifice to Athena, patron goddess of the city; here he made a gift of his armour to the temple, and took in exchange, from where they hung on the temple walls, some weapons which were still preserved from the Trojan war. These are supposed to have been carried before him by his bodyguard when he went into battle.[42] He is also said to have offered sacri-

39. Homer, *Iliad* 2.701; Herodotus 9.116.

40. North-west of Troy, near Cape Sigeium.

41. Diodorus (17.17.2) relates that Alexander, before leaping ashore first, threw his spear to claim Asia as a 'spear-won' prize. If this is true, it suggests that Alexander had already determined to conquer the Persian Empire.

42. The shield was carried by Peucestas in the attack on the citadel at the Malli town (p. 313 below).

fice to Priam on the altar of Zeus Herceius, to avert his anger against the family of Neoptolemus,[43] whose blood still ran in his own veins.

At Troy his sailing-master, Menoetius, crowned him with gold, as did Chares the Athenian, who came from Sigeium with a number of others, either Greeks or natives. One account says that Hephaestion laid a wreath on the tomb of Patroclus; another that Alexander laid one on the tomb of Achilles, calling him a lucky man, in that he had Homer to proclaim his deeds and preserve his memory.[44] And well might Alexander envy Achilles this piece of good fortune; for in his own case there was no equivalent: his one failure, the single break, as it were, in the long chain of his successes, was that he had no worthy chronicler to tell the world of his exploits.

No prose history, no epic poem was written about him; he was not celebrated even in such choral odes as preserve the name and memory of Hiero or Gelo or Thero, or many other men not in the same class as Alexander, with the result that the wonderful story of his life is less familiar today than that of the merest nonentities of the ancient world.[45] Even the march of the Ten Thousand under Cyrus against Artaxerxes, the fate of Clearchus and his fellow prisoners, and the return under Xenophon's command to the sea, are, thanks to Xenophon's history, much

43. The son of Achilles and founder of the Molossian dynasty. Alexander claimed descent from him through his mother, Olympias.

44. Hephaestion had been Alexander's dearest friend from boyhood. The crowning of the tombs of Achilles and Patroclus symbolizes their relationship. For Alexander's extravagant grief at his death see p. 371 below.

45. Hiero and Gelo ruled Syracuse and Thero Acragas (Agrigentum) in the early fifth century. Their achievements were celebrated by Pindar and Bacchylides.

better known than the grand achievements of Alexander[46];
yet, unlike Xenophon, Alexander did not hold a mere
subordinate command; he was not defeated by the Persian
King, or victorious only over the force which tried to stop
his march to the sea. On the contrary, there has never been
another man in all the world, of Greek or any other blood,
who by his own hand succeeded in so many brilliant enterprises. And that is the reason why I have embarked upon
the project of writing this history, in the belief that I am
not unworthy to set clear before men's eyes the story of
Alexander's life. No matter who I am that make this claim.
I need not declare my name – though it is by no means
unheard of in the world; I need not specify my country
and family, or any official position I may have held.
Rather let me say this: that this book of mine is, and has
been from my youth, more precious than country and kin
and public advancement – indeed, for me it *is* these things.
And that is why I venture to claim the first place in
Greek literature, since Alexander, about whom I write,
held first place in the profession of arms.

From Troy, Alexander marched to Arisbe, where his
entire force had taken up its position after crossing the
Hellespont; next day he proceeded to Percote, and the
day after passed Lampsacus and halted by the river Prac-
tius, which has its source in Mount Ida and flows into the
sea which connects the Black Sea with the Hellespont.
From there his route led past Colonae to Hermotus. On
the march he had scouts ahead of the army, under the
command of Amyntas, son of Arrabaeus, with the squadron of Companion cavalry from Apollonia under Socrates,
son of Sathon, and four squadrons of what were known
as advanced scouts. The town of Priapus, which lay on

46. The *Anabasis* of Xenophon. The fate of Clearchus is related
in the second book.

his route, surrendered to him, and he sent a party under Panegorus, son of Lycagoras, one of his Companions, to take it over.

The Persian forces were commanded by Arsames, Rheomithres, Petines, and Niphates in association with Spithridates, the satrap of Lydia and Ionia, and Arsites, the governor of northern Phrygia. They had taken up a position near the town of Zeleia with the Persian cavalry and the Greek mercenary troops. On receiving the report that Alexander had crossed into Asia, they met to discuss the situation. Memnon of Rhodes advised against risking an engagement: the Macedonian infantry, he pointed out, was greatly superior in numbers; Alexander was present in person, while Darius was not. It would be better, there-fore, to proceed at once to burn all growing crops, trample down and destroy grass and horse-feed, and even gut the towns, to prevent Alexander, by lack of supplies, from remaining in the country. Arsites, however, is said to have replied to this proposal that he would not consent to the destruction by fire of a single house belonging to any of his subjects. The other commanders supported him – no doubt because they had their suspicions of Memnon, and guessed that he was afraid of losing the position he held from Darius, if fighting started too soon.[47]

Alexander meanwhile was advancing in battle order upon the river Granicus. His infantry was massed in two groups, both wings protected by cavalry, while all trans-port had orders to follow in the rear. The reconnaissance

47. Memnon was not a mere *condottiere*, but had become one of the ruling class of Persia, married to the sister of Artabazus. In 335 he had succeeded in checking the Macedonian advance in Asia Minor, and at this time advocated carrying the war into Europe (Diod. 17.18.2). On his subsequent activities and death, see below p. 101..The satraps were (perhaps) actuated partly by jealousy in rejecting his plan.

parties were under the command of Hegelochus, with the lancers and about 500 light troops. Just short of the river the scouts galloped back to report that the Persian army had taken battle positions on the further bank, whereupon Alexander gave all necessary orders in preparation for an engagement. Parmenio, however, was opposed to this; presenting himself before Alexander, 'My lord,' he said, 'in my view our best plan in the present situation is to halt here, on this side of the river. The enemy infantry is heavily outnumbered by ours, and I do not think they will run the risk of remaining so close to us throughout the night; so if they withdraw, we can get across at dawn without opposition – indeed, we shall be over before they have a chance of getting into position to meet us. But to attempt the crossing in the present circumstances would, I think, be a grave risk. We cannot manage the crossing in line on a broad front, because in many places the river is obviously deep, the banks very high and, here and there, almost sheer. We should have to cross, therefore, in column, and in loose order at that, with the result that their massed cavalry will be upon us just as we are struggling out of the water and at the greatest possible disadvantage. A failure at the outset would be a serious thing now, and highly detrimental to our success in the long run.'

Alexander had his answer: 'Yes, Parmenio,' he said, 'but I should be ashamed of myself if a little trickle of water like this' (a very derogatory way of referring to the Granicus!) 'were too much for us to cross without further preparation, when I had no difficulty whatever in crossing the Hellespont. Such hesitancy would be unworthy of the fighting fame of our people and of my own promptitude in the face of danger. Without doubt it would give the Persians added confidence; nothing has yet happened to them to cause them alarm, and they would begin to think they were as good soldiers as we are.'[48]

Without further delay he sent Parmenio to take command of the left wing, and himself moved over to the right. Command of the right had already been given to Philotas, Parmenio's son, with the Companion cavalry, the archers, and the Agriane spearmen; Amyntas, son of Arrabaeus, was attached to him with the lancers, the Paeonians, and Socrates' squadron. On the left of these divisions were the Guards' battalions, commanded by Parmenio's son, Nicanor; next came the infantry battalions of Perdiccas, son of Orontes, of Coenus, son of Polemocrates, of Amyntas, son of Andromenes, in that order: finally the troops under Amyntas' son, Philip. The advance position of the left wing was held by the Thessalian cavalry under Calas, son of Harpalus, and these were supported – in the following order – by the allied cavalry under Philip, son of Menelaus, and the Thracians under Agathon. Immediately on their right was infantry – the battalions of Craterus, Meleager, and Philip, extending to the centre of the army as a whole.

The Persians had about 20,000 cavalry and nearly the same number of foreign mercenaries fighting on foot. Back from the river the ground rose steeply, and they had taken up a position with their mounted troops along the bank on a very broad front and with the infantry in the

48. Nothing could have suited Alexander better than the Persian decision to fight. He realised the moral effect a victory would have on the Greek cities of Asia Minor, and wished the Persian commanders to have no excuses for what he regarded as their certain defeat.

This is the first of a number of instances where Alexander rejects Parmenio's advice, some of which at least may be due to the imagination of Callisthenes, seeking, as official propagandist, to lessen the odium of Parmenio's murder by denigrating the old general.

rear.[49] At one point on the river-bank they had massed their squadrons in strength – for here it was that, threatening their left, they could see Alexander himself, an unmistakable figure in magnificent armour, attended by his suite with an almost ecstatic reverence.

There was a profound hush as both armies stood for a while motionless on the brink of the river, as if in awe of what was to come. Then Alexander, while the Persians still waited for the crossing to begin, that they might fall upon his men as they were struggling up the further bank, leapt upon his horse and called upon his bodyguard to follow and to play the man. His orders were that Amyntas, son of Arrabaeus, should lead off into the water with the advanced scouts, the Paeonians, and one infantry company, preceded by Ptolemy, son of Philip, with Socrates' squadron, which was the leading cavalry squadron for that day; then he himself, at the head of the right wing of the army, with trumpets blaring and the shout going up to the God of Battle, moved forward into the river. He kept his line oblique to the pull of the current as the troops went over, to prevent a flank attack as they emerged from the water, and to enable him to engage the enemy with a front as solid as he could make it.

The leading files under Amyntas and Socrates were met as they gained the river bank by volleys of missiles from the Persians, who kept up a continuous fire into the river both from their commanding position on the high ground above, and also from the comparatively flat strip right down by the water's edge. A hand-to-hand struggle developed, the Macedonian mounted troops trying to force their way out of the water, the Persians doing their utmost

49. Thereby depriving the cavalry of the opportunity to charge and the infantry (surely not as many as 20,000) of the opportunity to fight until it was too late. The reason for this blunder is not clear.

to prevent them. Persian lances flew thick and fast, the long Macedonian spears thrust and stabbed. In this first onslaught Alexander's men, heavily outnumbered, suffered severely; their foothold was insecure, and down there in the water they had to contend with an enemy in a strong position on the bank above them – not to mention the fact that they met there the fine flower of the Persian horse, with Memnon and his sons braving the fortune of battle in its midst.

The first to engage the Persians were cut down and died a soldier's death, though some of the leading troops fell back upon Alexander, who was now on his way across: indeed, he was almost over, at the head of the army's right wing. A moment later he was in the thick of it, charging at the head of his men straight for the spot where the Persian commanders stood and the serried ranks of enemy horse were thickest. Round him a violent struggle developed, while all the time, company by company, the Macedonians were making their way over the river, more easily now than before. It was a cavalry battle with, as it were, infantry tactics: horse against horse, man against man, locked together, the Macedonians did their utmost to thrust the enemy once for all back from the river-bank and force him into open ground, while the Persians fought to prevent the landings or hurl their opponents back into the water.

Things soon turned in favour of Alexander's men; their experience and the weight of their attack began to tell, added to the advantage of the long cornel-wood spear over the light lances of the Persians.

During the fight Alexander's spear was broken. He called on Aretis, one of his grooms, for another, but Aretis was himself in difficulties for the same reason, though still fighting gallantly enough with the remaining half of his

weapon. Showing it to Alexander, he called out to him to
ask someone else, and Demaratus the Corinthian, one of
Alexander's personal bodyguard, gave him his spear. The
fresh weapon in his hand, he caught sight of Mithridates,
Darius' son-in-law, riding with a squadron of horse in
wedge formation far ahead of the main body; instantly he
galloped out in front of his men, struck Mithridates in the
face with his spear, and hurled him to the ground. Rhoe-
saces then rode at Alexander with his scimitar and, aiming
a blow at his head, sliced off part of his helmet, which
nevertheless dulled the full force of the impact. A moment
later Alexander was on him, and he fell with a spear-thrust
through his cuirass into his breast. Now Spithridates had
his scimitar raised, ready for a blow at Alexander from
behind; but Cleitus, son of Dropidas, was too quick for
him, and severed his shoulder scimitar and all. Meanwhile
Alexander's party was being steadily reinforced by the
mounted troops as one after another they succeeded in
getting up out of the river and joining him.

The Persians were now in a bad way: there was no
escape for horse or rider from the thrust of the Macedonian spears; they were being forced back from their
position and, in addition to the weight of the main attack,
they were suffering considerable damage from the lightly
armed troops who had forced their way in among the
cavalry. They began to break just at the point where
Alexander in person was bearing the brunt of things.

Once the centre had failed to hold, both wings of the
Persian cavalry broke, too, and the rout was complete.
About 1,000 were killed – not more, because Alexander
soon checked the pursuit of them in order to turn his
attention to the foreign mercenaries, who had remained
in their original position, shoulder to shoulder – not, indeed, from any deliberate intention of proving their

courage, but simply because the suddenness of the disaster had deprived them of their wits. Ordering a combined assault by infantry and cavalry, Alexander quickly had them surrounded and butchered to a man, though one or two may have escaped notice among the heaps of dead.[50] About 2,000 were taken prisoner. Among the killed were the Persian commanders Niphates, Petines, and Spithridates, satrap of Lydia; Mithrobuzanes, governor of Cappadocia; Mithridates, son-in-law of Darius; Arbupales, son of Darius and grandson of Artaxerxes; Pharnaces, brother of Darius' wife, and Omares, commander of the foreign contingent. Arsites escaped to Phrygia, where he is said to have died by his own hand, because the Persians held him responsible for the defeat.

The Macedonian losses were small: about twenty-five of the Companion cavalry were killed during the first assault. Their statues in bronze now stand at Dium, executed, on Alexander's instructions, by Lysippus, who had been chosen from a number of competitors to make statues of Alexander.[51] Rather more than sixty of the other mounted troops were killed, and about thirty infantrymen.[52] By order of Alexander all the dead were buried with their arms and equipment on the day after the battle, and their parents and children were granted immunity from local taxes and all forms either of personal service or dues payable on property. For the wounded he

50. This massacre was a blunder, as was the sending of the Greek prisoners to hard labour, although in accordance with the decree of the Corinthian League. As early as the siege of Miletus Alexander realised this and allowed the 300 mercenaries, who were prepared to resist to the end, to enlist in his army.

51. Arrian seems to be wrong. According to Velleius (1.11.4) the statues were removed to Rome in 148 by Metellus Macedonicus.

52. The figures for Macedonian losses are suspiciously low, as they often are, in view of the resistance put up by the mercenaries.

showed deep concern; he visited them all and examined their wounds, asking each man how and in what circumstances his wound was received, and allowing him to tell his story and exaggerate as much as he pleased. He also gave rites of burial to the Persian commanders and the Greek mercenaries who fell fighting in the enemies' ranks; the Greek prisoners he sent in chains to hard labour in Macedonia, as a punishment for contravening the resolution of the League of Corinth by fighting in a foreign army against their own countrymen. As an offering to the goddess Athena, he sent to Athens 300 full suits of Persian armour, with the following inscription: *Alexander, son of Philip, and the Greeks (except the Lacedaemonians) dedicate these spoils, taken from the Persians who dwell in Asia.*[53]

Alexander appointed Calas to the satrapy previously held by Arsites, with orders to maintain the taxes at the same level as before; all natives who came out of hiding in the hills and surrendered he allowed to return to their homes; to the people of Zeleia he gave a free pardon, because he knew that they had fought with the Persians only under pressure. He sent Parmenio to take over Dascylium; and this was done without trouble, as the guards had abandoned the town.[54]

His next objective was Sardis. He was still some eight or nine miles away when he was met by Mithrines, the officer in command of the inner fortress; with him were

53. In view of the small part which the Greeks had played in the battle the inscription (with its omission of any mention of the Macedonians) must be regarded as propaganda designed for his Greek allies. Alexander does not fail to stress the absence of the Spartans.

54. Zeleia was a Greek city, but presumably paid the same taxes as the other inhabitants of the region. For the development of Alexander's policy towards the Greek cities see E. Badian, 'Alexander the Great and the Greeks of Asia', in *Ancient Society and Institutions. Studies Presented to Victor Ehrenberg* (Oxford, 1966), 37ff.

the leading men of the town, who had come to surrender it to Alexander, while Mithrines did the same for the fortress and the treasure. Alexander halted on the Hermus, a river about two and a half miles from Sardis, and sent on Amyntas, son of Andromenes, to take over the fortress; Mithrines he kept with his own suite, treating him in a way suitable to his rank, while the people of Sardis and the other Lydians he permitted to observe the old customs of their country and gave them their freedom.[55]

While he was in Sardis he went up into the acropolis, where the Persian garrison was stationed, and saw at a glance that this fortress, built as it was on a lofty and precipitous hill and defended by a triple wall, was an extremely strong position.

It occurred to him to build here a temple and altar in honour of Olympian Zeus, and while he was considering the best site a summer storm, breaking suddenly with violent thunder and a fall of rain over the palace of the Lydian kings, persuaded him that Zeus himself had indicated the spot where his temple should be raised; so he gave his orders accordingly.

He left Pausanias, one of his Companions, in charge of the fortress, and made Nicias responsible for the organization and payment of the tribute; the governorship of Lydia and the other territory formerly controlled by Spithridates was given to Asander, son of Philotas, with an adequate force of light infantry and mounted troops. Calas and Alexander, son of Aeropus, were sent to Memnon's part of the country[56] with the Peloponnesians and most of the other allied troops, with the exception of the Argives, who were left in Sardis to garrison the fortress.

55. Neither more nor less, as Alexander's arrangements show, than they had previously enjoyed.
56. Part of the Troad.

Meanwhile, news of the cavalry engagement had reached Ephesus. The mercenaries who formed the garrison of the town seized two warships and made their escape, accompanied by Amyntas, son of Antiochus, who had left Macedonia in order to avoid Alexander. He had not, to be sure, anything to complain of in Alexander's treatment; he merely disliked him and was disinclined to be made uncomfortable by his presence.

Alexander took three days to reach Ephesus; on his arrival he recalled everyone who had been expelled for supporting him, stripped the small governing clique of its power, and restored democratic institutions. All dues previously paid to Persia he transferred to the temple of Artemis.[57] The people of the town, freed from the fear of their political masters, were eager to put to death the men who had been responsible for calling in Memnon, and everybody else who had either ransacked the Temple, or helped to smash up the statue of Philip which stood there, or break open in the public square the tomb of Heropythus, the liberator. They dragged from the temple and stoned to death Syrphax and his son Pelagon and all his nephews. Alexander, however, who was well aware that the Ephesian populace, given the chance of continuing the hunt for guilty men and indulging its lust for revenge, would, out of personal hatred or greed, kill many who were innocent as well, firmly called a halt, with the result that his popularity never stood higher than it did on this occasion by his handling of the situation at Ephesus.

During the same period representatives came from the towns of Magnesia and Tralles to offer their submission; he accordingly dispatched Parmenio with a force consist-

57. Alexander had offered to dedicate the newly rebuilt temple – the old one had been burnt down on the night of his birth – but the Ephesians refused. Note that the tribute is not remitted.

ing of 2,500 allied foot, 2,500 Macedonians, and about 200 Companion cavalry, giving instructions for a similar force under Alcimachus, son of Agathocles, to proceed to the Aeolian towns and all the Ionian ones still subject to Persia. Throughout the country he dispossessed the ruling cliques and established popular government in their place, allowing every community to enjoy its own laws and customs and discontinue payment of the taxes it had previously paid to the Persians.[58] Meanwhile he remained in Ephesus, offered sacrifice to Artemis, and held a ceremonial parade of his troops, fully equipped and in battle order.

On the following day he marched for Miletus with a force made up of all the infantry not otherwise engaged, the archers, the Agrianes, the Thracian cavalry, the Royal Squadron of the Companion cavalry, and three other squadrons. What is known as the Outer City fell into his hands without a blow, as the garrison had withdrawn, whereupon he called a halt and proposed to establish a blockade of the inner defences, where Hegisistratus, who had been entrusted by Darius with the defence of the town, was still hoping to hold out. This officer had, some time before, written to Alexander to offer submission, but the proximity of the Persian fleet had subsequently encouraged him to make an effort to save the city for his masters. Nicanor, however, was too quick for him; he brought the Greek fleet to Miletus three days ahead of the Persians, and anchored, with 160 ships, at Lade, the island just off the town. The Persians had missed their opportunity; and the commanders, as soon as they found that

---

58. The establishment of democracies is not due to any preference on Alexander's part for democratic government (why, indeed, should he prefer it?), but because the Persians had supported oligarchies.

Nicanor's fleet had put in at Lade before their arrival, brought their own ships to anchor under Mount Mycale. Alexander, had, indeed, already made sure of Lade not only by anchoring his fleet there: he had also put ashore on the island his Thracian contingent, and some 4,000 other mercenary troops.

The Persians had about 400 ships, but Parmenio, in spite of their numerical superiority, urged Alexander to engage. He did, undoubtedly, believe that a sea-fight would go in favour of the Greeks, but the real reason for his confidence was a sign from heaven – an eagle which had been seen on the beach just astern of Alexander's ships. He pointed out that a victory in present circumstances would be of great strategic advantage, while a defeat would not be very serious, as Persia in any case had command of the sea. He was fully prepared, he said, to go aboard himself and share the perils of the day. Alexander replied that Parmenio was mistaken, and that he had wrongly interpreted the omen. In the first place, it was absurd to rush blindly into a naval engagement against greatly superior forces, and with an untrained fleet against the highly trained Cyprian and Phoenician crews; the sea, moreover, was a tricky thing – one could not trust it, and he was not going to risk making a present to the Persians of all the skill and courage of his men; as to defeat, it would be very serious indeed and would affect profoundly the general attitude to the war in its early stages, above all by encouraging the Greeks to revolt the moment they got news of a Persian success at sea. Secondly, having given his reasons for not risking an engagement, he went on to say that his interpretation of the omen was different from Parmenio's: the appearance of the eagle was, without doubt, a favourable sign; but the fact that it had been seen on shore surely indicated that it was his army, not his navy, which would render the Persian fleet powerless – he would, as it were, win his sea battle from the land.

At this juncture a distinguished Milesian named Glaucippus appeared before Alexander with a proposal from the people of the town and the foreign mercenaries who were chiefly responsible for guarding it in the Persian interest: this was that they were willing to grant free use of their harbours, and free entry within their walls, to Alexander and the Persians alike, and that on these terms the siege should be raised. Alexander's reply to this suggestion was to order Glaucippus to get back to his friends at the double and tell them to be ready to defend themselves at dawn next morning. He then proceeded to order up his siege engines; the walls were bombarded at close range, long stretches of the fortifications breached with battering-rams; he then brought his men up, to be ready to get a foothold at any point where the defences were sufficiently gapped or weakened to allow an entry, while the Persians at Mycale were so near that the progress of operations against their friends was almost visible to their eyes.

When Nicanor's men in Lade saw that Alexander's assault had begun, they got their ships under way and, rowing along shore, made for the harbour at Miletus, where they brought up in the narrowest part of the entrance, each vessel close aboard its neighbour, so that the harbour was effectively closed to the Persian fleet and the Milesians could no longer hope for assistance from that quarter. The Milesians and the mercenary troops in the town were already hard pressed by Alexander's attack; and now, at this fresh development, some of them plunged into the sea and paddled themselves over on their upturned shields to an islet (it has no name) just off the town, while others made a desperate effort to escape in boats before the Macedonian warships arrived; but they were too late and were caught at the harbour entrance. Most of them, however, were killed within the walls.

The town was now in Alexander's hands, and his next move was to turn his attention to the men who had escaped to the little island. Its shore was steep, and landing on it would be much like scaling a wall; so to facilitate the operation he had scaling-ladders fixed in the bows of his ships – when, however, he saw that the fugitives were preparing to fight to the death, he was moved to pity by their courage and loyalty and refrained from action on condition of their serving in future under his own command. They were Greek mercenaries, about 300 in number. All the Milesians who had not been killed when the town was taken he let go free.

The Persians continued for a while to use Mycale as a base for annoying the Greek fleet at Miletus. Every day they made a movement towards it in the hope of provoking a conflict; at night they remained in their station, which was not, however, a comfortable one, because they were obliged to water their ships from the Maeander, which was a long way off.[59] Alexander, still keeping his fleet on guard in the harbour, to prevent the Persians from forcing an entrance, sent Philotas round by land to Mycale with the mounted troops and three companies of infantry, with orders to stop the Persians getting ashore. The result was that lack of water and other supplies reduced the Persian crews to what was, to all intents and purposes, a state of siege; so they sailed for Samos, filled up there with whatever they needed, and returned to Miletus. Off the harbour they took up battle stations with the main body of their fleet, hoping to lure the Macedonians out into deep water, while five of their ships

59. Miletus lay nearly 10 miles from the mouth of the Maeander.

carried on into the sheltered water between Lade and the
Macedonian position on shore. There was a chance, they
thought, of surprising Alexander's ships with no one
aboard, because they had been told that most of the crews
had gone off on various jobs, such as collecting firewood
or foraging or fetching supplies. Some of the men were
actually away, but there were enough left on duty for
Alexander, when he saw the five enemy vessels approaching, to man ten of his own and send them out on the
instant with orders to ram. The five Persians found the
hostile approach of the Greek ships by no means according to plan; at first sight of them, still some way off, they
put about and hurried back to rejoin the fleet. One of
them, manned by Iassians, was a slow ship and failed to
get away; she and her crew were taken, but the other four
kept ahead of the pursuers and safely rejoined the fleet.
As a result of this episode the Persian fleet left Miletus,
with nothing to show for the time it had spent there.

Alexander now decided to disband his fleet. He had not,
at the moment, the money for maintaining it; he knew
that it was no match for the Persian navy, and he had no
wish to subject any part of his strength, in ships or men,
to the risk of disaster.[60] Moreover, now that his army was
master of the continent, he was well aware that a fleet was
no longer of any use to him: by seizing the coastal towns
he could reduce the Persian navy to impotence, for they
would then have no port on the Asian coast which they
could use, and no source of replacement for their crews.
Here, then, was the point of his interpretation of the
omen of the eagle – it meant that he would 'conquer the
ships from the land'.

60. Alexander doubtless also distrusted the loyalty of his Greek
allies. He retained the twenty Athenian ships whose crews may be
considered hostages.

Having settled affairs at Miletus, he started for Caria on a report that the Persians were in Halicarnassus with a considerable force of native and mercenary troops. The towns which lay upon his route surrendered without resistance, but on arriving at Halicarnassus he took up a position rather more than half a mile from the town in expectation of a long siege; for apart from the natural strength of the place, due to its geographical situation, any deficiencies in the means of assuring its safety had long before been supplied in person by Memnon, who had already been appointed by Darius controller of lower Asia and commander of the whole fleet; a powerful force of Persian troops and mercenaries had been left to garrison the town, and the presence of warships in the harbour meant that the sailors, too, could lend a helping hand, should the need for action arise.[61]

On the first day Alexander moved up towards the fortifications on the side of the town which faces Mylasa. As he approached the gates the defenders made a sortie and flung weapons at long range. A counter-attack by Alexander's men checked them without difficulty, and they were driven back within the walls. A few days later, with a force consisting of the Guards, the Companion cavalry, and the infantry battalions commanded by Amyntas, Perdiccas, and Meleager, supported by the Agrianes and archers, Alexander moved round to the part of the town which faces Myndus, his intention being to reconnoitre the state of the defences in that sector in the hope of finding that they offered an easier approach.[62] There was also, he thought, a chance that by an unexpected raid he might

61. For a somewhat different account of the siege, especially in its final stages, see Diodorus 17.23–27.

62. Myndus lay at the western end of the peninsula on which Halicarnassus stood.

take Myndus, the possession of which would greatly facilitate the siege of Halicarnassus. The plan was all the more attractive because some people in Myndus had suggested that they might open their gates to him if he came under cover of darkness. He accordingly took them at their word and approached the town about midnight. There was, however, no sign of surrender. Alexander, who had expected the place to be betrayed into his hands, was not prepared for a siege: he had brought with him neither rams, nor artillery, nor ladders; nevertheless, ill-equipped as he was, he ordered the Macedonian infantry to advance and begin sapping operations. They destroyed one fort, but its fall did not leave the wall defenceless; the troops in the town put up a vigorous resistance and, with the help of strong reinforcements which arrived by sea from Halicarnassus, successfully frustrated the surprise attack. Alexander accordingly, forced to withdraw with his object unaccomplished, turned his attention once more to the siege of Halicarnassus.

To enable him to bring into position his siege-engines – the towers from which to bombard the defenders of the wall, the artillery and battering-rams for breaching the defences – Alexander began by filling in the trench, about 45 feet wide and 23 feet deep, which had been dug outside the town. The work was done without difficulty and the towers soon brought into position. After dark a party of Halicarnassians made an attempt to set fire to the Macedonian siege artillery, including the towers, which were either already in position or about to be brought up; but the Macedonians on guard duty, with the help of others who were awakened by the noise during the action and joined them, had little trouble in driving them back within the town's defences. They lost 170 men, including Neoptolemus who, among others, had deserted to

Darius.[63] He was the son of Arrabaeus and brother of Amyntas. Alexander's losses were about 16 killed and 300 wounded – the comparatively large number of wounded being due to the fact that the attack took place in the dark, when it is more difficult to defend oneself.

A few days after this incident two Macedonian infantrymen of Perdiccas' battalion were drinking together in their tent and telling each other what stout fellows they were; as they warmed up with the drink, each bragging as hard as he could go, it soon developed into a competition between the pair of them, until at last they seized their weapons and, without any serious intention of risking their lives in a fight, but simply to prove to each other what mighty fellows they were, sallied out on their own to attack the wall of the town on the high ground facing Mylasa. Some soldiers in the town saw the foolish pair coming and promptly went for them. But the Macedonians killed those who came near, and hurled missiles at those who remained at a distance, although the Halicarnassians outnumbered them and the lie of the land was greatly in their favour since they could both shoot and move forward to the assault from high ground. More men from Perdiccas' battalion soon came hurrying to meet this threat, and, on the other side, reinforcements from the town. There was a sharp struggle, until once again the Macedonians succeeded in driving the attacking force back within their gates. Indeed, the town itself was very nearly taken; the walls, at the moment, were inadequately defended, and the collapse of two towers together with the intervening stretch of wall would have offered an easy entrance, had the assault been made in strength. Moreover a third tower had been badly damaged

63. According to Diodorus he was killed fighting on the Macedonian side.

and might easily have been brought down by mining; but before anything could be done, the men in the town made good the breach in their defences by building, from inside, a crescent-shaped wall of brick – and many hands made light work of it.

On the following day Alexander brought up his siege artillery to attack it, and his move was promptly countered by a party from the town. Their object was to set fire to his assault machines, and they succeeded in burning a part of the screen near the walls and of one of the wooden towers, though everything else was saved by the men under Philotas and Hellanicus, who were on guard there. During the raid Alexander appeared upon the scene in person, and the result was that the raiding party dropped their firebrands – most of them throwing away their weapons as well – and beat a hurried retreat into the town.

In spite of this set-back, in the first phases of the ensuing struggle the defenders had the advantage: their position, on the higher ground, was a commanding one; the troops forming a screen in front of Alexander's assault machines could be met by volleys of missiles not only in the direct line of their advance, but also from the flanks, where they could be enfiladed from the towers still standing on both sides of the breach in the original wall; indeed as they approached the newly built section, they could be shot at practically from the rear as well.

A few days passed before Alexander renewed his assault on the new brick wall inside the town. This time he took personal charge of the operation. His move was met by a counter-attack in full force from the town, by one division at the breach in the wall, where Alexander was, and by another at the Tripylum, or Triple Gate, where the Macedonians least expected it. Flaming brands and other inflammable material were flung at the assault machines to set them alight and spread the blaze; but the men under Alexander's immediate command made a strong counter-attack; the catapults mounted on towers kept up a continuous pressure by hurling heavy stones; javelins flew thick and fast, and the defenders of the town were without difficulty beaten back and forced to withdraw once more within their defences. The attempt had been a bold one, carried out with a considerable force, and their losses were, in proportion, heavy: some were killed in hand-to-hand fighting with the Macedonians, others among the debris of the breached wall: they could not get through because the gap was too narrow for such a press of men, and they could not get over because the fallen blocks of stone were an almost insuperable impediment.

The force which had made its sortie at the Tripylum was met by Ptolemy, Captain of the Royal Guard, with the troops under Addaeus and Timander, supported by light infantry. These had no greater trouble than the others in repelling the attack from the town. Like that of their comrades, the retreat of this force, too, was disastrous: for as they withdrew across a narrow bridge over the dyke, the bridge collapsed under the excessive weight. Many were flung into the dyke and were either trampled to death by their comrades or shot from above by the Macedonians. But the worst slaughter was at the gates of the town, which were shut too soon in blind fear of letting in the Macedonians on the heels of the fugitives; in this way the defenders shut out large numbers of their friends, who were cut down by the Macedonians right under the walls. Once again the town was almost in Alexander's hands; but even in this extremity he wished to save it, if only the people gave any sign of willingness to come to terms. So he called off the assault.

In this action Halicarnassus lost about 1,000 men, Alexander about forty, among whom were Ptolemy, Captain of the Royal Guard, Clearchus in command of the archers, Addaeus, a chiliarch – or battalion commander – and other well-known Macedonians.

The Persian commanders Orontobates and Memnon now met to discuss the situation. It was clear that in present circumstances it would not be possible to hold out much longer; part of the wall was already gone, other parts were seriously damaged, and in the recent sorties they had lost heavily, many men having been either killed or put out of action by wounds. Accordingly, somewhere near midnight they had the magazines set on fire together with the wooden tower which had been constructed as a counter to the enemy assault machines. The houses near the wall were also fired, while flames from the fiercely burning tower and magazines were spread by the wind to other buildings, which were soon ablaze as well. Their own surviving forces withdrew to the Arconnese, an island stronghold, and the high ground known as Salmakis.

These events were reported to Alexander by some Halicarnassians who had deserted after the fighting; accordingly, as the fire was still spreading before his eyes, he ordered up his Macedonian divisions, in spite of the fact that it was nearly midnight, with instructions to kill every man they could catch in the act of setting fire to buildings. Any of the townspeople found indoors were, on the contrary, to be rescued from the conflagration.

Daylight revealed the occupation by the Persians and their mercenaries of Salmakis and the Arconnese. Alexander, however, decided not to lay siege to these strongholds, because in addition to the fact that they would be awkward to take and much time would be wasted, he knew that, with the town itself already in his hands, they would not bring him any great advantage. So he buried the men killed in the night's fighting, ordered the troops in charge of the assault engines to move them to Tralles, and then razed the town to the ground. To garrison the place, together with the rest of Caria, he left a force of 3,000 infantry – mercenaries – and about 200 mounted troops under their commander Ptolemy. Then he made his preparations to move on into Phrygia.

He appointed Hecatomnus' daughter Ada to the governorship of Caria as a whole. This woman was the wife of Hidrieus – and also his sister, a relationship in accordance with Carian custom; Hidrieus on his death-bed had bequeathed her his power, government by women having been a familiar thing in Asia from the time of Semiramis onward.[64] She was subsequently deposed by Pixodarus, who seized power, and was succeeded after his death by his son-in-law Orontobates, who had been appointed to the position by a warrant from the King. Ada meanwhile remained in control of Alinda only, one of the most strongly defended places in Caria, and when Alexander invaded Caria she presented herself before him, surrendered the town, and offered to adopt him as her son. Alexander did not refuse the offer. He restored Alinda to her, and when, with the fall of Halicarnassus, he found himself master of Caria, he put the whole country under her control.

A number of the Macedonians serving in the campaign had been married just before the expedition started; feeling that some consideration was due to these men, Alexander dismissed them from Caria and sent them home to

64. Hecatomnus, the ruler of Caria, left three sons, Mausolus, Hidrieus, and Pixodarus, and two daughters, Artemisia and Ada. Artemisia married Mausolus and Ada Hidrieus, and all succeeded their father.

spend the winter with their wives; they were put in charge of Ptolemy, son of Seleucus, an officer of the Royal Guard, and of two other officers of high rank: Coenus son of Polemocrates, and Meleager son of Neoptolemus – both chosen because they, too, were newly married men. The officers' instructions were to raise levies of both horse and foot on as large a scale as possible on their rejoining the army with the party in their charge. No act of Alexander's ever made him better beloved by his native troops.

At the same time he sent Cleander, son of Polemocrates, to raise troops in the Peloponnese, while Parmenio was dispatched to Sardis with a force consisting of a regiment of the Companions, the Thessalian cavalry, the other allied contingents, and the baggage wagons. His orders were to proceed from Sardis to Phrygia. Alexander himself marched for Lycia and Pamphylia, to establish control of the coast and so immobilize the enemy's fleet. On the way the first place he took was the fortified town of Hyparna; it was held by a mercenary garrison, but on the offer of a truce they abandoned the citadel and marched out to surrender. There was no battle. On entering Lycia he took over Telmissus, the people agreeing not to resist him, after which he crossed the Xanthus and accepted the surrender of Pinara, Xanthus, Patara, and about thirty smaller places.[65]

It was now midwinter, and Alexander's next move was into what is known as Milyas – which actually belongs to greater Phrygia, but was reckoned at that period, by order of the Persian King, as part of Lycia.[66] Here he was met by representatives from Phaselis, bringing him a gold

65. The only resistance occurred at Marmara, where the inhabitants finally set fire to the town (Diodorus 17.28).
66. Milyas was the old name for Lycia, but was later applied to the high country extending north-eastwards to Pisidia.

crown and offers of friendship, and similar offers also reached him from the greater part of lower Lycia. Alexander in reply instructed the envoys from Phaselis, as well as those from Lycia, to surrender their towns to the proper authorities, which was duly done in every case. Soon afterwards he went in person to Phaselis and helped the people of the town to reduce a fortress which the Pisidians had built nearby as a base from which to annoy them – and annoy them they did, men at work on the land often suffering severely from their raids.

Before he had finished with Phaselis, a report reached him of the intended treachery of Alexander, son of Aeropus. This man was one of his Companions, in close contact with the King, and also, at the time, in command of the Thessalian cavalry; he was also a brother of Heromenes and Arrabaeus, both of whom had been involved in the murder of Philip.[67] On the occasion of his father's murder, Alexander, in spite of the fact that the evidence against his namesake looked black, did not prosecute the charge, because he had been among the first to support him on Philip's death, accompanying him into the palace, armed like his master; subsequently Alexander had given him an honourable position in his personal suite, sent him to direct operations in Thrace, and finally appointed him to the command of the Thessalian cavalry in place of Calas, who had been transferred to a provincial governorship.[68]

The plot was revealed to Alexander in the following way. Amyntas, who had deserted to the Persians, brought Darius certain written proposals from this fellow Alexandros (as I shall now call him). Thereupon Darius sent down to the coast a trusted member of his suite named

67. Both were executed.
68. Hellespontine Phrygia. Alexander had been sent to this region with Calas (p. 77 above).

Sisines, ostensibly on a visit to Atizyes, the satrap of Phrygia, but in reality to get into contact with Alexandros and promise him the throne of Macedonia and 1,000 talents of gold if he succeeded in assassinating the King. Sisines, however, fell into Parmenio's hands, revealed the purpose of his mission, and was sent on under guard to Alexander, to whom he repeated his story. Alexander called a meeting of his friends to discuss the situation, and the members of the Companions most closely in his confidence expressed the opinion that it was a mistake in the first place to have put an untrustworthy officer in command of the best cavalry regiments, and that he should now be summarily disposed of, before he became hand in glove with the Thessalians and plotted rebellion. Moreover, an ominous event had added to their anxiety; for it so happened that while Alexander, during the siege of Halicarnassus, was taking his siesta, a swallow flew round and round over his head twittering loudly in a way that seemed to express unusual alarm, and kept settling on various parts of his bed.

Alexander was too tired to wake up properly, but the noise the bird made disturbed him, so with his hand he tried to shoo it gently away, but without success; for, far from being scared off by the touch of Alexander's hand, it came and perched on his head, and refused to budge until he was fully awake.

Convinced that the incident was not without significance, Alexander reported it to the soothsayer Aristander of Telmissus, who declared that it portended a friend's treachery; and, in addition, that the plot would be revealed, for swallows are domestic birds, friendly to man and exceedingly talkative.

This clearly corroborated Sisines' story; so the king sent Alexander's son Amphoterus (he was brother to

Craterus) to Parmenio, accompanied by some natives of Perga to act as guides. To avoid recognition on the journey, Amphoterus wore native dress, and succeeded in reaching Parmenio without detection; he had no written instructions, for Alexander felt that in an affair of this sort it would be dangerous to commit anything to writing – he merely delivered a verbal message, as directed. In this way Alexandros was arrested and put into custody.

Alexander now left Phaselis. Part of his forces he dispatched over the mountains towards Perga, along tracks made for him by the Thracians to facilitate what was otherwise a long and difficult journey. He himself marched with his picked troops along the coast, a route which is practicable only in northerly winds – during southerlies the beach is impassable. It had been blowing hard from the south before he started; but (by the grace of God, as both he and his staff felt) the wind went round into the north and made the passage quick and easy.[69] Advancing from Perga he was met by plenipotentiaries from Aspendus, who offered to surrender the town, but begged, at the same time, that no garrison should be put in. As to the garrison, they got what they asked for; but Alexander demanded that the town should contribute fifty talents towards the men's pay and hand over all the horses bred there as tribute to Darius.[70] Both demands were agreed to, and the envoys returned home.

69. Plutarch (*Alexander* 17.6) remarks that many historians found in this incident an opportunity for 'striking and bombastic' treatment, and wrote of a 'heaven-sent stroke of fortune'. He cites a letter in which Alexander said nothing of this miraculous occurrence, but Callisthenes certainly began the process, presumably with Alexander's approval.

70. Badian (*Ehrenberg Studies*, 65, n. 50) comments that 50 talents was an enormous sum for a Greek city to pay and that the demand indicates Alexander's need for money at this time.

The next objective was Side, a town whose people came originally from Cyme in Aeolia. There is a tradition among them that when the first settlers from Cyme sailed thither and landed from their ships to found a new home, they promptly forgot their native Greek and began to talk in a foreign tongue – not the language spoken by the people of those parts, but an entirely new dialect of their own; and from then on the men of Side had remained foreigners, distinct in speech, as in everything else, from their neighbours.

Alexander left a party of men to occupy Side and then proceeded to Syllium, a fortified town garrisoned by mercenaries and native troops. He was unable, however, to take this place by assault, without regular siege operations, and this fact, combined with a report which he had received during his march, determined him to return to Aspendus. The report stated that the people of Aspendus had backed out of their agreement; they were refusing to hand over the horses to the proper authorities and to pay the money; moreover, they had taken their movable property inside the town's defences, shut their gates against Alexander's men, and were at work upon all necessary repairs to their walls.

The main part of the town of Aspendus is built upon a very steep and easily defended hill, the base of which is washed by the river Eurymedon. There were also a number of houses on the level ground round this central stronghold, all of them enclosed within a wall of no great height. This wall, together with all houses on the flat ground which seemed impossible to hold, was abandoned by the people of the place the moment they were aware of Alexander's approach. They hurriedly withdrew and took refuge within the fortified centre on the hill. Alexander, as soon as he reached the town, led his men inside the outer wall – now defenceless – and took up his quarters in the deserted houses.

The shock of Alexander's presence and the sight of his army surrounding them were too much for the people of the town: they sent their spokesmen to him and begged to be allowed their original terms. Alexander, however, in spite of the fact that the position of Aspendus was obviously a strong one and he was not himself prepared for a protracted siege, refused the request; he demanded, in addition to the horses they had previously agreed to hand over, 100 talents instead of the original fifty and the surrender as hostages of the leading men of the community; further, they were forced to obey the governor appointed by himself, to pay an annual tribute to Macedon, and submit to an inquiry into the rightful ownership of the land, which they were accused of holding by force, when it was really the property of their neighbours.

When this was settled to his satisfaction, Alexander moved on to Perga, and thence, by a route which led past Telmissus, to Phrygia.[71] The people of Telmissus are an Asiatic race of Pisidian blood; the town stands on a lofty and precipitous height, and the road which leads past it is an inconvenient one, because a ridge runs right down to it from the town above, breaking off short with the road at the bottom, while opposite to it, on the other side, the ground rises again in an equally steep ascent. The two cliffs make a sort of natural gateway on the road, so that quite a small force can, by holding the high ground, prevent an enemy from getting through. And this is precisely what the Telmissians did: they marched out with every available man and occupied the heights on either side of the road. Alexander, accordingly, gave the order to halt at once, convinced that when the enemy saw his

71. The town meant is Termessus, but the error may be Arrian's.

men taking up a position for the night they would no longer hold the road in force but withdraw the majority of their troops into the town near by, leaving only a small party on the hills to keep a watch. His guess proved right: the main body retired, and only the outposts remained. Alexander then promptly moved to the attack with a force consisting of the archers, the javelin battalions, and the more mobile infantry. The small force on the hills, unable to withstand the weight of his missiles, abandoned the position, and Alexander moved on through the narrow passage and took up a fresh position near the town.

It was at this juncture that representatives from the large town of Selga sought an interview with Alexander. The people of this place, too, are Pisidians – Asiatics – and are good soldiers. They were old enemies of Telmissus, and their object in sending to Alexander was to offer him their support. Alexander accepted the offer, and from that moment found them trustworthy in every respect.

Concluding that it would not be possible to reduce Telmissus without a long siege, he now proceeded to Sagalassus, another place of some size, belonging, like Telmissus, to people of Pisidian blood. The Pisidians are all fine soldiers, but the Sagalassians were conspicuous even among a nation of fighters. On this occasion they occupied the high ground in front of the town, a position no less good for defensive action than the wall itself, and there awaited the Macedonian assault. On the right wing of the attacking force Alexander had the Guards division under his personal command. In touch with them were the infantry battalions, forming the whole centre of the line and commanded by the various officers whose turn of duty happened to fall upon that day; command of the left he assigned to Amyntas, son of Arrabaeus. In advance of the right wing he stationed the archers and the Agrianes,

while his left was screened by the Thracian javelin battalions under Sitalces. Cavalry was useless, as the nature
of the ground was unsuitable for it. The enemy were reinforced by troops from Telmissus who had come to offer
assistance.

When Alexander's troops had reached the steepest part
of the ascent towards the Pisidians' position on the hill,
they were attacked on both wings by small parties of men,
who took advantage of the difficult ground to slip in
where they best could and the enemy had least chance to
retaliate; in this they were partially successful, for the
archers who were leading the assault, and were, moreover, only lightly protected, were forced to retreat. The
Agrianes, however, yielded nothing – encouraged, no
doubt, by the fact that the Macedonian infantry divisions
were already coming up, with Alexander in full view at
the head of them. A hand-to-hand struggle ensued; the
Pisidians, who had no defensive armour, found themselves matched with fully equipped heavy infantry, with
the result that they suffered severe losses and finally broke.
About 500 were killed; prisoners were few, because their
light equipment and knowledge of the country made
escape easy, while the Macedonians, for their part, with
their heavy gear and lack of local knowledge, were none
too eager to pursue them. None the less Alexander hung
on to the fugitives and stormed the town. Cleander, who
commanded the archers, was killed during these operations, as were about twenty others.

Alexander then proceeded against the other Pisidian
communities; some of their fortified places he took by
assault, others surrendered to him without resistance.

His next move was into Phrygia. His route lay past lake
Ascania – a lake from which the people of the neighbourhood collect natural salt, so that they have no need to

depend on supplies from the sea. Five days later he was at Celaenae.

The town of Celaenae has a lofty central stronghold, sheer all round, and this was garrisoned by 1,000 Carian troops and 100 Greek mercenaries, who took their orders from the Persian governor of Phrygia. The garrison sent Alexander an offer to surrender the town provided that no reinforcements arrived on a certain day on which they had agreed to expect them – which date they specified; and it seemed better to Alexander to accept this arrangement than to attempt the reduction by siege of such an unassailable position. Accordingly he left a force of some 1,500 men to watch the town, and after a wait of ten days marched for Gordium. Before he left he appointed Antigonus, son of Philip, to the governorship of Phrygia, promoting Balacrus, son of Amyntas, to the command of the allied contingents in his place.[72] To Parmenio he sent orders to meet him at Gordium with the troops under his command – and the orders were duly carried out. The recently married Macedonians who had been sent home on leave also rejoined at Gordium with a force of freshly levied troops – 3,000 Macedonian infantry and about 300 horse, 200 Thessalian horse, and 150 men from Elis under their own commander Alcias. The whole force was commanded by Ptolemy son of Seleucus, Coenus son of Polemocrates, and Meleager son of Neoptolemus.

Gordium is in Hellespontine Phrygia; the town stands on the river Sangarius, which rises in Phrygia and runs

72. Despite his great services in keeping Alexander's communications open – Curtius (4.1.35) mentions three victories over Persian forces after Issus – this is the only mention in the *Anabasis* of Antigonus 'the One-Eyed', the father of Demetrius the Besieger. Tarn (*Alexander* 2.110) attributes this silence to the fact that Ptolemy was his bitter enemy in the Wars of the Successors.

through Bithynian Thrace into the Black Sea. During his stay there Alexander was visited by envoys from Athens with a request for the liberation of Athenian prisoners of war, who had been captured on the Granicus fighting for Persia and were at that time in Macedonia under close confinement, with the other 2,000 prisoners. But for the moment, at any rate, the request was not granted, and the envoys were forced to return with their mission unfulfilled. For Alexander felt that, with the war against Persia still on his hands, it would be dangerous to relax his severity towards anyone of Greek nationality who had consented to fight for Asia against his own country. Nevertheless he did tell the Athenian envoys that they might approach him again on the matter when circumstances were favourable.[73]

73. They were released early in 331 after Alexander's return from Egypt (p. 156 below).

BOOK TWO

AFTER the events just related the island of Chios was betrayed into the hands of Memnon, whom Darius had made supreme commander of the Persian navy and responsible for the defence of the whole Asiatic coast. The object of Memnon's move was the hope of diverting the war to Greece and Macedonia. He then sailed to Lesbos and made himself master of all the towns in the island except Mitylene, the inhabitants of which refused to treat with him. He accordingly made a landing at Mitylene and blockaded it with a double stockade carried right to the sea on both sides; in addition to this he constructed five blockhouses, and was thus enabled to control the island without difficulty. Part of his fleet guarded the harbour; other ships he sent to the promontory of Sigrium,[1] the usual landing-place for merchantmen from Chios, Geraestus, and Malea, and was thus able to keep a watch on the coast and prevent any help from reaching Mitylene by sea.

Before his work was completed, however, he fell sick and died, and his death was the most serious setback which Persia received during this period of the war.

Memnon on his deathbed – and pending a further decision by Darius – had handed over his command to his nephew, Pharnabazus, Artabazus' son; and he and Autophradates vigorously prosecuted the siege. The people of Mitylene, finding themselves cut off on the landward side and blockaded by a powerful fleet, sent to Pharnabazus and agreed, first, to get rid of the mercenary troops sent

1. The most westerly point of the island.

to fight for them by Alexander; secondly, to rescind the pact they had made with him[2] and enter into alliance with Darius according to the terms of the peace of Antalcidas,[3] and, lastly, to allow their exiles to return and resume possession of half their original property. Such were the terms of the agreement; but Pharnabazus and Autophradates, once they had got inside the town, brought in a garrison under the command of Lycomedes of Rhodes and put one of the exiled party, named Diogenes, in general control with autocratic powers. At the same time they enforced the contribution of a sum of money, extorting a part of it from the wealthier men and raising the remainder by a general levy, after which Pharnabazus set sail for Lycia with the mercenary troops, while Autophradates proceeded to the other islands.

Meanwhile Darius sent Thymondas, son of Mentor, to fetch the mercenaries which were in Pharnabazus' charge and to order Pharnabazus himself formally to take over Memnon's command. The mercenaries were, accordingly, transferred to Thymondas,[4] and Pharnabazus sailed to rejoin Autophradates and the fleet. On his arrival they first dispatched ten ships under a Persian named Datames to the Cyclades islands, and then sailed with a squadron

2. *lit.* 'to destroy the pillars on which the treaty with Alexander was inscribed'. Arrian writes loosely; the treaty, as in the case of Tenedos (p. 103), was doubtless concluded with 'Alexander *and the Greeks*', i.e. the Mityleneans became members of the League of Corinth.

3. Called after the Spartan who was mainly responsible for negotiating the peace in 386. It is often (appropriately) called the King's Peace, since the Persian king gained control of the Greek states of Asia Minor, while the clause stipulating that all states in Greece should be autonomous prevented the creation of any hostile empire.

4. Thymondas took them by sea to Tripolis and thence to join Darius' army at Sochi. They fought in the B. of Issus. Their withdrawal effectively ruined any chance of a successful naval offensive.

a hundred strong for Tenedos, where they brought up in what is known as North Harbour. They then sent a demand to the islanders for the abrogation of their agreements with Alexander and the Greeks, and the observance of the terms of the Peace of Antalcidas, which they had concluded with Persia.

The people of Tenedos would have liked nothing better than to remain on good terms with Alexander and the Greeks; but in the circumstances they were forced to believe that their only hope of safety lay in accepting Persia's terms; even Hegelochus was a broken reed, for though he had had orders from Alexander once again to get a fleet together, he had not yet raised a sufficient force to give any prospect of speedy relief.[5] One might say, therefore, that Tenedos was scared into surrender by Pharnabazus and his men, against the true wishes of the people.

About this time it so happened that Proteas, son of Andronicus, upon orders from Antipater, had assembled a number of warships from Euboea and the Peloponnese to afford protection to the Greek coast and the islands in the event of a Persian attack by sea, which report said was not unlikely. Information reached Proteas that Datames had brought up off Siphnos with a squadron of ten ships, so with fifteen of his own he sailed at night for Chalcis on the Euripus. It was dawn when he reached the island of Cythnus, and throughout the day he remained there at anchor in order to get more definite information about the ten enemy ships, and also to give himself the chance of attacking their Phoenician crews with more devastating effect during the hours of darkness. As soon as all doubt about Datames' presence at Siphnos was removed,

5. Alexander's decision to disband his fleet might have proved costly had not Memnon opportunely died.

he made sail just before dawn, while it was still dark, delivered a surprise attack, and captured eight of the ten ships, together with their crews. Right at the start of the encounter with Proteas' squadron Datames slipped away with the remaining two vessels and succeeded in rejoining the rest of the fleet.

To return to Alexander at Gordium. Upon reaching this place he was irresistibly impelled to visit the palace of Gordius and his son Midas high up on the acropolis, in order to inspect the famous Wagon of Gordius and the Knot with which its yoke was fixed. There was a story about this wagon, widely believed in the neighbourhood. Gordius (so went the tale) lived in Phrygia in the ancient days; he was poor and had but two yoke of oxen and a small plot of land to till. With one pair of oxen he ploughed, with the other he drove his wagon. One day when he was ploughing an eagle perched on the yoke of his plough and stayed there until the oxen were loosed and the day's work done. Gordius was troubled, and went to the seers of Telmissus to consult them about what this sign from heaven might mean – for the people of Telmissus were skilled in interpreting God's mysteries, and their women and children as well as their men inherited the gift of divination. Near a village belonging to these people he fell in with a girl who was drawing water; he told her of the eagle, and she in reply, being herself sprung from a line of seers, advised him to return to the place where he had seen the sign and offer sacrifice to Zeus the King. Gordius urged her to go with him and show him the form the sacrifice should take, and he performed it as she directed, and afterwards married her, and they had a son whose name was Midas.

Now when Midas had grown to be a fine and handsome man there was trouble and strife among the Phrygians, and an oracle told them that a wagon would bring them a king, who would put an end to their quarrels. While they were still debating what to do about these things, Midas with his father and mother drove up in the wagon and came to a stop at their place of meeting. Taking this to be the fulfilment of the oracle, the Phrygians decided that here was the man whom the god had foretold that a wagon would bring. So they put Midas on the throne, and he made an end of their trouble and strife and laid up his father's wagon on the acropolis as a thank-offering to Zeus the King for sending the eagle.

There was also another traditional belief about the wagon: according to this, the man who undid the knot which fixed its yoke was destined to be the lord of Asia.[6] The cord was made from the bark of the cornel tree, and so cunningly was the knot tied that no one could see where it began or where it ended. For Alexander, then, how to undo it was indeed a puzzle, though he was none the less unwilling to leave it as it was, as his failure might possibly lead to public disturbances. Accounts of what followed differ: some say that Alexander cut the knot with a stroke of his sword and exclaimed, 'I have undone it!', but Aristobulus thinks that he took out the pin – a sort of wooden peg which was driven right through the shaft of the wagon and held the knot together – and thus pulled the yoke away from the shaft. I do not myself presume to dogmatize on this subject. In any case, when he and his attendants left the place where the wagon stood, the general feeling was that the oracle about the untying of the knot had been fulfilled. Moreover, that very night there was lightning and thunder – a further sign from heaven; so Alexander, on the strength of all this, offered sacrifice the following day to the gods who had sent the

6. In Alexander's day this meant the Persian Empire.

sign from heaven and proclaimed the Loosing of the Knot.

Next day he started for Ancyra in Galatia, where he was met by a deputation of Paphlagonians, who expressed a wish to be on terms of friendship with him, offering the submission of their people, and begging him not to march his troops into their territory. Alexander in reply instructed them to take their orders from Calas, the governor of Phrygia,[7] and then proceeded to Cappadocia, where he received the submission of all territory bounded by the river Halys and also of a large tract to the west and north beyond it. Then, leaving Sabictas[8] as governor of Cappadocia, he advanced to the Cilician Gates. When he reached the position where Cyrus had once encamped in the campaign with Xenophon, he found the Gates strongly held;[9] so he left Parmenio there with the heavy infantry, and marched under cover of darkness to the Gates with the Guards and Agrianes, with the intention of delivering a surprise attack upon the defending force. Actually, his approach was observed, but the bold move was none the less successful; for the knowledge that Alexander was coming upon them in person was too much for the enemy, who abandoned their posts and fled. At dawn the following morning he passed the Gates with all his men and entered Cilicia, where a report reached him that Arsames had abandoned his original intention of holding Tarsus for Persia: now, it appeared, having learned that Alexander had passed the Gates, he meant to give up the town,

7. Lesser Phrygia. Greater Phrygia (afterwards Galatia) was governed by Antigonus (p. 99).

8. Possibly a local chieftain. Nothing more is heard of him.

9. The modern Golek–Boghaz, the main pass over the Taurus Mts. between Cappadocia and Cilicia. See Xenophon *Anabasis* I.2.20–I.

and the townspeople were consequently afraid that he might strip the place before he left. Alexander, accordingly, brought up his cavalry and the most mobile of his light infantry with all possible speed, with the result that Arsames, the moment he was aware of his rapid approach, did not stop to plunder the town, but got out as fast as he could and made his way to the court of Darius.

About this time Alexander had a bout of sickness. The cause of it, according to Aristobulus' account, was exhaustion, but others say that he plunged into the river Cydnus for a swim, as he was sweating with heat and could not resist the pleasure of a bathe. The Cydnus runs right through Tarsus, and as it rises in Mount Taurus and flows through open country, its waters are clear and cold; the result was that Alexander was seized by a convulsion, followed by high fever and sleepless nights. All his doctors but one despaired of his life; but Philip of Acarnania, who attended him and was not only a trusted physician but a good soldier as well, proposed to give him a purgative. Alexander consented to take it, and just as Philip was preparing the draught, Alexander was handed a note from Parmenio. 'Beware of Philip', the note read; 'I am informed that he has been bribed by Darius to poison you.' Alexander read the warning, and with the paper still in his hand took the cup of medicine and then passed the note to Philip. Philip read it, and while he was reading Alexander swallowed the dose. It was immediately clear that there was nothing wrong with Philip's medicine; he showed no alarm at Parmenio's warning, but simply advised Alexander to continue to follow his instructions – for, if he did, he would recover. The dose had its due effect and brought relief, and from that moment Philip knew that Alexander was his faithful friend; it was evident also to everyone else about his person both that he was firm in his refusal to suspect treachery in friends and could look unmoved upon death.[10]

He now dispatched Parmenio to the other Gates which stand on the boundary between Cilicia and Assyria.[11] Parmenio's orders were to seize and hold the pass with the troops entrusted to him – the allied infantry, the Greek mercenaries, the Thracians under Sitalces, and the Thessalian cavalry. Alexander himself, leaving Tarsus after Parmenio had gone, in one day's march reached Anchialus, a town supposed to have been built by Sardanapalus the Assyrian. It is clear from the extent of the surrounding walls and the solidity of their foundations that it was originally a large town and grew to great importance. Close to the walls was the tomb of Sardanapalus, supporting a statue of him in the attitude of a man clapping his hands, with an inscription in Assyrian characters.[12] According to the Assyrians the inscription was in verse, but, whether verse or not, the general sense of it was this: 'Sardanapalus, son of Anakyndaraxes, built in one day Tarsus and Anchialus. O stranger, eat, drink, and play, for everything else in the life of a man is not worth this' – and by 'this' was to be understood a clap of the hands. They also said that 'play' was something of a euphemism for the original Assyrian word.

From Anchialus Alexander proceeded to Soli, where he installed a garrison and imposed upon the town a fine of 200 talents of silver for its support of the Persian cause; then with three battalions of Macedonian foot, the Agri-

10. Contrast his treatment of Philotas some four years later (p. 191).

11. The 'Syrian Gates' (called the 'Assyrian' Gates on p. 110) was the Beilan pass through the Amanus Mts., south-east of Alexandretta.

12. i.e. cuneiform writing.

anes, and all his archers he marched against those of the Cilicians who were holding the hills. Some he drove from their positions; others surrendered; and within a week he was back in Soli, where the news reached him that Ptolemy and Asander had won a victory over the Persian commander Orontobates, who was holding the acropolis in Halicarnassus together with the towns of Myndus, Caunus, Thera, and Callipolis, and had also taken possession of Cos and Triopium.[13] According to the dispatch, Orontobates had been defeated in a great battle; he had lost some 700 of his infantry and fifty of his mounted troops, with at least 1,000 prisoners.

To celebrate this success Alexander offered sacrifice to Asclepius[14] and held a ceremonial parade of all his troops, followed by a torch race and games which included contests in music and verse as well as athletics. The town of Soli he permitted to retain its own popular government. He then started for Tarsus and gave orders for the cavalry to proceed under the command of Philotas across the plain of Alea to the river Pyramus. With the infantry and the Royal Squadron of horse he then went to Magarsus, whence, after offering sacrifice to the local Athene, he proceeded to Mallus, where he performed all proper ceremonies in honour of the demi-god Amphilochus. In this latter place he found political troubles in progress, and settled them, remitting the tribute which the town paid to Darius on the ground that Mallus was a colony of Argos and he himself claimed to be descended from the Argive Heracleidae.

He was still at Mallus when a report reached him that Darius and the whole Persian army were at Sochi, a place

13. For Orontobates see pp. 89–90.
14. No doubt in gratitude for his recovery from the fever he had had at Tarsus.

in Assyrian territory about two days' march from the
Assyrian Gates. He at once called a meeting of his staff
and told them this important news. They urged unanimously an immediate advance. Alexander thanked them
and dismissed the meeting, and on the following day
moved forward with the evident intention of attack. Two
days later he was past the Gates. He took up a position
near Myriandrus, and during the night there was a storm
of such violent wind and rain that he was compelled
to remain where he was, with no chance of breaking
camp.

Meanwhile Darius had no apparent intention of making
a move; he had chosen for his position a part of Assyria
where the country was flat and open, good for cavalry
action, and suitable for manoeuvring the vast numbers
under his command. Amyntas, son of Antiochus, a deser-
ter from Alexander's army, urged him not to move from
such favourable ground, for plenty of space was precisely
what the Persian army most needed, its numbers and
equipment being what they were. Darius took Amyntas'
advice, but later, when there was still no sign of Alexander, who had been held up at Tarsus by his illness, and
again at Soli, for nearly as long, by the grand parade and
religious ceremonies he held there, and finally, by his
expedition against the hill tribes of Cilicia, he began to
have his doubts. Moreover, Darius was always ready to
believe what he found it most agreeable to believe, and on
this occasion flattering courtiers, such as always are, and
always will be, the bane of kings, had persuaded him into
thinking that Alexander no longer wished to advance
further into Asia: in fact, that the news of his own approach was the cause of Alexander's hesitation. First one,
then another of them blew up the bladder of his conceit
by saying that the Persian cavalry would ride over the

Macedonian army and trample it to pieces.[15] Only Amyntas opposed them, persistently affirming that Alexander
would seek out Darius in any place where he knew him to
be, and urging him not to shift his ground. But the worse
counsel prevailed – because it told him what at the
moment he liked to hear; more than that, there was surely
some supernatural power which led Darius to take up a
position where he could get little advantage either from
his cavalry or his superiority in numbers of men and
weight of missiles – a position where he had no chance of
dazzling the enemy with the splendour of his great host,
but was doomed to make a present of easy victory to
Alexander and the Macedonians. Destiny had decreed
that Macedon should wrest the sovereignty of Asia from
Persia, as Persia once had wrested it from the Medes, and
the Medes, in their turn, from the Assyrians.

Darius now moved; he crossed the high ground by
what are called the Amanian Gates – the pass across
Mount Amanus – and, making for Issus, established himself without being perceived in Alexander's rear.[16] Once in
possession of Issus he mutilated and put to death every
Macedonian he found left there as unfit for service, and
on the following day moved on to the river Pinarus. Alexander, not trusting the report that Darius was in his rear,

15. According to Aeschines, *Against Ctesiphon* 164, a similar statement was made by Demosthenes at this time.

16. From Cilicia the eastern countries could be reached by two
routes, through the Syrian Gates near Alexandretta and the Amanian
Gates (Bogtche Pass) in the north, leading to the Euphrates at
Apamea. Either Alexander had not been informed of the pass or he
thought it unimportant; certainly the news that Darius was astride
his communications came as a shock to him. Plutarch (*Alexander* 20)
writes that 'the two armies missed each other in the night'; in fact,
as Darius marched northwards from Sochi, they were separated by
the width of the Amanus Mts.

dispatched a party of his Companions in a galley with
orders to sail back to Issus and find out for themselves
whether or not it was true. The coast by Issus is deeply
indented, and this fact enabled the party in the galley the
more easily to see what they wished to see – that the Persians were there. So back they went to Alexander with
their news: Darius was indeed at hand.

Alexander now sent for his infantry and cavalry commanders and all officers in charge of allied troops and
appealed to them for confidence and courage in the
coming fight. 'Remember', he said, 'that already danger
has often threatened you and you have looked it triumph-
antly in the face; this time the struggle will be between a
victorious army and an enemy already once vanquished.
God himself, moreover, by suggesting to Darius to leave
the open ground and cram his great army into a confined
space, has taken charge of operations in our behalf. We
ourselves shall have room enough to deploy our infantry,
while they, no match for us either in bodily strength or
resolution, will find their superiority in numbers of no
avail. Our enemies are Medes and Persians, men who for
centuries have lived soft and luxurious lives; we of Macedon for generations past have been trained in the hard
school of danger and war. Above all, we are free men, and
they are slaves. There are Greek troops, to be sure, in
Persian service – but how different is their cause from
ours! They will be fighting for pay – and not much of it
at that; we, on the contrary, shall fight for Greece, and
our hearts will be in it. As for our foreign troops –
Thracians, Paeonians, Illyrians, Agrianes – they are the
best and stoutest soldiers in Europe, and they will find
as their opponents the slackest and softest of the tribes of
Asia. And what, finally, of the two men in supreme command? You have Alexander, they – Darius!'

Having thus enumerated the advantages with which they would enter the coming struggle, Alexander went on to show that the rewards of victory would also be great. The victory this time would not be over mere underlings of the Persian King, or the Persian cavalry along the banks of Granicus, or the 20,000 foreign mercenaries; it would be over the fine flower of the Medes and Persians and all the Asiatic peoples which they ruled. The Great King was there in person with his army, and once the battle was over, nothing would remain but to crown their many labours with the sovereignty of Asia. He reminded them, further, of what they had already so brilliantly accomplished together, and mentioned any act of conspicuous individual courage, naming the man in each case and specifying what he had done, and alluding also, in such a way as to give least offence, to the risks to which he had personally exposed himself on the field. He also, we are told, reminded them of Xenophon and his Ten Thousand, a force which, though not to be compared with their own either in strength or reputation – a force without the support of cavalry such as they had themselves, from Thessaly, Boeotia, the Peloponnese, Macedon, Thrace, and elsewhere, with no archers or slingers except a small contingent from Crete and Rhodes hastily improvised by Xenophon under pressure of immediate need – nevertheless defeated the King of Persia and his army at the gates of Babylon[17] and successfully repelled all the native troops who tried to bar their way as they marched down to the Black Sea. Nor did Alexander omit any other words of encouragement such as brave men about to risk their lives might expect from a brave commander; and in response to his address his officers pressed forward to clasp his hand and with many expressions

17. At Cunaxa, some 45 miles from Babylon.

of appreciation urged him to lead them to battle without delay.

Alexander's first order was that his men should eat, while at the same time he sent a small party of mounted men and archers to the narrow pass by the shore to reconnoitre the road by which he would have to return; then, as soon as it was dark, he moved off himself with the whole army to take possession once more of that narrow gateway. About midnight the passage was secured; for the remainder of the night he allowed his men to rest where they were, on the rocky ground, with outposts to keep exact and careful watch, and just before daylight next morning moved forward from the pass along the coast road. The advance was in column so long as lack of space made it necessary, but as soon as the country began to open up he gradually extended his front, bringing up his heavy infantry a battalion at a time, until he was moving in line with his right on the base of the hills and his left on the sea.

During the advance the mounted troops were kept in the rear, but as soon as open ground was reached Alexander ordered battle stations: the three battalions of the Guards, under Parmenio's son Nicanor, were sent to the right wing on the nearby rising ground, with Coenus' battalion on their left in close touch with Perdiccas' men, the whole forming a line from right wing to centre – the position of the heavy infantry. On the extreme left were stationed Amyntas' troops, and in touch with them, and working towards the centre, first Ptolemy's battalion, then Meleager's. Command of the infantry on the left was given to Craterus, of the left wing as a whole to Parmenio, whose orders were on no account to leave a gap between his extreme left and the sea; for if he did, they might well be surrounded, as the numerical superiority of the enemy would certainly enable them to outflank the Macedonians.[18]

When Darius received the report that Alexander was moving forward to the attack, he sent some 30,000 mounted troops and 20,000 light infantry across the river Pinarus, to give himself a chance of getting the main body of his army into position without molestation. His dispositions were as follows: in the van of his heavy infantry were his 30,000 Greek mercenaries, facing the Macedonian infantry, with some 60,000 Persian heavy infantry – known as Kardakes[19] – to support them, half on each of their flanks. These troops were drawn up in line, and the ground would not admit of a greater number. Hard on the rising ground on his left, and facing Alexander's right, was another division about 20,000 strong, some portions of which actually worked round to Alexander's rear; for the hills on their left receded to some distance so as to form a sort of bay, the further shore of which (so to put it) curved round back again, bringing the sections which were posted close under the hill to the rear of Alexander's right wing. In the rear of the Greek mercenaries and the Persians supporting them on either flank was the remainder of Darius' army – a great mass of light and heavy infantry. These were organized according to the countries of their origin and drawn up in greater depth than was likely to prove of much service; mere numbers made this unavoidable – indeed, it is on record that the army as a whole was some 600,000 strong.[20]

18. See, apart from the Alexander-historians, Polybius 12.17–22, who criticizes Callisthenes' account of the battle. Callisthenes gave the breadth of the plain as 14 stades, about a mile and three quarters.

19. For these troops see Strabo 14.3.18. Fuller regards it as almost certain that they were not heavy infantry but peltasts.

20. Plutarch gives the same number. Diodorus and Justin 400,000,

As soon as Alexander found the ground in front of him opening out a little more, he brought his cavalry – the Thessalian and Macedonian divisions,[21] together with the Companions – up from the rear to the right wing under his own personal command, and at the same time sent the Peloponnesian troops and other allied divisions round to Parmenio on the left. Darius, immediately his main infantry force was in position, recalled by signal the mounted troops which he had sent across the river to cover the movement, and ordered the greater number of them over to his right, to threaten Parmenio, on the seaward side, where the ground was rather more suitable for cavalry manoeuvre; some, however, he sent to the opposite flank under the hills, though, as lack of space at that end of the line made them obviously useless, he soon recalled nearly all of them and ordered them round to the right flank. Darius himself took the centre, the traditional position of the Persian Kings. (The general principle of the Persian order of battle has been explained by Xenophon.)[22]

Nearly all the Persian cavalry had now been transferred to a position on the seaward side facing Alexander's left, and opposing them he had nothing except the Peloponnesians and other allied cavalry; to meet this threat he sent his Thessalian cavalry with all speed to their support, with instructions to conceal their movement from the enemy by passing in the rear of the massed infantry battalions. At the same time, at the other end of the line he threw forward his advanced Scouts, under Protomachus' com-

---

and Curtius 250,000. All these numbers are fantastic, but we cannot now discover the truth.

21. Who were these Macedonians? Perhaps the 'advanced scouts', if these were a Macedonian unit. Alternatively, we may suppose that 'Macedonians' has replaced another word, e.g. Paeonians. Both units are mentioned below on the right.

22. *Anabasis* 1.8.21, 22.

mand, together with the Paeonians under Ariston, and the archers under Antiochus.

The Agrianes under Attalus, supported by a few units of mounted troops and archers, were ordered out towards the high ground at an angle to his main line of advance, thus splitting the right wing of the army into two separate prongs, one designed to engage Darius and the main body of the Persians on the further side of the river, the other the units which had worked round to the hill in the Macedonian rear. In the van of the infantry on the Macedonian left were the Cretan archers and the Thracians, under Sitalces, with the cavalry of the left wing in advance of them; all units had a proportion of foreign mercenaries assigned to them.

Observing a certain weakness on his right and also the danger of being outflanked at that end of his line, Alexander withdrew from the centre two squadrons of the Companions – namely, that from Anthemus commanded by Peroedas and the so-called Leugaean squadron, under Pantordanus, son of Cleander – and ordered them over to the right, with every precaution to conceal their movement; at the same time he further strengthened his right by a contingent of Agrianes and Greek mercenaries which he drew up in line, and so outflanked the Persian left. The Persians on the hills had made no aggressive move; indeed, when Alexander ordered a raid upon them by a small party of the Agrianes and archers, they had been easily dislodged from their position and had sought safety higher up the mountainside, so that Alexander decided that he could use the men originally intended to deal with them to strengthen his main attacking force. Three hundred mounted men were sufficient to keep an eye on the fugitives.[23]

23. These are *not* the two squadrons of Companions just

For a while Alexander's advance was slow and deliberate; every now and then he ordered a halt, giving the impression that time was on his side. Darius made no move as yet to attack, but kept his men in their original dispositions on the river-bank. In many places the bank was steep, and any sections of it which seemed less easy to defend he had strengthened with a stockade – at once by this precaution making it clear to Alexander's men that his was a craven spirit.

The two armies were now almost within striking distance. Alexander rode from one end of his line to the other with words of encouragement for all, addressing by name, with proper mention of rank and distinctions, not the officers of highest rank only but the captains of squadrons and companies; even the mercenaries were not forgotten, where any distinction or act of courage called for the mention of a name, and from every throat came the answering shout: 'Wait no longer – forward to the assault!'

The Persian army was in full view; still, however, Alexander moved forward in line at a deliberate pace, for a too-rapid advance might have thrown the line out of dressing and caused a break somewhere; but once within range of missiles, Alexander, at the head of his own troops on the right wing, rode at a gallop into the stream. Rapidity was now all in all: a swift attack would shake the enemy, and the sooner they came to grips the less damage would be done by the Persian archers. Alexander's judgement was not at fault: the Persian left collapsed the very moment he was on them – a brilliant local success for the picked troops under his personal command. In the centre, however, things did not go so well: here some of the

mentioned, but the 'units of mounted troops' mentioned with the Agrianians above, two squadrons according to Curtius (3.11.2). They were doubtless mercenaries.

troops had broken away towards the right and left a gap in the line, and, in contrast with Alexander, who had so swiftly crossed the stream and was already, in close combat, compelling the Persian left to withdraw, the Macedonian centre was much slower off the mark; in a number of places, moreover, the steep banks of the stream prevented them from maintaining a regular and unbroken front, and the result was that Darius' Greek mercenaries attacked precisely at that point in the line where the gap was widest. There was a violent struggle. Darius' Greeks fought to thrust the Macedonians back into the water and save the day for their left wing, already in retreat, while the Macedonians, in their turn, with Alexander's triumph plain before their eyes, were determined to equal his success and not forfeit the proud title of invincible, hitherto universally bestowed upon them. The fight was further embittered by the old racial rivalry of Greek and Macedonian. It was in this phase of the battle that Ptolemy, son of Seleucus,[24] and about 120 Macedonians of distinction met a soldier's death.

Alexander's victorious right wing, seeing the Persians opposite them already in flight, now swung left towards the centre, hard pressed as it was by Darius' Greeks; they forced them back from the river and then, outflanking the broken enemy left, delivered a flank attack on the mercenaries and were soon cutting them to pieces. The Persian cavalry facing Alexander's Thessalians refused, once the battle had developed, to remain inactive on the further side of the stream, but charged across in a furious onslaught on the Thessalian squadrons. The cavalry action which ensued was desperate enough, and the Persians broke only when they knew that the Greek mercenaries were being cut off and destroyed by the Macedonian

24. Commander of a battalion of heavy infantry.

infantry, and that Darius himself was in flight. That was
the signal for a general rout – open and unconcealed. The
horses with their heavily equipped riders suffered severely,
and of the thousands of panic-stricken men who struggled
in hopeless disorder to escape along the narrow mountain
tracks, almost as many were trampled to death by their
friends as were cut down by the pursuing enemy. The
Thessalians pressed the pursuit without mercy, and the
Persian losses in both arms, infantry, and cavalry were
equally severe.

The moment the Persian left went to pieces under
Alexander's attack and Darius, in his war-chariot, saw
that it was cut off, he incontinently fled – indeed, he led
the race for safety. Keeping to his chariot as long as there
was smooth ground to travel on, he was forced to abandon it when ravines and other obstructions barred his
way; then, dropping his shield and stripping off his
mantle – and even leaving his bow in the war-chariot – he
leapt upon a horse and rode for his life. Darkness soon
closed in; and that alone saved him from falling into the
hands of Alexander, who, while daylight held, relentlessly
pressed the pursuit; but when there was no longer light
enough to see what he was coming to, he turned back –
but not without taking possession of Darius' chariot together with his shield, mantle, and bow. In point of fact
his pursuit would have been more rapid had he not turned
back at the moment when his line of heavy infantry broke,
in the first stage of the battle; he had then waited until he
saw that both the Greek mercenaries and the Persian
cavalry had been forced back from the river bank.

Among the Persian dead were Arsames, Rheomithres,
and Atizyes – all three of whom had served as cavalry
officers at the battle on the Granicus; also Sabaces, governor of Egypt, and Bubaces, another person of distin-

guished rank; of the common soldiers, something like
100,000 were killed, including over 10,000 of the cavalry.[25]
Ptolemy, son of Lagus, who was serving with Alexander
at this time, says in his account of the battle that the Macedonians in their pursuit of Darius actually crossed a ravine
on the bodies of the Persian dead.

Darius' headquarters were stormed and captured; his
mother was taken, together with his wife (who was also
his sister) and his infant son; in addition to these, two of
his daughters fell into Alexander's hands with a few noble
Persian ladies who were in attendance upon them. The
Persian officers had sent their gear and womenfolk to
Damascus, and Darius, too, had sent thither most of his
treasure and the various paraphernalia which the luxurious
life of a great king seems to require, even on campaign;[26]
so that a mere 3,000 talents were found at his headquarters. In point of fact, however, the treasure at Damascus,
too, was seized not long afterwards by Parmenio, who
was ordered there for the purpose. Such, then, was the
result of the battle of Issus, fought in the month of November, during the archonship of Nicocrates at Athens.[27]

Alexander had been hurt by a sword-thrust in the
thigh,[28] but this did not prevent him from visiting the

25. Plutarch, Curtius, and Diodorus agree on the number of
casualties but it is as untrustworthy as the numbers given for the
Persian army. Macedonian casualties are given by Curtius (3.11.27)
as 450 killed and 4,500 wounded.

26. For some details see Plutarch, *Alexander* 20.11–13. As Fuller
remarks, Damascus lying some 200 miles to the south of Sochi was
a remarkable place to select.

27. 333 B.C.

28. That Alexander was slightly wounded is true enough. Chares,
however, asserted that the wound was inflicted by Darius himself,
a statement that Plutarch (*Alexander* 20.9) disbelieves, citing a letter
of Alexander to disprove it.

wounded on the day after the battle, when he also gave a splendid military funeral to the dead in the presence of the whole army paraded in full war equipment. At the ceremony he spoke in praise of every man who by his own observation or from reliable report he knew had distinguished himself in the fighting, and marked his approval in each case by a suitable reward. He appointed Balacrus, son of Nicanor, a member of the Royal Guard, as governor of Cilicia, promoting Menes, son of Dionysius, to fill the place thus left vacant, and Polysperchon, son of Simmias, was promoted to command the battalion of Ptolemy, son of Seleucus, who had been killed. The people of Soli still owed fifty talents of the fine imposed upon them, but he cancelled the debt and returned their hostages.[29]

His sympathy was extended, moreover, even to Darius' mother, wife, and children. According to some accounts, on the night when he returned from the pursuit he heard upon entering Darius' tent, which had been set aside as his own special portion of the spoils of war, the confused sound of women's voices raised in lamentation somewhere close at hand. He asked who the women were and why they should be in a tent so close to him. 'Sire,' he was told, 'they are Darius' mother and wife and children. They know that you have his bow and his royal mantle and that his shield has been brought back, and they are mourning for his death.' Alexander at once sent Leonnatus, one of his Companions, to tell them that Darius was alive – his mantle and weapons he had left, as he fled for safety, in his war chariot, and these, and nothing else, had fallen

29. This means that they had managed to find no less than 150 talents (see p. 108), a remarkable sum when one thinks that the estimated income of Athens in 431, including the tribute from subject states, was only about 1,000 talents.

into Alexander's hands. Leonnatus entered their tent, gave the message about Darius, and added that Alexander wished them to retain all the marks, ceremonies, and titles of royalty, as he had not fought Darius with any personal bitterness, but had made legitimate war for the sovereignty of Asia. This is the account given by Ptolemy and Aristobulus; there is also another story to the effect that Alexander on the following day entered the tent accompanied only by Hephaestion, and that Darius' mother, in doubt, owing to the similarity of their dress, which of the two was the King, prostrated herself before Hephaestion, because he was taller than his companion. Hephaestion stepped back, and one of the Queen's attendant's rectified her mistake by pointing to Alexander; the Queen withdrew in profound embarrassment, but Alexander merely remarked that her error was of no account, for Hephaestion, too, was an Alexander – a 'protector of men'. I record this anecdote not as necessarily true, though it is credible enough. If such were indeed the facts, I cannot but admire Alexander both for treating these women with such compassion and for showing such respect and confidence towards his friend; if the story is apocryphal, it was at least inspired by Alexander's character: thus he would have acted, thus he would have spoken – and on that account I admire him no less.[30]

Meanwhile Darius with a few followers made the best of his escape throughout the night, and with the coming of daylight was joined as he went along by parties of survivors, Persians or mercenaries, until he had in all a body of some 4,000 men; with these he pressed on with all speed towards Thapsacus and the Euphrates with the

30. Plutarch (*Alexander* 22.5) quotes a letter written by Alexander to Parmenio in which he claims never to have set eyes on the wife of Darius.

intention of putting the river between himself and Alexander as soon as he could.[31] Four men who had deserted to Darius – Amyntas son of Antiochus, Thymondas son of Mentor, Aristomedes of Pherae, and Bianor the Acarnanian – fled to the hills with the 8,000 troops under their command[32] and reached Tripolis in Phoenicia; finding hauled ashore there the ships which had brought them from Lesbos, they launched as many as they thought would serve their purpose, burnt the rest as they lay in the yards, to delay pursuit, and sailed first for Cyprus and thence to Egypt – where not long afterwards Amyntas was killed by the Egyptians for meddling in what did not concern him.[33]

All this time Pharnabazus and Autophradates had been hanging about in Chios. Now, after garrisoning the island, they dispatched a part of their fleet to Cos and Halicarnassus, and themselves put to sea with the hundred fastest ships they had; at Siphnos they were met by the Spartan King, Agis, who with a single trireme had come to raise money for the war and to ask that as many ships and men as possible should be sent to him in the Peloponnese. It was at this moment that the news of the battle of Issus came. The effect of it was shattering; Pharnabazus, fearing defeat might lead to trouble in Chios, at once sailed for

31. Many of the Persian cavalry escaped to Cappadocia, where they were joined by local troops in an attempt to recover Phrygia but were defeated by Antigonus. (Curtius 4.1.34–5, where 'Lydia' is a slip for 'Phrygia'.)

32. Greek mercenaries.

33. Diodorus (17.48.2–5) and Curtius (4.1.27–33) give more details of events in Egypt. As they mention only Amyntas and 4,000 mercenaries, it is probable that the force split up. Possibly the other 4,000 found their way into the service of Agis, the Spartan king; he is recorded to have hired 8,000 mercenaries who escaped from Issus. See E. Badian, *JHS* 1963, 25–6.

the island with twelve ships and 1,500 of the mercenaries, while Agis dispatched Hippias to Taenarum to deliver to his brother Agesilaus the ten ships and thirty talents of silver which he had received from Autophradates, adding instructions that he should tell Agesilaus to pay the seamen in full and sail immediately to secure Crete. Agis himself remained for a time in the islands, but subsequently joined Autophradates at Halicarnassus.[34]

Leaving Menon, son of Kerdimmas, as governor of Lowland Syria with the allied cavalry to keep the country under control, Alexander marched for Phoenicia. On the way thither he was met by Straton, the son of Gerostratus, who was the prince of Aradus and its neighbouring peoples; Gerostratus himself had sailed with Autophradates, as had the other petty kings of Phoenicia and Cyprus, so it was left to Straton to present himself before Alexander and to crown him with a gold crown, yielding him the sovereignty of the island of Aradus together with the large and prosperous town of Marathus on the mainland opposite, and Sigon, Mariamme, and everything else under his control.

While Alexander was at Marathus, envoys from Darius came with a request for the release of his mother, wife, and children. They also brought a letter from him, of which the substance was as follows:[35]

34. Undeterred by the result of Issus, Agis continued his preparations, and in spring 331 he 'issued an appeal to the Greeks to unite in defence of their freedom' (Diodorus 17.62.6). After initial successes he was finally defeated by Antipater at Megalopolis in the autumn of 331. For the evidence see Diodorus 17.48.1–2; 62.6–63.4; 73.5–6; Curtius 6.1; and, for a modern account of Agis, E. Badian, *Hermes* 1967, 170ff.

35. Diodorus (17.39.2) has a curious story that Alexander suppressed Darius' letter and substituted another 'more in accordance with his interests' which he put before his Companions to secure

Philip and Artaxerxes were on terms of friendship and alliance;[36] but upon the accession of Artaxerxes' son Arses, Philip
was guilty of unprovoked aggression against him.[37] Now,
since Darius' reign began, Alexander has sent no representa-
tive to his court to confirm the former friendship and alliance
between the two kingdoms; on the contrary, he has crossed
into Asia with his armed forces and done much damage to the
Persians. For this reason Darius took the field in defence of his
country and of his ancestral throne. The issue of the battle was
as some god willed; and now Darius the King asks Alexander
the King to restore from captivity his wife, his mother, and
his children, and is willing to make friends with him and be
his ally. For this cause he urges Alexander to send to him, in
company with Meniscus and Arsimas who have brought this
request, representatives of his own in order that proper
guarantees may be exchanged.

Alexander, having written his reply, ordered Thersip-
pus to accompany Darius' envoys on their return, giving
him strict instructions to deliver the letter to Darius but
to discuss no question whatever which might arise from
it. This was the letter:

---

the rejection of a negotiated peace. G. T. Griffith (*Proc. Camb. Phil.
Soc.* 1968, 33ff.) suggests that the letter in Arrian is this forged letter.
He points out that, e.g., Darius offers no financial or territorial
inducements (as he does in the letters of Diodorus 17.39 and Curtius
4.1.7), and that to raise the question of war-guilt would be bad
policy for one in Darius' position. For Griffith's other arguments
see the next two notes.

36. No such alliance is known to us in what is a relatively well-
documented period. Demosthenes, for example, does not mention
it.

37. Artaxerxes III (Ochus) ruled from 359–338, his son Arses
from 338 to 336. Darius refers to the Macedonian invasion of Asia
Minor in spring 336. This was not unprovoked, since Persia had
aided Perinthus against Philip in 340; Philip, however, had been the
aggressor in 342 by making an alliance with Hermeias of Atarneus
and one might expect a mention of this.

Your ancestors invaded Macedonia and Greece and caused havoc in our country, though we had done nothing to provoke them. As supreme commander of all Greece I invaded Asia because I wished to punish Persia for this act – an act which must be laid wholly to your charge. You sent aid to the people of Perinthus in their rebellion against my father; Ochus sent an army into Thrace, which was a part of our dominions; my father was killed by assassins whom, as you openly boasted in your letters, you yourselves hired to commit the crime;[38] having murdered Arses with Bagoas' help,[39] you unjustly and illegally seized the throne, thereby committing a crime against your country; you sent the Greeks false information about me in the hope of making them my enemies; you attempted to supply the Greeks with money – which only the Lacedae-monians were willing to accept,[40] your agents corrupted my friends and tried to wreck the peace which I had established in Greece – then it was that I took the field against you; but it was you who began the quarrel. First I defeated in battle your generals and satraps; now I have defeated yourself and the army you led. By God's help I am master of your country, and I have made myself responsible for the survivors of your army who fled to me for refuge: far from being detained by force, they are serving of their own free will under my command.

Come to me, therefore, as you would come to the lord of the continent of Asia. Should you fear to suffer any indignity at my hands, then send some of your friends and I will give them the proper guarantees. Come, then, and ask me for your mother, your wife, and your children and anything else you

38. There is no other evidence for this.

39. Alexander (or Arrian) is mistaken. Bagoas poisoned Arses and his children and secured the throne for Darius. Later, when he attempted to poison Darius, the king turned the tables on him. See Diodorus 17.5.3–6.

40. Aeschines (*Against Ctesiphon* 239) claims that Darius sent 300 talents to the Athenians who refused them, but that Demosthenes got his hands on 70 talents.

please; for you shall have them, and whatever besides you can persuade me to give you.

And in future let any communication you wish to make with me be addressed to the King of all Asia. Do not write to me as to an equal. Everything you possess is now mine; so, if you should want anything, let me know in the proper terms, or I shall take steps to deal with you as a criminal. If, on the other hand, you wish to dispute your throne, stand and fight for it and do not run away. Wherever you may hide yourself, be sure I shall seek you out.

Such were the terms of Alexander's answer.

When he learned that money and other valuables sent by Darius to Damascus in charge of Cophen, son of Artabazus, had been seized and removed together with all the Persians left to guard them, he instructed Parmenio to see that the whole treasure was taken back to Damascus for safe keeping. The envoys from Greece, who had visited Darius before the battle, had also fallen into Parmenio's hands; and these Alexander ordered should be sent to him. They were Euthycles, from Sparta; Thessaliscus, son of Ismenius, and Dionysidorus (the Olympic victor), from Thebes; and Iphicrates son of the distinguished general of the same name, from Athens. The four men were duly brought before Alexander; Thessaliscus and Dionysidorus, in spite of – or perhaps because of – the fact that they were Thebans, he at once dismissed: he was sorry for Thebes, and could not but feel that, as she had been reduced to slavery by a Macedonian army, her people had done nothing very reprehensible in sending to Darius; after all, they were only looking for what help they could get from Persia for themselves and their country, so he was inclined to take a lenient view of both these men. All the same, he privately declared that he released Thessaliscus out of respect for his family, which was one of the noble families of Thebes, and Dionysidorus because of his success at the Olympic games. Iphicrates, from affection for Athens and the memory of his father's fame, he retained in his personal suite, treating him with every mark of honour, and when he fell ill and died sent his bones to his relatives in Athens.[41] Euthycles, on the contrary, represented a city then bitterly hostile to him; and for that reason, and because he was unable to produce any reasonable claim to clemency, Alexander kept him for the time being under open arrest. Later, however, in the full tide of his success, he let Euthycles go free as well.

Alexander now resumed his advance from Marathus. Byblus and Sidon both surrendered to him – the people of Sidon, who hated Darius and the Persians, actually inviting him to enter the town.[42] He then proceeded in the direction of Tyre, and was met on the way by representatives from the town, who had been sent by its government to say that they had determined to abide by any instructions Alexander might give. The envoys were men of the best families in Tyre and included the son of the Tyrian king, Azemilcus, who himself was at sea with Autophradates; Alexander thanked them for their communication and directed them to return to Tyre and tell their people that he wished to enter the town and offer sacrifice to Heracles.

I must mention in this connexion that there is in Tyre the most ancient temple of Heracles known to man. This is not the Argive Heracles, Alcmena's son; for Heracles

41. Was Alexander influenced by the fact that his grandfather, Amyntas III, had adopted the elder Iphicrates? Aeschines, *On the Legation* 28. The occasion when Iphicrates rendered him military assistance is not certainly known.

42. At Sidon he deposed Strato, who favoured Persia, and appointed Abdalonymus king in his place (Curtius 4.3.4.).

was worshipped in Tyre many generations before Cadmus came from Phoenicia to Thebes and became the
father of Semele, who bore Dionysus to Zeus.[43] Dionysus
would seem to be in the third generation from Cadmus,
through Polydorus and Labdacus, while the Argive
Heracles was probably in the line of Oedipus, son of Laius.
The Egyptians also worship a Heracles, but not the
Heracles of Tyre or Greece; according to Herodotus he
is regarded by the Egyptians as one of the Twelve Gods.
Similarly, the Athenians worship a Dionysus who was the
son of Zeus and Kore – and it is to him, not to the Theban
Dionysus, that the *Iacchus* hymn is sung during the celebration of the Mysteries. I think that the Heracles who is
honoured at Tartessus by the Iberians (where are the so-
called Pillars of Heracles) is the Tyrian Heracles, because
Tartessus is of Phoenician origin and Heracles' temple
there and the ritual of sacrifice performed in it are both in
the Phoenician tradition. Moreover, according to the
chronicler Hecataeus, Geryones, whose oxen the Argive
Heracles was sent by Eurystheus to fetch to Mycenae, had
no connexion with Iberia; nor was Heracles sent to some
island or other called Erytheia beyond the Straits. It is
much more likely that Geryones was a mainland prince
somewhere in the region of Ambracia and Amphilochia,
and that Heracles' task – and no small one either – was to
steal the oxen from there. I know for myself that this
region still, today, contains excellent pasture and produces cattle of high quality, and it is likely enough that
Eurystheus was not unaware of the reputation of these
mainland cattle and of the name of the prince who ruled
in those parts; but he would surely not have known the
name of the Iberian king right away there in the remotest

43. In fact, this 'Heracles' was the Tyrian god Melcarth (the
Syrian Baal).

corner of Europe, or have had any idea whether or not there were good cattle in that distant land. Indeed, to make such an improbable story hang together, one would have to make a myth of it and drag in the goddess Hera, and say that it was she who told Heracles the secret through the mouth of Eurystheus.

It was, then, to this Tyrian Heracles that Alexander expressed a wish to offer sacrifice, and the envoys reported his request to the people of the town. In general, they were willing enough to accede to Alexander's wishes, but there was one thing which they firmly refused to do – and that was to admit any Persian or Macedonian within the walls of the town. This, they felt, was not only the most dignified attitude at the present juncture, but would also be the most likely to ensure their future safety, as the outcome of the war was not yet by any means assured.[44] The decision was duly reported to Alexander, who was very angry; he dismissed the envoys and at once called a meeting of his Companions and other officers of all ranks and addressed them in the following words.

'Friends and fellow soldiers, I do not see how we can safely advance upon Egypt, so long as Persia controls the sea; and to pursue Darius with the neutral city of Tyre in our rear and Egypt and Cyprus still in enemy hands would be a serious risk, especially in view of the situation in Greece. With our army on the track of Darius, far inland in the direction of Babylon, the Persians might well regain control of the coast, and thus be enabled with more power behind them to transfer the war to Greece, where Sparta is already openly hostile to us, and Athens, at the moment,

44. Diodorus (17.40.3) stresses their loyalty to Darius. They are said to have suggested that Alexander might sacrifice in a temple outside the city. Alexander's reasons for forcing the issue are given in the following speech.

is but an unwilling ally; fear, not friendliness, keeping her on our side. But with Tyre destroyed, all Phoenicia would be ours, and the Phoenician fleet, which both in numbers and quality is the predominant element in the sea-power of Persia, would very likely come over to us. The Phoenician seamen, ships' crews or fighting men, once their towns are in our hands, will hardly endure to face the perils of service at sea for the sake of others. The next step will be Cyprus: it will either join us without trouble on our part, or be easily taken by assault; then, with the accession of Cyprus and the united fleets of Macedon and Phoenicia, our supremacy at sea would be guaranteed, and the expedition to Egypt would thus be a simple matter, and finally, with Egypt in our hands we shall have no further cause for uneasiness about Greece: we shall be able to march on Babylon with security at home, with enhanced prestige, and with Persia excluded not only from the sea, but from the whole continent up to the Euphrates.'

Alexander had no difficulty in persuading his officers that the attempt upon Tyre must be made. He himself had further encouragement by a sign from heaven, for that very night he dreamed that as he was approaching the walls of the town Heracles greeted him and invited him to enter. The dream was interpreted by Aristander as signifying that Tyre would be taken, but with much labour, because labour was characteristic of all that Heracles had himself accomplished.

However – dreams or no dreams – it was obvious enough that the siege of Tyre would be a tremendous undertaking. The town was an island, and surrounded by strong and lofty walls, and, as things then were, with Persia in command of the sea and the Tyrian fleet still strong, any attack by sea would have been unlikely to succeed. In spite of all difficulties, however, Alexander's decision to attack it was accepted.

His plan was to construct a mole across the stretch of shallow water between the shore and the town.[45] In-shore there are patches of mud with little water over them, the deepest part of the channel, about three fathoms, being close to the town. There was an abundant supply of stones, which they used for the foundation of the mole, and plenty of timber, which they packed down on top. It was an easy matter to drive piles into the mud which itself acted as binding material to keep the stones in place. The men worked with as good a will as their commander, for Alexander was always on the spot giving precise instructions as to how to proceed, with many a word of encouragement and special rewards for conspicuously good work.

Little difficulty was encountered in constructing the in-shore portion of the mole, because the water was shallow and there was no opposition; but as they got out into the deeper water near the town, and within range of missiles from the lofty walls, their troubles began. The men were in working dress and not equipped for battle, and the Tyrians used their superiority at sea to make constant raids on various points along the mole, thus rendering the continuation of the work impossible. To counter these raids, the Macedonians built two towers on the mole (which was now of considerable length) and mounted artillery on them; they faced the towers with skins and hides to prevent damage from incendiary missiles and, at the same time, to afford some protection against arrows for the men working on them, hoping,

45. The island lay about half a mile offshore. According to Diodorus (17.40) the mole was about 200 feet wide. Stones were obtained from old Tyre and timber from Mt Libanus.

also, that the Tyrian crews who attempted to harass the men on the mole might be attacked by missiles from the towers and driven off without difficulty.

The Tyrians, however, soon had their answer: they filled a cattle-boat with dry brushwood and various sorts of timber which would burn well, set up twin masts in her bows, and, as far as they could, raised her bulwarks all round in order to make her hold as much inflammable material as possible, including pitch, sulphur, and anything else which would burn fiercely. Across the twin masts they rigged a yard double the usual length, and slung from it cauldrons full of any material which could be poured or flung on the fire to increase its fury, and, finally, heavily ballasted the vessel aft in order to lift her bows as high as possible. Then, having waited for a fair wind, they passed hawsers to a number of triremes and towed her stern-first to the mole. Near the two towers they started the fire, and the crews of the triremes pulled with all their might until they flung the blazing cattle-boat on the edge of the mole. Before she struck the men in her leapt overboard and swam to safety.

The towers were soon caught in a furious blaze; the yards burned through and collapsed, pouring into the fire the contents of the cauldrons which had been designed to increase its intensity. The triremes lay-to near the mole, their crews shooting continually at the towers so that no one could get near them with anything to extinguish the flames. Then, once the towers were well alight, the Tyrians in the town came swarming out, leapt into boats which they ran upon the mole at various points, and soon succeeded in wrecking the palisade built to protect it, and in setting fire to all the war-engines which had so far escaped the blazing cattle-boat.

The result of all this was that Alexander gave orders

for work to start again on the mole from the in-shore end; it was to be made broader, to give space for more towers, and the engineers were to set about the construction of fresh engines. In the meantime he himself with his Guards and Agrianes moved off for Sidon, in order to assemble there all the warships he possessed; for clearly, so long as the Tyrians were masters of the sea, the siege of Tyre would be no easy matter.

Meanwhile Gerostratus and Enylus, upon receiving a report that Aradus and Byblus were in Alexander's hands, left the fleet which was under Autophradates' command and sailed with their own contingents to join Alexander; the Sidonian warships accompanied them, so that Alexander received a reinforcement of about eighty Phoenician vessels. About the same time he was joined by the patrol ship from Rhodes and nine other vessels, three from Soli and Mallus, ten from Lycia, and a fifty-oared galley from Macedon under the command of Proteas, son of Andronicus. Shortly afterwards the alarming news of Darius' defeat at Issus, added to the fact that all Phoenicia was in Alexander's hands, induced the Cypriot kings to sail for Sidon with their fleet of some 120 ships.[46]

Alexander was aware that it was by necessity rather than choice that all of them had used their naval strength in support of Persia, and was quite willing, in consequence, to overlook the past.

While the war-engines were still under construction and the fleet was being put into order for active service, Alexander with some squadrons of cavalry, the Guards, the Agrianes, and the archers made an expedition to Mount Antilibanus in Arabia.[47] Within ten days he made himself

46. This was the turning-point in the siege.
47. Mt Antilibanus was the more easterly of the two mountain-ranges enclosing the valley of Coele-Syria proper; Arabia is used

master, either by force or agreement, of the country in that neighbourhood, and returned to Sidon, where he found that Cleander, son of Polemocrates, had arrived from the Peloponnese with about 4,000 Greek mercenary troops.

Once the fleet was fully mobilized, he embarked an adequate number of fighting men for the task in hand – on the assumption, that is, that in the coming engagement close fighting would be the order of the day rather than naval tactics. The fleet then sailed for Tyre in close order, with Alexander himself on the right wing to seaward, supported by the Cypriot kings and all the Phoenicians with the exception of Pnytagoras,[48] who, with Craterus, was in command of the left.

It had been the intention of the Tyrians to offer battle if Alexander attacked by sea; now, however, the situation was very different: here was a much more powerful fleet than they had expected in their ignorance of the fact that all the ships of Cyprus and Phoenicia had joined Alexander; the fleet had lain-to at sea a little way off the town as a challenge to battle, and now, when the challenge was not answered, it was coming on again in close order and at full speed. In these circumstances, therefore, the Tyrians decided not to risk an engagement; instead, they blocked their harbour entrances with as many ships as there was room for, and kept guard there to prevent the enemy fleet from coming to anchor in any of them.

On the refusal of the Tyrians to accept his challenge, Alexander continued his course towards the town. He did not intend to force an entry into the harbour on the Sidon side of the island, because the entrance was narrow and

---

loosely. The natives had killed some thirty of the Macedonians who were gathering timber for rafts and towers (Curtius 4.2.18; 4.3.1).

48. King of Salamis, one of the nine principal cities of Cyprus.

blocked by a number of warships lying bows-on to an approaching enemy; in spite of this, however, the Phoenicians rammed head-on the three outermost vessels and sank them, their crews swimming to safety on the friendly shore. After this incident the fleet brought up in-shore, not far from the mole, where there seemed to be shelter.

Next day Alexander gave orders for the blockade of the town: the Cyprian contingent under its commander Andromachus was to take station off the northern harbour (facing Sidon), and the Phoenicians off the southern harbour on the other side of the mole, where his own quarters were.

By this time Alexander had assembled a considerable body of workmen from Cyprus and various parts of Phoenicia, and many war-engines had been constructed; some were mounted on the mole, others on the transport vessels which he had brought from Sidon, others, again, on the slower-sailing triremes. When all was ready, they were ordered forward into action – not those on the mole only, but also those from the ships which were lying off the walls of the town at various points and already beginning the assault.

On the battlements overlooking the mole the Tyrians erected wooden towers for defensive action, and every threat from Alexander's artillery, wherever it might be, they met with missile weapons, using fire-arrows against the ships with such effect that their crews were afraid to approach within range. The walls of the town opposite the mole were about 150 feet high and proportionately thick, strongly built of large stone blocks cemented together. There was a further reason why it was difficult for the Macedonian transports and triremes to work in close to the town with their artillery, and this was the fact that blocks of stone in large numbers had been thrown into the

water, and obstructed their advance. Alexander determined to remove them, but the task proved a difficult one,
not only because the men had only the unsteady ships'
decks to work from, but also because the Tyrians in certain specially-armoured vessels kept driving athwart the
bows of the Macedonian triremes and cutting the anchor
cables, so that it was impossible for them to remain in their
station. Alexander, in reply, filled a number of thirty-
oared galleys with similar defensive armour and moored
them broadside-on ahead of the triremes' anchor ropes,
to repel the Tyrian attacks; but the Tyrians, not to be out-
done, sent down divers to cut the cables as before. Then
the Macedonians substituted chain for rope – and against
that, at any rate, the divers were useless. Finally, from the
mole, they managed to pass ropes round the blocks of
stone and to haul them out, after which they lifted them
with cranes and dropped them again into deep water,
where they were not likely to cause any further obstruc-
tion. Once the water by the wall was clear of obstacles,
the ships could lie there, close in, without much difficulty.

The Tyrians, now in serious trouble, decided to attack
the Cyprian contingent which was blockading the northern harbour. Some time previously they had rigged sails
across the harbour entrance to act as a screen behind which
they could man their vessels unobserved; and now, about
midday, when the crews of the Greek ships were dispersed upon whatever job they happened to have in hand,
and Alexander usually left the fleet on the other side of
the town to withdraw to his quarters, they completed
their preparations. Having manned three quinqueremes,
three quadriremes, and seven triremes with picked crews –
their smartest men, their best-armed marines, specially
selected for their courage in naval warfare – they slipped
quietly out of harbour in single file. No one called the

time to the men at the oars; they rowed in silence until just before they turned to come within sight of the Cyprians, when with a hearty shout and cheers of mutual encouragement they laid to their oars and bore down upon the enemy at their best speed.

It so happened that though Alexander had retired to his quarters that day, he had not taken his customary rest, but had almost immediately returned to the fleet. The Tyrian surprise proved successful: some of the blockading squadron they found without a single man aboard; others were being manned under difficulties with whoever was available at the last moment, with the enemies' battle-shout in their ears and the attack imminent; and the result was that Pnytagoras' quinquireme was rammed and sunk at the first encounter. The ships commanded by Androcles of Amathus and Pasicrates of Curium[49] suffered the same fate. The rest of the squadron was driven ashore and broken up.

As soon as it was reported to Alexander that the Tyrian triremes had been out, he ordered most of the ships on the south side of the town, the instant that each could be got ready for action, to lay-to off the south harbour entrance, in order to prevent another sortie; then with his quinquiremes and the five or six triremes which had been smartest in getting their crews aboard, he sailed round to the north side of the town in search of the Tyrian squadron which had made the attack. When the Tyrians on the battlements saw what was happening and that Alexander in person was with the enemy squadron, they shouted a warning to the men in their own ships to get back into harbour, and, when the din and clatter of action made their shouts inaudible, tried signals of various sorts to indicate the necessity of withdrawing to shelter. The Tyrian crews

49. Both cities on the south coast of Cyprus.

saw Alexander's ships coming; they put about and made
for the harbour – but too late: a few managed to get in
in time, but most of them were rammed; some were put
out of action and one quinquireme and one quadrireme
were captured right at the harbour entrance. Loss of life
was not severe; the men on board, once they knew their
ships were done for, swam off into the harbour and
escaped without difficulty.

All hope of protection by the fleet was now gone, and
this was the moment when the Macedonians began to
bring their artillery into action. From the mole the siege
engines could make little impression because in that sector
the city wall was too strong. Another attempt was made
on the north side, where a number of ships with artillery
aboard were brought into action; but their success was no
greater. Alexander, accordingly, turned his attention to
the southern sector of the defences, feeling methodically
for a weak spot, and it was here that he had his first success. A considerable length of the wall began to give
under the assault, and an actual breach was made, though
not a large one. Alexander then made a tentative attack –
a probing movement, not much more, in point of fact,
than the throwing of a bridge across the breach. The
movement was easily repulsed.

Three days later, when Alexander had the weather he
wanted, he addressed some words of encouragement to
his officers and ordered the ship-borne artillery into action.
Great damage was done to the defences, and as soon as he
thought that a breach of sufficient breadth had been made,
he withdrew the artillery carriers and ordered up two
other vessels equipped with gangways which he proposed
to throw across the breach. One of these vessels, commanded by Admetus, was taken over by a battalion of the
Guards, and the other by Coenus' battalion of heavy

infantry. Alexander himself was with the Guards ready to mount the breach wherever it was practicable. Some of his triremes he ordered round to the two harbours, on the chance that they might succeed in forcing an entrance while the enemy's attention was engaged in trying to repel the assault elsewhere; other vessels which had archers on board or carried ammunition for the artillery were instructed to cruise round the island and, wherever they could, close in with the wall, lying off but within range if it so happened that to get close in was impossible, so that the defenders might be threatened from every point and caught, as it were, in a ring of fire.

No sooner were Alexander's ships in under the city wall and the gangways lowered, than the men of the Guards sprang upon them and pressed powerfully forward into the breach. In the ensuing action Admetus played a soldier's part, and Alexander himself was in the thick of it, fighting like the rest, and ever on the watch for any act of conspicuous courage in the face of danger among his men. The section of the defences where Alexander had chosen to take personal command was, in fact, the first to fall; the attacking force were no longer faced by a sheer and precipitous ascent but had, for the first time, firm ground under their feet, and succeeded, in consequence, in driving the defenders from their position without difficulty. Admetus, leading the assault and calling to his men to follow, was killed by a spear-thrust while still upon the shattered wall, but Alexander, hot on his heels, seized the breach and, having established control of some of the towers together with the sections of wall connecting them, passed on through the battlements towards the royal quarters, this way appearing to offer the most practicable descent into the town.

Meanwhile the operations of the fleet had been no less

successful: the Phoenicians who were lying off the southern harbour smashed a way in through the defensive
booms and made short work of the shipping inside, ram-
ming some vessels where they lay afloat and driving others
ashore; and the northern harbour, which was not even
protected by booms, presented no difficulty to the Cyprians. They sailed straight in and quickly gained control of
that portion of the town. The main body of the Tyrian
defenders abandoned the wall once they saw it was in the
enemy's hands, and withdrew to the shrine of Agenor,[50]
where they turned to face the Macedonians. Alexander
and the Guards were soon upon them; some fell fighting,
others fled, with Alexander in pursuit. The troops from
the harbour were masters of the town; Coenus' battalion
was already in; the slaughter was terrible – for the Macedonians, sick as they were of the length of the siege, went
to work with savage ferocity.[51] There was another reason,
too, which roused them to rage; the Tyrians had taken
some prisoners on their way from Sidon; these men they
had subsequently dragged up on to the battlements, cut
their throats in full view of the Macedonian army, and
flung the bodies into the sea.

The Tyrian losses were about 8,000; the Macedonians,
in the actual assault, lost Admetus, who was the first to
mount the breach, and died as a soldier should, and
twenty men of the Guards who were with him. In the
siege as a whole they lost about 400.

Azemilcus, the King of Tyre, together with the dignitaries of the town and certain visitors from Carthage who
had come to the mother city to pay honour to Heracles

50. Agenor, the father of Cadmus, was reputed to be the founder
of Tyre and Sidon.
51. The siege lasted seven months, from January to August
332.

according to an ancient custom,[52] had fled for refuge to
Heracles' temple: to all of these Alexander granted a free
pardon; everyone else was sold into slavery. In all, including native Tyrians and foreigners taken in the town, some
30,000 were sold.[53]

After the victory Alexander offered sacrifice to Heracles
and held a ceremonial parade of his troops in full battle
equipment; the fleet also took part in the review in the
god's honour, and there were athletic contests in the
Temple enclosure and a torch-race. The piece of siege-
artillery which had made the breach was dedicated in the
Temple, and the Tyrian ship sacred to Heracles, which
had been captured in the naval action, was also solemnly
presented to the god. There was an inscription on the
vessel, composed either by Alexander himself or someone
else. In any case it is not worth remembering, so I have
not thought fit to record it here. In this way, then, Tyre
was taken; the year was that of the archonship at Athens
of Anicetus, and the month August.

While Alexander was still occupied with the siege, he
was visited by envoys from Darius, who in the King's
name offered a sum of 10,000 talents in exchange for his
mother, wife, and children; they further proposed that all
the territory west of the Euphrates right to the Aegean
Sea should belong to Alexander, who should seal his bond

52. According to Diodorus (20.14) the Carthaginians sent a tenth
part of their revenues to Melcarth, and envoys attended an annual
festival in Tyre. They are said to have promised the Tyrians help at
the start of the siege, but to have been unable to fulfil their promise
because of war with Syracuse (Curtius 4.2.10; 4.3.19).

53. Diodorus (17.46.4) gives the number of captives as 13,000,
but he mentions also that 2,000 men were crucified and Curtius
(4.4.15) adds (improbably) that 15,000 were smuggled to safety by
the Sidonians who took part in the final assault. Is it coincidence
that these figures total 30,000?

of friendship and alliance with Persia by marrying Darius' daughter.[54] These proposals were made known at a meeting of Alexander's personal advisers, and Parmenio, according to all reports, declared that were he Alexander he would be happy to end the war on such terms and be done with any further adventures. 'That,' replied Alexander, 'is what I should do were I Parmenio; but since I am Alexander, I shall send Darius a different answer.' And send it he did. He had no need, he wrote, of Darius' money, nor was there any call upon him to accept a part of the continent in place of the whole. All Asia, including its treasure, was already his property, and if he wished to marry Darius' daughter he would do so, whether Darius liked it or not. If, moreover, Darius wanted kindliness and consideration at his hands, he must come to ask for it in person. Upon receiving this reply, Darius abandoned all thought of coming to terms and began once more to prepare for war.

Alexander's next objective was Egypt. All of what is known as Syrian Palestine except the town of Gaza had already accepted Alexander's control. The master of this stronghold, however, a eunuch of the name of Batis, refused to join him. He had raised a force of mercenary Arab troops, and for some time past had been laying in stores sufficient for a protracted siege, and that, added to his confident belief that the town was too strongly defended ever to be taken by assault, induced him to refuse Alexander admission.

Gaza is about two and a half miles from the sea; the approach to it from the coast is over deep sand, and the

54. Diodorus (17.39.1) and Curtius (4.11.1) relate (probably incorrectly) that Darius sent envoys with similar terms shortly before the battle of Gaugamela. For the complicated story of the embassies see C. B. Welles in the Loeb edition of Diodorus (loc. cit.).

sea off-shore is all encumbered with shoals. It was a large town, standing high on an eminence, and encircled by a strongly-built wall – the last town, on the edge of the desert, as one travels south from Phoenicia to Egypt.

Once within striking distance, Alexander took up a position opposite that section of the defences which seemed most open to assault, and ordered the assembly of his siege engines. His engineers expressed the opinion that the mound, or artificial eminence, on which the town stood was so high that it would not be possible to carry it by assault; Alexander, however, was firm in his belief that the greater the difficulty, the more necessary it was to take it; for a success so far beyond reason and probability would be a serious blow to the morale of the enemy, while failure, once Darius and the Greeks got to know of it, would be an equally serious blow to his own prestige.

The plan of campaign was to enable the siege engines to be brought to bear upon the defences by ringing the town with a raised earthwork up to the level of their base, and mounting the engines upon it; the work was concentrated chiefly upon the southern sector, where the wall appeared more vulnerable than elsewhere, and when a sufficient height had been reached the engines were mounted and prepared for action. At this moment Alexander, the ceremonial wreath upon his head, was on the point of offering, according to precedent, the first victim of the sacrifice, when a bird of prey flew over the altar and dropped upon his head a stone which it was carrying in its talons, and when Alexander asked Aristander what the omen might mean, 'Sire,' the seer replied, 'you will capture the town, but today you must take care for your own safety.'[55]

55. Plutarch (*Alexander* 25.4) relates that the bird was subsequently entangled in the cords of a torsion catapult and caught, Curtius

Alexander, accordingly, kept out of range for a while, close to where his artillery was posted; before long, however, the defenders of the town made a sortie in strength; the Arab troops endeavoured to set fire to the siege engines, and heavy attacks with missile weapons delivered from their commanding position almost succeeded in thrusting the Macedonians back down the earthwork they had raised. At the sight of this reverse, Alexander forgot the seer's prophetic warning. Maybe he deliberately ignored it – perhaps the excitement of action put it out of his mind: in any case, at the head of his Guards he hurried to the support of the Macedonians at the very point where they were hardest pressed. For them, at any rate, his help was just in time: he saved them from being driven ignominiously from their position on the earthwork; but in the action a missile from a catapult pierced his shield and corselet and penetrated his shoulder. Aristander, then, had been right – he had foreseen the wound. Alexander was delighted, for he believed that the other prophecy would also be fulfilled, and that the town would fall. Meanwhile the wound was serious and did not easily yield to treatment.[56]

The artillery which had been instrumental in the capture of Tyre had already been sent for, and now arrived by sea. Alexander gave orders for the raised earthwork, two furlongs broad and fifty-five feet high,[57] to be carried right round the town. The artillery was assembled, mounted on the earthwork, and brought into action. Long stretches

---

(4.6.11) that it stuck fast on a tower smeared with bitumen and sulphur. Hence, presumably, Aristander's prediction that Alexander would capture the city.

56. Curtius tells how Alexander avoided an attempt at assassination by an Arab shortly before he was wounded.

57. A probable emendation of the manuscript reading '250 feet'.

of the wall suffered heavy damage; saps were dug at various points, the earth being removed unobserved by the enemy, until in many places the wall, having nothing to support it, collapsed and fell. Pouring in volleys of missile weapons, the Macedonians were soon in control of a wide sector, thrusting the defenders back from the towers. Three assaults the men of Gaza bravely resisted, in spite of heavy casualties in dead and wounded; but at the fourth Alexander brought into action the main body of his heavy infantry on all sides of the town, the wall, already undermined, was battered down or widely breached where the artillery had already done its work, so that it was now an easy matter to get ladders on to the shattered defences, and thus force an entry. Once the ladders were in position, every Macedonian soldier who had any claim to courage vied with his fellows to be the first man up. The honour fell to Neoptolemus, one of the Companions and an Aeacid by blood; hot on his heels came battalion after battalion, led by their officers, and no sooner had the leading sections penetrated the defences than they smashed down all the gates they could find and cleared an entrance for the whole army.

The defenders, though the town was taken, still stood shoulder to shoulder and fought to the last. Every one of them was killed at his post. Their women and children were sold as slaves.[58] People from neighbouring tribes were settled in the town and Alexander used it as a blockhouse for possible future operations.

58. We need not credit the story (Curtius 4.6.29) that Alexander had Batis, while still alive, dragged round the walls by his ankles at the rear of his chariot as Achilles had dragged Hector's corpse round the walls of Troy (Homer, *Iliad*, 22.395ff.)

The siege lasted two months (September/October 332), and cost the defenders 10,000 men.

BOOK THREE

ALEXANDER now made for Egypt, which was the original object of his southerly march, and a week after leaving Gaza arrived at Pelusium, where the fleet which had accompanied him, coasting along from Phoenicia, was already at anchor. Mazaces, the Persian governor of Egypt under Darius, had no native troops under his command, and this, added to the report of the battle of Issus and of Darius' ignominious scramble for safety, and the fact that Phoenicia, Syria, and most of Arabia were already in Macedonian hands, induced him to receive Alexander with a show of friendship and to offer no obstacle to his free entry into Egypt and its cities.[1]

Alexander garrisoned Pelusium[2] and, after giving orders to the fleet to proceed up the Nile to Memphis, set out northward along the east bank of the river, and, crossing the desert, arrived at Heliopolis. All the country along his route he secured without any native opposition. From Heliopolis he crossed the river to Memphis, where, among the other gods, he offered a special sacrifice to Apis and held Games with both athletic and literary contests.[3]

1. The previous governor, Sabaces, was killed at Issus. According to Curtius (4.7.4) Mazaces handed over the treasure amounting to 800 talents.

2. A very strong border fortress, the key to Egypt, where the Egyptians several times met invading armies.

3. Apis was the calf of Memphis, sacred to the god Ptah. Alexander treated the religion of the Egyptians (and other conquered peoples) with respect, and was enthroned as Pharaoh at Thebes. By contrast Cambyses had actually stabbed the Apis (Herodotus 3.27–8).

The most famous performers in Greece came over to take part. From Memphis he sailed down the river again with his Guards and archers, the Agrianes, and the Royal Cavalry Squadron of the Companions, to Canobus, when he proceeded round Lake Mareotis and finally came ashore at the spot where Alexandria, the city which bears his name, now stands. He was at once struck by the excellence of the site, and convinced that if a city were built upon it, it would prosper. Such was his enthusiasm that he could not wait to begin the work; he himself designed the general layout of the new town, indicating the position of the market square, the number of temples to be built, and what gods they should serve – the gods of Greece and the Egyptian Isis – and the precise limits of its outer defences. He offered sacrifice for a blessing on the work; and the sacrifice proved favourable.[4]

A story is told – and I do not see why one should disbelieve it – that Alexander wished to leave his workmen the plan of the city's outer defences, but there were no available means of marking out the ground. One of the men, however, had the happy idea of collecting the meal from the soldiers' packs and sprinkling it on the ground behind the King as he led the way; and it was by this means that Alexander's design for the outer wall was actually transferred to the ground. The soothsayers pondered the significance of this – especially, of course, Aristander of Telmissus, who had the reputation of having already proved a true prophet to Alexander on

4. This is the first, and greatest, of Alexander's many foundations, designed (unlike the majority) to be a great centre of trade. Plutarch (*Alexander* 26.4) agrees with Arrian that its foundation preceded Alexander's visit to Siwah, but another tradition (represented by Curtius, Diodorus, and Justin) places it after the visit. For arguments in favour of this latter view see C. B. Welles, *Historia* 11 (1962), 271ff.

many occasions – and their conclusion was that the new town would prosper and that, amongst its blessings, the chief would be the fruits of the earth.

Meanwhile Hegelochus arrived in Egypt by sea with the news that Tenedos, which had been forcibly annexed by Persia, had now revolted and come over to Macedon.[5] Chios, too, in spite of the puppet government introduced by Autophradates and Pharnabazus, had invited the Macedonians in; Pharnabazus had been captured in the island together with Aristonicus, the master of Methymna: the latter had entered the harbour at Chios with five pirate chasers, not being aware that it was already in Macedonian hands and misled by the statement of the men in charge of the defences that the vessels inside were Pharnabazus' fleet. All the pirate crews had been killed then and there, but he was bringing Aristonicus to Alexander, together with Apollonides, Phisinus, Megareus, and everyone else who had taken part in the original revolt of the island and had unlawfully seized control of its affairs. He further reported that he had taken the control of Mitylene from Chares[6] and that the other Lesbian towns had consented to support him; Amphoterus had been dispatched with sixty ships to Cos, at the invitation of its people – indeed, he had himself visited Cos and found it already in Amphoterus' hands. All the other prisoners he brought with him, with the exception of Pharnabazus, who had given his guards the slip in Cos and escaped.

Alexander sent the political bosses back to the towns in which they had exercised their power, to be dealt with

5. See p. 103 above.

6. The Athenian general, whose surrender was requested but not enforced in 335; last mentioned in the following spring when he presented Alexander with a golden crown at Sigeium. See pp. 63, 67.

by the people on the spot as the fancy took them; the
Chians with Apollonides he sent to Elephantine in Egypt
under regular guard.[7]

After these events Alexander suddenly found himself
passionately eager to visit the shrine of Ammon in
Libya.[8] One reason was his wish to consult the oracle
there, as it had a reputation for infallibility, and also because Perseus and Heracles were supposed to have con-
sulted it, the former when he was sent by Polydectes to
slay the Gorgon, the latter during his journeys in Libya
and Egypt in search of Antaeus and Busiris. But there was
also another reason: Alexander longed to equal the fame
of Perseus and Heracles; the blood of both flowed in his
veins, and just as legend traced their descent from Zeus,
so he, too, had a feeling that in some way he was descended from Ammon. In any case, he undertook this expedition with the deliberate purpose of obtaining more precise information on this subject – or at any rate to say that
he had obtained it.[9]

He began his journey, according to Aristobulus' ac-

7. Although an edict of Alexander to the Chians (Tod 192) about
a year earlier had provided that traitors should be tried by the
Council of the League of Corinth.

8. The shrine of Ammon, a god known to the Greeks for over a
century and equated by them with Zeus, was situated in the oasis of
Siwah some 400 miles west of Thebes. The visit is described by
Diodorus 17.49–51, Curtius 4.7.5–30, Plutarch *Alexander* 26–27,
and Strabo 17.1.43 (based on Callisthenes).

9. The author of the sceptical remark (given by Curtius also)
would appear to be Ptolemy, out of sympathy with Alexander's
belief in his divine sonship. On being enthroned Pharaoh at Thebes,
Alexander, like every Pharaoh, automatically became son of
Ammon.

Pseudo-Callisthenes (1.30) says that Alexander wished to gain
Ammon's approval before founding Alexandria; see Welles' article
(p. 149, n. 4).

count, by marching 200 miles along the coast to Paraetonium.[10] The country through which he passed was uninhabited but not waterless. At Paraetonium he turned
south towards the interior, where the oracle of Ammon
was situated. The way to it is across the desert, most of it
sandy and waterless. Fortunately for Alexander there was
much rain – the god's own gift, as he supposed. Now it
happens that a southerly wind in those parts buries the
track deep in sand so that it is impossible to see it; travellers
lose their bearings like sailors at sea; there are no marks
along the track, no hill, no tree, no eminence of solid
earth thrusting up through the sand, to enable the way-
farer to set his course, as seamen do by the stars. In fact,
the guides were lost and Alexander's army was going
astray. In this dangerous situation, however, the god had
another gift to give: according to Ptolemy, son of Lagus,
two snakes led the army, hissing as they went, and Alexander told his guides to trust in providence and follow
them. This they did, and the snakes led the way both to
the oracle and back again. There is a commoner version
of the story recorded by Aristobulus: according to this,
Alexander's guides were two crows which flew along in
front of the army; in any case I have no doubt whatever
that he had divine assistance of some kind – for what
could be more likely? But precisely what form it took we
shall never know because of the disparity in the various
records.

The shrine of Ammon[11] is surrounded on all sides by a
waterless desert of sand; but in the midst of this waste

10. Mersa Matruh. He was met there by envoys from Cyrene with
whom he concluded peace and alliance (Diodorus 17.49.2).

11. For a description of the oasis of Siwah and the temple of
Ammon see Diodorus 17.50, Curtius 4.7.16ff., and especially H.
W. Parke, *The Oracles of Zeus* (Oxford, 1967) 196ff.

there is a small plot of ground five miles wide at its broadest point, and thickly planted with fruit trees – olives and date-palms. This, the actual site of the temple, is the only spot in the surrounding desert which has any moisture. Dew falls, and there is a spring, quite unlike other springs elsewhere: its water at midday is cold to the taste and still more so to the touch – nothing could be colder; but as the sun goes down and evening draws in, it gets warmer, and continues to rise in temperature until midnight, when it reaches its peak. After midnight it cools again, and by dawn it is already cold, though coldest, as I have said, at noon. The same changes in temperature are repeated every day in a regular cycle. Natural salt is also mined in this region; some of it is taken to Egypt by priests of the Temple, who before they begin their journey pack it in palm-leaf baskets and then carry it as a present, sometimes to the king.[12] The salt is in large grains, some of which have been found to be more than three fingers broad,[13] and it is as clear as crystal. The Egyptians and other people who are particular about religious observance use it for their sacrifices in preference to sea salt, because of its greater purity.

It was with deep admiration that Alexander surveyed the Temple and its site. He put his question to the oracle and received (or so he said) the answer which his heart desired.[14] Then he began his return journey to Egypt,

12. Arrian presumably means the Ptolemies, indicating perhaps a Hellenistic source.

13. The 'finger' was the smallest unit of measurement, about seven-tenths of an inch in length.

14. It appears likely that the chief priest greeted Alexander (as Pharaoh) as 'son of Ammon' (or 'son of Zeus') and that the king then entered the temple alone. If so, the prophecies made by Ammon regarding his divine descent and his future world rule, given in Plutarch, Diodorus and Curtius, must be regarded as suspect,

following, according to Aristobulus, the same route as before. Ptolemy, son of Lagus, states that he took a different route and went direct to Memphis.

At Memphis he was visited by a number of deputations from Greece, and not a man of them did he send away without a favourable answer to his requests. He was joined here by a force of 400 Greek mercenaries sent by Antipater under the command of Menidas, son of Hegesander, and 500 Thracian cavalry commanded by Asclepiodorus, son of Eunicus. Here, too, he offered sacrifice to Zeus the King and held a ceremonial parade of his troops in battle order, followed by games with athletic and literary contests. He reorganized the country politically, appointing Doloaspis and Petisis, both Egyptians, as provincial governors, each to control one half of the country; but as Petisis declined the appointment, the whole was taken over by Doloaspis. To command the garrisons at Memphis and Pelusium respectively he posted two of his Companions, Pantaleon of Pydna and Polemon of Pella, son of Megacles; Lycidas, a Greek from Aetolia, was given the charge of the mercenaries. Other appointments were that of Eugnostus, son of Xenophantes, a member of the Companions, to be Secretary of foreign troops, and of Aeschylus and Ephippus of Chalcis to superintend the work of the two latter men. The governorship of the neighbouring country of Libya was given to Apollonius, son of Charinus, and of Arabia by Heröopolis

---

unless we suppose that the priests or Alexander himself subsequently revealed them.

Callisthenes evidently wrote up Alexander's divine origin (see e.g. Plutarch *Alexander* 33.1), doubtless with his approval. Plutarch (*Alexander* 28) and Arrian (7. 29) regard this as a political manoeuvre, to overawe the confused peoples, but while there is no doubt something in this view it seems probable that Alexander believed that he was in some way son of Ammon.

to Cleomenes of Naucratis;[15] the latter was instructed to permit the existing nomarchs, or district governors, to carry on as before except for the collection of tribute, which they, in their turn, were ordered to pay him. Peucestas son of Macartus and Balacrus son of Amyntas were posted to the command of the troops to be left in Egypt, and Polemon son of Theramenes to the command of the fleet. Leonnatus son of Onasus was taken into the King's personal bodyguard in place of Arrybas, who had died. Antiochus, the commander of the archers, had also died, and a Cretan named Ombrion was appointed to succeed him. Calanus took over the allied infantry in place of Balacrus, who was to remain in Egypt.

Alexander was deeply impressed by Egypt, and it is generally supposed that the potential strength of the country, which was greater than he expected, induced him to divide the control of it among a number of officers, as he judged it to be unsafe to put it all into the hands of one man. No doubt the Romans took a leaf from Alexander's book when they decided to keep Egypt under strict surveillance, and never to send a senator there as proconsul, but always a man from the class of Equites, or Knights.

At the first sign of spring Alexander left Memphis, crossing the Nile by a bridge which had been built for him over the river and all its canals, and marched for Phoenicia. At Tyre he found the fleet awaiting him, and here, once again, he did honour to Heracles by religious celebrations and games. While he was in Tyre, the Athenian State Galley arrived with Diophantus and Achilles on board – and indeed her entire crew, being all free citizens, were members of the deputation. Approaching Alexander, these men achieved all the objects of their mission, the

15. Naucratis was a Milesian foundation and remained a Greek city. For Alexander's letter to Cleomenes see p. 389.

most important of which was the return of the Athenian prisoners of war taken at the battle of the Granicus. News now came that things were on the move in the Peloponnese, and Amphoterus was sent with instructions to support all the Greek communities in that part of the country, which had sound views on the Persian war and did not take their orders from Sparta.[16] Phoenicia and Cyprus were to furnish 100 ships for the Peloponnese, in addition to the fleet which was being dispatched with Amphoterus.

The time had now come to be on the march again – inland, for Thapsacus and the Euphrates. Before starting, he entrusted Coeranus of Beroea with the collection of tribute in Phoenicia, and Philoxenus in Asia west of Taurus;[17] both these men had been in charge of the money actually with Alexander on campaign, and their office was now taken over by Harpalus, son of Machatas, who had recently been recalled from exile. Harpalus had twice fled the country: the first time was when Philip was still on the throne of Macedon, and he was then driven into exile for his loyalty to Alexander. Ptolemy son of Lagus, Nearchus son of Androtimus, Erigyius son of Larichus, and his brother Laomedon all shared the same fate for the same reason; for the fact was that at that period Alexander incurred Philip's suspicion when the king married Eurydice, in open contempt of Alexander's mother Olympias.[18] These men were recalled from exile

16. The first news of Agis' revolt (p. 125, n. 34).

17. Philoxenus' task probably included the collection of the 'contributions' of the Greek cities of Asia Minor so long as these continued to be levied. Later he possessed (or assumed) power to intervene in these cities. His title and functions are discussed most recently by Badian in *Ehrenberg Studies,* 55ff. Whether he is identical with the Philoxenus mentioned on p. 387 is uncertain.

18. Unlike Philip's other marriages, this marriage with a highborn Macedonian lady in 337 threatened the position of Olympias

after Philip's death, and raised by Alexander to important offices: Ptolemy was enrolled in the King's bodyguard; Harpalus, whose health was not good enough for active service, was given control of the treasury, Erigyius the command of the allied cavalry, and his brother Laomedon, who happened to be as fluent in the Persian language as in Greek, was put in charge of prisoners of war. Nearchus was appointed Governor of Lycia and the neighbouring territory as far as Mount Taurus. However, shortly before the battle of Issus, Harpalus was persuaded by a scoundrel named Tauriscus to desert – which they both did: Tauriscus made his way to Alexander of Epirus in Italy,[19] where he died; and Harpalus took refuge in the Megarid. In spite of this conduct Alexander urged him to return, assuring him that he would in no way suffer for his desertion. Nor, indeed, did he; on the contrary, Alexander restored him to the control of the treasury.

Finally, Alexander sent Menander, one of his Companions, as governor to Lydia,[20] appointing Clearchus to succeed to his command of the mercenaries; the governorship of Syria was given to Asclepiodorus, son of Eunicus, in place of Arimmas, who, in Alexander's opinion, had scamped his work of supplying and equipping the troops for their march into the interior.

---

and Alexander and a disgraceful scene at the wedding led to their flight from Macedonia. It was Alexander's attempt, after his return from Illyria later in the year, to ally himself with Pixodarus, the ruler of Caria, which led to the banishment of his friends. See chapters 9 and 10 of Plutarch's *Alexander*.

19. The uncle (and brother-in-law) of Alexander the Great. He aided the Tarentines against the Lucanians and Bruttians, but was defeated and killed in 331/0.

20. Superseding Asander, the brother of Parmenio, despite Asander's part in the defeat of Orontobates (p. 109); see E. Badian, *Transactions of the American Philological Association* 91 (1960) 329.

Alexander reached Thapsacus in August, during the archonship of Aristophanes in Athens.[21] Two bridges were already across the river. For some time previously Mazaeus, under orders from the Persian King, had been guarding the approaches to the river with a force of 3,000 mounted troops, two-thirds of them Greek mercenaries; and for this reason the Macedonians had not carried their bridge right to the further bank, lest the enemy should attack it at their end. Mazaeus, however, no sooner got wind of Alexander's approach than he made off at his best speed with all his men, whereupon the two bridges were promptly completed, and Alexander was able to use them to get his army across.

Thence he proceeded north and east, keeping the Euphrates and the Armenian mountains on his left, through Mesopotamia; for once across the river he preferred not to follow the direct route to Babylon, as by this other route supplies of all sorts, including fodder for the horses, would be more readily available; other needs for man and beast could be supplied by the country through which they passed, and, furthermore, the heat would be less intense.

During the march some prisoners were taken – men from Darius' army who had gone off on reconnaissance. They reported that Darius had taken up a position on the Tigris and intended to resist any attempt by Alexander to cross it. The force under his command greatly exceeded in numbers what he had had at the battle of Issus. Alexander's reply to this news was to push on for the Tigris at all speed. However, upon reaching it he found neither Darius nor the guard he had left there; so he crossed without opposition – except from the current, which was

21. 331 B.C. For the events of the next few months see E. W. Marsden, *The Campaign of Gaugamela* (Liverpool, 1964).

swift and made the operation a difficult one. Once over the river, he gave his men a rest.

While the troops were resting, there was an almost total eclipse of the moon, and Alexander offered sacrifice to Moon, Sun, and Earth, the three deities supposed to be concerned in this phenomenon. The opinion of Aristander, the seer, was that the moon's failure was propitious for Alexander and the Macedonians, and that the coming battle would be fought before the month was out; he concluded, moreover, that the sacrifices portended victory.[22]

Alexander now continued his advance through Aturia, keeping the Tigris on his right and the mountains of Gordyene on his left. Four days after the crossing of the river a report came in from his scouts that enemy cavalry had been sighted in open ground, but their numbers could not be accurately estimated; Alexander accordingly, before advancing further, made the necessary dispositions for an engagement, and immediately afterwards more scouts rode in; these had had a better view of the enemy force, and declared their belief that it was not above 1,000 strong, whereupon Alexander rode for it at the gallop with the Royal squadron, one squadron of Companions, and the Paeonian rangers. The main body of the army was ordered to follow at its own pace. The sight of Alexander's rapid approach was too much for the Persian cavalry, who incontinently fled, with Alexander in hot pursuit; most of them got away, but a few, whose horses could not stand the pace, were killed, and a few others were taken alive, horses and all. From these prisoners they learned that Darius was not far off, with a powerful force.

Darius' army had been reinforced by the Sogdians, the Bactrians, and the Indian tribes on the Bactrian border –

22. See p. 172 n. 34.

all under the command of Bessus, satrap of Bactria; their
lead had been followed by certain contingents of the
Sacae (a branch of the Asiatic Scythians) who, though
they owed no allegiance to Bessus, were in military alliance
with Persia. These troops were mounted archers, and
were commanded by Mauaces. The Arachotians and the
Indian hillmen were commanded by Barsaentes, satrap of
Arachotia; the Arians by their satrap, Satibarzanes; the
Parthians, Hyrcanians, and Tapurians, all mounted troops,
by Phrataphernes; the Medes, to whom were attached the
Cadusians, Albanians, and Sacesinians, by Atropates; all
contingents from the neighbourhood of the Persian Gulf
by Ocondobates, Ariobarzanes, and Orxines; the Uxians
and Susiani by Oxathres, son of Abulites; the Babylonians,
to whom were attached the Sitacenians and Carians, by
Bupares (these Carians had previously been resettled after
a mass transference of population); the Armenians by
Orontes and Mithraustes; the Cappadocians by Ariaces;
the lowland and Mesopotamian Syrians by Mazaeus.
Darius' total force was estimated at 40,000 cavalry,
1,000,000 infantry, 200 scythe-chariots, and a few elephants – the Indian troops from the hither side of the
Indus had about fifteen of them.[23]

This was the army which had taken up a position under
Darius at Gaugamela, near the river Bumodus,[24] about
seventy-five miles from Arbela. The country where it lay
was level and open, all places where a broken surface

23. Only Curtius (4.12.13) offers a reasonable figure, 200,000, for
the Persian infantry but although some scholars accept this, there
is no evidence that it rests on any reliable authority. His figure for
cavalry is 45,000. Marsden (pp. 31–7) calculates about 34,000.

24. The Khazir, a tributary of the R. Lycus (Great Zab).

The battle appears to have taken place near Tell Gomel, *north*
of the Persian royal road from Nineveh to Arbela (Erbil); see
Marsden, p. 20.

might obstruct the movement of cavalry having been worked on some time previously by the Persian troops, so that all of it was now good going for both chariots and cavalry. The reason for this precaution was the fact that it had been urged upon Darius that much of his trouble at the battle of Issus had been due to lack of space to manoeuvre in – an explanation which Darius was very ready to accept.

On receiving this information from the Persian prisoners, Alexander stayed where he was for four days, to rest his men after their march. He fortified his camp with a ditch and palisade, as he proposed to leave the pack-animals there together with all troops unfit for service, while he himself led to battle the remainder burdened with nothing but their weapons. The order to fall in was given, and at night, about the second watch, the advance began – so timed as to engage the enemy at dawn. The report that Alexander was on the move soon reached Darius, and he, too, ordered his men to battle stations. Meanwhile Alexander was drawing nearer, his troops ready to engage – but the opposing armies were still seven miles apart and had not yet seen each other, as each was screened by a ridge of high ground.

Past the crest of the ridge, just as he was beginning the descent, Alexander had his first sight of the enemy, about four miles away. He gave the order to halt, and sent for his officers – his personal staff, generals, squadron commanders, and officers of the allied and mercenary contingents – to consult upon the plan of action. The alternatives were either to advance at once with the main corps of infantry, as the majority urged him to do, or to accept the advice of Parmenio and stay where they were long enough to enable a careful reconnaissance of the ground to be made; for there might well be reasons for caution –

hidden obstructions, concealed trenches or stakes – and, in addition to that, it would be wise to get a more accurate knowledge of the enemy's dispositions. Parmenio's proposal appeared the better of the two; so for the moment there was no further forward move, the troops all remaining in the order in which they were to engage.

Alexander meanwhile carried out a wide reconnaissance with his light infantry and the Companion cavalry, minutely examining the whole terrain where the battle would be fought; he then returned and called a second meeting of his officers. There was no need, he said, for any words from him to encourage them to do their duty; there was inspiration enough in the courage they had themselves shown in previous battles, and in the many deeds of heroism they had already performed. All he asked was that every officer of whatever rank, whether he commanded a company, a squadron, a brigade, or an infantry battalion, should urge to their utmost efforts the men entrusted to his command; for they were about to fight, not, as before, for Syria or Phoenicia or Egypt, but this time the issue at stake was the sovereignty of the whole Asian continent. What need, then, was there for many words to rouse his officers to valour, when that valour was already in their own breasts? Let him but remind them each for himself to preserve discipline in the hour of danger – to advance, when called upon to do so, in utter silence; to watch the time for a hearty cheer, and, when the moment came, to roar out their battle-cry and put the fear of God into the enemy's hearts. All must obey orders promptly and pass them on without hesitation to their men; and, finally, every one of them must remember that upon the conduct of each depended the fate of all: if each man attended to his duty, success was assured; if one man neglected it, the whole army would be in peril.

With some such brief words of exhortation Alexander addressed his officers, and in reply they begged him to have every confidence in them. Orders were then given for the troops to rest and eat.

Some authorities state that Parmenio went to Alexander's tent and advised a night attack, because the enemy would not be expecting it, and it would naturally cause alarm and confusion. Alexander and Parmenio were not alone in the tent; others were listening, and that, perhaps, was one reason for Alexander's reply: 'I will not,' he said, 'demean myself by stealing victory like a thief. Alexander must defeat his enemies openly and honestly.' However, these lofty words probably indicated confidence in danger rather than vanity, and in my own own opinion they were based upon perfectly sound sense: night-fighting is a tricky business; unexpected things happen to both sides – to those who have carefully planned the attack as much as to those who are taken off their guard – and often enough the better men get the worst of it, while victory, contrary to everybody's expectation, goes to the weaker side.[25] More often than not Alexander took risks in his battles; but on this occasion he felt the chances of a night attack to be too unpredictable; moreover, the mere fact that it was delivered stealthily and under cover of darkness would save Darius, were he again defeated, the necessity of admitting inferiority, either in himself or in his men; while if they themselves suffered an unexpected reverse, they would be a defeated army in an unfamiliar

25. Apart from the dangers involved in a night attack (see Thucydides 7.43–4; Xenophon *Anabasis* 3.4.35), Alexander knew the propaganda value of defeating the Persian army on even terms. Darius could claim that at Issus he had suffered from lack of room (p. 161); on this occasion Alexander did not intend that he should have any excuse.

country among enemies thoroughly at home and surrounded by friends – and of those enemies not a few
would be the prisoners of war, who might well attack
them at night even after an indecisive victory, not to
mention a defeat.

These arguments were sound enough, and I therefore
commend Alexander's decision, and approve no less his
resounding claim to act openly.

During the night Darius' army kept the same dispositions as on the previous day, the reason for maintaining
battle stations being their fear of a night attack, added to
the fact that their position had no regular defence works.
One thing, at this critical moment, told against the Persians, more than anything else: their protracted stand
under arms, and the consequent fear, natural enough
when lives are at stake, but on this occasion rendered less
bearable by the fact that it did not come, as it were, in a
flash from the moment's crisis, but had been brooded on
hour after hour until their spirit was sapped.

We are informed by Aristobulus that Darius' written
orders for the disposition of his troops came into Greek
hands after the battle; we know, consequently, what his
order of battle was.[26] On his left was the Bactrian cavalry
supported by the Daae and Arachotians; in touch with
them were mixed Persian cavalry and infantry, followed
by Susian, and then by Cadusian contingents. These units
composed the left wing of the army as far as the centre.
On the right were the contingents from Lowland Syria
and Mesopotamia, and the Medes; then, in touch with
these, were the Parthians and the Sacae; then the Tapurian
and Hyrcanian contingents; lastly, next to the centre, the
Albanians and Sacesinians. In the centre, with Darius him-

26. This does not suggest that the *numbers* of the Persian forces
became known.

self and his kinsmen, were the royal Persian bodyguard with the golden apples on their spear-butts, the Indians, the so-called 'stateless' Carians,[27] and the Mardian archers. Uxians, Babylonians, troops from the Persian Gulf, and Sitacenians were drawn up in depth behind them. In advance of the left wing, facing Alexander's right, were the Scythian cavalry, about 1,000 Bactrians and 100 scythe-chariots – the elephants and fifty war-chariots were posted in close support of the Royal Squadron of the King's cavalry. In advance of the Persian right were fifty scythe-chariots and the Armenian and Cappadocian cavalry; the Greek mercenaries – the only troops likely to be a match for the Macedonian infantry – were drawn up facing them in two sections, one on each side of Darius and his Persian guard.

On the right wing of Alexander's army was the Companion cavalry, led by the Royal Squadron under the command of Cleitus, son of Dropidas; in touch with them, and working towards the centre, were the squadrons under the following officers and in the following order: Glaucias, Ariston, Sopolis son of Hermodorus, Heracleides son of Antiochus, Demetrius son of Althaemenes, and Meleager; finally there was the squadron commanded by Hegelochus son of Hippostratus. Parmenio's son Philotas was general officer in command of the Companions. Of the infantry, the shock troops of the Guards were posted in closest touch with the cavalry, and were supported on their own left by the other Guards units under the command of Nicanor, son of Parmenio; next to them was the battalion of Coenus son of Polemocrates, followed (working towards the left) by the units commanded respectively by Perdiccas son of Orontes, Meleager son of Neoptolemus, Polysperchon son of

27. They had been forcibly removed to Central Asia.

Simmias, and Amyntas son of Andromenes – the last being commanded by Simmias, as Amyntas had been sent to Macedonia to recruit.

The left of the Macedonian infantry line consisted of the battalion of Craterus son of Alexander – who commanded all the infantry in that sector; in touch with him were the allied cavalry units under Erigyius son of Larichus, supported by the Thessalian cavalry commanded by Philippus son of Menelaus. The Thessalian cavalry extended to the left wing of the army, the whole of which was under the general command of Parmenio son of Philotas. Close about this officer were grouped the mounted troops of Pharsalus, the finest and most numerous unit of the Thessalian cavalry.

Such was the disposition of Alexander's front line, in addition to which he posted reserve formations in order to have a solid core of infantry to meet a possible attack from the rear; the officers of the reserve had orders, in the event of an encircling movement by the enemy, to face about and so meet the threatened attack. One half of the Agrianes, commanded by Attalus and in touch with the Royal Squadron on the right wing, were, together with the Macedonian archers under Brison, thrown forward at an oblique angle, in case it should suddenly prove necessary to extend or close up the front line of infantry, and in support of the archers was the so-called 'Old Guard' of mercenaries under Cleander. In advance of the Agrianes and archers were the advanced scouts and the Paeonians, commanded by Aretes and Ariston; the mercenary cavalry commanded by Menidas were posted right in the van. The position in advance of the Royal Squadron and other units of the Companions was occupied by the other half of the Agriane contingent and of the archers, supported by Balacrus' spearmen who stood facing the Persian scythe-chariots. Menidas had orders to wheel and attack the enemy in the flank, should they attempt an outflanking movement.

So much for Alexander's right; on his left, forming an angle with the main body, were the Thracians under Sitalces supported, first, by the allied cavalry under Coeranus and, secondly, by the Odrysian cavalry under Agathon son of Tyrimmas. Right in the van of this sector was the foreign mercenary cavalry commanded by Andromachus son of Hieron. The Thracian infantry had orders to stand guard over the pack-animals. The total strength of Alexander's army was 7,000 cavalry and about 40,000 foot.

The two armies were now close together. Darius and his picked troops were in full view. There stood the Persian Royal Guard, the golden apples on their spear-butts, the Indians and Albanians, the Carians and the Mardian bowmen – the cream of the Persian force, full in face of Alexander as he moved with his Royal Squadron to the attack. Alexander, however, inclined slightly to his right, a move which the Persians at once countered, their left outflanking the Macedonians by a considerable distance. Meanwhile in spite of the fact that Darius' Scythian cavalry, moving along the Macedonian front, had already made contact with their forward units, Alexander continued his advance towards the right until he was almost clear of the area which the Persians had levelled during the previous days. Darius knew that once the Macedonians reached rough ground his chariots would be useless, so he ordered the mounted troops in advance of his left to encircle the Macedonian right under Alexander and thus check any further extension in that direction. Alexander promptly ordered Menidas and his mercenary cavalry to attack them. A counter-attack by the Scythian cavalry and their supporting Bactrians drove them back by weight of numbers, whereupon Alexander sent in against the Scythians Ariston's Paeonian contingent and the mercenaries. This stroke had its effect, and the enemy gave ground; but the remaining Bactrian units engaged the Paeonians and the mercenaries and succeeded in rallying the fugitives. A close cavalry action ensued, in which the Macedonians suffered the more severely, outnumbered as they were and less adequately provided with defensive armour than the Scythians were – both horses and men. None the less the Macedonians held their attacks, and by repeated counter-charges, squadron by squadron, succeeded in breaking the enemy formation.

Meanwhile as Alexander moved forward the Persians sent their scythe-chariots into action against him, in the hope of throwing his line into confusion. But in this they were disappointed; for the chariots were no sooner off the mark than they were met by the missile weapons of the Agrianes and Balacrus' javelin-throwers, who were stationed in advance of the Companions; again, they seized the reins and dragged the drivers to the ground, then surrounded the horses and cut them down. Some few of the vehicles succeeded in passing through, but to no purpose, for the Macedonians had orders, wherever they attacked, to break formation and let them through deliberately: this they did, with the result that neither the vehicles themselves nor their drivers suffered any damage whatever. Such as got through were, however, subsequently dealt with by the Royal Guard and the army grooms.[28]

Darius now brought into action the main body of his infantry, and an order was sent to Aretes to attack the

28. They had proved equally ineffective at Cunaxa (Xenophon *Anabasis* 1.8.19–20).

Persian cavalry which was trying to outflank and surround the Macedonian right. For a time Alexander continued to advance in column; presently, however, the movement of the Persian cavalry, sent to the support of their comrades who were attempting to encircle the Macedonian right, left a gap in the Persian front – and this was Alexander's opportunity. He promptly made for the gap, and, with his Companions and all the heavy infantry in this sector of the line, drove in his wedge and raising the battle-cry pressed forward at the double straight for the point where Darius stood. A close struggle ensued, but it was soon over; for when the Macedonian horse, with Alexander himself at the head of them, vigorously pressed the assault, fighting hand to hand and thrusting at the Persian's faces with their spears, and the infantry phalanx in close order and bristling with pikes added its irresistible weight, Darius, who had been on edge since the battle began and now saw nothing but terrors all around him, was the first to turn tail and ride for safety. The outflanking party on the Macedonian right was also broken up by the powerful assault of Aretes and his men.

On this part of the field the Persian rout was complete, and the Macedonians pressed the pursuit, cutting down the fugitives as they rode. But the formation under Simmias, unable to link up with Alexander to join in the pursuit, was forced to stand its ground and continue the struggle on the spot, a report having come in that the Macedonian left was in trouble. At this point the Macedonian line was broken, and some of the Indian and Persian cavalry burst through the gap and penetrated right to the rear where the Macedonian pack-animals were. There was some hard fighting; the Persians set about it with spirit, most of their adversaries being unarmed men who had never expected a break-through – at any rate here, where the phalanx was of double strength; moreover, the prisoners joined in the attack. However, the officers in command of the reserves on this sector, the moment the situation was clear, faced about according to orders and appeared in the Persian rear. Many of the Persians, as they swarmed round the baggage-trains, were killed; others did not stay to fight, but made off.

Meanwhile the Persian right, not yet knowing that Darius had fled, made a move to envelop Alexander's left and delivered a flank attack on Parmenio. The Macedonians being caught, as it were, between two fires, Parmenio sent an urgent message to Alexander that his position was desperate and that he needed help. Alexander at once broke off the pursuit, wheeled about with his Companions and charged the Persian right at the gallop.[29] Coming first into contact with those of the enemy cavalry who were trying to get away, he was soon heavily engaged with the Parthians, some of the Indians, and the strongest and finest cavalry units of Persia.[30] The ensuing struggle was the fiercest of the whole action; one after another the Persian squadrons wheeled in file to the charge; breast to breast they hurled themselves on the enemy. Conventional cavalry tactics – manœuvring, javelin-throwing – were forgotten; it was every man for himself, struggling

29. As it is inconceivable that a messenger could have caught Alexander if he were in hot pursuit of Darius, the question arises 'Where was Alexander?' G. T. Griffith, *JHS* 1947, 87, suggests that he had wheeled right to help his hard-pressed right wing, Marsden, 58ff., that he was already moving left to encircle the Persian centre and right wing.

30. These Indians and Persians are distinct from 'some of the Indian and Persian cavalry' mentioned in the previous paragraph. The latter were a small body and could not possibly have plundered the Macedonian camp, some five miles away, and returned to meet Alexander in the time available.

to break through as if in that alone lay his hope of life. Desperately and without quarter, blows were given and received, each man fighting for mere survival without any further thought of victory or defeat. About sixty of Alexander's Companions were killed; among the wounded were Coenus, Menidas, and Hephaestion himself.

In this struggle Alexander was once again victorious. Such Persians as managed to fight their way through galloped off the field to save their skins.

Alexander was now on the point of engaging the Persian right; but his help was not needed, as in this sector the Thessalian cavalry had fought hardly less magnificently than Alexander himself. The Persians were already in retreat by the time he made contact with them, so he turned back and started once more in pursuit of Darius, continuing as long as daylight served. Parmenio, in chase of his own quarry, was not far behind him. Once across the Lycus, Alexander halted for a brief rest for men and horses, and Parmenio went on to take possession of the Persian camp and all its contents; baggage, elephants, and camels.

Allowing his troops to rest till midnight, Alexander then pressed on to Arbela in the hope that he might catch Darius there and seize his treasure and all the other stuff with which a King of Persia takes the field. But though he reached this place on the following day, after a chase since the battle of some seventy-five miles, he failed to find Darius, who in his efforts to escape had kept going without a single break; his treasure, however, and all his valuables fell into Alexander's hands, including his chariot, shield, and bow – all captured for the second time.[31]

Alexander's losses in this battle amounted to about 100

31. The first occasion was at Issus (p. 120).

men killed;[32] over 1,000 horses – nearly half of them belonging to the Companions – perished either from
wounds or from exhaustion in the pursuit. The Persian
losses were reckoned at about 300,000 dead, a figure
greatly exceeded by the number of prisoners.[33] The elephants and such war-chariots as escaped destruction were
also captured. Such was the end of the battle of Gaugamela, fought in the month of October during the archonship at Athens of Aristophanes. Aristander had foretold
that before the month which saw the moon's eclipse was
over, the battle would be fought and Alexander would
win it. He was a true prophet.[34]

Upon leaving the field, Darius made straight for Media
by way of the Armenian mountains; with him was the
Bactrian cavalry, which had been posted at his side during
the fight, and certain Persians – his kinsmen and a small
number of the Royal Guard. He was joined on the way by
about 2,000 foreign mercenary troops under the command of Paron of Phocis and Glaucus of Aetolia. The
reason why he made for Media was his belief that Alexander, once the battle was over, would take the road to
Susa and Babylon, which was a fairly easy one for his transport; moreover, all that part of the country was inhabited,
and, which was more important, Babylon and Susa were
obvious prizes for a victorious army. The route to Media,
on the other hand, was an awkward one for a large force.[35]

32. Surely an underestimate. Curtius (4.16.26) gives 300, Diodorus (17.61.3), 500, with 'very many wounded'.

33. Diodorus (90,000) and Curtius (40,000) are more reasonable.

34. The eclipse (p. 159) occurred on the night of September 20/21
and the battle was fought on October 1, i.e. on the 26th day of the
Attic month Boedromion. (Plutarch *Alexander* 31.4; *Camillus* 19.5).

35. Alexander considered that the occupation of Babylon and
Susa was more important politically than the pursuit of a defeated
army over difficult country.

Darius' guess was right, for Alexander did, in point of fact, make straight from Arbela to Babylon. Not far from the city, which he took the precaution of approaching in battle order, he was met by the people of the place who with their priests and magistrates came flocking out to bring him various gifts and to offer to put the city, with the citadel and all its treasures, into his hands. He marched in accordingly, and instructed the people to restore the temples which had been destroyed by Xerxes, in particular the temple of Bel, the god held by the Babylonians in the greatest awe.[36] He appointed Mazaeus to the governorship of the city, Apollodorus of Amphipolis was put in command of the troops to be left there, and Asclepiodorus, son of Philo, was entrusted with the collection of tribute. Mithrines, the man who had surrendered to Alexander the inner defences of Sardis, was sent as governor to Armenia.[37]

It was here in Babylon that Alexander came into contact with the Chaldaeans;[38] in all matters of religious ceremonial he took their advice, offering sacrifice to Bel in particular, according to their instructions.

His next objective was Susa. He was met on the way there by the governor's son and a messenger with a letter from Philoxenus, whom he had sent to Susa immediately after the battle; the letter stated that the people of Susa had opened their gates and that all the treasure was secured. The march from Babylon took twenty days, and the treasure which Alexander took over upon entering the

36. The temple of Bel (Marduk) had not been rebuilt by the time that Alexander re-entered Babylon in 323 (p. 377).

37. Mazaeus was the first Oriental to be appointed governor. Was this a reward for the part he had played at Gaugamela (see Tarn (*Alexander* 2.109), citing Curtius 5.1. 18), or for surrendering Babylon?

38. By 'Chaldaeans' Arrian means the priests of Marduk.

city amounted to 50,000 talents of silver in addition to other valuables formerly in possession of the King; nor was this by any means all that Susa yielded, for there also fell into Alexander's hands all the treasures which Xerxes had brought there from Greece, among them bronze statues of Harmodius and Aristogeiton. These statues Alexander sent back to Athens, where they now stand in the Cerameicus, on the way to the Acropolis opposite the Metröon and not far from the altar of the Eudanemi.[39] This altar stands on the level ground, as everyone knows who has been initiated into the mysteries of the Two Goddesses at Eleusis.[40]

Here in Susa, Alexander offered the traditional sacrifices and celebrated games and a torch race; before leaving he appointed a Persian named Abulites as governor of the province,[41] made Mazarus, one of the Companions, garrison commandant of the city, and promoted Archelaus, son of Theodorus, general of the forces. Before setting out for the province of Persia, he sent Menes to the coast as governor of Syria, Phoenicia, and Cilicia,[42] giving him 3,000 talents of silver with instructions to pay over to Antipater as much of that sum as he should need for the expenses of the Lacedaemonian war. Here too he was joined by Amyntas, son of Andromenes, with the fresh

39. Arrian says later (p. 381) that these statues were sent back to Athens in 323. For Harmodius and Aristogeiton see p. 218, n. 25.

40. Demeter and Persephone.

41. Arrian is misleading. Abulites was the governor who sent his son, Oxathres, to Alexander. He was *retained* in his post.

42. The Greek word translated 'governor' is 'Hyparchos', a utility word which can denote a variety of positions; see Tarn, *Alexander* 2.173 n. 1. 'Menes was ... a general in charge of a very important sector of communications' (Tarn, op. cit., 2.177).

troops from Macedonia, both horse and foot,[43] the former he attached to the Companion cavalry and distributed the latter according to nationality among the various infantry units. He also – this was an innovation – formed two companies in each cavalry squadron and put them under the command of such officers of the Companions who had distinguished themselves.

He then set out for the province of Persia, and after crossing the Pasitigris entered the territory of the Uxians, a part of whom – those, namely, who occupied the plains and owed allegiance to the Persian satrap – surrendered to Alexander. The hill tribes, on the contrary, who had never recognized Persian dominion, sent a message to Alexander to the effect that they would not allow him or his army to pass through into Persia unless they first received what they always used to receive from the Persian King, whenever he chanced to come that way.[44] Alexander dismissed the messengers with an invitation to meet him at the pass, the control of which also gave them – or so they supposed – the control of the route into Persia. At the pass, he declared, he would give them what they asked for. Then with a force consisting of his personal guard, the remainder of the Guards, and about 8,000 other troops, and with a party of guides from Susa, he set out under cover of darkness by a route no one would be likely to expect him to take; the going was rough and difficult, and within a single day he swooped down on the villages, carried off a great deal of plunder, and killed a number of the villagers before they could rise from their

43. Almost 15,000 in all, including 6,000 Macedonian infantry and 500 Macedonian cavalry. For details see Diodorus 17.65.1, Curtius 5. 1. 40–2.

44. Fuller (p. 227) compares the toll sometimes paid by the British to the tribesmen on the north-west frontier of India.

beds – the rest escaped to the hills. He then hurried on to the pass, where the Uxians counted upon meeting him with all the force they could muster, to receive payment of the customary dues. Craterus, meanwhile, had been sent in advance to seize the high ground to which the Uxians would in all probability try to make their escape, when they found themselves hard pressed.

Alexander's advance was rapid and unhesitating; he · seized the pass before the natives could reach it, and from this commanding position began, in battle order, to move down to the attack. So swiftly had he acted that the Uxians were taken hopelessly by surprise: robbed of the position in which their chief advantage lay, they made no attempt at resistance, but incontinently fled. Some were killed as they tried to get away, and many more on the rough and precipitous mountain track; most of them, however, managed to reach the hills, where they perished at the hands of Craterus and his men. Such were the 'dues' paid by Alexander to the Uxians; they had hard work, moreover, in persuading him to allow them to keep possession of their territory upon payment of an annual tribute. Ptolemy, son of Lagus, states that Darius' mother begged Alexander on their behalf to let them remain in their old homes. The tribute was assessed at 100 horses a year, 500 mules, and 30,000 sheep – the Uxians possessed no money and no arable land, being for the most part herdsmen.

After this Parmenio was given orders to proceed by the main road into Persia with the Thessalian cavalry, the allied and mercenary contingents, all the other more heavily armed units, and the baggage-trains; Alexander himself, at the head of a force consisting of the Macedonian infantry, the Companion cavalry, the Agrianes, archers, and advanced scouts, set off with all speed

through the hills.[45] At the Persian Gates he encountered
Ariobarzanes, the satrap of the province, who had already
built defences across the pass and with a force of about
40,000 foot and 700 horse had taken up a position there to
prevent Alexander from getting through. Alexander
checked his advance, but on the following day moved to
the assault of the pass. It proved a hard task, as the enemy
were in a commanding position and the ground was far
from favourable to an attacker; they suffered severely
from missiles hurled or catapulted from above, and Alexander was compelled to make a temporary withdrawal to
his original position. His prisoners, however, undertook
to show him another way round by which he could reach
the further side of the pass; the track he was to follow was,
he understood, a rough and narrow one, so he instructed
Craterus to remain behind with his own and Meleager's
battalion, a few archers, and about 500 mounted troops,
and to attack the defences of the pass as soon as he was
sure that the advanced party were safely round to the
further side and were actually approaching the Persian
position. The timing of this movement would cause no
difficulty, as he would get a signal from the trumpeters.

Alexander moved off under a cover of darkness and
after a march of some twelve miles detached a force consisting of the Guards, Perdiccas' battalion, the most lightly armed of the archers, the Agrianes, the Royal Squadron
of the Companions, and one double squadron of cavalry;
with these troops he then made a turning movement and,
still guided by the prisoners, went straight for the pass.
Amyntas, Philotas, and Coenus had orders meanwhile to
take the remainder of the troops down the hills and to
bridge the river which would have to be crossed before

45. Alexander's object was to prevent Ariobarzanes from re-
moving the enormous treasure from Persepolis.

entering the province of Persia. The track Alexander had
to follow was still a rough and difficult one; however, he
lost no time, taking most of it at the double. He was on
top of the first enemy outpost before daylight, over-
whelmed it and most of the second as well; nearly all the
men in the third got away – not, however, back to the
army, which they made no attempt to rejoin, but in panic
flight to the hills – so that Alexander was enabled just
before dawn to make a surprise attack on Ariobarzanes'
main position. As he fell upon the trench, the trumpets
sounded, and Craterus, accordingly, immediately moved
to the assault of the outer defences on the other side. The
enemy were properly caught; making no attempt at resistance, they would have fled for their lives had it been possible, but the Macedonians were all round them, on one side
Alexander pressing his attack, on the other Craterus and
his men rapidly thrusting forward, so that most of them
had no option but to turn back to the inner defences in
the hope of saving themselves there. But these defences
too were already in Macedonian hands, for Alexander,
having foreseen how things would go, had left Ptolemy
there with 3,000 infantrymen, who in some close fighting cut the greater part of the enemy to pieces. A few
escaped, but in their desperate efforts to avoid destruction
leapt to their death over the edge of the cliffs. Ariobarzanes and a few mounted men got clear away into the hills.

Alexander now pressed on with all speed to the river.
It was already bridged and the army crossed without
difficulty. Thence he marched to Persepolis with such
rapidity that the garrison had no time to plunder the city's
treasure before his arrival.[46] He also captured the treasure

46. This amounted, according to Diodorus (17.71) and Curtius
(5.6.9), to 120,000 talents, according to Plutarch (*Alexander* 37) and
Strabo (15.3.9), to 40,000 talents.

of Cyrus the First at Pasargadae.[47] He appointed Phrasaortes son of Rheomithras, to the governorship of Persepolis. He burnt the palace of the Persian kings, though
this act was against the advice of Parmenio, who urged
him to spare it for various reasons, chiefly because it was
hardly wise to destroy what was now his own property,
and because the Asians would, in his opinion, be less
willing to support him if he seemed bent merely upon
passing through their country as a conqueror rather than
upon ruling it securely as a king. Alexander's answer was
that he wished to punish the Persians for their invasion of
Greece; his present act was retribution for the destruction
of Athens, the burning of the temples, and all the other
crimes they had committed against the Greeks. My own
view is that this was bad policy; moreover it could hardly
be considered as punishment for Persians long since dead
and gone.[48]

Having learned that Darius was in Media, Alexander
made that country his next objective. Darius had decided,
in the event of Alexander's stopping in the neighbourhood of Susa and Babylon, to remain in Media and to
watch for any new move which he might make; if, on the
other hand, Alexander advanced directly to attack him, he
proposed to withdraw up-country to Parthia and Hyrcania

47. Pasargadae was the old capital of Persia, founded by Cyrus.
6,000 talents were captured there.

48. This is the official version, connected with the ostensible
Pan-Hellenic character of the expedition. Plutarch (*Alexander* 38),
Diodorus (17.72), and Curtius (5.7) say the burning of the palace
was the result of a suggestion made at a drinking party by the Athenian courtesan Thais. According to Curtius' precise chronology it
took place in mid May near the end of Alexander's four months'
stay at Persepolis. For the ruins of Persepolis see the excellent illustrations in Sir Mortimer Wheeler's *Flames over Persepolis,* or in Jean-
Louis Huot's *Persia* (London, 1965) in the series *Archaeologia Mundi.*

and on to Bactria, scorching the earth as he went in order to impede any further advance by his enemy. His women and covered waggons and such other gear as he still had with him he sent to the pass known as the Caspian Gates, while he himself held on in Ecbatana with such troops as he had managed, in the circumstances, to get together.[49] It was the report of this which induced Alexander to start for Media without delay. On the way he invaded and subdued the Paraetacae and left as governor there Oxathres son of Abulites, the governor of Susa; then, a report reaching him that Darius who had been reinforced by troops from Scythia and Cadusia had determined upon risking another encounter, he proceeded in full battle order with the main body of his army, leaving the baggage-trains to follow on with their guards and all the rest of the stores.

Within twelve days he was in Media, where he learned that no Scythian or Cadusian reinforcements had reached Darius; his army was too weak to risk a battle, and he had determined upon a further withdrawal. Alexander, accordingly, increased the speed of his advance. About three days' march from Ecbatana he was met by Bisthanes son of Ochus, Darius' predecessor on the throne, and was informed by him that Darius had already been in retreat for five days; he was taking with him his treasure from Media amounting to 7,000 talents, and had a force of 3,000 cavalry and about 6,000 infantry.

At Ecbatana Alexander dismissed his Thessalian cavalry and the other allied contingents and ordered them back to the Aegean.[50] The agreed amount of pay was settled in

49. Ecbatana is the modern Hamadan. The Caspian Gates, the principal pass through the Elburz mountains from Media into Hyrcania and Parthia, are about 40 miles east of Teheran.

50. He now considered the League war at an end.

full, with a sum of 2,000 talents added by Alexander as gratuity. Any man who wished on his own account to continue his service as a paid soldier was to have his name entered on the pay-roll, and a considerable number thus voluntarily enlisted; the remainder were put under the command of Epocillus son of Polyeides with orders to march back to the Aegean. They were given a mounted guard, as the Thessalians had sold their horses. Instructions were added that when they reached the coast, Menes should attend to their transport by sea to Euboea. Parmenio was ordered to transfer the captured Persian treasure to the citadel in Ecbatana and hand it over for safe keeping to Harpalus, who had been left in charge of it with a guard of 6,000 Macedonians, a few light troops, and some cavalry.[51] Parmenio was then to proceed through Cadusia to Hyrcania with the mercenaries, the Thracians, and all cavalry units except those of the Companions; Cleitus, the commander of the Royal Squadron, who had been left behind on the sick-list in Susa, was ordered, as soon as he should arrive in Ecbatana, to start for Parthia with the Macedonian troops which had been left to guard the treasure. Alexander himself also proposed to make for Parthia.[52]

Without delay Alexander's march began, its objective Darius. His force consisted of the Companion cavalry, the advanced scouts, the mercenary cavalry under Erigyius' command, the Macedonian heavy infantry (all of it except those sections detailed to guard the treasure), the archers, and the Agrianes. So rapid was the march that many of

51. The treasure assembled at Ecbatana is said to have amounted to 180,000 talents (Diodorus 17.80; Strabo 15.3.9.)

52. Parmenio remained in Ecbatana until his death. His orders were presumably countermanded. The 6,000 Macedonian infantry appear to have rejoined Alexander at Susia in Aria (p. 189).

the men, unable to stand the pace, dropped out, and a number of horses were worked to death; but Alexander pressed on regardless of loss, and in eleven days reached Rhagae, a day's march – at this speed – from the Caspian Gates.[53] Darius, however, had already passed through.

Many of Darius' men had deserted during the course of his retreat and dispersed to their homes, and a considerable number had surrendered to Alexander, who now, abandoning hope of overtaking Darius, halted for a five days' rest. He appointed to the governorship of Media a Persian named Oxodates, a man who had been arrested by Darius and confined in Susa – a circumstance which induced Alexander to trust him. Then he moved on towards Parthia. At the end of the first day's march he halted close to the Caspian Gates; on the second day he passed through, and advanced to the limit of cultivated land; then, on a report that the country beyond was uninhabited, he dispatched Coenus with a party of mounted troops and a few infantrymen to forage for supplies.

At this juncture two important persons in Darius' army, Bagistanes, a Babylonian nobleman, and Antibelus, one of Mazaeus' sons, sought an interview with Alexander. Admitted to his presence, they reported that Darius had been forcibly seized and put under arrest by Nabarzanes, commander of the cavalry which had accompanied his retreat, Bessus, satrap of Bactria, and Barsaentes, satrap of Arachotia and Drangiana. Instantly Alexander was on the march again, with greater rapidity than ever; he did not even wait for Coenus' foraging party, and the only troops he took with him were the Companions, the advanced scouts, and a picked body of the toughest of his light infantry. His other men he put under Craterus' com-

53. Rhagae (Rei) is situated 5 miles south-east of Teheran, no less than 44 miles from the Caspian Gates.

mand, with orders to follow on at their own pace. His own force carried nothing but their weapons and two days' rations. Marching all night and half the following day, he stopped at noon for a brief rest; then he was off again and, after a second all-night march, reached at daybreak the camp where Bagistanes had been before his visit. It was empty – the enemy had gone. He learned, however, that the story of Darius' arrest was true; he was being taken off in a covered wagon and Bessus had assumed power in his place. Bessus had received the royal salute from the Bactrian cavalry and all the Persians who had been with Darius on his retreat, except Artabazus and his sons – and the Greek mercenaries – who remained loyal. These, unable to prevent what had taken place, had left the main road and made for the hills on their own, refusing to take any part in the action of Bessus and his supporters. Darius' captors had determined to hand him over if they heard that Alexander was after them, and thus get favourable terms for themselves; if, on the other hand, there should be no pursuit, they proposed to muster as large a force as they could and unite in preserving their power. For the time being Bessus was in command, as he was related to Darius, and also because it was in his province that this daring act had taken place.

The news made it plain to Alexander that he must continue to press his pursuit without a moment's delay. His men and horses were both pretty well exhausted already by their unremitting exertions, but Alexander drove them forward none the less, and after covering a great deal of ground during the night and the following morning reached about noon a village where Darius and his captors had stopped the previous day. Learning that they had resolved to continue their journey by night, he asked the natives of the place if they knew a short cut by which he could catch up with them. They said they did – but the way was through uninhabited country and there was no water – but no matter: Alexander at once ordered them to act as guides.

He knew that the pace would be too much for his infantry, so he dismounted about 500 cavalrymen and mounted in their place the toughest and fittest officers of his infantry and other units, ordering them to keep their own arms and equipment; Nicanor and Attalus, who commanded, respectively, the Guards and Agrianes, were instructed to take the remainder of the force by the way already followed by Bessus and his party; they were to proceed as lightly equipped as was possible, and the rest of the infantry were to follow in their regular formation. Alexander himself then started off again at dusk with all the speed he could make, and covering some fifty miles in the course of the night, came up with the Persians just as dawn was breaking. They were straggling along unarmed; only a few made any offer of resistance; most of them incontinently fled the moment they saw it was Alexander himself who was upon them. Those who attempted to fight also made off after losing a few men. Bessus and his friends did not at once abandon the attempt to get Darius away in the wagon, but when Alexander was close upon them, Nabarzanes and Barsaentes struck him down and left him and made their escape with 600 horsemen. The wound proved fatal, and Darius died shortly afterwards, before Alexander could see him.[54]

Alexander sent Darius' body to Persepolis to be buried in the royal tombs, like the kings before him.[55] He ap-

54. Darius was murdered near Damghan or Shahrud. Alexander had covered either 210 or 250 miles from the Caspian Gates in just over a week in mid-summer over country that was largely desert.
55. For the royal tombs see Diodorus 17.71.2.

pointed a Parthian named Amminapes as Governor of
Parthia and Hyrcania – he was one of Mazaces' party who
had surrendered Egypt to Alexander. Tlepolemus, son of
Pythophanes, one of the Companions, was given a post to
assist him in keeping an eye on things in the two provinces.

Such was the end of Darius; he died in July, during the
archonship of Aristophon in Athens.[56] In military matters
he was the feeblest and most incompetent of men; in
other spheres his conduct appears to have been moderate
and decent – though the truth may well be that, as his
accession to the throne coincided with the declaration of
war by Macedon and Greece, he had no opportunity to
play the tyrant. In the circumstances, being himself in
greater peril than his subjects, he could hardly have
treated them with the usual cruelty of an Oriental despot,
even had he wished to do so. His life was an unbroken
series of disasters from the moment of his accession to the
throne. He was immediately faced by the defeat of his
satraps and their mounted troops on the Granicus; the
loss of Ionia and Aeolis swiftly followed, with the two
Phrygias, Lydia, and all Caria except Halicarnassus; soon
afterwards Halicarnassus, too, was gone, and the whole
coast as far as Cilicia; then came his own defeat at Issus,
and the bitter sight of his mother, wife, and children as
prisoners in enemy hands. The loss of Phoenicia and
Egypt was followed by the *débâcle* at Arbela, his own
shameful flight from the field, and the destruction of the
mightiest army of the whole East; then, a homeless fugi-
tive in the land he once ruled, ruthlessly betrayed by his
own guards, a monarch in chains contemptuously
smuggled away from the scene of his former glory, he
was finally murdered by the treachery of those most

56. 330 B.C.

bound in duty to serve him. Such was the unhappy life of Darius; dead, he was more fortunate; for he was buried in the royal tomb, his children were given by Alexander the same upbringing and education they would have had if he had still been king – and his daughter became Alexander's wife.[57] He was about fifty when he died.

The troops left behind during the pursuit of Darius now rejoined, and Alexander advanced into Hyrcania, a country which lies on the left of the road to Bactria. One side of it is bounded by high wooded hills; on the other the plains extended to the Caspian Sea. He chose this route because of a report that it was the way taken by Darius' mercenaries in their escape to the mountains of Tapuria, and also because he intended to subdue the Tapurian people. Dividing his force into three, he took charge of the largest and most mobile section himself, and proceeded by the shortest but most difficult road; Craterus was sent against the Tapurians with his own and Amyntas' contingent, some of the archers, and a small group of mounted men, while Erigyius had orders to take the mercenaries and the rest of the cavalry by the better, though longer, route, accompanied by the baggage-wagons and non-combatant units.

Alexander halted after crossing the first range of hills, and then went on with the Guards, some of the archers, and the most mobile of the Macedonian infantry. The going was rough and difficult; as he proceeded, he left parties of men to guard the tracks at dangerous points, to prevent the possibility of his own troops, who were coming along behind, being set upon by the enemy who held the hills. Once through the pass with his archers, he halted on level ground by a small river.

57. Barsine, usually called Stateira. For her marriage to Alexander see p. 353.

While he was there, Nabarzanes, commander of Darius'
cavalry, Phrataphernes, satrap of Hyrcania and Parthia,
and other high-ranking Persian officers, came and gave
themselves up. Alexander stayed four days in camp at this
spot; by that time all the men left behind on the march
had rejoined: most of them came through safely, though
the Agrianes, who formed the rearguard, had been attacked by the hill-tribes. However, their long-range fighting was too good for the enemy, who had the worst of it
and withdrew.

On the march again. Alexander now advanced to
Zadracarta, a town in Hyrcania,[58] where he was rejoined
by Craterus' division; they had not encountered Darius'
mercenaries, but had managed to take over all the territory through which they had marched, either by force or
surrender. Erigyius also rejoined at this point with the
baggage-wagons and gear. Shortly afterwards Artabazus
came over to Alexander with three of his sons – Cophen,
Ariobarzanes, and Arsames; with them were delegates
from the mercenary troops who had served under Darius,
and Autophradates, the satrap of Tapuria. Autophradates
was permitted to retain his satrapy, and Artabazus and his
sons, not only because of their rank but especially because
of their loyalty to Darius, were kept in close attendance
upon his person and treated with every mark of respect.
The Greek delegates asked for terms for all Greek mercenaries now prisoners of war; this, however, Alexander
categorically refused: Greek soldiers, he maintained, who
fought for Persia against their own country were little
better than criminals and had acted contrary to the resolutions of the Greeks. Far from agreeing upon terms, he
gave orders that they should all put themselves into his
hands to be dealt with as he saw fit – or, if they preferred,

58. The modern Asterabad.

to take what measures they could for their own safety. They chose the former alternative, and at the same time asked for an officer, to give the prisoners safe conduct. The number of prisoners was reckoned to be about 1,500. Alexander sent them Artabazus and Andronicus, son of Agerrhus.

He now marched for Mardia, his force consisting of the Guards, the archers, the Agrianes, the battalions of Coenus and Amyntas, half the Companions, and the mounted javelin-men, a brigade of which had by now been formed. He overran the greater part of Mardia, and the people of the province suffered severely: many were killed either attempting to escape or, in some cases, offering resistance, and many prisoners were taken. Mardia is a rugged and difficult country; its people, although poor, are sturdy fighters, and it was many years since an invader had set foot upon their soil; they had not the least apprehension of an attack by Alexander, especially as he already appeared to have by-passed their territory, so for these reasons they were caught off their guard even more than they would otherwise have been. Many of them did succeed in escaping to the mountains, which are very lofty and precipitous in this part of the world, confident that there, at least, Alexander would not come after them; however, he did; so they had nothing for it but unconditional surrender. The spokesmen who brought the offer of surrender were allowed by Alexander to return to their people, and Autophradates was made governor of the province, as well as of Tapuria.

Returning to the spot whence he had started upon his expedition to Mardia, Alexander found the Greek mercenaries awaiting him. Dropidas the Athenian, and the Spartans Callicratidas, Pausippus, Monimus, and Onomas, – envoys from Greece on their way to Darius' court – h..d also arrived. They were all arrested. The envoys from Sinope were dismissed, as Sinope was not a member of the League of Corinth, and the fact that, as Persian subjects, they were sending a delegation to the Persian King seemed to Alexander reasonable enough. Of the other Greeks those who had been serving with the Persians before the conclusion of the peace and alliance with Macedon were also dismissed, as was Heracleides, the delegate from Calchedon; the remainder were ordered to serve under Alexander at the same rate of pay. Andronicus was made their commander: it was he who had brought them to Alexander, and he had made it clear that he considered the safety of his men a matter of the first importance.

This business completed, Alexander went on to Zadracarta, the chief town of Hyrcania and site of the royal palace. He remained there fifteen days, sacrificed to the gods in accordance with custom, celebrated Games, and then moved on by way of Parthia to the frontiers of Aria. At Susia, a town in this province,[59] he was visited by the satrap, Satibarzanes, whose office he confirmed, sending Anaxippus, one of the Companions, to accompany him on his return with about forty mounted javelin-men. This force was to enable him to set guards to save the people of Aria from molestation at the hands of the troops passing through.

About this time some Persians came with a report that Bessus was proclaiming himself King of Asia: he was wearing the royal mantle and the cap with the point erect, in royal fashion, and had changed his name to Artaxerxes. He already had with him the Persian troops who had escaped into Bactria, besides a considerable number of the Bactrians themselves, and was expecting reinforcements from Scythia. Alexander marched at once for Bactria with his whole force, which had now reassembled, and was met

59. Probably Meshed.

there by Philip, son of Menelaus, who had come from Media with the mercenary cavalry under his own command, the Thessalian volunteers, and Andromachus' contingent of foreign troops. Parmenio's son Nicanor, the commander of the Guards, had already died of sickness.

On the way to Bactra[60] news came in that Satibarzanes, satrap of Aria, had murdered Anaxippus and the forty men with him; he was arming the Arians and concentrating them at Artacoana (where the palace was), and had resolved, as soon as he should learn that Alexander had put sufficient space between them, to join Bessus with the force at his disposal and assist him in attacking the Macedonians wherever an opportunity should present itself. Alexander changed his plans accordingly: leaving Craterus in command on the spot, he took the Companions, the mounted javelin-men, the archers, the Agrianes, and Amyntas' and Coenus' battalions, and marched with all speed against Satibarzanes and the Arians, reaching Artacoana after covering some seventy-five miles in two days.

The rapidity of the march took Satibarzanes completely by surprise, and he fled as soon as he heard that Alexander was coming. A few horsemen got away with him, but the majority of his men, once they, too, knew that Alexander was approaching, had deserted immediately the attempt to escape began. All who had had any hand in the revolt or had left their villages at the time of its occurrence were rapidly hunted down and rounded up in various places. Some were killed, others sold into slavery. Arsaces, a Persian, was appointed to the governorship of Aria.

The troops left in charge of Craterus now rejoined Alexander, and, marching for Zarangia,[61] he arrived at

60. Also called Zariaspa (Strabo 11.11.2), the modern Balkh.
61. Arrian also calls the country Drangiana, as on p. 182. It lay to the west of Arachotia.

the town where the palace was situated. This region was then under the control of Barsaentes, one of the conspirators who had fatally wounded Darius during the attempt to get him away; and when he learned of Alexander's approach, he fled for refuge to the Indians west of the Indus. But they arrested him and sent him back to Alexander, who had him executed for his treachery to Darius.

It was here, too, that Alexander learned of Philotas' plot against his life.[62] According to Ptolemy and Aristobulus, information of what was going on had come to his ears before, while he was in Egypt, but he had refused to believe it;[63] for Philotas had long been his friend, he had trusted him, and had also bestowed the highest honours upon his father, Parmenio. Ptolemy's account of what now occurred is this: Philotas was brought before the Macedonians to stand his trial; Alexander made his accusation in no uncertain terms, and Philotas answered the charge. Then the persons who had reported the affair came forward, with various irrefutable proofs of his own guilt and that of his fellow-conspirators, of which the most damning was that he admitted knowledge of a plot against Alexander but had said nothing about it, in spite of the fact that he was in the habit of visiting Alexander's tent twice a day.[64] Thereupon he was shot[65] by the

62. At Phrada, later called Prophthasia ('Anticipation') with reference to the detection of the plot. For Philotas' alleged plot see Plutarch *Alexander* 48–9, Diodorus 17.79. 1–80.2, Curtius 6.7–11, who all say that Philotas was tortured to extract a confession.

63. According to Plutarch, Alexander had Antigone, Philotas' mistress, report his utterances to him.

64. In fact, there was *no* evidence against Philotas, except that he twice failed to arrange an audience for a Macedonian named Cebalinus who claimed that he had important information to give the king. It transpired that this concerned a plot against Alexander.

65. Or stoned to death (Curtius 6.11.38).

Macedonians, and the others who were concerned in the conspiracy shared the same fate. Parmenio was executed as well: Polydamas, one of his Companions, was sent to him with a letter from Alexander addressed to Cleander, Sitalces, and Menidas, three generals in Media who had been posted to the army which Parmenio commanded. It was they who put him to death.[66]

The reason for Parmenio's execution may have been that Alexander could not believe that he had no share in his son's conspiracy; on the other hand, even granting his innocence, his living on after his son's execution was already in fact a danger; for he was a man of immense prestige: he had great influence not only with Alexander himself but also with the army – and not alone with the Macedonian units, but also with the mercenary soldiers, whom so often by Alexander's orders and with Alexander's approbation he had led on special missions or in the ordinary course of duty.[67]

It is said that Amyntas, son of Andromenes, and his brothers, Polemon, Attalus, and Simmias, were brought to trial at the same time for complicity in the plot against Alexander, on the grounds of the closeness of their association with Philotas.[68] Most people were the more inclined to believe in their guilt because Polemon deserted to the enemy when Philotas was arrested. In any case, Amyntas stood his trial with his other two brothers, and after making a vigorous defence was acquitted, whereupon he immediately asked permission of the Court to go and find his brother and bring him back. Permission was granted,

66. Details in Curtius 7.2.11–35.

67. See, e.g., pages 78 and 91. The Thessalian cavalry were particularly his command, the Pharsalian squadron corresponding to Alexander's Royal Squadron (p. 166).

68. For the trial of Amyntas see Curtius 7.1.10–2.10.

and he started out the same day, returning later with Polemon. This was a strong additional proof of Amyntas' innocence. Soon after, however, during the siege of some village or other, he died of a wound from an arrow, so that all the benefit he got from his acquittal was death without dishonour.

In view of these events Alexander split the Companions into two separate divisions and appointed, respectively, Hephaestion son of Amyntor and Cleitus son of Dropidas[69] to command them. The reason for this step was that he did not think it advisable that one man – even a personal friend – should have control of so large a body of cavalry – especially as the Companions were the most famous and formidable of all his mounted troops. This done, he proceeded to the territory of the Ariaspians (this, by the way, was their original name: later they came to be known as the Benefactors in recognition of the help they gave Cyrus, son of Cambyses, in his expedition to Scythia). These people Alexander treated with every courtesy; he honoured them for the service rendered to Cyrus in the old days and also for the fact, which he observed for himself, that their political institutions were different from those of other tribes in that part of the world: like the best of the Greeks, they claimed to know the distinction between right and wrong. He accordingly allowed them to retain their freedom, and offered to give them as much of their neighbours' territory as they wanted – and they asked only for a small slice.

There Alexander sacrificed to Apollo – and arrested one of his personal guards named Demetrius on suspicion of complicity in Philotas' plot. Ptolemy, son of Lagus, was appointed in his place.

69. i.e. Cleitus 'the Black', who had saved Alexander's life at the Granicus.

These difficulties settled, Alexander advanced against Bessus in Bactria. On the way to Bactria he subdued the Drangae, the Gedrosians, and the Arachotians, appointing Menon as governor of Arachotia. In fact, he got as far as the neighbouring Indian tribes. The march was all the way through deep snow, and his men suffered severely from exhaustion and lack of supplies.

A report came in that, Satibarzanes having entered Aria with a force of 2,000 cavalry which he had received from Bessus, the Arians had again revolted; Alexander accordingly sent the Persian officer Artabazus there, accompanied by Erigyius and Caranus, two of the Companions, with further orders to Phrataphernes, the satrap of Parthia, to assist them in dealing with the Arians. The troops of Erigyius and Caranus fought a brisk engagement with Satibarzanes, the Persians holding their ground until Satibarzanes in hand-to-hand fight with Erigyius was struck in the face with a spear and killed; then they broke, and fled in confusion.

Alexander's route now led him to the Indian Caucasus. Here he founded a city and named it Alexandria;[70] then, after the traditional religious observances, he crossed the Caucasus range. A Persian called Proexes was made governor of the district, and Neiloxenus, one of the Companions and son of Satyrus, was appointed overseer, and left there with a body of troops at his disposal.

According to the testimony of Aristobulus, the Caucasus range is as lofty as any in Asia, and most of it, at any rate on its hither side, is barren. It extends for a very great distance – so far, indeed, that the Taurus range,

70. By the 'Indian Caucasus' Arrian means the Hindu Kush; see pp. 262-3, and cf. Strabo 11.8.1. The city is generally known as 'Alexandria by the Caucasus', founded perhaps on the site of Begram, 25 miles north-east of Kabul.

which forms the boundary of Cilicia and Pamphylia, is supposed to be part of it, as are other great mountains distinguished from it by various names according to the countries in which they are situated. Here – that is, in the Indian Caucasus – nothing grows (to quote Aristobulus once more) except silphium and terebinth; nevertheless the region was by no means sparsely inhabited; large numbers of sheep and other cattle grazed there, for sheep like silphium, and if they smell the plant in the distance make straight for it and bite off the flower, and even grub up and eat the root. For this reason the people of Cyrene keep their flocks as far away as they can from the places where silphium grows; sometimes they fence the ground to keep the sheep out out should they approach, so valuable is this plant to them.[71]

Bessus did his utmost to prevent Alexander from advancing further: he had with him, besides the Persians who had taken part in the arrest of Darius, about 7,000 Bactrians and the Daae from the hither side of the Tanais,[72] and with these troops he proceeded to lay waste the country round the foothills of the Caucasus, in the hope that if all crops and everything edible between Alexander and himself were destroyed, Alexander would be halted by sheer lack of supplies. The hope, however, was vain; Alexander, in spite of everything, continued to advance. Snow and privation made it a laborious task – but they could not stop him.

When the report reached Bessus that Alexander was already close at hand, he crossed the Oxus in boats, which he then burned, and withdrew to Nautaka in Sogdiana; he was accompanied by the troops of Spitamenes and Oxyartes, together with the mounted troops of Sogdiana

71. It is represented on the coins of Cyrene.
72. For the 'Tanais' see p. 199.

and the Daae from the Tanais. The Bactrian cavalry dispersed to their homes as soon as they knew that Bessus had made up his mind to avoid a conflict.

At Drapsaka, Alexander halted to rest his men, and then went on to Aornos and Bactra, the two chief towns of Bactria; both of them were surrendered without resistance.[73] He left a garrison in Aornos under the command of Archaelaus son of Androcles, one of the Companions. From the rest of Bactria he met with little opposition, and appointed the Persian officer Artabazus as governor of the district. His next objective was the river Oxus.

The source of the Oxus is in the Indian Caucasus; it is greater than any other Asian river reached by Alexander's army, except the rivers of India, which are the greatest in the world. It empties itself into the Caspian Sea in Hyrcania.[74] At Alexander's first attempt to cross it, it seemed an impossible task: it was about six furlongs wide and much deeper than its breadth would lead one to expect; the combination of a rapid current and a sandy bottom made it impossible to drive piles securely into its bed: they could get no grip on the soft sand and were quickly loosened by the force of the stream. Moreover, timber was scarce, and it seemed a great waste of time to go far afield in search of enough to construct a bridge. Accordingly Alexander had all the hides collected which served the men for tents, and gave instructions that they should be filled with chips and other dry rubbish, and then tied up and carefully sewn to make them water-tight.[75] When

73. For Bactra see p. 190 n. 60. The other towns are the modern Kunduz and Tashkurgan respectively. Alexander crossed the Hindu Kush by the Khawak pass, 11,600 ft high.

74. Arrian is mistaken. The Oxus (Amu Darya) flows into the Aral Sea, of which he had no knowledge.

75. Repeating his manoeuvre on the Danube in 335 (p. 47).

they were filled and sewn, there were enough of them to get the men across in five days.

Before the crossing, Alexander sent home all Macedonians whose age rendered them no longer fit for service, and also the Thessalian volunteers who had remained with the army. He sent Stasanor, one of the Companions, to Aria with orders to put Arsaces, the satrap, under arrest for suspected treason and to take over the governorship in his place.

Once over the river, he pressed on with all speed to where Bessus and his army were reported to be. Meanwhile a message arrived from Spitamenes and Dataphernes to the effect that if a body of troops – not necessarily a large one – under command of an officer were sent them, they would arrest Bessus, and hand him over to Alexander. In fact, they already had him under open arrest. On receipt of this message Alexander slackened the speed of his advance, halting frequently, and ordered Ptolemy, son of Lagus, to go on ahead with forced marches and make contact with Spitamenes and Dataphernes with the least possible delay: he was to take with him a force consisting of three regiments of the Companions, all the mounted javelin-men, Philotas' infantry battalion, one regiment of the Guards, all the Agrianes, and half the archers. With these troops Ptolemy covered in four days a distance which would normally take ten, and reached the spot where Spitamenes' men had bivouacked on the preceding day. There he learned that Dataphernes and Spitamenes were in two minds about the surrender of Bessus, so leaving his infantry with instructions to follow in marching order, he rode off with his cavalry to a village not far away where Bessus and a few soldiers were. Spitamenes had already left the place, he and his men feeling the actual betrayal of Bessus to be too much for their conscience.

The little settlement was fortified more or less, having an outer wall with gates in it. Ptolemy cordoned it off with his mounted troops and announced to the Persians inside that if they gave Bessus up they would be allowed to go without molestation; he was accordingly admitted, whereupon he seized Bessus and again withdrew, sending off a messenger to ask Alexander how he wished to be brought into his presence. Alexander replied that he must be stripped of his clothes and led in a dog-collar and made to stand on the right of the road along which he and his army would pass. The order was obeyed, and when Alexander saw him there, he stopped his chariot and asked him why he had treated Darius, his king, kinsman, and benefactor, so shamefully, first seizing him, then hurrying him off in chains, and finally murdering him. Bessus answered that the decision to do what he had done was not his alone: everyone close to Darius at that time had shared in it, and their object was to win Alexander's favour and so save their lives. At this Alexander ordered him to be scourged; and at every lash a crier was to repeat the words of reproach he had himself used as he asked the reason for his treachery. After this humiliating punishment he was sent away to Bactra to be executed.

The foregoing account of the fate of Bessus is Ptolemy's. Aristobulus states that he was brought along, on Ptolemy's behalf, and handed over to Alexander by Spitamenes and Dataphernes. He confirms the details of the stripping and the dog-collar.

Many of Alexander's horses had died of exhaustion in the long climb over the Caucasus and during the marches to and from the Oxus; he therefore brought his cavalry units up to strength with fresh horses taken from the neighbouring country, and then marched for Marakanda, the royal city of Sogdiana,[76] moving on thence to the Tanais. Like the Oxus, this river, too (according to Aristobulus the natives call it the Orexartes) rises in the Indian Caucasus and flows into the Caspian Sea;[77] it can hardly be the Tanais which the historian Herodotus describes as the eighth of the Scythian rivers, having its source in a great lake and flowing into a greater, called Maeotis: this other Tanais is regarded by some as the boundary between Asia and Europe, on the supposition that from this corner of the Black Sea Lake Maeotis and the river flowing into it actually divide Asia from Europe in the same way as the straits between Gadeira and the nomad Libyans divide Libya from Europe – and in the same way, presumably, as Libya is divided from the rest of Asia by the Nile.[78]

It was on this river (call it Tanais, or Jaxartes) that a party of Macedonians foraging for supplies was cut up by natives. After their attack the tribesmen, who were some 30,000 in number, withdrew to a position in the hills, where the ground was not only excessively broken but as steep as a cliff on every side. None the less Alexander, with his most mobile troops, moved to the assault. Again and again the Macedonians struggled for a foothold on the precipitous ascent, but without success: the missiles of the natives drove them back. Many were wounded, including Alexander himself, who was shot through the leg

76. The modern Samarcand.

77. Orexartes is Aristobulus' form for the R. Jaxartes (Syr Darya), which, like the R. Oxus, flows into the Aral.

78. The Tanais of which Herodotus speaks (4.45.57) is the Don and Lake Maeotis is the Sea of Azov. Alexander and his followers identified the Jaxartes with the Tanais (Plutarch *Alexander* 45.5), and Strabo (11.7.4) regards the identification as part of a 'stratagem' to prove that Alexander has conquered all Asia. Gadeira is now called Cadiz. Like many ancient writers, Arrian considers Libya a part of Asia.

with an arrow and had the fibula broken. But despite every obstacle he at length took the place; some of the enemy were killed by his troops, and many others leapt to death over the edge of the cliffs. Of their 30,000 not more than 8,000 escaped with their lives.

BOOK FOUR

A FEW days after the events previously recorded Alexander was visited by a deputation from the tribe known as the Abian Scythians – Homer, by the way, mentioned these people with approval, calling them 'the most righteous of mankind'.[1] They are Asiatics and have kept their independence, thanks, as much as anything, to their poverty and fair dealing. Another deputation came from the European Scythians, the most numerous of all the European peoples. Alexander instructed certain officers of the Companions to return with the delegates ostensibly to conclude formally a pact of friendship with their country, though his actual purpose was rather to gather information about Scythia – its geographical peculiarities, the customs of its people, their numbers, and military equipment.

It was his intention to found a city on the Tanais and to name it after himself. The site, he considered, was a good one; a settlement there would be likely to increase in size and importance, and would also serve both as an excellent base for a possible future invasion of Scythia and as a defensive position against raiding tribes from across the river. Without doubt both its numbers and the splendour of its name would one day turn the new settlement into a great city.[2]

Meanwhile, however, the native tribes along the Tanais took the offensive: they seized and killed the Macedonian garrisons in their towns and began to look to their safety

1. *Iliad* 13.6.
2. 'Alexandria the furtherest', the modern Chojend.

by strengthening their own defences.[3] They were joined
in this hostile move by most of the people of Sogdiana,
who were incited to it by the party which had arrested
Bessus, and these, in their turn, drew into the movement
some of the Bactrians as well. The reason for it may have
been simply fear of Alexander; on the other hand, they
may have justified the movement by the fact that Alexander had issued an order for the leading men of that
country to meet for a conference at Zariaspa, the capital –
an order which might well conceal some sinister purpose.[4]

The report of the revolt led to immediate counter-
measures; each section of infantry was ordered to prepare
a definite number of scaling-ladders, and Alexander himself at once moved forward to Gaza, the nearest of the
native settlements to his own position – there were,
according to report, seven of these towns in which the
natives had shut themselves up. At the same time he sent
Craterus to Cyropolis, the largest of the seven and now
occupied by the greatest number of natives. His instructions were to take up a position close to the town, surround it with a ditch and stockade, and then assemble such
siege engines as might suit his purpose, in order to concentrate the defenders' attention upon himself and his
troops, and thus prevent them from sending assistance to
their friends elsewhere.

Arrived at Gaza, Alexander ordered an immediate
assault with scaling-ladders on every side of the town's
defences, which consisted of an earthen wall of no great
height; as the infantry moved forward, the slingers,
archers, and javelin-throwers poured their missiles into

3. Arrian has not mentioned the occupation of these seven frontier posts.

4. More probably Alexander optimistically thought of arranging
a general settlement.

the defenders on the wall and at the same time the catapults went into action. Under the storm of missiles the
wall was soon cleared; the ladders were fixed and the
Macedonians were up in a moment. All males in the town
were killed, by Alexander's orders; the women and children were treated as prizes of war, and carried off with anything else of value. Then, without delay, Alexander proceeded to the next settlement, took it the same day and in
the same manner, and dealt with the inhabitants with the
same severity. Thence he went on to the third, and on the
day following took this, too, at the first assault.

While the infantry was engaged in these operations, the
cavalry was dispatched to the next two towns with orders
to take strict measures to prevent any of the people there
from getting away; for it was likely enough that, when
they learned of the fall of the neighbouring towns and of
Alexander's impending approach, they would scatter in
flight and pursuit might be impossible. Alexander's guess
was right, and the dispatch of the cavalry came in the nick
of time; for the men in the two settlements which had not
yet fallen, as soon as they saw the smoke rising from the
settlement nearest to them and got direct news of its capture from a few survivors, in a confused and desperate
attempt to get out in time, ran straight into the cordon of
mounted troops and were nearly all killed.

Five of the seven towns were thus taken in two days,
and their women and children sold into slavery. Alexander
then moved on to the largest of the seven, Cyropolis. This
place had been founded by Cyrus, and it was defended by
a loftier wall than the other towns; moreover the natives
who had shut themselves up in it were more numerous,
and the best fighters of the district, so its capture presented the Macedonians with a much tougher problem.
Alexander's first move was to order up the siege engines,

intending to batter the defences and force an entrance
through the breaches, as and wherever they were made;
but he soon observed something which induced him to
change his tactics. A stream ran through the town, but
there was water in it only in winter; now it was dry, and
in each of its several channels, at the points where they
emerged, its bed was below the base of the surrounding
wall, leaving just room enough for men to crawl through
and so get into the town. Alexander, therefore, while the
enemy's attention was engaged by the siege engines and
the attempted assault within their sector, ordered the
Guards, the archers, the Agrianes, and his personal guard
to hold themselves in readiness, and himself, with a few
men only, crept unobserved by the dried-up water-course,
under the wall, into the town. Once inside he broke open
the nearest gates and admitted the rest of the troops without difficulty.

The enemy saw that the town was already taken; none
the less they turned to fight and fell furiously upon Alexander's men. Alexander himself received a violent blow
from a stone upon his head and neck; Craterus was
wounded by an arrow, and many other officers were hurt.
But in spite of strong opposition they cleared the centre
of the town, while at the same time the assault on the
outer defences was equally successful; the defenders were
all driven off and the wall was taken without further
resistance.

The enemy force in this town amounted to about
15,000 fighting men; of these, in the first phase of the
operations about 8,000 were killed. The rest took refuge
in the central fortress. Alexander stationed troops all
round the fortress, and kept a close watch on the fugitives.
After one day they surrendered for lack of water.

The seventh town was taken without trouble. In this

case, however, accounts differ: Ptolemy says they surrendered; Aristobulus that the place was stormed and
everyone in it massacred. Ptolemy also states that Alexander distributed the prisoners among the various units
of his army with orders that they should be kept bound
and under constant supervision all the time he should remain in that part of the country; not one, in fact, who had
taken part in the revolt was to be allowed his liberty.

About this time a force of Asian Scythians arrived at
the Tanais. Most of them had heard that some of the
tribes beyond the river had declared their hostility to
Alexander and intended to join in an attack upon the
Macedonians in the event of a serious rising. A report also
came in that Spitamenes was blockading the troops which
had been left behind in the fortress of Marakanda. To
meet this situation, Andromachus, Menedemus, and
Caranus were dispatched with a force consisting of sixty
Companions, 800 of Caranus' mercenaries, and some
1,500 mercenary infantry. Pharnuches the interpreter was
attached to the troops: he was a Lycian, thoroughly familiar with the language of this part of the country, and had
often shown a skilful touch in dealing with the natives.

Alexander spent twenty days on the work of fortifying
the site of his proposed new town and arranging for the
settlement there of any Greek mercenaries and neighbouring tribesmen who expressed a wish to avail themselves
of the opportunity, and also of a number of Macedonians
no longer fit for active service.[5] To mark the occasion,
after his customary religious observances he held games,
with athletic and equestrian contests.

Meanwhile the Scythians made no move to leave the
Tanais. The river was not broad at that point; they could
be seen shooting arrows into the water, and heard calling

5. Chojend, mentioned on p. 201.

out, in their barbarous way, insulting remarks to Alexander and boasting that he would never dare to lay a finger upon men like them – or, if he did, that he would soon find out the difference between Scythians and Asiatic savages. To Alexander such an exhibition was most annoying, so he proposed to cross the river and deal with them as they deserved. The skin floats were being prepared for the crossing when he found that the omens, at the preliminary sacrifice, were against him. In spite of his vexation, he nevertheless made the best of it and abandoned the enterprise. The Scythians, however, continuing their insufferable behaviour, he sacrificed again; but this time, too, Aristander the seer declared that the omens portended danger. Thereupon Alexander replied that it was better to face the worst of perils than for the conqueror of nearly all Asia to make himself ridiculous to a pack of Scythians – as Darius, the father of Xerxes, had done long ago.[6] None the less, Aristander refused to misinterpret the divine prediction merely because Alexander wished it otherwise.[7]

When all the skin floats were ready and the army in full equipment drawn up on the river-bank, the catapults, at the word of command, opened up on the Scythians who were riding along the edge of the water on the further side. Some of them were hit; one was pierced through both shield and breastplate and fell dead from his horse. The Scythians were taken completely aback by the long range of the catapults, and that, together with the loss of a good man, induced them to withdraw a short distance from the river, whereupon Alexander, seeing their consternation, ordered the trumpets to sound and himself led

6. See Herodotus 4.122–142.
7. Curtius 7.7.24–9 relates that Aristander changed his prophecy and declared that the sacrifices had never been more favourable.

the way over the water, followed by his men. First to be put ashore were the archers and slingers, who were then ordered to open up on the enemy to prevent them from closing on the main infantry units before the mounted troops were all safely over; then, as soon as every man was across and the army massed on the river-bank, a regiment of mercenaries and four squadrons of lancers were ordered forward to lead the attack. The Scythians met the challenge; their numbers were for the moment superior; they made circles round the small attacking force, shooting as they rode, and then galloped off to a safe distance. At this Alexander ordered an advance by a mixed force consisting of the cavalry together with the archers, the Agrianes, and the other light troops under Balacrus, and, when they were almost within striking distance, gave the word for three regiments of the Companions and all the mounted javelin-men to charge, while he himself at the head of the remaining cavalry came on at the gallop with his squadrons in column.[8]

This effectually put a stop to the enemy's circling movements; the Macedonian cavalry, with the light troops mixed with it in close support, was now right on top of them, and it was no longer possible for them to repeat their former manœuvre without the certainty of destruction. Indeed, from this moment they were well and truly beaten; in their attempt to get away, about 1,000 were killed, including Satraces, one of their commanders, and some 150 were made prisoner.

The rapid pursuit, in the great heat, was exhausting; every man suffered acutely from thirst, and Alexander

8. This is the first mention (apart from p. 91) of 'regiments' (Hipparchies) of the Companion cavalry; see the Introduction, p. 38. For the operations against the Scythians see especially Fuller pp. 236–41.

himself, as he rode, was forced to drink whatever water he could find. Unfortunately it was not pure, and gave him a severe attack of dysentery. This proved the salvation of some, at any rate, of the Scythians; for had not Alexander had this trouble, I do not think a single one of them would have escaped with his life.

Alexander did, in fact, become very seriously ill, and was carried back to camp – so Aristander was a true prophet after all.

Not long after this Alexander was visited by an embassy from the Scythian King. Its purpose was to offer an explanation of what had occurred and to make it clear that the recent incident was merely a casual raid by a pack of brigands and in no sense the deliberate policy of the Scythian State. The King, moreover, was willing to carry out such instructions as Alexander might give him. Alexander returned a polite answer, for the situation was an awkward one: clearly it was his duty to continue the campaign if he distrusted the protestations of the King; but, at the same time, the moment was not propitious for doing so.

The Macedonian garrison,[9] beset in the fortress at Marakanda, in reply to an attempted assault by Spitamenes made a successful sortie, killing a number of the enemy without loss to themselves; they then resumed their position in the fortress. Then, when it was reported to Spitamenes that the troops which Alexander had dispatched to the town were already near, he abandoned his siege and withdrew to the capital of the district. Pharnuches and the officers with him, pressing on with all speed with the intention of getting him right out of the country, followed his withdrawal towards the frontier of Sogdiana, and in the course of the pursuit came to blows with the Nomad Scythians. This wholly unpremeditated

9. 1,000 according to Curtius (7.6.10).

action had serious consequences: for Spitamenes, having now an accession to his force of some 600 Scythian mounted men, was emboldened by this unexpected assistance to stand and take the offensive. He took up a position on level ground near the Scythian desert, then, at the approach of the Macedonians, with whom he had no intention of risking a close engagement, he dispatched his cavalry to gallop round the Macedonian infantry formations, discharging their arrows as they rode. Pharnuches' men attempted to charge, but to no purpose; the enemy, on their swifter horses, were out of range in a moment. Their horses, moreover, were fresh, while those of Andromachus' men were in poor condition from long, forced marches and inadequate feeding. The Macedonians tried now to stand their ground, now to withdraw; but all to no effect: in either case the weight of the Scythian cavalry was too much for them. Many were wounded, some killed, until finally the officers formed the men into a square and withdrew to the river Polytimetus. Near the river there was a little wood, which would give some cover against the enemy's arrows and at the same time enable them to make better use of their own infantry.

Caranus, who was in command of the cavalry, without a word to Andromachus of his intention, attempted to cross the river to get his men and horses into safety; the infantry without orders promptly followed suit, scrambling down the steep bank into the water in a panic-stricken and disorderly rabble. The Scythians soon turned this fatal error to their own advantage: galloping up from all directions, they plunged into the stream; some rode hard on the heels of the Macedonians already across and trying to get away; others confronted the fugitives in mid-stream and dragged them down; or flung themselves upon those not yet in the water, while all the time from

the flanks showers of arrows were poured in. The Macedonians were helpless, and all who survived took refuge
on a small island in the river; but this did not save them,
for Spitamenes' cavalry and the Scythians surrounded the
island and shot them down to a man. The few prisoners
taken were promptly butchered.

Aristobulus' account of this disaster is somewhat different: according to him, most of the Macedonian force was
caught and destroyed by an ambush.[10] The Scythians had
concealed themselves in a park, and fell unexpectedly on
the Macedonians when they were already engaged. This
happened to be the moment when Pharnuches was offering to surrender his command to the Macedonian officers
who had been sent with him on the expedition – on the
ground that he was ignorant of military tactics and had
been sent by Alexander not to command troops in battle,
but to establish relations with the natives, while the others,
unlike him, were true-born Macedonians and Companions of the King. But Andromachus, Caranus, and Menedemus refused to accept the command, partly to avoid the
responsibility of a personal decision not covered by Alexander's explicit orders, and partly because, in the present
dangerous situation, they did not wish to incur individual
blame in the event of defeat, much less to expose themselves to the general charge of inferior leadership. It was
in this situation, when everything was at sixes and sevens,
that the Scythian attack occurred – with results so disastrous that only about forty of the cavalry and 300 infantrymen escaped with their lives.

News of the *débâcle* caused Alexander great distress,

10. Curtius (4.7.30–9) agrees with Aristobulus that the Macedonians fell into an ambush; otherwise his account differs considerably from those in Arrian. Of an original force of 3,000 infantry and
800 cavalry, 2,000 and 300 were killed respectively.

and he determined to march with all speed against Spitamenes and the tribesmen with him. Accordingly, with
half the Companion cavalry, all the Guards, the Agrianes,
the archers, and the most active of the infantry units, he
proceeded towards Maracanda, whither he knew that
Spitamenes had returned and was again besieging the
garrison in the fortress. In three days he covered about
185 miles, and at dawn on the fourth was close to the
town. At the report of his approach Spitamenes and his
men abandoned the town and fled; Alexander followed in
close pursuit, passing the scene of the battle, where he
paused to give such burial to the dead as circumstances
permitted. At the edge of the desert he turned back and
began the work of systematic destruction; a number of
natives had fled for refuge to the forts, and on a report
that they had joined in the attack on the Macedonians, he
had them all butchered. He covered in this way the whole
region watered by the Polytimetus.[11]

The country is desert beyond the spot where the Polytimetus disappears – for disappear it does, in spite of the
fact that it is a river of some size. It vanishes into the sand.
The same phenomenon can be observed with other rivers
in this part of the world – rivers, too, of considerable
volume, not mere streamlets such as dry up in the summer: the Epardus, for instance, which flows through
Mardia, and the Areius, from which the country of Aria
takes its name, and the Etymandrus, which runs through
the country of the 'Benefactors'.[12] All these are larger
than the Peneus in Thessaly, which reaches the sea
through the pass of Tempe. The Polytimetus is much
larger than the Peneus.

Having brought these operations to an end, Alexander

11. Now the Zarafshan.
12. For the 'Benefactors' see p. 193.

went to Zariaspa, where he stayed for the worst of the winter.[13] He was visited there by Phrataphernes, satrap of Parthia, and Stasanor, the officer who had been sent to Aria to arrest Arsaces; they brought Arsaces with them under close guard, and also Barzanes, who had been appointed to the satrapy of Parthia by Bessus, and a number of other prisoners, all men who had assisted Bessus in his movement to depose Darius. At about the same time Epocillus, Menidas,[14] and Ptolemaeus, general of the Thracians, returned from their mission of escorting to the coast the allies and the treasure sent with Menes.[15] Alexander was also joined in Zariaspa by Asander and Nearchus with a force of Greek mercenaries, and by further reinforcements from the coast in charge of the satrap of Syria (also named Bessus) and of Asclepiodorus, the provincial governor.[16]

Alexander had Bessus brought before a full meeting of his officers and accused him of treachery to Darius. He then gave orders that his nose and the tips of his ears should be cut off, and that thus mutilated he should be taken to Ecbatana to suffer public execution before his own countrymen, the Medes and Persians.[17]

13. 329/8 B.C.

14. For their departure from Nautaka a year later see p. 232.

15. Arrian is writing loosely. Menes had been sent from Susa late in 331 (p. 174), Epocillus from Ecbatana some months later (p. 181).

16. It is generally agreed that the name Bessus here is due to the mention of Bessus, the murderer of Darius, immediately before. A probable emendation would read 'Asclepiodorus, the satrap of Syria, and of Menes, the "governor"' (see Tarn, *Alexander* 2.179–80). The Greek word translated 'governor' is again 'Hyparchos'; see p. 174, n. 42.

For the details of the reinforcements, totalling 19,000 men, see Curtius 7.10.11–12.

17. For this 'barbarous', i.e. non-Hellenic, form of mutilation see, e.g., Herodotus 3.154.

I do not myself approve the excessive severity of this punishment; for mutilation of that sort is, I think, a barbarous custom. I admit, moreover, that Alexander came to allow himself to emulate Eastern extravagance and splendour, and the fashion of barbaric kings of treating their subjects as inferiors; regrettable, too, was the assumption by a descendant of Heracles of Median dress in place of what Macedonians have worn from time immemorial, and the unblushing exchange of his familiar head-gear, so long victoriously worn, for the pointed bonnet of the vanquished Persians.[18] I have no praise for such conduct; but in my opinion, at least, the splendid achievements of Alexander are the clearest possible proof that neither strength of body, nor noble blood, nor success in war even greater than Alexander's own – not even the realization of his dream of circumnavigating Libya and Asia and adding them both to his empire, together with Europe too[19] – that none of these things, I say, can make a man happy, unless he can win one more victory in addition to those the world thinks so great – the victory over himself.

In connexion with this I may as well relate here an incident which actually took place a little later: I mean the death of Cleitus, son of Dropides, and its effect upon Alexander.[20] The Macedonians used to celebrate a festival

18. Plutarch *Alexander* 45 more accurately says that Alexander adopted a mixed Persian and Median dress, avoiding the most 'barbarous' elements of the latter. Arrian later (p. 397) acknowledges that the motive for its adoption was political.

19. See also Arrian's remarks on pp. 348f., 382; cf. Alexander's speech on p. 293.

20. It took place at Marakanda in the autumn of 328. For somewhat different accounts of what took place see Plutarch *Alexander* 50–2 and Curtius 8.1.20–2.12. The various versions are analysed by T. S. Brown, *AJP* 1949, 236 ff.

in honour of Dionysus, and it was Alexander's custom to
offer sacrifice each year on the sacred day. The story is
that on this particular occasion Alexander, for some
reason best known to himself, sacrificed not to Dionysus
but to Castor and Polydeuces, the Dioscuri. There had
been some pretty heavy drinking (another innovation –
in drink, too, he now tended to barbaric excess), and in
the course of talk the subject of the Dioscuri came up,
together with the common attribution of their parentage
to Zeus instead of to Tyndareus. Some of the company –
the sort of people whose sycophantic tongues always have
been and always will be the bane of kings – declared with
gross flattery that, in their opinion, Polydeuces and Castor
were not to be compared with Alexander and his achievements; others, being thoroughly drunk, extended the
invidious comparison to Heracles himself: it was only
envy, they maintained, which deprived the living of due
honour from their friends.

Now Cleitus for some time past had quite obviously
deprecated the change in Alexander: he liked neither his
move towards the manners of the East, nor the sycophantic expressions of his courtiers. When, therefore, he heard
what was said on this occasion (he, too, had been drinking
heavily), he angrily intervened; it was intolerable, he
declared, to offer such an insult to divine beings, and he
would allow no one to pay Alexander a compliment at the
expense of the mighty ones of long ago – such a compliment was not for his honour but for his shame. In any
case, he continued, they grossly exaggerated the marvel-
lous nature of Alexander's achievements, none of which
were mere personal triumphs of his own; on the contrary,
most of them were the work of the Macedonians as a
whole.

Alexander was deeply hurt – and I, for my part, feel

that Cleitus' words were ill-judged; in view of the fact that most of the party were drunk, he could, in my opinion, have quite well avoided the grossness of joining in the general flattery simply by keeping his thoughts to himself. But there was more to come: for others of the company, hoping, in their turn, to curry favour with Alexander, brought up the subject of Philip, and suggested, absurdly enough, that what he had done was, after all, quite ordinary and commonplace. At this Cleitus could control himself no longer; he began to magnify Philip's achievements and belittle Alexander's; his words came pouring out – he was, by now, very drunk indeed – and, among much else, he taunted Alexander with the reminder that he had saved his life, when they fought the Persian cavalry on the Granicus.

'This is the hand,' he cried, holding it out with a flourish, 'that saved you, Alexander, on that day.'

Alexander could stand no more drunken abuse from his friend. Angrily he leapt from his seat as if to strike him, but the others held him back. Cleitus continued to pour out his insulting remarks, and Alexander called for the Guard. No one answered.

'What?' he cried, 'have I nothing left of royalty but the name? Am I to be like Darius, dragged in chains by Bessus and his cronies?'

Now nobody could hold him; springing to his feet, he snatched a spear from one of the attendants and struck Cleitus dead.

Accounts of this incident differ. Some authorities say it was not a spear but a pike; Aristobulus does not mention the occasion of the drinking bout: according to him, Cleitus need not have been killed but for his own action; for when Alexander sprang up in rage to kill him, Ptolemy, son of Lagus, a member of the King's personal guard, hurried him out of the door and over the wall and ditch of the fortress. However, he did not stay there, but went back to the banquet room and met Alexander just at the moment when he was calling his name.

'Here I am, Alexander!' he cried, and, as he spoke, the blow fell.

Personally, I strongly deprecate Cleitus' unseemly behaviour to his sovereign; and for Alexander I feel pity, in that he showed himself on this occasion the slave of anger and drunkenness, two vices to neither of which a self-respecting man should ever yield. But when the deed was done, Alexander immediately felt its horror; and for that I admire him. Some have said that he fixed the butt of the pike against the wall, meaning to fall upon it himself, because a man who murdered his friend when his wits were fuddled with wine was not fit to live. Most writers, however, say nothing of this; they tell us that Alexander lay on his bed in tears, calling the name of Cleitus and of his sister Lanice, who had been his nurse. 'Ah,' he cried, 'a good return I have made you for your care, now I am a man! You have lived to see your sons die fighting for me, and now with my own hand I have killed your brother.' Again and again he called himself the murderer of his friends, and for three days lay without food or drink, careless of all personal comfort.

One result of these painful events was that soothsayers began to suggest that the god Dionysus was angry because Alexander had failed to offer him sacrifice; and when at last he was with difficulty persuaded by his friends to take food and attend in some measure to his bodily needs, he did offer the neglected sacrifice. Doubtless he was not unwilling that what had happened should be attributed rather to the wrath of God than to his own wickedness. Here again, I have nothing but admiration for him: he made no attempt to justify his crime; he never added to his guilt by becoming champion and advocate in his own defence; he quite simply admitted that, being no more than human, he had done wrong.

There is a story that Alexander sent for the sophist Anaxarchus,[21] in the hope he might give him comfort, and was still on his bed, bewailing his fate, when he came in.

Anaxarchus laughed. 'Don't you know,' he said, 'why the wise men of old made Justice to sit by the side of Zeus? It was to show that whatever Zeus may do is justly done. In the same way all the acts of a great king should be considered just, first by himself, then by the rest of us.'[22]

This was some consolation, at any rate for a time – though in my opinion he did Alexander a wrong more grievous than his grief, if he seriously, as a philosopher, put forward the view that a king need not act justly, or labour, to the best of his ability, to distinguish between right and wrong – if he really meant that whatever a king does, by whatever means, should be considered right.

In this connexion it is widely believed that Alexander wished people to prostrate themselves in his presence. This was due partly to the notion that his father was not Philip but Ammon, and partly to his growing admiration, expressed also by the change in his dress and in the general etiquette of his court, of Median and Persian extravagance. There were plenty of people, moreover, who, to

21. A native of Abdera in Thrace and the teacher of Pyrrhon the sceptic. His attitude is frequently contrasted with that of Callisthenes; see, e.g., Plutarch *Alexander* 52–3.

22. The connexion of Justice (*Dike*) with Zeus is at least as old as Hesiod (*Works and Days*, 256ff.); cf. Sophocles, *Oedipus at Colonus*, 1381f; Anaxarchus interprets the old myth to suit himself.

flatter him, submitted to this servile behaviour: Anaxarchus the sophist was one of the worst – and the Argive
poet Agis.[23]

There was one man, however, who did not approve of
these innovations. This was Callisthenes of Olynthus, a
pupil of Aristotle. Thus far I agree with Callisthenes; but
he was a somewhat tactless man, and his remark (if it has
been rightly reported) that, without the history he was
writing, Alexander and his work would be forgotten, was,
I feel, most unfortunate. He used to declare that he had
come not in the hope of honour for himself, but merely to
spread Alexander's fame throughout the world; adding
that if Alexander was destined to have a share of divinity,
it would not be owing to Olympias' absurd stories about
his birth,[24] but to the account of him which he would
himself publish in his history. According to another anecdote, Callisthenes was once asked by Philotas who he
thought was held in the greatest honour by the Athenian
people.

'Harmodius and Aristogeiton,' Callisthenes replied,
'because they killed one of the tyrants and abolished
irresponsible government.'[25]

'And do you think,' Philotas went on, 'that a tyranni-
cide could find asylum in any Greek community he liked
to choose?'

'Even if no one else would have him,' said Callisthenes,

23. It is very probable that Alexander's attempt to introduce
prostration (*proskynesis*) as a court practice, like his adoption of a
mixed dress, was due to his desire to place Macedonians and Persians on an equal footing. The best discussion is J. P. V. D. Balsdon's article in *Historia* 1950, 371ff. See also T. S. Brown, *AJP*
1950, 242ff.

24. For these see Plutarch *Alexander* 2–3.

25. Hipparchus was killed in 514 and Hippias was expelled from
Athens in 510; see Thucydides 6.54–9.

'he would be safe in Athens; for the Athenians once fought for the children of Heracles even against Eurystheus, who was at that time absolute master of Greece.'

I will now relate a widely accepted story about Callisthenes' opposition to Alexander in this matter of prostration. Alexander had arranged with the sophists and the Persian and Median noblemen at his Court that the subject should be brought up one day at a party. The discussion was begun by Anaxarchus, who declared that Alexander had a better claim upon them to be considered divine than Dionysus or Heracles. The reason for this was not merely his brilliant and successful career, but also the fact that neither Dionysus nor Heracles was connected with Macedon: Dionysus belonged to Thebes, and Heracles to Argos – the latter's only connexion with Macedon was through Alexander, who had his blood in his veins. This being so, there would be greater propriety in the Macedonians paying divine honours to their own King. In any case there was no doubt that they would honour him as a god after he had left this world; would it not, therefore, be in every way better to offer him this tribute now, while he was alive, and not wait till he was dead and could get no good of it?

Those who were, so to put it, 'in the know' expressed their approval of what Anaxarchus said, and were only too willing to begin prostrating themselves forthwith; but the Macedonians – or most of them – who were present, strongly dissented, and said nothing. Suddenly Callisthenes intervened. 'For my part,' he said, 'I hold Alexander fit for any mark of honour that a man may earn; but do not forget that there is a difference between honouring a man and worshipping a god. The distinction between the two has been marked in many ways: for instance, by the building of temples, the erection of statues; the dedication of sacred ground – all these are for gods; again, for gods sacrifice is offered and libations are poured; hymns are composed for the worship of gods, while panegyrics are written for the praise of men. Yet of all these things not one is so important as this very custom of prostration. Men greet each other with a kiss; but a god, far above us on his mysterious throne, it is not lawful for us to touch – and that is why we proffer him the homage of bowing to the earth before him.[26]

'Again, for the worship of gods we perform the ceremonial dance and sing the song of praise. There is nothing surprising in this, for even the gods are worshipped by varying forms of ceremonial; and heroes and demi-gods, remember, have, again, their own peculiar, and quite different, rites.

'It is wrong, therefore, to ignore these distinctions; we ought not to make a man look bigger than he is by paying him excessive and extravagant honour, or, at the same time, impiously to degrade the gods (if such a thing were possible) by putting them in this matter on the same level as men. Suppose some fellow or other, by some quite unjustified vote or show of hands, were brought to enjoy royal honours: would Alexander tolerate it? Of course he would not. By the same reasoning there are much better grounds for the gods' resentment against men who invest themselves with divine honours, or allow other people to do it for them.

'Now Alexander deserves his reputation of being incomparably the bravest of the brave, the most kingly of kings, the worthiest to command of all commanders. And you, Anaxarchus – you who are admitted to Alexander's

26. The Persians did not consider their kings to be gods, although the Greeks regarded prostration as an act of worship; see especially Herodotus 7.136.

presence for the express purpose of instructing him in the truth – you, above all people, should have been the first to speak as I am speaking; you should have stopped the mouth of anyone who dared argue on the other side. To take the lead in the way you did was a disgraceful thing: you ought to have remembered that you are not the attendant and adviser of Cambyses or Xerxes, but of Philip's son, a man with the blood of Heracles and Aeacus in his veins,[27] a man whose forefathers came from Argos to Macedonia, where they long ruled not by force, but by law.

'Again, not even Heracles was accorded divine honours by the Greeks while he was alive – nor when he was dead either, until the command to do so was given by an oracle of Apollo at Delphi. Well, here we are in a foreign land; and if for that reason we must think foreign thoughts, yet I beg you, Alexander, to remember Greece; it was for her sake alone, that you might add Asia to her empire, that you undertook this campaign. Consider this too: when you are home again, do you really propose to force the Greeks, who love their liberty more than anyone else in the world, to prostrate themselves before you? Or will you let the Greeks off and impose this shameful duty only on the Macedonians? Or will you make a broad and general distinction in the matter, and ordain that barbarians only should keep their barbarous manners, while Greeks and Macedonians honour you honourably as a man, according to the traditions of Greece?

'It is said that Cyrus, son of Cambyses, was the first man to receive the homage of prostration, and that this humiliating custom thereafter became an accepted thing

27. Alexander's mother, Olympias, was the daughter of Neoptolemus, the king of Epirus, who traced his descent from his namesake, the son of Achilles, the grandson of Aeacus.

in Persia. So be it; none the less you must remember that the great Cyrus was cured of his pride by a tribe of Scythians – poor men but free; that Darius was humbled by Scythians too,²⁸ as Xerxes was by Athens and Sparta, and Artaxerxes by the Ten Thousand of Clearchus and Xenophon. And now Alexander has robbed another Darius of his pride – though no man has yet bowed to the earth before him.'

This speech vexed Alexander profoundly, but not the Macedonians, who found what he said very much to their mind. Alexander was aware of this, and told the Macedonians accordingly to forget the matter: the need to prostrate themselves would not in future arise.

For a moment there was silence; then the senior Persian officials rose from their seats and one by one grovelled on the floor before the King. Leonnatus, a member of the Companions, thought one of them bungled his bow, and burst out laughing at his attitude, which was, indeed, hardly dignified.²⁹ Alexander was angry – but his anger passed and he was afterwards willing to make friends again.

One more story on this subject is on record.³⁰ Alexander sent round a golden loving-cup, passing it first to those with whom the agreement about the act of prostration had been made. The first to drink rose from his seat, prostrated himself, and then received a kiss from Alexander.³¹ The rest followed suit; but Callisthenes, when his

28. See Herodotus 1.204–14 and 4.83–144.

29. According to Curtius (8.5.22) it was Polyperchon who mocked the Persian.

30. This is the version given by Chares, the Royal Chamberlain (Plutarch, *Alexander* 54.4–6).

31. The Persian king customarily kissed his 'kinsmen' on the mouth (Xenophon, *Cyropaideia* 1.4.27, 2.2.31; cf. Herodotus 1.134); see below, p. 364.

turn came, first drank, then rose to his feet, and then, without prostrating himself, walked up to Alexander and offered to kiss him. Alexander, at the moment, was talking to Hephaestion, and did not trouble to observe whether or not Callisthenes had properly performed the act of obeisance, but one of the Companions – Demetrius, son of Pythonax – mentioned the fact that he had omitted to do so before going up for his kiss. Thereupon Alexander refused to allow him to kiss him.

'Well then,' Callisthenes exclaimed, 'I must go back to my place one kiss the poorer.'

In my opinion all these stories are deplorable in so far as they reflect upon Alexander's growing arrogance and Callisthenes' bad manners. It is enough, I think, once a man has consented to enter a king's service, that he should exalt his master as much as he can, while at the same time preserving a decent modesty in his own behaviour; and for that reason I feel that Alexander was not unjustified in being angry with Callisthenes both for his absurd conceit and for letting his tongue run away with him. And this, I imagine, is why credit was so readily given to the story that Callisthenes had a hand in the plot which was laid against Alexander by his young attendants – or indeed that he was actually the prime mover of it.[32]

It was Alexander's father, Philip, who first instituted the custom of making the adolescent sons of Macedonian nobles personal attendants upon the king. These boys were entrusted with the general care of his person and also with the duty of guarding him when he was asleep; when he went riding, they would receive the horses from

32. Plutarch (*Alexander* 55.1–2) relates that Hephaestion maintained that Callisthenes had agreed to perform prostration and had gone back on his word, and that certain flatterers of Alexander sought to increase Callisthenes' unpopularity.

the grooms, lead them up and assist him to mount in the Persian manner, and share with him the friendly rivalry of the hunt.[33]

One of these boys was named Hermolaus; he was the son of Sopolis, and was supposed to be interested in philosophy, an interest which brought him into close touch with Callisthenes. Now the story is that during a hunt Alexander was charged by a boar and, before he could strike, was forestalled by Hermolaus, who himself struck the boar and killed it. Alexander was furious at missing his chance, and ordered Hermolaus to be whipped in front of the other boys, and then took his horse from him.[34]

Bitterly hurt by this high-handed treatment, Hermolaus told Sostratus, son of Amyntas and his bosom friend, that life would not be worth living till he had had his revenge for this brutal insult, and Sostratus, who adored him, was easily persuaded to take a hand in planning it. The two boys then obtained the support of Antipater, son of Asclepiodorus, a former governor of Syria, and of three others: Epimenes son of Arseus, Anticles son of Theocritus, and Philotas son of a Thracian named Carsis. It was agreed between them that, when Antipater's turn of night duty came round, they should murder Alexander in his sleep.

It so happened that on the night in question Alexander sat up drinking until dawn. This may have been pure chance, though Aristobulus has a different explanation. According to him,[35] there was a certain Syrian woman

33. See also Curtius 8.6.2–6.

34. This took place at Bactra early in 327. cf. pp. 238–9.

Curtius (8.6.8–8.23) relates the story of the plot at length. He gives a slightly different list of conspirators and differs from Arrian in a number of details.

35. And to Curtius.

with the gift of second sight, who kept following Alexander about. He and his friends used to laugh at her; but, as time went on and everything she foretold in her trances turned out to be true, Alexander began to feel differently. He no longer found her a figure of fun, but let her come to him whenever she wished, by day or night, and on many occasions allowed her to watch over him while he slept.

This woman, in one of her prophetic trances, met him as he was coming away from his potations. She begged him to go back and drink the night out, and Alexander, convinced that there was something more than human in the warning, took her advice. So the boys' plot fell through.

Epimenes, one of the guilty ones, also, like Hermolaus, had a bosom friend, Charicles, son of Menander; and to him, on the following day, he told the whole story. Charicles told Epimenes' brother, Eurylochus, who went to Alexander's tent and passed everything on to Ptolemy son of Lagus, of the King's Guard, who, in his turn, told Alexander. Alexander ordered the arrest of all the boys whose names were given him by Eurylochus. Questioned under torture, they admitted their guilt, and at the same time implicated certain others as well.

Aristobulus declares – and Ptolemy supports him – that the boys said that Callisthenes had urged them to commit the crime. Most authorities, however, have no mention of this; they merely suggest that Alexander was ready enough to believe the worst about Callisthenes, first, because he already disliked him, and, secondly, because of his close association with Hermolaus.[36]

36. Plutarch (*Alexander* 55.6) cites a letter written by Alexander to his generals, Craterus, Attalus, and Alcetas, who were campaigning in Pareitacene (p. 238), in which he says that only the Pages were involved in the conspiracy. For the authenticity of this letter see *CQ* 1955, 219ff.

In some writers,[37] moreover, we find the story that
Hermolaus, when he was brought to stand his trial, openly confessed his guilt, declaring that it was no longer
possible for an honourable man to endure Alexander's
inhuman arrogance; and then went on to give a list of his
crimes – the lawless killing of Philotas, the still more
arbitrary execution of his father Parmenio and the other
officers who were put to death on the same occasion,
the murder in his cups of Cleitus, his assumption of Persian dress, the duty of prostration he had planned, and
was still planning, to impose, his heavy drinking and his
drunken sleeps: what he desired was to free himself and
the Macedonians from evils such as these, which were no
longer to be borne. Hermolaus and the other boys arrested
with him were then stoned to death on the spot.[38]

Callisthenes' fate is variously reported: Aristobulus
writes that he was dragged about in chains wherever the
army went, till his health broke and he died. According to
Ptolemy he was first tortured and then hanged. So we see
that even the most trustworthy writers, men who were
actually with Alexander at the time, have given conflicting
accounts of notorious events with which they must have
been perfectly familiar.[39] Many other details of this affair
have been handled by other writers, too, in a most con-
fusing and contradictory manner – so I can do no better
than leave the story as I have told it. I have, indeed, anticipated events a little; but I do feel that, for the purposes
of my narrative, the story of Hermolaus is closely connec-

37. Curtius (8.7) follows this tradition.

38. Plutarch (*Alexander* 55.7) confirms the manner of their death.
Curtius (8.8.20) says that they were tortured.

39. Plutarch (loc. cit.) reports both versions, and adds that
Chares said Callisthenes was kept in confinement for seven months
until he died.

ted with the story of Alexander and Cleitus; so for that reason I have related it here, as an immediate sequel.

Alexander was now for the second time visited by envoys from the European Scythians, who arrived in company with the envoys he had himself sent to Scythia.[40] The reigning King of Scythia at the time of their dispatch had died; he had been succeeded by his brother, and the purpose of the present embassy was to express the willingness of Scythia to accede in every point to Alexander's instructions; they brought as presents from the King such things as are reckoned most valuable in their country, and communicated to Alexander their King's desire to cement the friendship and alliance between their countries by giving him his daughter in marriage. Should Alexander be unwilling to marry the Scythian Princess, the King was none the less anxious to do the next best thing and to give as brides to his most trusted officers the daughters of the governors and other personages of rank in Scythian territory. He would, moreover, visit Alexander in person, if he were called upon to do so, and thus be enabled to take his instructions from Alexander's own lips.

About the same time the King of the Chorasmians, Pharasmanes, arrived at the Court with 1,500 mounted troops.[41] He told Alexander that his territory had common frontiers with the Colchians and the Amazon women,[42] and that if Alexander should ever contemplate an invasion of those countries with the object of reducing the various peoples in that part of the world as far as the Black Sea, he was willing to act as his guide and to provide all the necessary supplies for his army.

40. For the first occasion see p. 201.
41. The Chorasmians inhabited the country (Khiva) between the Caspian and Aral seas.
42. For the Amazons see p. 369.

To the envoys from Scythia, Alexander gave a polite and suitable reply: he had no need, he said, of a Scythian marriage. He thanked Pharasmanes for his offer and concluded a pact of friendship with him, adding that an expedition to the Black Sea was not at the moment convenient; and, before dismissing him, he put him in touch with Artabazus, the Persian, to whom he had given charge of affairs in Bactria, and also with the various governors of the neighbouring provinces. His own thoughts were at present occupied with India, and he pointed out that once India was his he would be master of all Asia, after which his intention was to return to Greece and to make from thence an expedition to the Black Sea region by way of the Hellespont and the Propontis with all his land and sea forces combined. Pharasmanes, therefore, would oblige him if he deferred the fulfilment of his offer until that occasion should arise.

Alexander now returned to the Oxus. His intention was to proceed to Sogdiana, as a report had come in that many of the people there were refusing to obey the governor he had appointed and had shut themselves up in the forts. While he was in camp on the Oxus, a spring of water and another of oil quite near it came up from the ground close to his tent. Ptolemy, son of Lagus, was informed of this remarkable event, and Ptolemy told Alexander, who, to mark his sense of its miraculous nature, offered sacrifice according to the form prescribed by his soothsayers. Aristander declared that the spring of oil was a sign of difficulties to come and of eventual victory.[43]

Four officers – Polysperchon, Attalus, Gorgias, and Meleager – were left in Bactria with instructions to destroy all natives who had refused submission and to keep a sharp look-out for any further trouble; and Alexander

43. The first mention of petroleum in Greek literature.

himself, after crossing into Sogdiana, divided his remaining strength into five, one division to be commanded by Hephaestion, another by Ptolemy, son of Lagus, a third by Perdiccas, a fourth by Coenus and Artabazus. The fifth he took over himself and proceeded with it in the direction of Marakanda, while the other four commanders carried out offensive operations as opportunity offered, storming the forts where some of the native tribesmen were trying to hold out, or receiving the voluntary surrender of others.

The greater part of Sogdiana was covered by these operations, and when the whole force was reunited at Marakanda, Alexander sent Hephaestion to plant settlements in the various towns, and at the same time dispatched Coenus and Artabazus to Scythia, where Spitamenes, according to report, had taken refuge. Meanwhile Alexander with the remainder of his force marched against those parts of Sogdiana which were still in rebel hands, and had no difficulty in subduing them.

Spitamenes, while all this was going on, had made his way with a number of fugitives from Sogdiana to that branch of the Scythian people known as the Massagetae;[44] there they got together 600 native horsemen and presented themselves at one of the forts in Bactria. Neither the garrison nor its commander had expected any hostile move; Spitamenes took them by surprise, killed the men, and captured their officer, whom he kept under guard. This success emboldened him a few days later to approach Zariaspa. They did not venture an assault upon the town, though they rounded up a lot of livestock and carried it off as booty.

44. The Massagetae were a Scythian tribe, living east of the Caspian, who had defeated and killed Cyrus the Great (Herodotus 1.201–16).

A few men of the Companion cavalry had been left behind sick in Zariaspa, and among them were Sosicles' son, Peitho, who had charge of all arrangements for the King's personal comfort in that town, and the harp-player, Aristonicus. These two had sufficiently recovered to ride and bear arms when the Scythian raid occurred; so as soon as they knew of it, they got together about eighty mounted men – mercenaries, left to garrison the town – and with them and a few of the King's boy squires rode out to the attack. The Scythians were taken by surprise, and the first charge was successful: they recovered all the stolen cattle and killed a number of the men who were driving them off; but as they were straggling back to the town, in a more or less go-as-you-please fashion, Spitamenes and his Scythians caught them in an ambush. Seven of the Companions were lost, and sixty mercenaries. Aristonicus, too, was killed – having fought, however, not like a harpist but like a man;[45] and Peitho was wounded and taken prisoner.

As soon as he got the news of this action, Craterus lost no time in marching against the Massagetae, who withdrew hastily towards the desert when they observed his approach. Craterus followed them up, and not far from the edge of the desert made contact with them and another force of their mounted troops, over 1,000 strong. A sharp engagement ensued, in which the Macedonians were victorious. The Scythians lost 150 mounted men; the rest of them got safely away into the desert, Craterus finding it impracticable to continue his pursuit.

About this time Artabazus asked to be relieved of the governorship of Bactria on account of his age. Alexander

45. Because of his heroism Alexander had a bronze statue of him erected at Delphi, holding his lyre and a levelled spear (Plutarch, *Moralia* 334f.).

granted his request and appointed Amyntas, son of Nicolaus, in his place.[46] He left Coenus in that part of the country with a force consisting of his own and Meleager's battalions, about 400 Companions, all the javelin-men, and such troops from Bactria and Sogdiana as were attached to Amyntas. His instructions were that they should all take their orders from Coenus and winter in Sogdiana, partly as a precautionary measure, and partly on the chance that they might succeed in laying a trap for Spitamenes, should he be riding around in the neighbourhood in the course of the winter.

When Spitamenes found that the whole country was held by Macedonian garrisons and that there was little likelihood of escape for himself or his men, he determined to make a move against Coenus, in the hope of making a better fight of it in that part of the country. At Bagae, a stronghold of Sogdiana on the Massagetaean frontier, they had no difficulty in inducing a force of some 3,000 Scythian mounted troops to join them in a raid on Sogdiana. These Scythians are always ready at a word to take part in any fighting which may be going on: their extreme poverty might be reason enough; but, in addition to that, they have no towns, no settled homes, and consequently no cause to fear the loss of what is dearest to them.

Learning of the approach of Spitamenes' cavalry, Coenus went out to meet them. There was a vigorous engagement, in which the Macedonians were successful; over 800 enemy horsemen were killed, while Coenus' losses amounted to about twenty-five mounted men and twelve

46. Artabazus is said by Curtius (6.5.4.) to have been 95 years old in 330, but this is either an exaggeration or else we should read 55 for 95.

Alexander had intended Cleitus to succeed Artabazus, but he had not lived to take up his post.

infantrymen. While Spitamenes was trying to make his escape, he was deserted by most of the Bactrians and such troops from Sogdiana as were still with him. All these surrendered to Coenus. The Massagetae marked their defeat by plundering the baggage-trains of their late companions in battle, and then made off with Spitamenes for the desert; but no sooner had they learned that Alexander, too, was on the move towards the desert than they cut off Spitamenes' head and sent it to him, in the hope that by this friendly act they might keep him from molesting them.

Meanwhile Alexander was rejoined at Nautaka by Coenus and Stasanor, satrap of Aria, and also by the troops under the command of Craterus and Phrataphernes, satrap of Parthia. These officers had successfully carried out all Alexander's instructions.[47] As it was now mid-winter, Alexander rested his men at Nautaka, and dispatched Phrataphernes to fetch Autophradates, the satrap of Mardia and Tapuria, who on a number of previous occasions had ignored Alexander's orders to come and report himself. He sent Stasanor to take over the governorship of the Drangae, and Atropates to replace Oxodates in Media, as the latter appeared to be unreliable. Mazaeus, the governor of Babylon, being reported dead, Stamenes was sent to succeed him. Sopolis, Epocillus, and Menidas were ordered home to Macedonia to fetch reinforcements.

News had come in that a large number of the natives had taken refuge on the Rock of Sogdiana, and among them the wife and daughters of Oxyartes the Bactrian, who had himself refused to submit to Alexander and had

47. What these were is not known, unless, as has been suggested, the report of their arrival at Bactra in the previous winter (p. 212) is a mistake and they now brought with them Arsames and Barzanes.

chosen this refuge for his family in the belief that the Rock was impregnable. It was the last stronghold of Sogdiana: should it fall, there would be nothing left for those who still hoped to offer resistance. To the Rock, therefore, Alexander advanced, at the beginning of spring.[48]

He found, on a near approach, that it rose sheer on every side against attack. The natives had provisioned it for a long siege, and deep snow on its summit caused the double disadvantage of making the ascent more awkward for the Macedonians and of ensuring the defenders an unlimited supply of water. None the less, Alexander determined on assault.

In point of fact the reason for his determination was something the natives had said, an offensive bit of bragging which made him angry and put him on his mettle. He had called on them to discuss terms, and offered to allow them to return unmolested to their homes on condition of surrendering the stronghold; but their answer to the offer was a shout of laughter. Then in their barbaric lingo they told Alexander to find soldiers with wings to capture the Rock for him, as no other sort of person could cause them the least anxiety. As a result of this, Alexander proclaimed that he would give a prize of twelve talents to the first man up, and of eleven to the second, and ten to the third, and so on to the twelfth, who would receive 300 gold darics.[49] The men were keen enough already, but this proclamation was an added spur.

There were some 300 men who in previous sieges had had experience in rock-climbing. These now assembled. They had provided themselves with small iron tent-pegs,

48. Curtius (7.11) also describes the capture of the Rock, which he calls the Rock of Ariamazes. He relates, with evident exaggeration, that it was about 18,000 ft high. The year was 327 B.C.

49. The equivalent of one talent.

which they proposed to drive into the snow, where it was frozen hard, or into any bit of bare earth they might come across, and they had attached to the pegs strong flaxen lines. The party set off under cover of darkness to the steepest part of the rock-face, which they knew was least likely to be guarded; then, driving their pegs either into bare ground or into such patches of snow as seemed most likely to hold under the strain, they hauled themselves up, wherever each could find a way. About thirty lost their lives during the ascent – falling in various places in the snow, their bodies were never recovered for burial – but the rest reached the top as dawn was breaking, and the summit of the Rock was theirs. Then, in accordance with Alexander's orders, they signalled their success to the troops below by waving bits of linen, and Alexander sent a crier to shout the news to the enemy's advanced posts that they might now surrender without further delay, as the men with wings had been found and were already in possession of the summit. And, as the crier gave them this information, Alexander pointed to his men, where they stood on top of the Rock.

The unexpectedness of the sight was a severe shock to the natives; indeed, they were so much alarmed by the handful of Macedonian troops they could actually see, that, imagining a larger force, and fully armed at that, must be in possession, they surrendered. Many women and children were among the prisoners – notably the wife and daughters of Oxyartes.

One of these daughters was named Roxane. She was a girl of marriageable age, and men who took part in the campaign used to say she was the loveliest woman they had seen in Asia, with the one exception of Darius' wife. Alexander fell in love with her at sight; but, captive though she was, he refused, for all his passion, to force her to his will, and condescended to marry her.[50] For this act I have, on the whole, more praise than blame.

As for Darius' wife, said to be the most beautiful woman in Asia, either he felt for her no desire, or, if he did, he controlled it, in spite of the fact that he was both young and on top of the world – a combination of circumstances which leads most men to all sorts of excess. But he respected her and let her alone. In this he showed great restraint – and also, no doubt, a quite natural anxiety to be well spoken of.[51]

There is a story about Darius[52] that shortly after the battle of Issus the eunuch who had charge of his wife succeeded in making his way to him. Darius' first question was whether his mother, wife, and children were still alive, and hearing that they not only were, but were also addressed by the title of princess and treated with as much ceremony as when he was on the throne, he proceeded to inquire if his wife still preserved her chastity.

'She does,' replied the eunuch.

'And has Alexander offered her no violence – no insult?'

'My lord,' exclaimed the eunuch with an oath, 'your wife is as you left her, and Alexander is the best of men and the least ready to yield to temptation.'

Darius raised his hands to heaven in prayer. 'My lord Zeus,'[53] he cried, 'to whom it is given to order the affairs

50. Whatever his feelings for Roxane may have been, Alexander doubtless hoped by this marriage to conciliate the Bactrian barons.

51. For Alexander's treatment of the Persian royal family see pp. 122–3. Darius' wife, Stateira, died in childbirth early in 332 B.C. (Plutarch, *Alexander* 30).

52. Told also by Curtius (4.10.25–34) and by Plutarch (*Alexander* 30), who notes that most writers related it.

53. i.e. Ahura Mazda. In Plutarch Darius more appropriately calls on his ancestral gods.

of kings in this world, keep safe for me now the empire over the Medes and Persians, even as once you gave it me; but, if it is no longer your will that I be King of Asia, then entrust my throne, I pray, to no man but Alexander'. Thus even enemies are not indifferent to honourable deeds.

When Oxyartes learned that his daughters were prisoners, the further intelligence that Alexander was interested in Roxane emboldened him to present himself, and Alexander as was only proper in these happy circumstances, treated him with all respect.

With the capture of the Rock, the operations in Sogdiana were successfully concluded, and Alexander's next move was to the territory of the Pareitacae, where a large force of natives were said to be holding another rock fortress, the Rock of Chorienes.[54] Chorienes himself, with many others of eminence in the country, had taken refuge there. This rock, some 12,000 feet high and about seven miles in circumference, rose sheer on every side; there was only one way up, by a narrow and difficult track hewn out of the rock-face and consequently awkward to ascend even in single file and without opposition. The fortress was further defended all round by a deep ravine, so that any attempt to assault it would have to be preceded by the labour of filling this up, to enable the attack to be launched from level ground. However, the reckless courage engendered by success had by this time brought Alexander to believe that there was no place where he might not set his foot and no fortress which could hold out against him; so, despite the difficulties, he set to work. Felling some of the lofty pine-trees, which grew in large numbers round the base of the hill, he had ladders constructed to enable his men to descend into the ravine,

54. The Pareitacae lived between the rivers Oxus and Jaxartes. Curtius (8.2.19) calls Chorienes Sisimithres.

which would have been impracticable by other means. Alexander personally superintended the work during the day, half his men being on duty; at night the other half came on, divided into three shifts, under the respective command of his Guards, Perdiccas, Leonnatus, and Ptolemy, son of Lagus. It was such an awkward spot to work in, and the work itself so hard, that about thirty feet was all they could manage in a daylight shift, and rather less at night, though the entire army was employed. The method they used was to climb right down to the narrowest part of the ravine and drive in stakes properly spaced to carry the load to be laid on them, which consisted of wattles (as in bridge-building) bound firmly together, with a layer of soil on top. In this way the troops would be enabled to get to the base of the rock across level ground.

In its early stages the enemy contemptuously ignored the whole thing as a hopeless undertaking; but as the work proceeded arrows began to find their mark; all attempts to dislodge the Macedonians by missile attacks from above proved abortive, and the work continued in perfect security under the protection of screens. Faced by this unexpected situation, Chorienes lost his nerve, and sent a messenger to Alexander with a request that Oxyartes should be allowed to come to him. Alexander agreed, and Oxyartes urged Chorienes to give up the stronghold and surrender to Alexander. Against Alexander and his men no place in the world, he declared, was impregnable; on the other hand, should the question of a loyal and friendly agreement arise, he had nothing but praise for Alexander's sense of honour and justice. Of this there were many examples, if proof were wanted, and not least the treatment he had himself received. Chorienes allowed himself to be persuaded; he came to Alexander together with some of his kinsmen and friends, and received from him a kindly assurance of friendship. Alexander kept him at his side, and told him to send back to the fortress with a demand for its surrender certain of the men he had brought down with him. The troops holding out there duly surrendered it, and Alexander himself subsequently ascended the rock, out of curiosity to see it, with a party of some 500 Guards. Chorienes he treated with the utmost consideration, actually putting the control of the rock into his hands and letting him continue to administer the same territory as before.

The winter had brought Alexander's men considerable distress, as much snow had fallen during the course of the siege, and supplies were short. Chorienes, however, offered a gift of two months' rations for the whole army; from his stores on the rock he distributed grain, wine, and dried meat – so much for each tent, or mess – and declared that, even so, he had not used a tenth part of what had been laid in for the siege. Alexander's respect for him was much increased by this, for it clearly indicated that the surrender had been a matter not of necessity but of deliberate policy.

Alexander's next move was for Bactra. Craterus, with a force consisting of 600 Companions, his own and Alcetas' infantry battalions, and those commanded by Polysperchon and Attalus, was ordered to march against Catanes and Austanes, the last two in the territory of the Pareitacae to be still refusing submission. There was a sharp clash, in which Craterus was victorious; Catanes was killed in action, and Austanes was taken prisoner and brought to Alexander. Of the native forces under their command, about 120 cavalrymen were killed and 1,500 infantry. After this success Craterus proceeded with his men to join Alexander in Bactra. It was in Bactra that Alexander had his unpleasant experience with Callisthenes and the boys.

Towards the end of spring[55] Alexander began his march for India, leaving Amyntas in Bactria with a force of 3,500 mounted troops and 10,000 infantry. He crossed the Indian Caucasus, and in ten days reached Alexandria, the town he had founded in the territory of the Parapamisadae during his first expedition into Bactria.[56] The governor, whom he had appointed on that occasion, he dismissed for incompetence, and increased the population of the settlement by the addition of families from the neighbourhood and such of his own men as were unfit for service. Nicanor, one of the Companions, was put in control of the actual settlement, and Tyriaspes was made governor of the territory of the Parapamisadae and of the rest of the country as far as the river Cophen.[57] Then, by way of Nicaea, where he offered sacrifice to Athene, Alexander marched for the Cophen, having first sent instructions to Taxiles[58] and the Indians west of the Indus to meet him at whatever time each might find it convenient. Taxiles and the other chiefs obeyed the summons, bringing with them the sort of presents which are most valued in their country, and offering to give Alexander the twenty-five elephants they had with them.

Alexander now divided his force. Hephaestion and Perdiccas, with the battalions of Gorgias, Cleitus, and Meleager, half the Companions and all the mercenary cavalry, were ordered forward to Peucelaotis, in the direction of the Indus. Their instructions were to take over

55. Of the year 327.

56. See p. 194 n. 70.

57. The modern R. Kabul.

58. The ruler of the great city of Taxila, north-west of Rawalpindi, and the territory between the rivers Indus and Hydaspes. Taxiles was his official title, his personal name being Omphis (Ambhi); see Curtius 8.12.14.

either by force or agreement all places on their march, and on reaching the Indus to make suitable preparations for crossing.[59] Taxiles and the other Indian chiefs were sent with them, and Alexander's orders were duly carried out when the force arrived at the river.

Astes, the governor of Peucelaotis, caused some trouble, but lost his life in the process and involved in his own ruin the town in which he had attempted to hold out. It was taken by Hephaestion after a thirty days' siege. After Astes' death, Sangaeus was put in control of the town – he had deserted Astes some time previously and joined Taxiles, a circumstance which enabled Alexander to trust him.

Alexander's next objective was the territory of the Aspasians, Guraeans, and Assacenians.[60] The force he took with him consisted of the Guards, all the Companion cavalry not at the moment serving under Hephaestion, the so-called Foot Companions, the archers, the Agrianes, and the mounted javelin-men. The route, which followed the river Choes, was rough and mountainous, and the crossing of the river was no easy task. Once over, he ordered the main body of the infantry to follow at their own pace and himself with the mounted troops and about 800 Macedonian foot, whom he also mounted still carrying their infantrymen's shields, pressed on with all speed, following a report that the natives thereabouts had taken up defensive positions either in the hills or in such towns as were strong enough to offer a chance of resistance. Attacking the first of these towns which lay on his route, he had no trouble in driving in the force which was stationed outside, and compelling the men to take refuge

59. At Ohind, 16 miles above Attock.
60. The modern territories of Bajaur and Swat. Alexander was making for the Indus above Attock.

within the defences; but during the operation he was
wounded in the shoulder by a missile which pierced his
corselet. The wound was not serious, as the corselet prevented the missile from going right through his shoulder.
Ptolemy, son of Lagus, and Leonnatus were also hurt.
Alexander then took up a position opposite the section of
the town's defences which appeared most promising for
an assault, and moved foward at dawn the following day.
There was a double ring of defence-works round the
town, and the outer one, which was carelessly constructed, was forced by the Macedonians without trouble; at
the second the enemy maintained a brief resistance, but
once the ladders were in position and the defenders began
to suffer losses from the missile weapons concentrated
upon them, they abandoned the town and made a dash for
the hills. Some were killed as they were trying to get
away, and all prisoners were butchered by the Macedonians in revenge for the wound they had given Alexander;
the greater number, however, escaped to the hills, which
were not far off. Alexander razed the town, and moved
on to another – Andaca – which was surrendered to him.
Craterus and the other infantry commanders were left in
the district to organize affairs as the situation demanded,
and to reduce any other towns which refused submission,
while Alexander himself continued his advance with the
Guards, the archers, the Agrianes, Coenus' and Attalus'
battalions, the picked cavalry squadron and some four
regiments of the other mounted Companions, and half the
mounted Archers. His route lay towards the river Euaspla,
and after a long march he reached on the second day the
town where the governor of the Aspasians was. The
natives were no sooner aware of his approach than they
fired the town and made their escape to the hills, with
Alexander's men in hot pursuit all the way. Many were

cut down before the rough hill-country enabled them to
shake off their pursuers.

During the pursuit, Ptolemy, son of Lagus, actually
spotted the chief of the Indians of this district: he had already reached a hill and was trying to get away with some
of his guards. Ptolemy, though he had a much inferior
force, nevertheless rode for him; but it was too steep and
too rough going for his horse, so he dismounted, gave it
to a man to lead, and continued to chase the Indian on
foot. Seeing him coming, the Indian and his guards
turned to face him. They met; and the chief struck
Ptolemy in the breast with his long spear, which pierced
his corselet but did not penetrate his body. With a blow
clean through the Indian's thigh, Ptolemy laid him flat,
and began to strip him, whereupon his guards, seeing that
their chief was down, turned and fled. Other Indians, however, on the neighbouring hills, grieved at the sight of
their leader's body being carried off by the enemy, came
hurrying down, and a fierce struggle ensued over the
corpse. By then Alexander and his cavalrymen, now dismounted, were not far from the hill; they joined in the
mêlée and finally succeeded in driving the Indians into the
hills and getting possession of the body.

Having crossed the range, Alexander came down at a
settlement called Arigaeum.[61] He took the place, though
it had been burnt and deserted by the inhabitants. He was
rejoined there by Craterus and his troops, all his instructions having been successfully carried out. It occurred to
him that the site of Arigaeum had much to recommend it,
so he ordered Craterus to fortify the place and settle in it
any of the natives in the vicinity who were willing to go
there, and such of his own men as were unfit for service.

61. 'Possibly Nawagai, the present capital of Bajaur' (Fuller
p. 126).

That done, he moved on towards the region where report had it that most of the native forces had concentrated, with an eye to their own defence, and came to a halt at the foothills of a range of mountains.

While he was encamped at this spot, Ptolemy, who had been sent foraging and had gone ahead of the army with a small party to reconnoitre, reported that he had seen the enemy camp-fires, and that they were more numerous than their own. Alexander received this report with some scepticism, convinced as he was that the number of camp-fires was a ruse; he determined, therefore, to advance. Part of his force he left where they were at the foot of the mountains, and himself moved forward with a body of troops which he thought sufficient to meet the situation according to the report he had received. As soon as they got a close view of the fires, he split his force into three, putting one section, consisting of the units of Attalus and Balacrus, under Leonnatus, a member of his personal guard, another, consisting of one third of the Guards, the units of Philip and Philotas, two regiments of archers, the Agrianes, and half the cavalry, under Ptolemy, son of Lagus, while the third section he took charge of in person and advanced with it to where the natives appeared to be concentrated in the greatest numbers.[62]

The Indians were rendered confident both by their numbers and by their position, which was a commanding one; so when they saw the Macedonians coming, contemptuous of their apparently inadequate strength they began to leave the high ground and advanced to meet them. A fierce battle followed, the result of which, however, was not long in dispute where Alexander's section

62. Leonnatus was given Attalus' infantry battalion and Balacrus' javelin-men, Ptolemy Philotas' infantry battalion and Philip's unit, probably light-armed (see Tarn, *Alexander* 2.144).

was concerned. Ptolemy's section did not wait to be attacked on the level ground; the natives held a hill, and Ptolemy pressed forward in column to what appeared the best point for assault; he then surrounded the hill, leaving a gap in his line for the enemy to get through, should they wish to make their escape. Here, too, there was a hard struggle – for the Indians' position itself presented a tough problem, and they happened to be much the best and most courageous fighters of all the tribes in that part of the country. None the less, they, too, were driven from their hill, while the third section, under Leonnatus, was equally successful. According to Ptolemy's account, the total number of prisoners was over 40,000, and more than 230,000 oxen were taken. Alexander picked out the finest of them, as they seemed to be of uncommon size and beauty, and expressed a wish to send them to Macedonia to work on the land.

From there he marched to the territory of the Assacenians, who were reported to be prepared for resistance with 2,000 cavalry, over 30,000 infantry, and thirty elephants at their disposal. His force consisted of the Companions, the mounted javelin-men, the battalions of Coenus and Polysperchon, the thousand Agrianes, and the archers, while Craterus, who by now had completed the fortification of the town the settlement of which he had been left to organize, brought along for him the more heavily armed units and the siege engines, in case of need. Alexander's route lay through the country of the Guraeans. The river which gives the district its name proved difficult to cross, being both deep and rapid; and the large round stones with which its bed is strewn gave a treacherous foothold. None the less, the native troops, when they saw Alexander coming, had no heart to stand massed to meet him, but broke up and straggled away in groups to their various towns, where they proposed to defend themselves and to save their homes – if they could.

Alexander's first move was against Massaga,[63] the largest town in this neighbourhood. On his approach to the walls, the natives were so confident in the effectiveness of some 7,000 mercenary troops from the interior of India, whom they had in their pay, that they advanced at the double as soon as they saw the Macedonian army begin to take up its position. It was clear to Alexander that the fight would take place close to the town; he determined, therefore, to draw the enemy on, in order to ensure that, if they were repulsed – as he was certain they would be – they would not have a short and easy way of retreat within the protection of their walls. Accordingly, the moment he saw them come pouring out of the town, he gave the order for withdrawal to a piece of high ground rather less than a mile from the position he had originally intended to take up. This apparent sign of defeat put fresh fire into the enemy; and in a disorderly rabble they came charging on. But as soon as his men were within range of their arrows, Alexander gave the signal to face about and brought the phalanx at the double to meet them. The first to go into action were the mounted javelin-men, the Agrianes, and the archers, and, while they were engaged, Alexander steadily advanced at the head of his infantry. The Indians were badly shaken by this unexpected reversal, and in the close fighting which ensued they broke and withdrew to the town. About 200 of them were killed, and the rest shut themselves up within their defences.

Alexander advanced his infantry close under the walls, and an arrow, shot from them, wounded him slightly in the ankle.

The following day he brought his machines into action

63. Its site has not been identified.

and had no difficulty in making a breach. The Macedonians tried to force their way through, but, as the Indians
offered stout resistance, the assault was temporarily called
off. The day after that, the attack had more power behind
it: a wooden tower was brought up; from it the archers
shot with greater effect, and that, added to the weight of
missiles from the catapults, did much to keep the defenders within bounds. Even so, the Macedonians were unable to force their way in.

On the third day Alexander once more brought his infantry into action, and from one of the siege engines threw
a bridge across the breach in the wall. Over this he led his
Guards, the unit which, by the same tactics, had helped
him to the capture of Tyre.[64] The men, their blood being
up, pressed forward in great numbers, but their weight
was too much for the bridge, which broke under them
and let them down. At this the enemy with a shout of
triumph poured in a hail of missiles – stones from the
wall, arrows, or anything else they had or could lay their
hands on – while others rushed out through the little gates
between the towers and rained blows upon the Macedonians before they could recover themselves.

At this juncture Alexander sent Alcetas with his battalion to pick up the wounded and to recall the men who
were still engaged. On the fourth day of the battle the
procedure was repeated – another engine was brought
into action, and another bridge laid.

So long as their chief survived, the Indians fought with
great courage; but when he was killed by a missile from a
catapult, what with their own losses in the four days' continuous siege and the large numbers of men wounded or
put out of action, they sent to Alexander to ask for a truce.
For him it was a pleasure to save the lives of such brave

64. See p. 141.

men, and he agreed with the Indian mercenaries that they should serve under himself, as a part of his own army. These troops, accordingly, marched with their arms out of the town and went into camp by themselves on a hill facing the Macedonian position. Their intention was not what Alexander expected; for, having no desire to fight against other Indians, they meant to desert under cover of night and disperse to their homes. Their purpose, however, was reported to Alexander, and that same night he stationed his whole force in a ring round the hill, caught the Indians in a trap, and butchered them.[65] He then seized the town, now undefended. Assacenus' mother and daughter were among the prisoners.[66] During the operation as a whole Alexander's losses amounted to about twenty-five men.

From Massaga, Alexander sent Coenus to Bazira, on the supposition that the people of that town, when they learned of the fate of Massaga, would surrender to him. At the same time Attalus, Alcetas, and Demetrius, the cavalry commander, were dispatched to Ora, with instructions to blockade it with a ring-wall pending his own arrival. The Indians in Ora made a sally against Alcetas' troops, but were repulsed without difficulty and forced to withdraw within the wall again. At Bazira, meanwhile, Coenus was unsuccessful; the natives there were encouraged to resist by the natural strength of the town's position – it stood very high and was well fortified on every side – and showed no sign of surrender.

65. Diodorus (17.84) attributes gross treachery to Alexander, who attacked the mercenaries without provocation; cf. Plutarch *Alexander* 59.3–4.

66. Diodorus (loc. cit.) and Curtius (8.10.22) relate that the beautiful Queen Cleophis was reinstated in her kingdom. It was even said that Alexander had a son by her (Curtius).

Alexander started for Bazira as soon as he learned of this check; he was diverted, however, by a further report that some of the Indians of the neighbourhood, upon instructions from Abisares, were preparing to make their way secretly into Ora.[67] So he made Ora his first objective, sending an order to Coenus to construct a blockhouse outside Bazira, garrison it sufficiently to prevent the people of the town from making free use of the surrounding country, and then join him with the remainder of his troops.

When the Indians in Bazira saw the greater part of Coenus' forces moving off, they were not unnaturally contemptuous: the Macedonians – evidently – were no match for them. So out they all came, and a brisk engagement ensued. During the course of it about 500 of the Indians were killed and more than seventy captured; the remainder withdrew within the town. After this incident the garrison of the blockhouse took still stronger measures to bar access to the surrounding country.

The siege of Ora gave Alexander very little trouble; in fact, he took the place at the first assault – including the elephants which had been left there.

The news from Ora soon persuaded the Indians at Bazira that their position was hopeless. At midnight they abandoned the town. The other Indians of the district all followed their example: without exception they left their towns and fled for refuge to what was known as the Rock of Aornos.[68] This rock is a really tremendous thing; and the story goes that Heracles himself, the son of Zeus, was

67. Bir-kot and Ude-gram respectively, according to Sir Aurel Stein, *On Alexander's Track to the Indus* (London, 1929) 43, 59ff.

68. Identified in 1926 by Stein (op. cit., 129ff.) as Pir-Sar, a flat-topped ridge just over 7,000 ft. high, commanding the Indus about 75 miles north of Attock. See Fuller pp. 248–54.

unable to capture it.[69] Personally, of course, I should not like to state categorically that the Theban, or the Tyrian, or the Egyptian Heracles did, in fact, go to India. I incline to fancy that he did not; for it seems to me that people like to make difficulties look much more difficult than they really are, and to this end start a legend about Heracles' failure to overcome them. That, at any rate, is my opinion about this rock: the name of Heracles was introduced simply to make the story more impressive. The circumference of Aornos is said to be about 25 miles, and its height, not including the peaks, nearly 8,000 feet. There is only one way up it, a difficult path, hewn from the rock. On the summit there is an abundant supply of pure water from a spring – it comes streaming out – and also woodland and enough good arable land to keep 1,000 men busy.

The description of this remarkable place awakened in Alexander a passionate desire to capture it, and the story about Heracles was not the least of his incentives.[70]

Ora and Massaga he converted into blockhouses for keeping order in the neighbourhood. Bazira was fully fortified. Hephaestion and Perdiccas, having fortified and garrisoned another town, called Orobatis, started for the Indus, where they set about the construction of the bridge according to Alexander's orders. Nicanor, one of the Companions, was appointed governor of the territory west of the Indus.

On his march to Aornos, Alexander started in the direction of the Indus; the town of Peucelaotis, which stood not far from the river, he took over by surrender

69. For this legend see also Diodorus 17.85.2 and Curtius 8.11.2. Arrian recounts other legends about Heracles at pp. 258–9 below.

70. Fuller points to its strategic importance and the effect its capture would have on the neighbouring Indian tribes.

and garrisoned with Macedonian troops under the command of Philip.[71] A number of other small places on the river also fell into his hands. He was accompanied on his march by the chiefs of the district, Cophaeus and Assagetes. Arrived at Embolima, a town close to Aornos, he detached a portion of his forces, under the command of Craterus, with orders to lay in supplies of all kinds in sufficient quantity for a long period of time, as his intention was to use the town as a base from which he could, by a protracted siege, little by little break the resistance of the Indians on Aornos, should it prove impossible to take the Rock by assault. Then, with the archers, the Agrianes, Coenus' battalion, the best-armed and most active of the other infantry units, 200 Companions and 100 mounted archers, he moved on towards the Rock.

Before the day was over he halted in what he judged to be a convenient spot, and on the morrow advanced a little further; then halted again. While he waited there, some natives sought an interview with him. They put themselves into his hands, and then declared that they would guide him to the most vulnerable point of the Rock and from there he would be able to secure a valuable offensive position without difficulty. Alexander accepted the offer and ordered Ptolemy, son of Lagus, of his personal Guard, with the Agrianes, the other light-armed units, and a picked company of Guards, to go with the guides, seize the position they mentioned, make sure to secure it strongly, and inform him by signal in the event of his success.

The rough track made difficult going, but Ptolemy, unperceived by the enemy, reached the position and occupied it. He at once proceeded to secure it by a ditch and stockade, and raised a fire-signal on an eminence where

71. Perhaps Charsadda, the capital of Gandhara.

Alexander would be sure to see it. Alexander did see it, instantly, and on the following day began his own advance, but, meeting resistance from the enemy and great difficulty from the broken ground, achieved, for the time being, nothing. The Indians no sooner perceived that Alexander's offensive was getting nowhere than they turned their attention to Ptolemy. They moved to the attack, and there was a fierce struggle, the Indians doing all they could to tear down the stockade, while Ptolemy fought to maintain his hold. The weight of the Macedonian missiles overpowered the Indians, who at nightfall were forced to withdraw.

Wishing to get a message through to Ptolemy, Alexander chose as his messenger one of the Indian deserters, a trustworthy fellow with the further recommendation of an intimate knowledge of the locality. Under cover of darkness he sent this man with a letter containing instructions to Ptolemy, not to rest content with holding the position he had occupied, but to take the offensive: his attack, moreover, should be simultaneous with his own, so that the Indians would be caught between two fires. Next day at dawn Alexander moved; he marched for the track by which Ptolemy had made his secret ascent, in the belief that if once he could get through and join Ptolemy, what remained to do would be comparatively easy. All went according to plan: there was a hard struggle lasting until noon, the Macedonians trying to force their way up and the Indians doing what they could to stop them by all the missiles they could muster. Company by company the Macedonians pressed relentlessly up the slope, the leading files pausing till their companions below could join them, and at last, just as the light was going, they managed to get through and made contact with Ptolemy. The whole force, now united, then moved forward to the assault of the actual Rock. The assault, however, proved abortive, and for what remained of the day nothing else was accomplished.

The following dawn Alexander issued an order for every man to cut a hundred stakes. This was done, and he then began the construction of an extensive earthwork, to reach from his present position on the crest of the hill across to Aornos itself. From the top of this he judged that the defenders of the Rock would be within range both of arrows and of catapults. Every man set to and took a hand, while Alexander himself kept an eye upon things and was as quick to punish shoddy work as to praise what was well and truly done.

During the first day the earthwork was carried forward about 200 yards; by the second, slingers and catapults operating from the portion already completed were able to check enemy raids on the men still working; within three days the entire space was filled. Then, on the fourth day, a small party of Macedonians stormed and secured another height, of no great extent, the summit of which was level with the Rock, and Alexander promptly began to extend the earthwork in this direction, in order to make it run without a break right up to this new position.

The seizure of this second height was an act of daring wholly beyond the Indians' experience; they were badly shaken, and when they saw the earthwork completed and continuous, they abandoned any further hope of resistance, and sent an offer to Alexander to surrender the Rock upon terms. They expected to be able to protract the discussion of terms throughout the day, and their plan was to slip away during the night and disperse to their various homes. Alexander, however, was informed of their intention; giving them plenty of time to get away and to remove the pickets which were stationed all round the Rock, he waited till the actual withdrawal began, and then, with a party of 700 of the Guards and his personal guard, moved forward to that part of the Rock which was now undefended. He was himself the first to set foot upon it, and his men followed, hauling each other up.

At a given signal they turned upon the retreating Indians and killed many of them as they tried to escape; others in sudden desperation flung themselves over the cliffs.

Thus Alexander was left in possession of the Rock which had baffled Heracles himself. Upon it he offered sacrifice, and then garrisoned it with troops under the command of Sisicottus, an Indian who some time previously had deserted to Bessus in Bactria and had subsequently taken service under Alexander, after his conquest of Bactria, and proved himself highly trustworthy.

Leaving Aornos, Alexander entered the territory of the Assacenians on the strength of a report that Assacenus' brother with his elephants and a large number of natives proposed to defend themselves in the mountains there. The town of Dyrta he found empty and abandoned, as was the country in the immediate neighbourhood, and the day after his arrival there he detached Nearchus with the light-armed units and the Agrianes, and Antiochus with his own regiment of Guards and two others and sent them out to reconnoitre. Their orders were also to capture and question any natives they could lay hands on, and, in particular, to get what information they could about elephants, as this interested him more than than anything.

He now marched for the Indus. It was difficult country, and troops went on ahead to make a practicable route. A few natives were captured, and from them he learned that the Indians of the district had fled to Abisares,[72] leaving

72. The ruler of Kashmir.

their elephants where they were to feed by the river. He ordered the men to take him to the elephants.

Many Indians hunt elephants, and Alexander greatly liked to have elephant-hunters in his retinue. On this occasion, too, he went hunting with his guides; two of the beasts, in the course of the hunt, jumped over a cliff and were killed, but the rest were caught. They permitted riders to mount them and were attached to the army.

There was a wood by the river, and as the timber was of good quality Alexander had it felled and boats built. The boats were taken down-river to the bridge, the construction of which Hephaestion and Perdiccas had some time ago completed.[73]

73. See p. 240 n. 59.

BOOK FIVE

IN the country on Alexander's route between the river Cophen and the Indus lay the city of Nysa, supposed to have been founded by Dionysus, at the time of his conquest of the Indians.[1] Nobody knows, however, who this Dionysus was, nor the date of his invasion of India, nor where he started from, and I myself should hardly care to say if this Theban deity marched with his army against the Indians from Thebes or from Tmolus in Lydia, or how it was that after passing through the territories of so many warlike peoples unknown to the Greeks of that date, he fought and conquered only the Indians.[2] However, one should not inquire too closely where ancient legends about the gods are concerned; many things which reason rejects acquire some colour of probability once you bring a god into the story.

The people of Nysa, upon Alexander's approach, sent their chief, Acuphis, to him accompanied by thirty of their most distinguished men with instructions to ask him to leave their city to its god. The story is that when they entered Alexander's tent, they found him sitting there dusty and travel-stained, still wearing his equipment, his helmet on his head and a spear in his hand. The sight of

1. Arrian embarks upon a digression, strategically placed at Alexander's crossing of the Indus, to clarify his attitude to the legends told about the king in the fabulous country of India.

Nysa appears to have been situated in the Kabul Valley, perhaps near Jalalabad. Alexander's visit is narrated by Curtius (8.10.7–18) immediately after the events related by Arrian at 4.23; cf. the Table of Contents in Diodorus, whose account has not survived.

2. On Dionysus compare Strabo's remarks at 15.1.7.

him sitting thus surprised them so much that they prostrated themselves upon the ground and for a long time
spoke never a word. At last, however, Alexander bade
them get up and not be alarmed; whereupon Acuphis
addressed him in the following words: 'Sire, it is the
request of the people of Nysa that you show your reverence for Dionysus by leaving them free and independent.
For when Dionysus, after his conquest of the Indians, was
on his way homeward towards the Grecian sea, he
founded this city as a memorial of his long journey and
his victory, leaving to inhabit it those of his men who
were no longer fit for service – who were also his Priests.
He did but as you have done; for you too founded Alexandria in the Caucasus and Alexandria in Egypt and many
other cities as well, and will found yet more hereafter,
in that you will have surpassed the achievements of
Dionysus.

'Dionysus named this city Nysa and this land Nysaea
in memory of his nurse, who bore that name; and to the
mountain near the city he gave the name Merus – or the
Thigh – because legend has it that he grew in the thigh of
Zeus. Ever since that time Nysa has been free; we who
live in it have made our own laws – and obeyed them, as
good men should. If you wish for a proof that Dionysus
was our founder, here it is: this is the only place in India
where ivy grows.'

Alexander found what Acuphis said highly agreeable;
he would have liked very much to believe the old tale
about Dionysus' journey and his foundings of Nysa, for
then he would have had the satisfaction of knowing that
he had already penetrated as far as Dionysus did, and
would presently advance yet further; he felt moreover
that his Macedonian troops would consent to share his
hardships a little longer, if they knew they were in com-

petition with Dionysus. Accordingly he granted to the people of Nysa the continuance of their freedom and autonomy.

He inquired about the nature of their institutions, and on being told that the government was aristocratic in form, he expressed approval and asked that 300 of their mounted troops should be sent to join him together with 100 men chosen from the most distinguished in the governing class (which also happened to consist of 300 men). Acuphis, whom Alexander appointed governor of Nysaea, was to select them. Acuphis is said to have smiled at this request, and on being asked by Alexander what it was that amused him, the story goes that he replied: 'But how, my lord, do you suppose that a city can lose a hundred good men and still be well governed? If you have our interest at heart, we will, indeed, send for the three hundred cavalrymen, and more, if you want them; but instead of the hundred able and distinguished citizens whom you ask me to select, take, I beg you, double the number of the inferior sort, so that when you come again to visit us you may find us as well governed as we are now.'

Alexander acceded to the request, which he thought a sensible one. He repeated his order that Acuphis should send the cavalrymen to accompany him, but neither the select hundred nor any substitutes for them. Acuphis, however, sent him his son and grandson.

There was a certain spot which the people of Nysa were very proud of because of its connexions with Dionysus. Alexander was extremely anxious to visit it; he longed to go with the Companion cavalry and his Guard of infantry to Mount Merus and see with his own eyes the ivy and laurel which grew there in such abundance, the groves of various trees which covered it, and the dense woodland full of game of all kinds for hunting. Accordingly they went, and the Macedonians were delighted with the ivy, which they had not seen for so long – there is none in India elsewhere, not even in districts where the vine grows – and at once eagerly set themselves to make wreaths of it which they put on their heads while they sang songs of praise to Dionysus and called upon him by his many names. Alexander offered sacrifice on the sacred spot and made merry with his friends – and there is a story (which you may believe if you like) that a number of distinguished Macedonian officers, once the ivy crown was on their heads and the god invoked, were possessed by his spirit and with cries of *Euoi, Euoi*, lost their wits in the true Bacchic frenzy.

These tales, however, you may believe or not, as you think fit. Personally I do not completely accept the view of Eratosthenes of Cyrene, who tells us that everything attributed by the Macedonians to the divine influence was grossly exaggerated in order to please Alexander.[3] For instance, there is the case of the cave in the territory of the Parapamisadae: according to Eratosthenes, the Macedonians saw this cave and on the strength of some local legend – which they may well have invented – put it about that it was the cave where Prometheus was hung in chains when the eagle used to come to feed on his guts, and that Heracles came thither to kill the eagle and set Prometheus free; so that by means of this tale the Macedonians transferred Mount Caucasus from Pontus to the far east, fixing it in India in the country of the Parapamisadae, and gave the name Caucasus to what was in reality the Parapamisus

3. The great polymath of the third century B.C., head of the library at Alexandria from *c.*246, whose jealous critics called him second-rate. His greatest achievement was his *Geography*, used extensively by Strabo.

range simply to flatter Alexander by the inference that he had crossed Caucasus. Again, having seen Indian cattle branded with the image of a club, they used this as an argument to prove that Heracles had visited India. Eratosthenes is equally sceptical about similar tales of Dionysus' wanderings – but, for my own part, I am content to maintain neutrality in these matters.[4]

On reaching the Indus, Alexander found that Hephaestion had already bridged it and collected a large number of small boats and two thirty-oared galleys. Gifts from Taxiles the Indian were awaiting him: 200 talents of silver, 3,000 oxen and over 10,000 sheep for sacrificial purposes, and some thirty elephants. A cavalry contingent 700 strong also came from Taxiles to join Alexander's forces, and the town of Taxila, which is the most considerable between the Indus and the Hydaspes, was given into his hands.[5] Here Alexander offered sacrifice to the gods whom it was his custom to honour, and held a contest of athletics and horsemanship by the river. The omens from the sacrifice were favourable for the crossing.

The Indus is bigger than any river in Europe, and than any other in India except the Ganges; it rises somewhere west of the Parapamisus (or Caucasus) range[6] and flows into the Indian Ocean to the southward; it has two mouths and in both of them the lower reaches are swampy like the five mouths of the Danube; it forms a delta (called Pattala in the Indian language) similar to the delta

4. We may compare what Strabo says at the beginning of Book 15 of his *Geography*, especially in chapters 7–9. He is a good deal more sceptical than Arrian. See, however, Arrian's remarks in his *Indica* (1.7; 5.10–13).

5. Taxila, some 20 miles north-west of Rawalpindi, has been thoroughly excavated by Sir John Marshall. See his *Taxila* (Cambridge, 1951).

6. In fact, it rises in the Himalayas.

of the Nile in Egypt: all these are accepted facts, and I take the opportunity of recording them here. The four Indian rivers, Hydaspes, Acesines, Hydraotes, and Hyphasis,[7] though much greater than the other Asian rivers, are nevertheless smaller – indeed much smaller – than the Indus, as the Indus itself is smaller than the Ganges. Ctesias indeed (if his report is worth anything as evidence) says that at its narrowest part the breadth of the Indus is about five miles, at its widest about twelve miles, while for most of its course it is somewhere between the two.[8] This, then, was the river which early one morning Alexander crossed with his army, and so entered India.

I have not included in this book an account of the Indian way of life, or any description of the strange animals to be found, or of the variety and size of the fish and other aquatic creatures in the Indus, the Hydaspes, the Ganges, and elsewhere: nor have I mentioned gold-mining ants and gold-guarding griffons[9] and other queer things which people have invented rather for diversion than as serious history, in the belief that none of the absurd stories they tell about India are likely to be brought to the test of truth. Actually, however, most of these fables were indeed proved or disproved by Alexander and his men – except in a few cases where they themselves were guilty of invention. They proved, for instance, that the Indians have no gold – at any rate the very considerable section of them which Alexander visited in the course

7. The Jhelum, Chenab, Ravi, and Beas respectively. The Punjab is 'the land of the Five Rivers'.

8. Ctesias, a native of Cnidos, was court physician to Artaxerxes II (404–359). He wrote a history of Persia and a book on India which are preserved only in brief extracts. He had a reputation in antiquity for romancing; see, e.g., Aristotle, *History of Animals* 8.27.

The Indus is nowhere broader than two and a half miles.

9. See Herodotus 3.102, 4.13; Strabo 15.1.44.

of his campaign – and that their domestic arrangements are far from luxurious. The men are taller than any other Asiatics, most of them being over seven feet, or not much less; they are darker-skinned than any other race except the Ethiopians, and the finest fighters to be found anywhere in Asia' at that time. I cannot satisfactorily compare them with the ancient Persians who marched with Cyrus, son of Cambyses, when he wrested the sovereignty of Asia from the Medes and established his control either by force or by consent over so many other peoples as well; for the Persians at that period of their history were a poor nation and lived in a harsh land, and their way of life was as near as may be to the stern discipline of Sparta;[10] nor can I make any certain inference from the Persian disaster in Scythia, not knowing if the cause of it was the unfavourable nature of the ground where the battle was fought, or some mistake made by Cyrus, or the actual military inferiority of the Persian soldiers to the Scythians of those parts.

However, about India it is my intention to write a special account[11] based on the most reliable reports from Alexander's expedition and the discoveries of Nearchus, who sailed along the northern coasts of the Indian Ocean,[12] and including facts recorded by the two distinguished writers Megasthenes and Eratosthenes. My account will cover the Indian way of life, any strange creatures to be found in the country, and the actual coastal voyage in the Southern Ocean. For the present I must be content with what I have felt to be adequate simply for the illustration of Alexander's achievements: namely, that

10. cf. Xenophon, *Cyropaideia* 7.5.67.

11. This is *The History of India* (*Indica*), which is still extant.

12. This account, which has perished, was used extensively by Arrian in the *Indica*. For the voyage see chapters 17–43.

the boundary of Asia is the Taurus range, beginning at Mycale opposite the island of Samos, running north of Pamphylia and Cilicia, and thence to Armenia, whence it continues by way of Parthia and Chorasmia to Media, and in Bactria joins the Parapamisus range. It was this latter range which Alexander's men called the Caucasus, apparently for the purpose of magnifying his achievement by the suggestion that he reached the further side of the Caucasus in his triumphant advance. It is possible, however, that there is no real break between this Indian Caucasus and the Scythian Caucasus, any more than there is between it and Taurus, and it is for that reason that I have already used the name Caucasus for it, and shall continue to do so. It runs down to the Indian Ocean.

Thus all the important rivers of Asia rise either in the Taurus or in the Caucasus Mountains, some of them flowing north and entering either Lake Maeotis or the so-called Hyrcanian Sea[13] itself a gulf of the Ocean[14] – others flowing south, such as the Euphrates, Tigris, Indus, Hydaspes, Acesines, Hydraotes, Hyphasis, and all the rest between these and the Ganges, which either empty themselves into the sea or disperse into swamp and disappear, as the Euphrates does.

Imagine Asia as divided by the Taurus and Caucasus ranges, running in an east–west direction, and you will see that the two main divisions are formed by the Taurus, one lying north of it, the other south; the southern part may then again be divided into four, the largest of which

13. The sea of Azov and the Caspian sea.

14. This was the prevalent view in antiquity. Herodotus (1.202 ff.) and Aristotle (*Meteorology* 2.1.10) knew the truth, but after Patrocles, who was sent to explore the Caspian about 284/3, reported that it was a gulf of the Ocean this view was adopted by Eratosthenes and prevailed, with a few exceptions, until the 14th century. For Alexander's intended exploration see p. 375.

is, according to Eratosthenes and Megasthenes, India;
(Megasthenes, by the way, spent much time in Arachotia
with its governor Sibyrtius, and tells us that he frequently
visited the Indian King Sandracottus);[15] the smallest
division, bounded on the east by the Euphrates, lies towards the Aegean, and the two remaining divisions, lying
between the Euphrates and the Indus, can hardly, when
put together, be compared in extent with India. India itself, east and west and right down to the south, is bounded
by the Indian Ocean, and on the north by the Indian Caucasus as far as its junction with the Taurus range; from
these mountains to the Indian Ocean its western boundary is the Indus. Most of the country is plain, generally
supposed to be alluvial; and it is a fact that elsewhere, too,
the majority of coastal plains have been formed by the silt
of rivers – which was also, presumably, the reason why in
ancient times the name of the country was the same as
that of its river: for example, there is a plain of Hermus,
a river which rises in the mountain of Dindymene the
Great Mother,[16] in Asia, and flows into the sea near
Smyrna in Aeolia; then there is the Cayster, which gives
its name to a plain in Lydia, the Caïcus in Mysia, and the
Maeander in Caria, after which is named the whole coastal
strip as far as Miletus in Ionia. The historians Herodotus
and Hecataeus (if the latter is indeed the author of the
book in question) both call Egypt 'the gift of the river',
and Herodotus has proved the point by very clear evi-

15. Sandracottus is Chandragupta, the founder of the Mauryan
dynasty, who expelled the Macedonians from the Punjab after
Alexander's death, and eventually ruled much of India, including
territory west of the Indus ceded to him by Seleucus in 304.
Megasthenes was Seleucus' ambassador, and his account formed
the basis of Greek knowledge of India; see Strabo Book 15 and
Arrian's *Indica*.

16. Cybele, to whom Mt Dindymus in Phrygia was sacred.

dence.[17] In this case, too, the river gave its name to the country, for that Aegyptus was originally the name of the river now known both in Egypt and elsewhere in the world as the Nile there is sufficient evidence in Homer, where we find the statement that Menelaus brought up 'at the mouth of the Aegyptus'.[18]

If, therefore, in various parts of the world one river, and a comparatively small one at that, can on its course to the sea build up a large area of land by means of the mud and silt which it brings down from the uplands where it rises, there is surely no reason why one should not admit that India, too, is for the most part an alluvial plain; for if one added together the Hermus, Cayster, Caïcus, Maeander, and all the other Asian rivers which flow into the Aegean, they would not, for sheer volume of water, compare with any single one of the rivers of India – to say nothing of the greatest, the Ganges, with which not even the Egyptian Nile or the great European river the Danube is to be mentioned in the same breath: indeed, combine all those rivers into one and they would not equal in volume even the Indus, which is a mighty stream right from its source and receives the waters of fifteen tributaries, all of them bigger than the rivers of Asia,[19] and imposes its name upon the country as it flows down to meet the sea. That is all I will say here about this great country. I must keep the rest for my other book, *The History of India*.

There is no mention in the accounts either of Aristobulus or Ptolemy (my two principal authorities) of the method employed by Alexander in bridging the Indus, and I should myself hesitate to express an opinion as to

17. See Herodotus 2.5, and 2.10–34.
18. *Odyssey* 4.477, 581.
19. Arrian gives the names of these rivers in his *Indica* (4.8–12).

whether a permanent bridge was constructed or a bridge of boats such as Xerxes made for crossing the Hellespont or Darius for crossing the Bosphorus and the Danube.[20] Nevertheless I am inclined to think that the latter method was used, if only because the depth of water is too great to allow the construction of a permanent bridge, and because, even had so astonishing a feat been accomplished, it could not possibly have been completed so quickly. Again, granting that boats were used, I still cannot say for certain whether they were lashed together and moored in line as in the bridge over the Hellespont which Herodotus describes, or whether the method was that employed by the Romans in their bridges over the Danube and the Celtic Rhine, or on the various occasions when they had to bridge the Tigris and the Euphrates; in any case, the Roman method of bridging by boats is the quickest I know of, and I shall describe it here, if only for its interest.

At the word of command, the boats are allowed to float downstream, stern first, while their way is checked by a rowing-boat which manœuvres them into position. Once they are in position, pyramid-shaped wicker baskets filled with rough stones are lowered from the bows to hold them against the current. As soon as one vessel is securely moored, another is brought up alongside of it, bows-on to the current, at the proper distance to ensure a sufficiently strong base for the superstructure; then timbers are rapidly laid athwartships from one vessel to the other with planks across them to make the structure rigid. The same process is repeated from vessel to vessel, as many as are needed to complete the bridge. On both sides of it ladders are fixed to serve as a bulwark and render the passage safer for horses and pack-animals, and also to

20. Herodotus 7.33–6; 4.83, 97.

strengthen the structure still further. The whole operation takes little time, and is carried out in an orderly
manner, in spite of much noise and bustle; shouts of
encouragement there may be, on one vessel or another, or
loud comments on bad work – but through it all the words
of command can be heard well enough, and the rapid
progress of the work is not impaired.

Such, then, is the traditional method employed by the
Romans. Precisely how Alexander bridged the Indus I do
not know, for there is no contemporary account; none
the less, I expect it was by some very similar method.
Perhaps it was not – but no matter.

Once across the river, Alexander offered his customary
sacrifice and continued his march to Taxila, a large and
prosperous town – indeed, the largest between the Indus
and the Hydaspes. Here he was courteously received by
Taxiles, the governor, and the Indians of the district, and
he granted them, in return, as much of the territory
bordering on their own as they asked for. He was also
visited by representatives from Abisares, King of the
Indian hill-tribes, with his brother and other distinguished
personages among them, and by representatives from the
local governor Doxareus. All of them brought presents.
Here as elsewhere Alexander offered his usual sacrifices
and held public games with contests in athletics and
riding; then, after appointing Philip, son of Machatas, as
governor of this district, he proceeded to the Hydaspes,
leaving in Taxila any men who were sick and unfit for
service.

News had already reached him that Porus[21] with all the
troops he could muster was on the other side of the Hydaspes, determined either to prevent his crossing or to

21. King of the Pauravas, whose kingdom lay between the
Hydaspes and the Acesines.

attack him should he attempt it. Alexander, accordingly, sent Coenus, son of Polemocrates, back to the Indus with orders to cut into sections the boats which had been used at the crossing of that river and transport them to the Hydaspes; the order was carried out, the smaller vessels being cut in half, the thirty-oared galleys into three, and the sections carried in carts to the bank of the Hydaspes, where they were re-assembled, so that the whole flotilla was once again to be seen, as it had been seen upon the Indus. Then, with the force he had brought to Taxila and 5,000 Indian troops under Taxiles and the local chieftains, he marched for the Hydaspes.

From the position he took up on the bank of this river he was able to see Porus, with all his forces, including his squadron of elephants, on the further side.[22] At the point immediately opposite Alexander, Porus remained on guard in person, and sent pickets, each under command of an officer, to the various other points along the river where a crossing was practicable; for he was determined to stop the Macedonians from getting over. Alexander's answer was by continual movement of his own troops to keep Porus guessing: he split his force into a number of detachments, moving some of them under his own command hither and thither all over the place, destroying enemy possessions and looking for places where the river might be crossed, and putting others under the command of various officers with instructions to keep constantly on the move, now in this direction, now in that. As supplies

22. The location of Alexander's camp and his place of crossing are not certainly known. The most probable view is that of Sir Aurel Stein, who argues that Alexander encamped at Haranpur and crossed at Jalalpur. For a discussion of the various theories see Fuller, pp. 181–5. For the operations against Porus see Diodorus 17.87–89; Curtius 8.13–14; Plutarch, *Alexander* 60.

continued to come in for his army from all parts of the country west of the Hydaspes, it was clear to Porus that he meant to remain in the neighbourhood of the river, until in the course of the winter the water fell sufficiently to enable him to effect a crossing at any one of a number of places. Morever, the continual movement of Alexander's boats up or down stream, the manufacture of skin floats filled with hay, and the sight of troops, cavalry and infantry, constantly massed on the river-bank, gave Porus no chance to relax his vigilance or to concentrate his defensive preparations upon any one point rather than another.

The water was high at that time of year – the summer solstice[23] – in all the Indian rivers, and the current in them swift and turbulent; for there are heavy rains at this season, and these, added to the melting snow from the Caucasus, where most of the rivers rise, greatly increase the volume of water, while during the winter the flow is checked again, the water becomes less turbid, and the level of it drops, so that here and there it is possible to get across. The Indus and the Ganges (and perhaps one other) are never fordable – but what I have said is certainly true of the Hydaspes.

Alexander openly declared his intention of waiting for the season in which the water in the river should fall, if he were prevented from crossing immediately; nevertheless he remained in the neighbourhood and kept a sharp look-out for any possible opportunity of getting his men over by a swift and unexpected movement. It was clear to him that he could not effect the crossing at the point where

23. Arrian is mistaken. Indeed, he later (p. 282) states that the battle was fought in May. According to Nearchus (Strabo 15.1.18; Arrian, *Indica* 6.5.) at the summer solstice, i.e about 21 July, Alexander was encamped on the Acesines.

Porus held the opposite bank, for his troops would certainly be attacked, as they tried to gain the shore, by a powerful and efficient army, well-equipped and supported by a large number of elephants; moreover, he thought it likely that his horses, in face of an immediate attack by elephants, would be too much scared by the appearance of these beasts and their unfamiliar trumpetings to be induced to land – indeed, they would probably refuse to stay on the floats, and at the mere sight of the elephants in the distance would go mad with terror and plunge into the water long before they reached the further side.

The river had to be crossed, so, as it could not be done openly, Alexander determined to attain his object by cunning. Every night he kept moving the greater part of his mounted troops up and down the bank of the river, making as much noise as possible – shouts, war-cries, and every sort of clatter and shindy which might be supposed to precede an attempted crossing. Porus, bringing up his elephants, followed these movements, guided by the noise, and Alexander gradually led him to make these marches, parallel to his own, a regular thing. This went on for some time, until Porus, finding that the Macedonians never went beyond shouts and yells, gave it up. Clearly, it was a false alarm; so he ceased to follow the movements of the enemy cavalry and stayed where he was, in his original position, with look-outs posted at various points along the river. Thus Porus, no longer expecting a sudden attempt under cover of darkness, was lulled into a sense of security – and this was Alexander's opportunity.

At a sharp bend in the river there was a projecting spit of land, thickly wooded with different sorts of timber; and just off this promontory lay an uninhabited island, also well wooded. Alexander did not fail to observe the opportunity which this offered: the dense woodland both on the island and on the river-bank beyond it was just the thing to conceal his attempt, so this was the spot where he determined to make the crossing. It was some eighteen miles from his main position, and all along the river he had stationed pickets, close enough to enable them to keep contact with each other both by sight and sound and to hear without difficulty any orders passed from any point along the line. For several nights in succession over a wide area noise and bustle were kept going and fires burning.

The decision once made, Alexander began his preparations openly. Craterus was left in charge of the original position with his own cavalry regiment, the mounted contingents from Arachotia and the Parapamisadae, part of the Macedonian infantry consisting of the battalions of Alcetas and Polysperchon, the local Indian chieftains, and the 5,000 troops under their command. His orders were not to attempt a crossing until Porus had moved from his position to attack Alexander, or until he was sure that Porus was in retreat and the Macedonians victorious. 'But if,' Alexander added, 'Porus opposes me with a part only of his force and leaves the rest, together with elephants, where it now is, you must stay where you are; if, on the other hand, he moves his whole contingent of elephants against me, leaving in his present position only some portion of his other forces, then you must lose no time in getting across. The only real danger to our horses, as we put them ashore, is elephants. Nothing else will worry them.'

Between the island and the main camp of which Craterus was left in charge, Meleager, Attalus and Gorgias were posted with the mercenary cavalry and infantry;[24]

24. As well as their own infantry battalions (Tarn, *Alexander* 2.191).

their instructions, too, were to effect a crossing in sections as soon as they saw that the Indians were fairly engaged. The mounted troops which Alexander selected to operate under his own command consisted of the special squadron of the Companions, the cavalry regiments of Hephaestion, Perdiccas, and Demetrius, the contingents from Bactria and Sogdiana, the Scythian cavalry, and the mounted archers of the Daae; from the infantry units he chose the Guards, the battalions of Cleitus and Coenus, the archers, and the Agrianes. He took the precaution of moving at some distance from the river, in order to conceal his march to the point where he proposed to cross – the island, namely, and the spit of land opposite to it. To this point the floats had already been conveyed some time previously, and now, under cover of darkness, they were filled with hay and carefully sewn up. During the night a deluge of rain helped to conceal the preparations for the coming attempt; the clatter of arms, shouted orders, and the commotion they caused could not be heard across the river through the noise of the storm and the claps of thunder. Besides the skin-floats, most of the boats, including the thirty-oared galleys, had already arrived. These had been cut into sections, and were now re-assembled and concealed among the trees.

Just before dawn the rain stopped and the wind fell light. The mounted troops were embarked on the floats, the boats taking as many of the infantry as they would hold, and the crossing began – screened by the island, to prevent discovery by Porus' scouts before the island was passed and the whole flotilla already near the opposite bank. Alexander himself crossed in one of the galleys with half of the Guards, the remainder following in other galleys. He was accompanied by three officers of his personal guard – Ptolemy, Perdiccas, and Lysimachus – and by Seleucus (the Seleucus who afterwards became King).[25]

Once past the island, the approach to the river-bank was in full view of the enemy patrols, who galloped off with all the speed their horses could muster, to report to Porus. Alexander was the first ashore, and promptly took charge of the troops from the other galleys; the cavalry had had orders to disembark first, and these he proceeded to marshal as each squadron came off the floats. He then moved forward in battle order.

To Alexander this was all strange country, and it so happened that he had, without knowing it, landed on another island, and not on the mainland at all. It was an island of considerable extent – and therefore all the more difficult to recognize as such – and was separated from the mainland beyond by a branch of the river of no very great size. Nevertheless the torrential rain throughout the previous night had increased the volume of water, and the mounted troops were unable to find a practicable place for crossing. For a time they were faced with the disagreeable prospect that all the labour they had gone through would have to be repeated; at last, however, a ford was found, and Alexander led the way over. It was no easy task, as the water in the deepest part was up to the men's armpits and the horses' necks.

Once this second crossing was successfully accomplished, Alexander again marshalled his troops. His Royal Squadron and the best of the other mounted regiments he brought round to the right wing, stationing the mounted archers in the van; in the rear of the cavalry he posted the Royal Regiment of Guards under Seleucus, then the Royal regiment of the heavy infantry, in close touch with the other Guards divisions, according to their

25. Seleucus Nicator founded the Seleucid dynasty, which at times ruled much of Alexander's Asiatic empire. cf. p. 387.

precedence for that day.[26] The archers, Agrianes, and javelin-men took their position on either wing of the main body of infantry. Having thus made his dispositions, he gave orders for the infantry, nearly 6,000 strong,[27] to follow in order of march, while he himself, with only the cavalry (numbering some 5,000) in which he thought he had the advantage over the enemy, moved forward rapidly. Tauron, captain of the archers, was instructed to advance in the rear of the cavalry with all the speed he could make.

The idea in Alexander's mind was that if Porus' army should attack in force he would either settle them straight away by a cavalry charge,[28] or, failing that, fight a delaying action until his infantry could come to his support; if, on the other hand, the Indians proved to be so badly shaken by the bold and unexpected crossing of the river that they took to their heels, he would be able to press hard on the retreating army, and the more men they lost during their withdrawal, the lighter his own task would subsequently be.

There are, however, somewhat conflicting accounts of these operations. According to Aristobulus, Porus' son arrived on the scene with sixty chariots before Alexander effected his second crossing – from the island, that is; and in view of the fact that the crossing was no easy matter

26. Arrian's text is faulty. Tarn (*Alexander* 2.191–2) suggests that Ptolemy wrote 'he posted the Royal regiment of Guards and the other Guards regiments under Seleucus, and in close touch with them the battalions of the phalanx, according as each (Guards regiments and infantry battalions) had precedence on that day'.

27. The infantry units enumerated above (p. 271) clearly amounted to more than 6,000. As Arrian (loc. cit.) writes that the boats took as many of the infantry as they could, perhaps not all had been transported across the river by this time.

28. It seems incredible that Alexander can have hoped to defeat Porus' full force with his cavalry alone. Plutarch (*Alexander* 60.7), whose account is based on a letter of Alexander, writes that the king envisaged the possibility of an attack by the Indian cavalry.

even without opposition, he might have prevented it altogether if his Indians had left their chariots and attacked on foot Alexander's leading troops as they were trying to get on shore. But in point of fact he merely drove past, and permitted Alexander to cross without molestation. Against this force Alexander sent his mounted archers, and it was broken up without difficulty, many of the men being wounded. Other writers state that there was a fight at the actual landing between Alexander's cavalry and a force of Indians commanded by Porus' son, who was there ready to oppose them with superior numbers, and that in the course of the fighting he wounded Alexander with his own hand and struck the blow which killed his beloved horse Bucephalus.

Ptolemy, son of Lagus, gives a different account, which I myself accept. According to him, Porus did, as other writers relate, send his son, but not with only sixty chariots. For it is hardly likely that, on a report from his scouts that either Alexander himself or, at any rate, some portion of his army, had crossed the Hydaspes, he would have sent his own son to oppose the landing with so trivial a force – a force, on the one hand, unnecessarily large for mere reconnaissance and unsuitably equipped for a rapid withdrawal, and, on the other, totally inadequate either to prevent a proposed crossing or to attack an enemy which had already succeeded in getting over.[29] Ptolemy's actual statement is that Porus' son had with him 2,000 mounted troops and 120 chariots[30] when he reached the spot; but

29. This criticism of Aristobulus appears to be Arrian's own, not Ptolemy's, as is sometimes said. The passage, therefore, is not evidence that Ptolemy wrote after Aristobulus.

30. According to Plutarch (*Alexander* 60.8), Porus' son had 1,000 cavalry and 60 chariots. He agrees with Arrian that the Indian losses were 400 cavalry and all the chariots. Curtius (8.14.2) says that Porus' brother was sent with 4,000 cavalry and 100 chariots.

Alexander had been too quick for him and had already effected his final crossing from the island. Against this force Alexander first sent his mounted archers, while he himself moved on with the cavalry, thinking that Porus was on the way to engage him with the main strength of his army, and that this cavalry contingent, posted in the van, preceded the rest of the Indian troops. But as soon as Alexander received an accurate report of the enemies' numbers, he attacked at once, and the Indians, seeing Alexander there in person and his massed cavalry coming at them in successive charges, squadron by squadron, broke and fled. The Indians' losses in the action were some 400 mounted men, Porus' son being himself among the killed; their chariots and horses were captured as they attempted to get away – speed was impossible, and the muddy ground had rendered them useless even during the fight.

The Indians who did succeed in getting away reported to Porus that Alexander had crossed the river in force and that his son had been killed in the action. Porus was faced with a difficult choice, for the troops under Craterus, who had been left behind in Alexander's original position opposite the main Indian army, could now be seen making their way over the river. Swiftly he made up his mind; he determined to move in force against Alexander, and to fight it out with the King of Macedon himself and the flower of his men. Then, leaving behind a small force with a few elephants to spread alarm among Craterus' cavalry as they attempted to land on the river-bank, he marched to meet Alexander with all his cavalry, 4,000 strong, all of his 300 chariots, 200 elephants, and the picked contingents of his infantry, numbering some 30,000 men.[31]

31. Curtius (8.13.6) agrees with Arrian's figures for infantry and chariots, but has 85 elephants. He does not mention cavalry; but see last note. Diodorus (17.87.2) gives 50,000 infantry, 3,000

Much of the ground was deep in soft mud, so he continued his advance till he found a spot where the sandy soil offered a surface sufficiently firm and level for cavalry manœuvre, and there made his dispositions. In the van he stationed his elephants at intervals of about 100 feet, on a broad front, to form a screen for the whole body of the infantry and to spread terror among the cavalry of Alexander. He did not expect that any enemy unit would venture to force a way through the gaps in the line of elephants, either on foot or on horseback; terror would make the horses uncontrollable, and infantry units would be even less likely to make the attempt, as they would be met and checked by his own heavy infantry and then destroyed by the elephants turning upon them and trampling them down. Behind the elephants were the foot-soldiers, though not on a front of equal extent: the various units, forming a second line, were so disposed as to fill the intervals in the line of elephants. There was infantry on both wings as well, outflanking the elephants, and, finally, on both flanks of the infantry were the mounted units, each with a screen of war-chariots.

Noting that the enemy was making his dispositions for battle, Alexander checked the advance of his cavalry to allow the infantry to come up with him. Regiment by regiment they made contact, moving swiftly, until the whole force was again united. Alexander had no intention of making the fresh enemy troops a present of his own breathless and exhausted men, so he paused before advancing to the attack. Meanwhile he kept his cavalry manœuvring up and down the line, while the infantry units were allowed to rest until they were once more in good heart for battle.

cavalry, over 1,000 chariots, and 130 elephants; Plutarch (*Alexander* 62.1) 20,000 infantry and 2,000 cavalry.

Observation of the Indian dispositions decided him against attempting an assault upon their centre, where the heavy infantry was massed in the intervals of the protecting screen of elephants, and his reluctance to take this course was based precisely upon Porus' own calculations; relying, instead, on his superiority in cavalry, he moved the major portion of his mounted troops towards the enemy's left wing, to make his assault in that sector. Coenus was sent over to the Indians' right with Demetrius' regiment and his own, his orders being that when the enemy moved their cavalry across to their left to counter the massed formations of the Macedonian mounted squadrons, he should hang on to their rear. The heavy infantry was put in charge of Seleucus, Antigenes, and Tauron, with orders not to engage until it was evident that the Indians, both horse and foot, had been thrown into confusion by the Macedonian cavalry.

Once the opposing armies were within range, Alexander launched his mounted archers, 1,000 strong, against the enemy's left wing, hoping to shake it by the hail of their arrows and the weight of their charge, and immediately afterwards himself advanced with the Companions against the Indian left, intent upon making his assault while they were still reeling under the attack of the mounted archers and before their cavalry could change formation from column into mass.

The Indians meanwhile withdrew all the cavalry from other sections of their line, and moved it across to meet and counter Alexander's movement towards their flank, and it was not long before Coenus' men could be seen following, according to orders, close in their rear. The Indians were thereupon compelled to split their force into two; the larger section, containing the best troops, continued to proceed against Alexander, while the remainder wheeled about in order to deal with Coenus. This, of course, was disastrous not only to the effectiveness of the Indians' dispositions, but to their whole plan of battle. Alexander saw his chance; precisely at the moment when the enemy cavalry were changing direction, he attacked. The Indians did not even wait to receive his charge, but fell back in confusion upon the elephants, their impregnable fortress – or so they hoped. The elephant-drivers forced their beasts to meet the opposing cavalry, while the Macedonian infantry, in its turn, advanced against them, shooting down the drivers, and pouring in a hail of missiles from every side upon the elephants themselves. It was an odd bit of work – quite unlike any previous battle; the monster elephants plunged this way and that among the lines of infantry, dealing destruction in the solid mass of the Macedonian phalanx, while the Indian horsemen, seeing the infantry at one another's throats, wheeled to the assault of the Macedonian cavalry. Once again, however, the strength and experience of Alexander's mounted troops were too much for them, and they were forced back a second time on the elephants.

During the action all the Macedonian cavalry units had, by the exigencies of the fighting rather than deliberate orders, concentrated into a single body; and now its successive charges upon this sector or that inflicted heavy losses on the enemy. By this time the elephants were boxed up, with no room to manœuvre, by troops all round them, and as they blundered about, wheeling and shoving this way and that, they trampled to death as many of their friends as of their enemies. The result was that the Indian cavalry, jammed in around the elephants and with no more space to manœuvre than they had, suffered severely; most of the elephant-drivers had been shot; many of the animals had themselves been wounded, while others, riderless and bewildered, ceased altogether to play their expected part, and, maddened by pain and fear, set indiscriminately upon friend and foe, thrusting, trampling, and spreading death before them. The Macedonians could deal with these maddened creatures comfortably enough; having room to manœuvre, they were able to use their judgement, giving ground when they charged, and going for them with their javelins when they turned and lumbered back, whereas the unfortunate Indians, jammed up close among them as they attempted to get away, found them a more dangerous enemy even than the Macedonians.

In time the elephants tired and their charges grew feebler; they began to back away, slowly, like ships going astern, and with nothing worse than trumpetings. Taking his chance, Alexander surrounded the lot of them – elephants, horsemen, and all – and then signalled his infantry to lock shields and move up in a solid mass. Most of the Indian cavalry was cut down in the ensuing action; their infantry, too, hard pressed by the Macedonians, suffered terrible losses. The survivors, finding a gap in Alexander's ring of cavalry, all turned and fled. Craterus and the other officers who had been left on the bank of the river began to cross as soon as they saw Alexander's triumphant success, and their fresh troops, taking over the pursuit from Alexander's weary men, inflicted upon the vanquished Indians further losses no less severe.

Nearly 20,000 of the Indian infantry were killed in this battle, and about 3,000 of their cavalry. All their war-chariots were destroyed. Among the dead were two sons of Porus, Spitaces the local Indian governor, all the officers in command of the elephants and chariots, and all the cavalry officers and other commanders of high rank. The surviving elephants were captured. Out of Alexander's original 6,000 infantry, some eighty were killed; in addition to these he lost ten of the mounted archers, who were the first unit to engage, about twenty of the Companions, and 200 of the other cavalry.[32]

Throughout the action Porus had proved himself a man indeed, not only as a commander but as a soldier of the truest courage. When he saw his cavalry cut to pieces, most of his infantry dead, and his elephants killed or roaming riderless and bewildered about the field, his behaviour was very different from that of the Persian King Darius: unlike Darius, he did not lead the scramble to save his own skin, but so long as a single unit of his men held together, fought bravely on. It was only when he was himself wounded that he turned the elephant on which he rode and began to withdraw. The wound was in his right shoulder, the only unprotected part of his body; no missile, as he moved here and there in the thick of the fighting, could touch him anywhere else because of the corselet which he wore – a corselet exceedingly tough and closely fitting, as all who subsequently saw him could observe.

Alexander, anxious to save the life of this great and gallant soldier, sent Taxiles the Indian to him. Taxiles rode up as near as he dared and requested him to stop his elephant and hear what message Alexander sent him, as escape was no longer possible. But Taxiles was an old enemy of the Indian King, and Porus turned his elephant and drove at him, to kill him with his lance; and he might indeed have killed him, if he had not spurred his horse out of the way in the nick of time. Alexander, however, far from resenting this treatment of his messenger, sent a

32. Diodorus (17.89.1–3), the only other writer to mention casualties, gives over 12,000 Indians killed and 9,000 captured, and 280 cavalry and over 700 infantry killed on the Macedonian side.

number of others, the last of whom was an Indian named Meroes, a man he had been told had long been Porus' friend. Porus listened to Meroes' message, stopped his elephant, and dismounted; he was much distressed by thirst, so when he had revived himself by drinking, he told Meroes to conduct him with all speed to Alexander.

Alexander, informed of his approach, rode out to meet him, accompanied by a small party of his Companions. When they met, he reined in his horse, and looked at his adversary with admiration: he was a magnificent figure of a man, over seven feet high[33] and of great personal beauty; his bearing had lost none of its pride; his air was of one brave man meeting another, of a king in the presence of a king, with whom he had fought honourably for his kingdom.

Alexander was the first to speak. 'What,' he said, 'do you wish that I should do with you?'

'Treat me as a king ought,' Porus is said to have replied.

'For my part,' said Alexander, pleased by his answer, 'your request shall be granted. But is there not something you would wish for yourself? Ask it.'

'Everything,' said Porus, 'is contained in this one request.'

The dignity of these words gave Alexander even more pleasure, and he restored to Porus his sovereignty over his subjects, adding to his realm other territory of even greater extent.[34] Thus he did indeed use a brave man as a

33. Diodorus (17.88.4) agrees with Arrian that Porus was five cubits tall, i.e. seven feet six inches if the Attic cubit is meant. However, Tarn (*Alexander* 2.170) argues that the short Macedonian cubit of about 14 inches is meant. If so, Porus will have been about six feet tall.

34. cf. Diodorus 17.89.6; Curtius 8.14.45; Plutarch *Alexander* 60.15. Additions to his territory are mentioned on pp. 283, 286, 291, 299, and 302.

king ought, and from that time forward found him in every
way a loyal friend. Such was the result of the battle with
Porus and the Indians beyond the Hydaspes. It was fought
in the month of May, during the archonship of Hegemon
at Athens.[35]

Near the scene of the battle and the spot where he
crossed the Hydaspes, Alexander founded two cities; one
he called Nicaea, to commemorate his victory, the other
Bucephala, in memory of his horse Bucephalus, who died
in that country – not of hurts received in battle, but of old
age and exhaustion. He was about thirty and worn out.[36]
In former days he had shared with Alexander many a
danger and many a weary march. No one ever rode him
but his master, for he would never permit anyone else to
mount him. He was a big horse, high-spirited – a noble
creature; he was branded with the figure of an ox-head,
whence his name – though some have said that the name
came from a white mark on his head, shaped like the head
of an ox. This was the only bit of white on his body, all
the rest of him being black. In Uxia,[37] once, Alexander
lost him, and issued an edict that he would kill every man

35. 326 B.C. Diodorus (17.87.1) wrongly says that the battle was
fought in the archonship of Chremes, i.e. July 326–June 325; see
p. 268 n. 23.

36. Plutarch (*Alexander* 61) tells us that the majority of writers
maintained that Bucephalus died of wounds, but that Onesicritus
stated that he died of old age when he was 30.

We need not suppose that his age has been arbitrarily equated
with Alexander's or that Alexander cannot have 'broken' him until
he was sixteen. Bucephalus may well have lived to the age of 30,
and Alexander could have ridden him at the age of (say) seven or
eight. For a description of the 'breaking' of Bucephalus see Plutarch, *Alexander* 6.

37. i.e. between Susa and Persepolis. Plutarch (*Alexander* 44.3–4)
places the incident in Hyrcania, Diodorus (17.76.5) and Curtius
(6.5.18) among the Mardians, to the west of Hyrcania.

in the country unless he was brought back – as he promptly was. The story is evidence both of the fear which Alexander inspired and of his devotion to Bucephalus. But I
must say no more: what I have written in Bucephalus'
praise, I have written for Alexander's sake.

When the funeral rites for the men who fell in the battle
had been duly performed, Alexander offered the customary sacrifices in thanksgiving for victory and celebrated
games, with athletic and equestrian contests, at the place
of his first crossing of the Hydaspes.[38] Then, leaving
Craterus with part of the army to superintend the building and fortification of the newly founded settlements, he
proceeded against the Indians across the border of Porus'
kingdom. Aristobulus calls this tribe Glauganicae, Ptolemy Glausae – but never mind that; the name hardly matters. Alexander entered their territory with half of the
Companions, picked troops from each battalion of heavy
infantry, the archers, the Agrianes, and the whole contingent of the mounted archers. The natives surrendered
to a man. Some thirty-seven towns were taken, the smallest having not less than 5,000 inhabitants and many of
them more than double that; a large number of villages
hardly less populous also fell into Alexander's hands. All
this territory he handed over to Porus. He also brought
about a reconciliation between Porus and Taxiles, and
sent Taxiles back to his own people.

About this time Alexander was visited by a delegation
from Abisares offering the surrender of himself and his
territory, and this in spite of the fact that before the battle
on the Hydaspes his intention had been to join Porus.[39]
His own brother was now among the envoys, entrusted

38. Diodorus (17.89.6) mentions a halt of thirty days.
39. Arrian has earlier (p. 266) mentioned the arrival of envoys
from Abisares, the ruler of Kashmir.

with a gift of money and forty elephants for Alexander. The free Indians also sent a delegation, and yet another came from a chieftain who also bore the name Porus.[40] Alexander promptly sent for Abisares, adding a threat that, should he fail to appear, he would soon see the Macedonian army and its commander-in-chief in an unwelcome spot.

Meanwhile Phrataphernes, the satrap of Parthia and Hyrcania, arrived with Thracians left there under his command, and at about the same time a message came through from Sisicottus, the satrap of Assacenia, that the Greek governor had been assassinated, and the people had thrown off their allegiance to Alexander.[41] Alexander, accordingly, dispatched a force under the command of Philip and Tyriaspes to restore order in the province. He then marched for the river Acesines.

The Acesines is the only Indian river of which Ptolemy, son of Lagus, has mentioned the size. By his account, at the point where Alexander's men crossed it on boats and floats it is a little under two miles wide and very swift; it is fouled by large jagged rocks over which the water pours violently with much noise and commotion. The floats got over easily enough, but of the boats a number came to grief, being swept on to the rocks, where they were broken up and their occupants drowned. From this description it is reasonable to infer that other writers are pretty accurate when they give the average breadth of the Indus as five miles, contracting to two at the points where

40. Said by Strabo (15.1.30) to have been a nephew of Porus, the Paurava monarch.

41. As Nicanor had been appointed satrap of the territory west of the Indus (p. 249) and Sisicottus is last mentioned as commander of a fort near Aornus (p. 253), it is probable that Sisicottus was a subordinate of the murdered satrap, Nicanor.

it is narrowest and deepest. Indeed, two miles is its breadth over a good part of its course. I am inclined to think, moreover, that Alexander deliberately crossed the Acesines at its widest point, to take advantage of the slower current.[42]

After crossing he left Coenus with his own battalion to superintend the passage of the remainder of the troops who were to bring up the grain and other supplies from those parts of the country which were already in his hands. Porus was then sent back to his people with instructions to rejoin later with the pick of his troops and any elephants he happened to have. The other Porus – the one who had disgraced himself, and was reported to have fled his country – Alexander proposed to pursue with the most mobile units of his army. This second Porus, so long as there was hostility between Alexander and his nobler namesake, had sent Alexander repeated offers to surrender himself and his territory – not, indeed because he liked Alexander, but because he hated his namesake; then, learning that the latter had not only been released but had also been granted a large accession of new territory, he became alarmed, and fled his country with as many fighting men as he could persuade to share his fortunes. What frightened him was not Alexander so much as the threat to himself of his rival's increase in power.

Alexander's route in pursuit of him brought him first to the Hydraotes, a river as broad as the Acesines but not so swift. At all strategic points throughout the territory on the hither side of the Hydraotes he left troops, so that Craterus and Coenus in their foraging expeditions might be able to go pretty well anywhere without risk. He then

42. In the *Indica* (3.10) Arrian gives its breadth at the junction with the Indus at about four miles, but this is after it has been joined by the Hydaspes and the Hydraotes.

instructed Hephaestion to proceed with two battalions of
infantry, his own and Demetrius' cavalry regiment, and
half the contingent of archers to the territory of the rene-
gade Porus, which he was to hand over to the other Porus,
together with any independent Indian tribes he might find
on the Hydraotes; these, too, were to be taken over and
submitted to Porus' authority. These arrangements made,
he crossed the Hydraotes, which, unlike the Acesines,
caused him no trouble, and advanced along the further
bank. Most of the tribes in this region surrendered to him
without resistance, including a few who had begun by
offering a certain show of hostility; a few others tried
to elude him, but were caught and subdued by force of
arms.

It was reported to Alexander that a tribe of independent Indians known as Cathaei was, among certain others,
preparing resistance in the event of an invasion, and calling for the support of its neighbours. Sangala,[43] the town
where they were proposing to make their stand, was said
to be a strong one, and they themselves were reputed to
be excellent soldiers and brave men. The defiant attitude
of these people was shared by two other tribes, the Oxydracae and Malli. Not long before, Porus and Abisares
had undertaken an expedition against these people; they
had induced a number of other independent tribes to support the attempt, but even so they had achieved nothing –
nothing, at any rate, commensurate with the magnitude
of their preparations.

The effect of this report was to put Alexander on the
move against the Cathaei without an instant's delay. Two
days' march from the Hydraotes he reached a town named

43. Neither Sangala nor Pimprama (below) has been identified;
they were evidently situated in the Amritsar district. The Malli and
the Oxydracae lay further to the south.

Pimprama, belonging to a tribe known as the Adraistae. They offered no resistance. On the following day he rested his men, and then proceeded against Sangala. The Cathaei with the neighbouring tribes who had joined them had taken up a position on a hill in front of the town; the hill was less steep in some places than in others, and all round it they had put carts to form a triple defensive ring, within which they lay encamped.

Alexander modified his tactics to suit the circumstances. In view of the enemy's strength and the nature of his position, he immediately ordered forward the mounted archers with instructions to ride along the enemy's front, shooting at long range, to prevent a sortie before the rest of his troops were in position, and to cause as much damage as possible before they left their defensive position to engage in force. Meanwhile he brought Cleitus' mounted regiment and the special cavalry squadron round to the right wing of his army, with the Guards and Agrianes in close touch; and on the left posted Perdiccas' cavalry regiment and the battalions of heavy infantry. The archers were in two divisions, one on each wing. Before his dispositions were completed, the rear-guard, both horse and foot, arrived on the scene; the cavalry was used to strengthen the wings, and the additional infantry units to increase the solidity of the phalanx. This done, Alexander took control of the mounted troops on his right and advanced against the line of baggage-carts on the Indian left, where they were spaced out somewhat more widely and the conformation of the ground seemed to offer not too awkward an approach.

The cavalry threat did not draw the Indians out from their defences; they climbed on to the carts and met the advance with bows and arrows at long range. Alexander saw that cavalry in these circumstances would be

ineffective, so he promptly dismounted and in person led
his infantry to the assault. The enemy was driven without
difficulty from the first line of carts, but, falling back on
the second, they rallied and were better able to defend
themselves. Holding a smaller ring, they were consequently in closer order, and the Macedonians had no
longer the advantage of advancing over open ground; on
the contrary, they had to clear the outer ring of carts out
of their way and push through individually as best they
could, wherever there was room. They managed it, however, and once again the Indians were forced to withdraw.
This time they made no further stand; without attempting
to hold the third line of carts, they hurriedly retreated and
shut themselves up in the town.

Alexander did not press his offensive any more that day.
So far as he could with the number of infantry troops at
his disposal he surrounded the town, but the extent of its
defences was too great to allow a complete encirclement.
At one point there was a break in the defences, and in
front of this at no great distance was a lake; round this
lake Alexander took the precaution of posting his mounted men, as the water was evidently shallow, and he
guessed that the Indians, severely shaken as they were by
their previous defeat, would attempt to get out of the
town under cover of darkness. His guess proved right:
about the second watch most of them slipped out, and
fell into the arms of the cavalry patrols. Many were killed,
and the rest, realizing that there were enemy patrols all
round the lake, retired into the town again.

All round the town, except where the lake formed a
natural barrier, Alexander now erected a double stockade,
and saw to it that the lake itself was more efficiently
guarded. His intention had been to bring up siege-engines
to breach the town's defences, but he was informed by

deserters that the Indians had decided to make their escape
that very night: their purpose was to slip out by the lake,
where there was a break in the stockade. Accordingly he
ordered Ptolemy, son of Lagus, to take up his position at
that point with the three Guards' regiments, all the Agrianes, and a brigade of archers. Pointing to the place where
he guessed the enemy would make their attempt to get
through. 'The instant,' he said to Ptolemy, 'you see them
at it, stop them, and order the trumpeter to sound the
alarm. On this signal, the rest of you officers will take your
men promptly to the scene of action, wherever the trum-
pet calls you. And, mark you, I shall be there myself.'

Ptolemy collected all the carts he could out of those the
Indians had left behind after their initial repulse and sent
them across the line of the Indians' escape, to act as booby
traps in the darkness and confusion; he also gave orders
that the posts which had been cut for the stockade but not
yet erected should now be used to construct a barrier on
either side between the lake and the wall of the town. His
men completed the work, despite the fact that most of it
was done in darkness.

At approximately the fourth watch[44] the Indians, just
as Alexander's informants had said they would do, opened
the town gates which led to the lake and made their way
with all speed towards it. Ptolemy and his guards were
ready for them. At once the trumpeters sounded the
alarm, and Ptolemy led his men fully armed and in good
order against the enemy; their way of escape was already
blocked by the carts and the new section of palisade, and
when the trumpets sounded and they found Ptolemy's
troops on top of them, cutting down every man who managed to struggle through between the carts, they gave it

44. The Greeks divided the night into three watches, the Romans
into four. Arrian here writes as a Roman.

up and withdrew once more into the town, with a loss during their retreat of some 500.

By this time Porus had arrived with the rest of his elephants and 5,000 Indian troops. Alexander had had his siege-engines assembled and they were already being brought into position; but they proved unnecessary, for before a breach was made in the wall – which was of brick – the Macedonians undermined it, erected scaling-ladders at numerous points all round, and took the town by assault. Up to 17,000 Indians were killed in this operation and over 70,000 taken prisoner. Five hundred mounted men and 300 war chariots were also captured. Throughout the siege Alexander lost a little under 100 men; the number of wounded, however, was disproportionately large – over 1,200 – among them being Lysimachus, of Alexander's personal guard, and other officers.

After the burial of the dead with all customary ritual, Alexander sent his secretary, Eumenes,[45] with 300 mounted men to the two towns which had joined Sangala in refusing submission. His instructions were to report the capture of Sangala and to give the people an assurance that if they stayed where they were, and admitted Alexander as a friend within their gates, they would have nothing to complain of in their treatment – no more, indeed, than any of the other independent tribes which had voluntarily submitted to him. Both towns, however, had already had the news that Sangala had been taken by assault, and such was the consternation it caused that the

45. Eumenes, of Cardia in Thrace, had been Philip's secretary. After Alexander's death he obtained Cappadocia and Paphlagonia, and played a prominent part in the wars of the Successors until put to death by Antigonus in 316. Both Cornelius Nepos and Plutarch wrote biographies of him. This is the only time on the expedition when he is recorded to have commanded troops.

people had fled. Alexander pursued them hotly as soon as he knew that they were on the move, but, as the report took some time to reach him, most of them had had time to get clear away. A certain number of sick, perhaps 500, had been abandoned by their comrades in their dash for safety, and these were caught and killed. Alexander soon broke off the pursuit, returned to Sangala, and razed it to the ground. The land belonging to it he handed over to the Indian tribes who had given up their former independence and voluntarily attached themselves to his cause. Porus was then sent with his troops to the towns which had surrendered, with orders to garrison them, and Alexander himself marched for the river Hyphasis, bent upon still further conquest. So long as a single hostile element remained, there could, he felt, be no end to the war.

Reports had come in that the country beyond the Hyphasis was rich and productive; the people were good farmers and fine soldiers and lived under an orderly and efficient social system. The governments in that region were mostly aristocratic, but by no means oppressive. The elephants there were more numerous than elsewhere in India, and conspicuous both for size and courage. Such stories could not but whet Alexander's appetite for yet another adventure; but his men felt differently. The sight of their King undertaking an endless succession of dangerous and exhausting enterprises was beginning to depress them.[46] Their enthusiasm was ebbing; they held

46. Strabo (15.1.27) comments that they suffered most of all from the drenching rain. This had fallen incessantly since they left the Hydaspes: see Diodorus 17.94.3.

For the story of the mutiny see also Diodorus 17.93–5; Curtius 9.2.1–3.19 (with speeches by Alexander and Coenus); Plutarch, *Alexander* 62.

meetings in camp, at which even the best of them grumbled at their fate, while others swore that they would go no further, not even if Alexander himself led them. This state of affairs was brought to Alexander's notice, and before the alarm and despondency among the men could go still further, he called a meeting of his officers and addressed them in the following words:[47]

'I observe, gentlemen, that when I would lead you on a new venture you no longer follow me with your old spirit. I have asked you to meet me that we may come to a decision together: are we, upon my advice, to go forward, or, upon yours, to turn back?

'If you have any complaint to make about the results of your efforts hitherto, or about myself as your commander, there is no more to say. But let me remind you: through your courage and endurance you have gained possession of Ionia, the Hellespont, both Phrygias, Cappadocia, Paphlagonia, Lydia, Caria, Lycia, Pamphylia, Phoenicia, and Egypt; the Greek part of Libya is now yours, together with much of Arabia, lowland Syria, Mesopotamia, Babylon, and Susia; Persia and Media with all the territories either formerly controlled by them or not are in your hands; you have made yourselves masters of the lands beyond the Caspian Gates, beyond the Caucasus, beyond the Tanais, of Bactria, Hyrcania, and the Hyrcanian sea; we have driven the Scythians back into the desert; and Indus and Hydaspes, Acesines and Hydraotes

47. Tarn (*Alexander* 2.287 ff.) considers Alexander's speech a late patchwork, since it cannot be separated from Coenus' reply and Coenus, he holds, had been left behind on the Acesines (see p. 285), where he later died. But Coenus was to arrange for the forwarding of supplies and, like Porus (p. 290), he doubtless rejoined Alexander. He died on the Hydaspes (see p. 302 below). Nevertheless the speech contains statements whose genuineness seems doubtful; see Tarn.

flow now through country which is ours. With all that accomplished, why do you hesitate to extend the power of Macedon – *your* power – to the Hyphasis and the tribes on the other side? Are you afraid that a few natives who may still be left will offer opposition? Come, come! These natives either surrender without a blow or are caught on the run – or leave their country undefended for your taking; and when we take it, we make a present of it to those who have joined us of their own free will and fight at our side.

'For a man who *is* a man, work, in my belief, if it is directed to noble ends, has no object beyond itself; none the less, if any of you wish to know what limit may be set to this particular camapaign, let me tell you that the area of country still ahead of us, from here to the Ganges and the Eastern ocean, is comparatively small.[48] You will undoubtedly find that this ocean is connected with the Hyrcanian Sea, for the great Stream of Ocean encircles the earth. Moreover I shall prove to you, my friends, that the Indian and Persian Gulfs and the Hyrcanian Sea are all three connected and continuous.[49] Our ships will sail round from the Persian Gulf to Libya as far as the Pillars of Hercules, whence all Libya to the eastward will soon be ours, and all Asia too, and to this empire there will be no boundaries but what God Himself has made for the whole world.[50]

48. That Alexander knew of the Ganges is likely enough, but it may be doubted whether he still thought of the Eastern Ocean as near, as Aristotle may have taught him. Nearchus, at any rate, writes that the journey through the plains of India took four months (Strabo 15.1.12).

49. The view that the Hyrcanian (Caspian) sea was a gulf is not Alexander's but Eratosthenes' (and Arrian's) geography; see p. 262 n. 14.

50. For this unlikely proposal see p. 348.

'But if you turn back now, there will remain uncon-
quered many warlike peoples between the Hyphasis and
the Eastern Ocean, and many more to the northward and
the Hyrcanian Sea, with the Scythians, too, not far away;
so that if we withdraw now there is a danger that the
territory which we do not yet securely hold may be stirred
to revolt by some nation or other we have not yet forced
into submission. Should that happen, all that we have
done and suffered will have proved fruitless – or we shall
be faced with the task of doing it over again from the
beginning. Gentlemen of Macedon, and you, my friends
and allies, this must not be. Stand firm; for well you know
that hardship and danger are the price of glory, and that
sweet is the savour of a life of courage and of deathless
renown beyond the grave.

'Are you not aware that if Heracles, my ancestor, had
gone no further than Tiryns or Argos – or even than the
Peloponnese or Thebes – he could never have won the
glory which changed him from a man into a god, actual
or apparent? Even Dionysus, who is a god indeed, in a
sense beyond what is applicable to Heracles, faced not a
few laborious tasks; yet we have done more: we have
passed beyond Nysa and we have taken the rock of Aornos which Heracles himself could not take. Come, then;
add the rest of Asia to what you already possess – a small
addition to the great sum of your conquests. What great
or noble work could we ourselves have achieved had we
thought it enough, living at ease in Macedon, merely to
guard our homes, accepting no burden beyond checking
the encroachment of the Thracians on our borders, or the
Illyrians and Triballians, or perhaps such Greeks as might
prove a menace to our comfort?

'I could not have blamed you for being the first to lose
heart if I, your commander, had not shared in your ex-

hausting marches and your perilous campaigns; it would
have been natural enough if you had done all the work
merely for others to reap the reward. But it is not so. You
and I, gentlemen, have shared the labour and shared the
danger, and the rewards are for us all. The conquered
territory belongs to you ; from your ranks the governors
of it are chosen; already the greater part of its treasure
passes into your hands, and when all Asia is overrun, then
indeed I will go further than the mere satisfaction of your
ambitions: the utmost hopes of riches or power which
each one of you cherishes will be far surpassed, and whoever wishes to return home will be allowed to go, either
with me or without me. I will make those who stay the
envy of those who return.'[51]

When Alexander ended, there was a long silence. The
officers present were not willing to accept what he had
said, yet no one liked to risk an unprepared reply. Several
times Alexander invited comment, should any wish to
give it and genuinely hold different views from those he
had expressed; but in spite of his invitation nothing was
said, until at last Coenus, son of Polemocrates, plucked
up his courage to speak.

'Sir,' he said, 'we appreciate the fact that you do not
demand from us unreasoning obedience. You have made
it clear to us that you will lead us on only after winning
our consent, and, failing that, that you will not use compulsion. This being so, I do not propose to speak on behalf of the officers here assembled, as we, by virtue of our
rank and authority, have already received the rewards of
our services and are naturally concerned more than the
men are to further your interests. I shall speak, therefore,
for the common soldiers, not, by any means, with the
purpose of echoing their sentiments, but saying what I

51. cf. Xenophon, *Anabasis* 1.7.4.

believe will tend to your present advantage and our future security. My age, the repute which, by your favour, I enjoy among my comrades, and the unhesitating courage I have hitherto displayed in all dangers and difficulties give me the right to declare what I believe to be the soundest policy. Very well, then: precisely in proportion to the number and magnitude of the achievements wrought by you, our leader, and by the men who marched from home under your command, I judge it best to set some limit to further enterprise. You know the number of Greeks and Macedonians who started upon this campaign, and you can see how many of us are left today: the Thessalians you sent home from Bactra because you knew their hearts were no longer in their work[52] – and it was wisely done; other Greeks have been settled in the new towns you have founded, where they remain not always willingly,[53] others, again, together with our own Macedonians, continue to share with you the dangers and hardships of war, and of these some have been killed, some, disabled by wounds, have been left behind in various parts of Asia, and more still have died of sickness, so that only a few from that great army are left, a small remnant broken in health, their old vigour and determination gone. Every man of them longs to see his parents again, if they yet survive, or his wife, or his children; all are yearning for the familiar earth of home, hoping, pardonably enough, to live to revisit it, no longer in poverty and obscurity, but famous and en-

52. The Thessalians were said (p. 180) to have been sent home from Ecbatana, and we should probably read 'Ecbatana' here instead of 'Bactra'.

53. Early in 325, when the rumour reached Bactria that Alexander had been killed among the Malli, 3,000 mercenaries rose in revolt and eventually made their way back to Greece (Curtius 9.7.1–11). Soon after Alexander's death a much greater mercenary revolt broke out in Bactria (Diodorus 18.4.8; 7.1–9).

riched by the treasure you have enabled them to win. Do not try to lead men who are unwilling to follow you; if their heart is not in it, you will never find the old spirit or the old courage. Consent rather yourself to return to your mother and your home. Once there, you may bring good government to Greece and enter your ancestral house with all the glory of the many great victories won in this campaign, and then, should you so desire it, you may begin again and undertake a new expedition against these Indians of the East – or, if you prefer, to the Black Sea or to Carthage and the Libyan territories beyond. It is for you to decide. Other troops, Greek and Macedonian, will follow you – young, fresh troops to take the place of your war-weary veterans. Still ignorant of the horrors of war and full of hope for what the future may bring, these men will follow you with all the more eagerness in that they have seen your old campaigners come safely home again no longer poor and nameless but loaded with money and fame. Sir, if there is one thing above all others a successful man should know, it is *when to stop*. Assuredly for a commander like yourself, with an army like ours, there is nothing to fear from any enemy; but luck, remember, is an unpredictable thing, and against what it may bring no man has any defence.'

Coenus' words were greeted with applause. Some even wept, which was proof enough of their reluctance to prolong the campaign and of how happy they would be should the order be given to turn back. Alexander resented the freedom with which Coenus had spoken and the poor spirit shown by the other officers, and dismissed the conference. Next day he summoned the same officers to his presence and angrily declared that, though he would put pressure on no Macedonian to accompany him, he himself was resolved to go on.

'I shall have others,' he cried, 'who will need no compulsion to follow their King. If you wish to go home, you are at liberty to do so – and you may tell your people there that you deserted your King in the midst of his enemies.'

Thereupon he withdrew to his tent, and for the rest of that day, and for two days following, refused to allow anyone to see him, even his Companions; his hope was that the various commanders, both of his Macedonian and allied contingents, might change their minds and become readier to listen to him – for, after all, in a crowd of soldiers such sudden reversals of feeling are common enough. The silence, however, remained absolute and unbroken; the men were angry at Alexander's burst of temper and determined not to let it influence them. But in spite of their obvious hostility Alexander (according to Ptolemy's account of the incident) none the less offered sacrifice in the hope of favourable omens for the crossing. When, however, the omens proved to be against him, he at last submitted, and, having sent for the most senior officers of his Companions and those who were his own closest friends, made a public announcement that, as all circumstances combined to dissuade him from a further advance, he had decided upon withdrawal.

One can imagine the shouts of joy which rose from the throats of that heterogeneous host. Most of them wept. They came to Alexander's tent and called down every blessing upon him for allowing them to prevail – the only defeat he had ever suffered.

The decision made, Alexander divided his men into companies and ordered the construction of twelve altars, as high as the loftiest siege-towers and even broader in proportion, as a thank-offering to the gods who had brought him so far in his victorious progress, and as a

memorial of all he had so laboriously achieved.[54] The
altars were duly raised, and he offered sacrifice upon them
as his custom was, and held games with contests for both
horse and man. The territory as far as the river Hyphasis
he added to Porus' dominions, and then began his own
withdrawal towards the Hydraotes. Crossing this river,
he retraced his steps to the Acesines, where he found already complete the settlement which Hephaestion had
been instructed to build and fortify.[55] Here he settled
volunteers from the neighbouring Indian tribes and those
of his mercenary troops who were disabled by wounds or
sickness, and then began his preparations for the voyage
down-river to the Indian Ocean.

Meanwhile Arsaces, governor of the territory which
bordered on that of Abisares, presented himself. He was
accompanied by Abisares' brother and other relatives,
and brought presents for Alexander of the kind most
esteemed by the Indians, together with thirty of Abisares'
elephants. Abisares himself, he reported, was too ill to
come in person.[56] At the same time Alexander's envoys to
Abisares also presented themselves. Alexander readily
believed that the facts were as stated, and allowed Abisares
to continue to govern his own province, with Arsaces
attached to the administration. He assessed the amount of

54. Diodorus (17.95.1) and Curtius (9.3.19) confirm the erection
of twelve altars to the twelve Olympians. According to Diodorus
they were 75 ft high. No trace of them has been found, but as the
course of the Indian rivers has changed greatly since Alexander's
day this is not surprising.

Diodorus, Curtius and Plutarch (*Alexander* 62) all add that
Alexander gave orders for the construction of beds for his troops
and stalls for their horses larger than normal in order to impress
posterity.

55. Not previously mentioned.

56. For the order to Abisares to report to Alexander see p. 284.

tribute they should pay, and again offered sacrifice; then, having crossed the Acesines, he marched to the Hydaspes, where he made good the damage done by heavy rains to the two settlements of Nicaea and Bucephala, and saw to any other matters which required attention in that part of the country.

BOOK SIX

On the Hydaspes, Alexander's preparations were now complete. The various craft for the passage included a number of galleys, some of thirty oars, some smaller, barges for horse transport, and other craft likely to be of service in moving an army by river. The decision was accordingly made to begin the voyage down the Hydaspes to the Indian Ocean.

Alexander fancied at this time that he had discovered the source of the Nile, his reasons being that he had, on a previous occasion, seen crocodiles in the Indus, and in no other river except the Nile, and had also observed a kind of bean like the Egyptian bean growing on the banks of the Acesines, which, he was told, flowed into the Indus. His notion was that the Nile (under the name of Indus) rose somewhere in that part of India and then flowed through a vast desert tract, where it lost its original name and received that of Nile from the Ethiopians and Egyptians at the point where it began to flow through inhabited country again, ultimately debouching into the Mediterranean. Homer, he remembered, called it Aegyptus, after the country through which it ran.[1]

Indeed, in a letter to Olympias on the subject of India, Alexander made a special point of mentioning his belief that he had found the source of the Nile, though in actual fact he based this important conclusion upon the slenderest evidence. Later he went more thoroughly into the question of the geography of the Indus, and learned from the natives that the Hydaspes ceases to be so named at its

1. See p. 264 n. 18.

junction with the Acesines, just as the latter does at its junction with the Indus, which, in its turn, flows out by two channels into the Indian Ocean, and has no connexion with Egypt whatever. This information led him to cut out the passage about the Nile from his letter to his mother.[2] He then gave orders for the preparation of the fleet for the proposed voyage down the rivers to the Ocean. The crews of the various craft were drawn from the Phoenicians, Cyprians, Carians, and Egyptians serving in the forces.

It was at this time that Coenus fell sick and died. He was one of his most loyal and trusted Companions, and so far as circumstances permitted Alexander gave him a splendid funeral.[3] He then summoned to his presence his Companions and such Indian envoys as happened to be present to pay their respects, and proclaimed Porus monarch of all the Indian territory he had by that time conquered. This included seven nations and a grand total of over 2,000 towns.

The army for the coming expedition was organized in three divisions:[4] all the Guards, the archers, the Agrianes, and the picked cavalry squadron were embarked in the transports under Alexander's personal command; Craterus was instructed to march a part of the infantry and cavalry along the right bank of the Hydaspes, while the bulk of the best fighting troops, together with the ele-

2. Historians generally accept this letter as genuine, but it is difficult to know who would have had knowledge of this deletion.

3. Curtius (9.3.20) places his death on the Acesines, but as he and Diodorus wrongly think of Alexander returning to this river to find his fleet ready, there is no reason to doubt Arrian. On Coenus see Badian, *JHS* 1961, 20ff., although we need not suppose that Coenus' death was other than natural.

4. According to Nearchus (Arrian, *Indica* 19.5) this amounted to 120,000 fighting men including 'barbarians'.

phants, now about 200 in number, were to proceed along
the left bank under the command of Hephaestion. These
officers had orders to march with all speed for the palace
of Sopeithes.[5] Philip, governor of the territory on the
west, or Bactrian, side of the Indus, was to wait three days
and then follow with his troops. The mounted troops
from Nysa were sent home. Nearchus was appointed
Admiral of the fleet, and the helmsman of Alexander's
own vessel was Onesicritus, the man who wrote a memoir
about Alexander full of lies – among them the statement
that he was an admiral. However, he wasn't: he was just a
helmsman.[6] According to Ptolemy, son of Lagus, my
principal authority, the river fleet consisted of eighty
thirty-oared galleys, while the total number of boats, of
all sorts, including horse-transports, light galleys, and
other river craft, some already in service, others specially
built for the occasion, was not far short of 2,000.[7]

The final preparations made, the embarkation began at
dawn, and Alexander offered his customary sacrifice, not
omitting a special offering to the river Hydaspes according to the soothsayers' instructions. Stepping aboard, he
stood in the bows of his vessel and from a golden bowl
poured a libation into the water, solemnly invoking the
river and joining with its name the name of Acesines,
which he now knew to be the greatest of its tributaries,
with the meeting of the waters not far away, and, finally,

5. Its location is unknown. Diodorus (17.91.4) and Curtius (9.1.
24) wrongly place Sopeithes' kingdom east of the Cathaeans, between the rivers Hydraotes and Hyphasis. cf. Strabo 15.1.30.

6. cf. Arrian, *Indica* 18.9–10. Strabo (15.1.28) remarks that Onesicritus deserved to be called the chief pilot of marvels rather than of
Alexander, and that he surpassed all Alexander's followers in the
telling of monstrosities.

7. In the *Indica* Arrian gives a total of 800 ships, evidently Nearchus' figure. Diodorus and Curtius have 1,000.

calling upon the Indus too, into which both Acesines and
Hydaspes run. Then, after a libation to Heracles his ancestor and to Ammon and the other gods it was his custom
to honour,[8] he ordered the trumpets to sound the signal
for departure, and the whole fleet, each vessel in her
proper station, began to move down-river. To avoid the
danger of running foul of each other, all craft – carriers,
horse-transports, and warships – had instructions to keep
their exact distances, the faster vessels being ordered to
check their speed so as not to break formation. One may
imagine the noise of this great fleet getting away under
oars all together: it was like nothing ever heard before,
what with the coxswains calling the *in . . . out: in . . . out*
for every stroke and the rowers' triumphant cries as, like
one man, they flung themselves upon the swirling water.
The lofty banks, often towering above the ships, caught
the clamour, and held it and intensified it, tossing it to and
fro across the stream, echoing and re-echoing, while silent
and deserted glens on one side or other of the river rever-
berated with the din and helped to swell it. The natives
(who had no tradition that Dionysus' expedition to India
had been by water) had never before seen horses on ship-
board, and the sight of them crowding the barges filled
them with such amazement that all who witnessed the
departure of the fleet followed it along the banks for
miles, and other friendly tribesmen who were near enough
to hear the cries of the rowers and the dash and clatter of
the oars came running to the river-bank and joined in the

8. Nearchus (*Indica* 18.11) says that Alexander sacrificed to his
ancestral gods, to those to whom the seers instructed him to sacrifice, to Poseidon, Amphitrite, the Nereids, and the Ocean, as well
as to the three rivers.

According to Aristobulus (Strabo 15.1.17), Alexander set out
'a few days before the setting of the Pleiads', i.e. at the beginning
of November 326.

procession, singing their barbaric songs, For the Indians, be it said, are an extremely musical race and have loved dancing ever since the days when Dionysus came with his wild revellers to their country.[9]

On the third day the fleet brought up at the spot where Hephaestion and Craterus had been ordered to halt their forces, one on each side of the river. Alexander waited there two days, and when Philip joined him with the rest of the troops, he sent him to the Acesines with orders to proceed with his men along its banks. Craterus and Hephaestion were also ordered on again, with careful instructions on the route they were to follow. Then the descent of the Hydaspes was resumed, and was found to be nowhere less than two and a half miles wide. In the course of the voyage Alexander put in, when opportunity offered, to the river-bank, to deal with the natives of the vicinity. Some surrendered voluntarily; others, who offered resistance, he subdued.

He was, however, anxious to hurry on to the territory of the Mallians and Oxydracae. Information had reached him that these people were the most numerous and warlike of the Indians in that part of the country,[10] and it was further reported that they had shut up their women and children in their most strongly fortified towns with the intention of making a stand against him. Accordingly he made all possible speed, in order to get at them before they were ready to receive him, and while their preparations were still inadequate and incomplete.

Getting under way again, on the fifth day he reached

9. cf. *Indica* 7.8–9.

10. According to Curtius, they could put into the field 90,000 infantry, 10,000 cavalry, and 900 chariots. Diodorus says 80,000, 10,000 and 700 respectively. Arrian (p. 311) mentions 50,000 Mallians.

the junction of the Hydaspes and the Acesines. At the
place where the two streams unite, the river is very narrow, and the current, in consequence, extremely rapid;
the surface is roughened and broken, there are dangerous
eddies and whirlpools, and the roaring of the water can
be heard for many miles. Alexander had been forewarned
of these conditions by the natives, and he had told his
men what to expect; none the less, when the flotilla
approached the junction, the water made such an appalling shindy that the men at the oars stopped rowing in
sheer panic, and the coxswains, dumb with astonishment,
ceased to call the time. Presently, however, just above the
actual point of meeting, the men at the helm of the various
craft shouted orders to the rowers to put their backs into
it and drive through the narrows with all speed, in the
hope that if they kept good way on they might prevent
their vessels from being spun round by the swirling
eddies. The barges and short, beamier craft were, indeed,
spun about like tops, but, apart from the anxiety of their
crews, came to no harm, as the current swept them, stern-
first or broadside-on, in a direct line through the narrows;
the warships, on the contrary, got off by no means so
lightly: their inferior buoyancy made it harder for them to
cope with the hubbub and those with two banks of oars
had great difficulty in keeping the lower tier clear of the
water. Some, unable to keep sufficient way on to shoot the
rapids successfully, were badly caught and got their oars
broken off as they came broadside on to the eddies, and
many other craft were in distress, two of them running
foul of one another and sinking with the loss of many
lives. At last, when the narrows were passed, the stream
slackened and the swirls and eddies were much less violent, so that Alexander was able to land his men on the
right bank of the river just below a headland where the

force of the current was not felt and the ships could be beached and floating wreckage collected, together with any survivors who might still be clinging to it.[11] These were accordingly brought to safety and the damaged vessels repaired, after which Nearchus was ordered to continue down-stream as far as the territory of the Mallians, while Alexander himself carried out a rapid raid against the natives who had not submitted to him, and thus prevented them from bringing help to the Mallians. That done, he returned to the flotilla.

At this point he was rejoined by Hephaestion, Craterus, and Philip. Sending the elephants, Polysperchon's battalion, the mounted archers, and Philip's contingent over to the other side of the river, he put them under Craterus' command and at the same time instructed Nearchus to proceed down the river, keeping three days' march ahead of the army, which he then split into three divisions: Hephaestion was ordered to march five days in advance, with the object of intercepting and capturing any native troops which, in their attempt to escape Alexander's own contingent, might be moving rapidly forward; Ptolemy, son of Lagus, with another division, had orders to wait three days and then follow, in order to be in a position to catch any of the enemy who, to avoid Alexander, turned back upon their tracks. Further instructions were that, on reaching the junction of the Acesines and Hydraotes, the leading division was to wait till Alexander should himself arrive and Craterus and Ptolemy join up with him.

Under his personal command Alexander took the Guards, archers, Agrianes, Peitho's battalion of heavy infantry, all the mounted archers, and half of the Companions. With these troops he marched for the territory

11. Diodorus (17.97.2) compares the episode with Achilles' fight with the river Scamander (*Iliad* 21.228ff.)

of the Mallians, a branch of the independent Indians. His
route lay over almost waterless country,[12] but in the
course of the first day's march he halted by a pond about
a dozen miles from the Acesines; there, after a meal and a
brief rest for the men, he ordered every available recep-
tacle to be filled with water before proceeding, when,
having covered fifty miles during the remainder of the day
and the whole of the following night, he reached a town
where many of the Mallians had taken refuge. The last
thing they expected was that Alexander would come by
way of this waterless region, and most of them were, in
consequence, unarmed and outside the defences of their
walls. Obviously this was the very reason why Alexander
had chosen this route: it was a difficult one, and the enemy
never thought it possible that he would choose it. He took
them completely by surprise, and most of them, unarmed
as they were, offered no resistance and were killed. Some
shut themselves up in the town, whereupon Alexander,
whose infantry had not yet arrived upon the scene,
blocked them up there by throwing a cordon of mounted
troops round the walls. As soon as the infantry joined
him, he dispatched Perdiccas with his own and Cleitus'
cavalry regiments and the Agrianes to another Mallian
town at which large numbers of the Indians had concentrated, and ordered him not to attack till he himself should
arrive, but to keep his eyes open to prevent anyone from
slipping out of the town and informing the other natives
that he was already on the way.

He then launched his own attack. The Indians, who had
already lost a great many men either killed or wounded in
the first surprise attack, abandoned their outer defences,
which they had no hope of holding, and took refuge within their inner fortifications, where, as the position was a

12. The Sandar-Bar desert.

commanding one and difficult to assault, they managed for
a time to hold out; but the strong pressure exerted on
every side by the Macedonians and the ubiquitous pressure of Alexander in the thick of the fighting soon proved
too much for them. The inner fortress was stormed
and all its defenders, about 2,000 in number, were
killed.

Perdiccas, meanwhile, had reached his objective. He
found the town deserted, and learning that it was not long
since the inhabitants had fled, he rode with all speed in
pursuit of them, his light infantry following at the best
pace they could make. Some of the fugitives managed to
escape into the marshes; the rest were overtaken and
killed.

After his meal and a rest for his men, Alexander set
forward again at about the first watch. He covered many
miles in the course of the night, and at daybreak reached
the Hydraotes, where he learned that most of the Mallians
had already crossed to the other side; some were still on
their way over, and many of these he caught and destroyed
– indeed, without a moment's hesitation he went over the
river among them and then continued to press his pursuit
of those who had got away ahead of him. Many of these
too he caught and killed, and took a number of prisoners;
but the majority of them succeeded in making their escape
to a strongly fortified position. Against these, as soon as
the infantry rejoined him, he sent Peitho with his own
battalion and two regiments of cavalry. The attack was
successful; they captured the position and reduced to the
status of slaves every man who survived the assault. After
this exploit Peitho and his troops rejoined the main body
of the army.

A report had reached Alexander that a Mallian force
was preparing to defend itself in one of the Brahmin

towns and he was now on his way thither.[13] On reaching
it, he stationed his infantry in a ring round the outer defences and moved up in close formation. The defenders
soon saw that their walls were being sapped, and this,
together with the weight of the enemy missiles, induced
them (as in Alexander's previous operation) to abandon
their position and take refuge in their inner stronghold;
here they continued to resist, and not without some success, for they turned and fell upon a small party of Macedonians who had forced their way in with them, driving
some of them out again and killing about twenty-five
before they could get away.

Alexander meanwhile brought the scaling-ladders into
position all round the inner stronghold and ordered sapping operations to begin. A tower soon fell and the collapse of a section of the wall laid the fortress open to
assault, whereupon Alexander, ahead of his men, was up
in the moment, and stood there alone, a conspicuous
figure, holding the breach. The sight of him struck shame
into his troops, so up they went after him in scattered
groups, some here, some there. Soon the fortress was in
their hands. Some of the Indians set fire to their houses or
were caught in them and killed; most died fighting. In all
they lost about 5,000 men; they had fought too well for
more than a handful to be taken alive.

After waiting there a day to rest his troops Alexander
began his advance against the remaining Mallian forces.
He found their settlements deserted and gathered by report that they had all fled into uninhabited country; accordingly, after another day's rest for his men, he sent

13. Fuller points out that these 'towns' probably resembled
many present-day Indian villages – 'conglomerations of mud-huts,
the circumference of which formed a protective wall of no great
height or thickness'.

Peitho and Demetrius, the cavalry officer, back to the
river with the troops already under their command together with some companies of light infantry sufficient
for the task in hand: this was, to march along the river
and keep a look out for any of the enemy who might have
fled to the woods there (they were very extensive along
the river-bank) and to kill all of them who refused to give
themselves up. They did, in fact, catch and kill a great
many of them.

Alexander's own next objective was the principal town
of the Mallian people. It had been reported to him that
many of the Mallians had left their own settlements and
joined their kinsmen there; nevertheless, on the news of
Alexander's approach, this town, too, was abandoned,
and the Indians, having crossed the Hydraotes, took up a
strong position on the high ground of the opposite bank,
evidently intending to prevent Alexander from coming
over. Learning of this movement, Alexander at once
advanced with all his available cavalry to the point on the
Hydraotes where the Mallians had massed, and gave
orders for the infantry to follow. Reaching the river and
observing the enemy in position on the further bank,
though he still had only the cavalry with him, he plunged,
without even waiting to reform after his march, into the
ford. When he was halfway over, the enemy withdrew
from the river-bank rapidly but in good order. Alexander
followed them up, and as soon as they realized that he had
only mounted troops with no infantry in support, they
checked their withdrawal, turned, and offered a vigorous
resistance. Their force was some 50,000 strong. Alexander's infantry had not yet joined him; accordingly, as
the Indians were massed in close formation, he held off
for the time being, keeping his cavalry continually
manœuvring and making an occasional probe; presently,

however, the Agrianes arrived on the scene together with
the archers and some picked units of light infantry which
were serving under his personal command, while at the
same time the heavy infantry was already visible at no
great distance. Faced by these simultaneous threats the
Indians broke and hurriedly withdrew to the shelter of
one of the neighbouring settlements which was strongly
fortified. Alexander followed close on their heels, inflict-
ing a number of casualties, and when the fugitives had
shut themselves up inside the defences of the town, he
promptly ordered his cavalry to draw a cordon round it;
then, when his infantry joined him, he took up a position
completely encircling the outer defences, and suspended
operations for the day. There were two reasons for the
pause: insufficient daylight left for an immediate attack,
and the fact that all his men were pretty well exhausted –
the infantry by their long march, the mounted troops by
their protracted pursuit, and both not least by their crossing of the river.

Next day when the attack began, with Alexander himself in command of one division of the army and Perdiccas
of the other, the Indians did not hold their positions on
the outer defences to receive the Macedonian onset, but
withdrew their entire force to the inner fortress of the
town. Alexander and his men by wrenching a gate from
its hinges penetrated into the town far in advance of the
troops under Perdiccas, who had met trouble in trying to
get over the wall and were, in consequence, slow off the
mark; most of them, moreover, carried no ladders, as the
sight of the wall bare of defenders led them to believe that
the town was already taken. But they soon realized their
mistake, and seeing that the enemy held the inner fortress,
with large numbers of men posted in front of it bent upon
its defence, they at once began sapping operations and got

scaling-ladders into position wherever they could, in an attempt to force their way in. The men with the ladders were not quick enough to satisfy Alexander; in his impatience he snatched one from the fellow who carried it and with his own hands reared it against the fortress wall; then, crouched under his shield, up he went. Peucestas followed him with the 'sacred shield' – the shield from the temple of Athene at Troy, which Alexander kept by him and had carried before him in battle.[14] Peucestas was followed by Leonnatus, an officer of the Guard; then Abreas, one of the picked soldiers on double pay, mounted by a second ladder.

The King had now reached the top. Laying his shield on the coping of the wall, he forced some of the defenders back into the fortress, cut down others with his sword, till he stood there on the battlements alone, not one of the enemy within his reach. The sight of him filled the men of the Guards with terror for his safety; scrambling for precedence, they made a dash for the ladders, but under the excessive load they broke and hurled the climbers to the ground. The rest were helpless.

No Indian ventured to approach Alexander as he stood on the fortress wall; but he was the target of every marksman in the neighbouring towers; men in the town shot at him too – and from no great distance either, as raised ground near the fortress wall brought them within closer range. That it was indeed Alexander who stood there was plain to all: his almost legendary courage no less than his shining armour proclaimed him.

Suddenly a thought crossed his mind: by staying where he was he might well be killed with nothing accomplished; but if he leapt down into the fortress, he might by that very act spread consternation among the enemy, or at

14. See p. 66.

least, if it was his fate to die, death would come not without a struggle and as the crown of an exploit which would
live upon the lips of men. To think was to act: without
further hesitation he made his leap.

Once inside the fortress, he put his back to the wall and
made ready to fight. A party of Indians came at him, and
he cut them down; their commander rushed forward, all
too rashly, and he, too, fell. First one, then a second, who
tried to approach him he stopped with a well-aimed stone.
Others pressed within striking distance, and fell victims
to his sword. After that none ventured again to attack
him hand to hand; keeping their distance, they formed a
half-circle round where he stood and hurled at him whatever missiles they had or could find.

By this time Peucestas, Abreas, and Leonnatus, the only
men who succeeded in scaling the wall before the ladders
collapsed, had got inside the fortress and were fighting in
defence of their King. Abreas was shot in the face and
killed and Alexander himself was hit, the arrow penetrat-
ing his corselet and entering his body above the breast.
Ptolemy tells us that the blood from the wound was mixed
with air breathed out from the pierced lung. Despite the
pain he continued to defend himself so long as the blood
was warm; but there was soon a violent haemorrhage, as
was to be expected with a pierced lung, and overcome by
giddiness and faintness he fell forward over his shield.
Peucestas stood astride of his body holding up before him
the sacred shield from Troy, and Leonnatus took his stand
on the other side, both men being now the target for the
enemy missiles, while Alexander himself was almost un-
conscious from loss of blood.

The Macedonian assault upon the fortress was by now
thoroughly out of hand; the men had seen Alexander as
he stood on the battlements, the mark of the enemy's

missiles; they had seen him leap down on the other side; and now, afraid lest his rash act should be the end of him and eager to bring help in time, they made a rush for the fortress wall. The ladders were smashed and useless, but, on the spur of the moment, they used whatever means they could to get up and over: some drove stakes into the clay of the wall and dragged themselves slowly and laboriously up; others struggled up by standing on their comrades' shoulders. Each man as he got to the top flung himself down on the further side into the fortress. There they saw the King on the ground, and a cry of grief and a shout of rage rose from every throat. Soon a fierce battle was raging, one man after another holding his shield over Alexander's prostrate body, until at last the troops outside had smashed the bolt of the gate in the curtain-wall and were beginning to come in, a few at a time. Others then got their shoulders to the half-opened gate, forced it inwards, and so laid the fortress open.

Now the slaughter began; neither women nor children were spared. A party of men carried away the King on his shield; his condition was critical and no one, at this time, thought he could live. Some writers have stated that the arrow which hit him was cut out by Critodemus, a doctor from the island of Cos, of the family of Asclepius; others that Perdiccas, of the King's Guard, cut it out with his sword at Alexander's request, no doctor being at hand in this emergency. There was a rush of blood as the arrow was drawn out, and Alexander fainted again, thus checking the haemorrhage. All sorts of other stories about this grave incident have been put on record, most of them false, and tradition has taken them over in their original form and still preserves them; and doubtless it will continue to pass them on to future generations, unless a stop is put to it by the account I give in this book.

In the first place, it is universally supposed that it was among the Oxydracae that Alexander received his almost fatal wound:[15] but it was not – it was in the territory of the Mallians, an independent Indian tribe. The town was a Mallian town, and it was the Mallians who shot Alexander. They had, to be sure, intended to join the Oxydracae and to continue hostilities in concert with them, but Alexander had been too quick for them: he had come upon them by the desert route before either they or the Oxydracae could do anything to help each other. Nor is this the only point in which popular tradition is at fault: for instance, it is generally said that the final battle with Darius, in which he fled for his life until he was caught and killed by Bessus, with Alexander pressing hard upon his heels, took place at Arbela, while the previous battle was fought at Issus, and the one before that, the first – cavalry – battle, on the Granicus. Now it is true enough that there was a cavalry engagement on the Granicus and that the next encounter with Darius took place at Issus, but the historians have stated that Arbela was, at the largest estimate, seventy-five and, at the smallest, rather more than sixty miles from the scene of the final battle between Darius and Alexander. Actually, both Ptolemy and Aristobulus declare that this battle was fought at Gaugamela near the river Bumodus. Now Gaugamela was only a large village, not a town; it was not a well-known place, and the name itself has a somewhat unpleasing sound, and I fancy that it was for these reasons that the town of Arbela was allowed to have the honour of being the scene of this great battle.[16] How absurd! If we are

15. See Curtius 9.4.26.

16. Strabo (16.1.3) gives a similar account. He explains how Gaugamela, 'the grazing-place of the camel', came to get its name.

expected to believe that the battle was fought at Arbela, miles and miles from its actual scene, we might as well pretend that the sea-fight at Salamis took place at the Isthmus of Corinth, or that the engagement at Artemisium in Euboea took place at Aegina or Sunium.

Again, all writers agree that Peucestas was one of the men who held his shield over Alexander during those critical moments, but there is no agreement either about Leonnatus or Abreas.[17] One story is that Alexander reeled and fell from a blow on the helmet with a club, but got to his feet again and was then shot in the breast, the arrow piercing his corselet; but Ptolemy, son of Lagus, states that he was shot in the breast only. The most glaring error of all is, in my opinion, the statement of some writers about Alexander's campaigns to the effect that Ptolemy, son of Lagus, went up the ladder with Alexander, accompanied by Peucestas, and protected him with his shield when he lay wounded on the ground, thereby winning the title of Saviour, whereas Ptolemy himself has made it quite plain that he was not present at this action at all, but was, at the time, commanding his own division in other actions elsewhere.[18] I think I must be allowed this digression; these events are of the highest importance, and what I have said should help future historians to record less carelessly the facts connected with them.

For some time Alexander was kept where he was, under

17. Curtius (9.5.14 ff.) mentions Timaeus and Aristonus as well as Peucestas and Leonnatus, Plutarch (*Moralia* 327 b, 344 d) Ptolemy and Limnaeus. Peucestas and Leonnatus later (p. 355) received gold crowns for their part in saving Alexander's life.

18. Curtius (9.5.21) censures Cleitarchus and Timagenes for stating that Ptolemy was present. He tells us that Ptolemy wrote in his *History* that he was away on an expedition.

Ptolemy received his title of 'Saviour' from the Rhodians in 304 for his help during the siege of Rhodes by Demetrius.

medical treatment, and the first report to reach the base camp was that he had died of wounds. The bad news swiftly spread, and the whole army was in the deepest distress. Recovering from the first shock of grief, the men were plunged into helpless despair: who would be their new commander – as both in Alexander's view and in their own a number of officers had an equal reputation for ability? How could they get safely home, encircled as they were by many warlike tribes, some of which had not yet submitted and seemed likely to fight hard for their freedom, while other seemed certain to revolt now that the dread of Alexander's name was a thing of the past? They were, or so they thought, hemmed in by impassable rivers, and every difficulty seemed hopelessly insoluble without Alexander to get them through. When at last the news came that he was alive, they could hardly believe it, and were unable at first to persuade themselves that he would really recover. Then he wrote them a letter saying that he would soon be visiting them at headquarters, but such was their state of mind that they could not believe it was genuine, and most of them thought it had been forged by his officers and Guards.

Alexander's first thought on learning of this state of affairs was to prevent a breakdown of discipline among the men; so at the first possible moment he had himself carried to the Hydraotes, and proceeded to travel downstream. The troops were in camp at the junction of the Hydraotes and the Acesines, where Hephaestion was in charge of the land forces and Nearchus had the fleet, and when his vessel had nearly reached them, he ordered the awning over the stern to be taken down so that everyone might see him. Even then the troops were incredulous, and supposed that what they saw on board was Alexander's body. At last, however, the vessel was brought in to the river-bank; Alexander raised a hand in greeting to the men, and immediately there was a shout of joy, and arms were stretched towards him in welcome or lifted to heaven in thankfulness. So unexpected was the sense of relief that many, despite themselves, burst into tears. As he was being moved from the ship, a party of his Guards brought him a stretcher; but he refused it and called for his horse. He mounted, and at the sight of him, once more astride his horse, there was a storm of applause so loud that the river-banks and neighbouring glens re-echoed with the noise. Near his tent he dismounted, and the men saw him walk; they crowded round him, touching his hands, his knees, his clothes; some content with a sight of him standing near, turned away with a blessing on their lips. Wreaths were flung upon him and such flowers as were then in bloom.

We are told by Nearchus that he was annoyed with some of his friends, who blamed him for exposing himself in advance of his men and taking risks which no commander ought to take;[19] and I fancy that his resentment was due to the fact that he was well aware that their criticism was justified. The truth is that he was fighting mad, and such was his passion for glory that he had not the strength of mind, when there was action afoot, to consider his own safety; the sheer pleasure of battle, as other pleasures are to other men, was irresistible. Nearchus goes on to say that a Boeotian soldier, an oldish man whose name he does not mention, aware of Alexander's resentment at his friends' criticism and observing the glum expression on his face, came and said to him in his rustic dialect: 'Action is a man's job, my lord'; and then quoted a line of verse – something to the effect that 'he who acts

19. Curtius (9.6.6) says that Craterus spoke on behalf of the senior officers, and was supported by Ptolemy and others.

bravely must expect his meed of suffering'.[20] The fellow's stock went up immediately, and from that time on he enjoyed Alexander's warm approval.

Representatives of the remaining Mallians now came to Alexander with the offer of surrender. A similar offer came at the same time from the Oxydracae, the deputation consisting of the governors of their various towns and districts, accompanied by 150 other dignitaries, all acting as plenipotentiaries to discuss a settlement and bringing with them the most precious Indian gifts. They urged that their failure to treat with him earlier was a pardonable offence, as, like certain other tribes though in a greater degree, they desired to be independent and to keep the freedom which they had enjoyed from the time when Dionysus visited India right up to the present day. However, as it was generally believed that Alexander, too, was of divine descent, they were willing, if that were his pleasure, to accept any governor he should appoint, pay any tribute he should please to demand, and give as many hostages as he should require. Alexander asked for a thousand of their leading men and said he would either keep them as hostages or, if it proved more convenient, make them serve in his army until the end of his Indian campaign. The men were duly sent, all being chosen for their influence and importance, and with them, as an unsolicited gift, 500 war chariots with their drivers. Alexander then appointed Philip as governor of these people and of the surviving Mallians. The hostages he returned, but retained the chariots.

During Alexander's convalescence many new rivercraft had been built, and now, when the matters just mentioned were satisfactorily settled, he ordered aboard 1,700 of the Companion cavalry, the same number as before of

20. A fragment of one of the lost tragedies of Aeschylus.

the light infantry, and about 10,000 regular infantry, and set off down the Hydraotes. Actually, the voyage down the Hydraotes was a short one, for at its junction with the Acesines it takes the name of the latter river – so it was down the Acesines that he found himself sailing as far as its junction with the Indus.

Four great rivers, all navigable, pour their waters into the Indus – but some of them lose their original names before they get there: the Hydaspes joins the Acesines, by which name, after the junction, the united streams are known; the Acesines keeps its name after its meeting with the Hydraotes, and also after receiving the tributary waters of the Hyphasis, until its junction with the Indus, when it surrenders it. From that point on I can well believe that the Indus before it splits into its delta is as much as twelve or thirteen miles wide, and perhaps more in its lowest reaches, where it is more like a lake than a river.

Alexander waited at the junction of the Acesines and Indus until the arrival of Perdiccas' contingent. Perdiccas, on his way to rejoin, had subdued the Abastani, an independent people. About this time, too, the fleet was reinforced by the addition of some new galleys and cargo vessels, built for Alexander in the territory of the Xathri – another independent tribe which had submitted to him – and envoys from the Ossadians, also an independent people, presented themselves with an offer of surrender. He fixed the Acesines and Indus, where they converge to their point of meeting, as the boundaries of Philip's province, and left under his command the whole Thracian contingent and such troops from the other units as seemed sufficient to garrison the country. He instructed Philip to found a settlement at the actual junction of the two rivers in the hope that the place would grow and become a world-famous town. He also ordered the construction of dockyards there.

During this period he was visited by Oxyartes the Bactrian, father of his wife, Roxane; he conferred upon him the governorship of the Parapamisadae in place of Tyriaspes, the former governor, whom he removed from office on a report of mismanagement.[21]

Before moving on he sent Craterus over to the left bank of the Indus with the elephants and most of the troops, as it appeared to be easier going for an army with heavy equipment on that side and the neighbouring tribes were not everywhere friendly; then he set off down-stream for the royal palace of Sogdia. There he built and fortified a new settlement, had dockyards constructed and his damaged vessels repaired. He appointed Peitho to govern the country from the junction of the Indus and Acesines to the sea, together with the whole coastal region of India.

Having given Craterus orders once again to proceed by land, he then went on down the river to the kingdom of Musicanus, which according to report was the richest in India.[22] Musicanus had not as yet presented himself with an offer of submission, nor had he sent representatives to establish relations; he had, indeed, ignored Alexander, neither sending him such tokens of courtesy as might befit a great king, nor making him any sort of request. Alexander's voyage down the Indus was so rapid that before Musicanus even knew that he had started he was on the boundaries of his kingdom. This was something of a shock; and Musicanus, in consequence, hastened to present himself before Alexander with all his elephants and such gifts as are considered by Indians to be of the

21. Curtius (9.8.9), who calls him Terioltes, says he was put to death.

22. For Onesicritus' description of this country see Strabo 15.1.34.

greatest value. He offered the submission of himself and his people and acknowledged the error of his previous conduct. With Alexander to acknowledge an error was always the best way to get what one wanted, and the case of Musicanus was no exception: Alexander freely pardoned him. He admired his country and his capital city, and permitted him to retain his sovereignty. Craterus received orders to fortify the inner stronghold of this city, and the work was done and a garrison established there while Alexander was still present; for the neighbouring tribes needed watching, and this seemed a convenient base from which to control them.

The governor of this district, a man named Oxycanus, had not yet made any contact with Alexander, either in person or by sending a deputation with offers of surrender. Alexander accordingly undertook an expedition against him with a force consisting of the archers, the Agrianes, and the cavalry he had brought with him down the river. The two largest towns in Oxycanus' province he took by assault without much trouble, and in one of them Oxycanus himself was taken prisoner. All the plunder Alexander distributed among his men; the elephants he added to his own force.[23] Other towns in this district surrendered at his approach, and there was no attempt at resistance – an indication of the extent to which the Indians had been cowed by the unbroken chain of Alexander's success.

His next move was against Sambus, whom he had himself appointed governor of the Indian hill-tribes. Sambus and Musicanus were at enmity, and a report had come in that Sambus had fled on learning that Alexander had treated Musicanus with leniency and allowed him to retain

23. Diodorus (17.102.5) and Curtius (9.8.11–13) report that Oxycanus, whom they call Porticanus, was put to death, that the prisoners were sold, and the towns in his kingdom destroyed.

his kingdom. The gates of Sindimana, the capital of Sambus' territory, were opened at Alexander's approach; Sambus' relatives made an inventory of his treasure and came out to meet him with the elephants, and pointed out to him that the reason why Sambus had abandoned his capital was not hostility to Alexander, but alarm at his clemency towards Musicanus. Alexander captured another town in the course of this expedition; it had thrown off its allegiance, and he executed the Brahmins (the Indian teachers of philosophy) who had been responsible for the revolt.[24] The Brahmin philosophy, such as it is, I will discuss in my book on India.[25]

News now came that Musicanus had revolted. The district governor, Peitho, son of Agenor, was dispatched to deal with him at the head of an adequate force, while Alexander proceeded against the various towns in his dominions; some of these he destroyed, selling the people into slavery; others he fortified and garrisoned. He then returned to his base, where the fleet was awaiting him. Musicanus, who had been taken prisoner by Peitho, was brought there, and Alexander had him hanged in his own country, together with the Brahmins who had instigated his rebellion.

Alexander was also visited at the base by the ruler of Pattala, the territory which, as I have already mentioned, consists of the delta of the Indus – larger in extent than the Nile delta in Egypt. He offered surrender of the whole territory and put himself and all he possessed into Alexander's hands. Alexander sent him back to his country

24. According to Diodorus and Curtius (who gives Cleitarchus as his source) 80,000 Indians were killed and many captured in this region.

25. See his *Indica*, chapter 11. Strabo (15.1.59) gives a better description of the Brahmins, based on Megasthenes.

with instructions to make all necessary preparations for receiving the army, and then ordered Craterus to proceed to Carmania by way of Arachotia and Zarangia[26] with the battalions of Attalus, Meleager, and Antigenes, some of the archers, and the members of the Companion cavalry and other Macedonian units whom he was already sending home as unfit for further service. Craterus was also given charge of the elephants, and Hephaestion was put in command of all the remaining units except those which were sailing with Alexander down the Indus to the sea. Peitho with the mounted javelin-men and the Agrianes was ordered across the river – the opposite side to Hephaestion – with further instructions to settle the towns which had already been fortified and to deal with any trouble which might occur in the neighbourhood, before joining Alexander at Pattala.[27]

On the third day of Alexander's passage down-stream news was brought that the Indian chief in charge of Pattala had made off with nearly all his people, leaving his territory empty and undefended. Alexander, in consequence, redoubled his speed and found, on reaching Pattala, that the town was indeed deserted and that not a labourer was left working on the land. He at once sent his most mobile units in pursuit of the fugitives, caught a few of them, and sent them off to tell their friends to come back to their homes without fear, as they were at liberty to live in their town and cultivate their lands as before. Most of them took Alexander at his word and returned.

26. i.e. Drangiana. Craterus probably travelled by way of the Mulla pass (Fuller).

27. At the apex of the Indus delta as it existed in Alexander's day. It is generally thought to be either Hyderabad or Bahmanabad. Alexander arrived there about the middle of July 325.

Hephaestion was then ordered to construct a fortress in the town, and parties of men were sent out to dig wells where there was a shortage of water and to make the surrounding country fit to live in. While the men were at work, they were set upon by natives; the attack was unexpected and a few were killed, but the natives suffered heavy losses and made their escape into the wilds. The working party was then able to finish its task, with the assistance of fresh troops which Alexander sent out to lend a hand as soon as he heard of the attack.

At Pattala the Indus divides into two mighty streams, both of which retain the name of Indus till they reach the sea. At the point of division Alexander began the construction of a harbour and dockyards, and as soon as the work was well under way he decided to sail down the right-hand, or westerly, stream as far as its mouth. Leonnatus with 1,000 mounted troops and about 8,000 light and heavy infantry was ordered to move on to the delta – or island – of Pattala, ready to follow by land the progress of the flotilla down the river, and the voyage began. Alexander had selected for the purpose his fastest vessels – all the thirty-oars, the one-and-a-half bankers, and some of the light galleys; but, as the natives of these parts had all made off, he was unable to procure a pilot, and this resulted in serious difficulties. The day after he started it blew very hard, and the wind[28] being against the tide raised a steep hollow sea which gave the vessels a thorough shaking; most of them were badly strained, and some of the thirty-oars had their timbers started. However, they managed to run them ashore before they actually fell to pieces. Other ships, therefore, were built.

A party of light infantry was then sent out to bring in some prisoners from the country adjacent to the river, and

28. The south-west monsoon; see p. 330.

for the remainder of the passage these men acted as pilots. But their troubles were not over, for near the mouth of the river, where it attains its greatest breadth of some twenty-five miles, they encountered a hard wind blowing in from the open sea, and the water was so rough that it was hardly possible to lift the oars clear of the crests and they were compelled to run for shelter into a small creek, under their pilots' direction. Lying in the creek, they were caught by the ebb tide and left high and dry. The tide is, of course, a regular feature of the ocean, but the ebb came as a surprise to Alexander's men, who had had no previous experience of it, and it was an even greater surprise when, in due time, the water returned on the flood and the vessels were refloated. Some of them had settled on soft mud; these were floated again without sustaining any damage and were able to continue their voyage; but others, which had been caught on a rocky bottom and were not evenly supported when the tide left them, did not fare so well; as the flood came in with a rush, they either fell foul of one another or bumped themselves to pieces on the hard bottom.

Alexander effected such repairs as circumstances permitted, and sent two light pinnaces down-stream with a party of men to take a look at the island – called Cilluta[29] – where his native pilots said he would find an anchorage on his passage to the sea. The men reported that there was, indeed, good shelter, and that the island itself was large and well supplied with fresh water; the rest of the flotilla, accordingly, brought up there, while Alexander himself went on beyond it with some of his fastest vessels, to get a view of the river-mouth and to find out if there was a practicable passage into the open sea. They went on some

29. According to Plutarch (*Alexander* 66.1), Alexander called it Scillustis, others Psiltucis.

twenty-five miles below Cilluta, and then observed, out at sea, another island, whereupon they put back to Cilluta, and Alexander, bringing his vessel to under a headland, offered sacrifice to those gods which he liked to say Ammon had instructed him to honour. On the following day he sailed down to the second island – beyond the mouth of the river – brought up there, and once more offered sacrifice, this time to other gods and with a different ritual, though still, by his own account, in accordance with the oracular utterance of Ammon.[30] Then, leaving the estuaries of the Indus behind him, he set sail for the open ocean, with the professed object of finding out if there was any other land near by – though I dare say his chief object was the mere achievement of having sailed in the Great Sea beyond India. There on the ocean he slaughtered bulls as a sacrifice to Poseidon and flung their bodies overboard, and poured a libation from a golden cup, and flung the cup, too, and golden bowls into the water for a thank-offering, and prayed that Poseidon might grant safe conduct to the fleet which he proposed to send under Nearchus' command to the Persian Gulf and the mouths of the Tigris and Euphrates.[31]

This done, he returned to Pattala, where he found the construction of the fortress complete and Peitho already arrived with his mission successfully accomplished. Hephaestion was ordered to make all necessary prepara-

30. These sacrifices, the counterpart of those offered at the start of the voyage down the Indus (p. 303), are Alexander's thank-offering for his successful journey.

31. cf. *Indica* 20.10. Wilcken, *Alexander* 196, regards the sacrifice and libation as a thank-offering made by Alexander for having reached 'a limit of the world', as well as a prayer for the future. This seems to read too much into Arrian's text.

Nearchus' voyage is described in the *Indica*, chapters 21–43.

tions for fortifying the harbour and for the installation of docks, as it was Alexander's intention to leave a considerable fleet stationed at Pattala, at the junction of the two estuaries of the Indus.

He now undertook a second voyage to the Ocean, this time by the other branch of the Indus, for the purpose of informing himself which of the two offered the easier passage (the mouths of the Indus are about 225 miles apart).[32] On the way down he came to a great lake; it is really a part of the estuary, and its vast extent is due to the spreading waters of the river assisted, possibly, by other tributary streams flowing in on this side or on that, so that it resembles, in effect, a gulf of the sea. Moreover, deep-sea fish were to be seen in it, larger than those we find in our own waters at home.

Alexander came to an anchor at a spot in the lake which his pilots recommended; then, leaving behind all the light pinnaces and most of his men in charge of Leonnatus, he proceeded with the thirty-oars and one-and-a-half-bankers down to the mouth of the river, and so, once again, out into the open sea. The passage by this branch proved the easier of the two.

Bringing up close off-shore, he landed and went three days' march with a party of mounted troops along the coast, making observations of the nature of the country along which the coasting voyage would have to be made and arranging for wells to be dug, to provide the fleet with water. Then he returned to his ships, and having sailed up to Pattala, sent off a strong working-party to the coast with orders to rejoin him when the task was complete. This done, he once again went down-river to the

32. This is Nearchus' figure; Aristobulus made it 125 miles (Strabo 15.1.33). The eastern arm of the Indus is thought to have run into the Rann of Cutch at this time.

lake, where he had another harbour and more docks constructed. Finally, leaving a garrison there, he laid in four months' supplies for the troops and made all other necessary preparations for the coastal voyage.

At the moment, however, it was the wrong time of year for a sea voyage. The monsoon was blowing, and, unlike our own seasonal winds, the monsoon is not a northerly wind, but blows in off the ocean from the south; but according to the information Alexander received conditions were suitable for sailing from the setting of the Pleiades at the beginning of winter[33] to the winter solstice, as throughout that period the heavy inland rains give rise to constant light off-shore winds, convenient for a coastal voyage under either sails or oars.

While Nearchus, admiral of the fleet, was waiting at Pattala for weather,[34] Alexander moved on with his whole force to the river Arabius,[35] and then turned towards the coast and proceeded along it in a westerly direction, taking with him half the total number of Guards and archers, the battalions of footguards, the picked squadron of the Companions, a squadron from each of the other cavalry regiments, and all the mounted archers. His object was, first, to have wells dug in order to ensure a good supply of water for Nearchus' men during their coastal passage, and, secondly, to make a surprise attack on the Oreitae, a local Indian tribe which had long been independent and had hitherto made no gesture of friendship towards

33. About the beginning of November.

34. He left Pattala about 21 September 325, but had to wait in the eastern arm of the Indus for 24 days until the arrival of the north-east monsoon (*Indica* 21).

35. The river Hab, not the Purali. For this identification and Alexander's route generally see Sir Aurel Stein, *Geographical Journal* 1943, 193–227.

Alexander and his army.[36] Hephaestion had command of the troops left behind at Pattala.

The Arabitae, another independent tribe near the Arabius, thought they were no match for Alexander; they did not, however, surrender when they learned of his approach, but made off into the wilds. Alexander, accordingly, crossed the river, which was hardly more than a shallow stream, crossed in the course of the night the greater part of the uninhabited country, and by dawn found himself close to the occupied regions again; then, instructing his infantry to follow in marching order, he entered the Oreitan territory with his mounted troops, dividing them into squadrons to enable them to cover as much ground as possible. All the natives who attempted resistance were killed; many were taken prisoner.[37] He then made a temporary halt near a small stream, and as soon as he was rejoined by Hephaestion continued his advance as far as the village called Rhambacia, the largest settlement in the Oreitan territory. The site of this place impressed him favourably, and feeling that if a town were built there it might well become great and prosperous, he left Hephaestion on the spot to put the work in hand.[38]

His next objective was the frontiers of the Oreitae and Gedrosians, and thither he now proceeded with a force consisting of one half of the Guards and Agrianes, his crack cavalry regiment, and the mounted archers. A

36. For Alexander's motives in marching through Gedrosia, the modern Makran, see also p. 335.

37. The squadrons were led by Leonnatus, Ptolemy, and himself (Diodorus 17.104.6). Diodorus doubtless exaggerates when he writes that 'many myriads' were killed.

38. The site of Rhambacia is unknown. Diodorus (17.104.8) says that the new Alexandria lay on the coast, but Stein (op. cit., p. 215) locates it inland, near the modern Bela.

report had come in that the approach was by a narrow pass, and that the combined forces of these two peoples had taken up a position in front of it with the purpose of stopping Alexander from getting through. This was, in fact, true; but as soon as they knew of his approach most of them abandoned their post and left the pass undefended, while the chiefs of the Oreitae came to Alexander with an offer of surrender for themselves and their people. Alexander ordered them to round up the scattered members of their tribe and send them back to their homes, adding an assurance that they should come to no harm. As governor there he appointed Apollophanes, and left Leonnatus, officer of the Guard, in the territory of the Orians[39] to support him; he put under Leonnatus' command all the Agrianes, certain units of archers and cavalry, and a number of Greek mercenary troops, both horse and foot, and added instructions that he was to wait for the arrival of the fleet off the coast in those parts, to attend to the new settlement, and help to introduce such order and discipline among the Oreitae as might induce them to be more obedient to their governor. Then, when Hephaestion had rejoined him with the troops left behind at Rhambacia, he moved forward with the greater part of his army towards Gedrosia, mostly through desolate and uninhabited country.

In this wild region (Aristobulus records) myrrh grows in great abundance, the trees being larger than the common species; the Phoenicians, who accompanied the expedition for what they could make out of it, used to collect the gum and load their pack-animals with it – it was, indeed, extremely plentiful, for it had never been collected before and the trunks which exuded it were of such uncommon size. The country also produces nard,

39. Arrian uses 'Oreitae' and 'Orians' indiscriminately.

both abundant and sweet-smelling, and this, too, was
gathered by the Phoenicians.[40] This grew in such pro-
fusion that much of it was trampled underfoot by the
marching men, and the crushed plants spread a delicious
fragrance for miles around. Other trees grow there too;
one, with a leaf like laurel, is found growing below high-
water mark on the sea-shore: this tree is left high and dry
by the ebb tide, and on the succeeding flood looks as if it
were growing in the sea. Some of them, growing in hol-
lows which do not dry at low tide, are never out of the
water, but even so take no harm from the constant im-
mersion of their roots. Some trees are as much as forty-
five feet in height and were in blossom when Alexander
saw them; the flower is rather like the white violet, but
much more fragrant. The region also produces a sort of
thistle with great strong spikes – sometimes, as the men
rode by, the spikes would catch their clothes, and so tough
were they that rather than break off they pulled the rider
from his horse. It is said that passing hares get these thorns
entangled in their fur; and indeed they used to be caught
in this way, as birds are with lime or fish with hooks.
The stem of this plant could be easily cut through; and
when it was, it exuded juice, more in quantity and more
pungent than that of early figs.

From there Alexander marched through Gedrosian
territory.[41] The route was a difficult one, and no supplies
were to be had; worst of all, in many places there was not
even water for the men. They were forced to cover great
distances at night, going some way inland, in spite of the
fact that Alexander was anxious to work along the coast

40. This plant, from which the costly ointment frequently mentioned in the Bible was prepared, was so plentiful that the Macedonians used it for bedding (Strabo 15.2.3).

41. See also Strabo 15.2.6–7.

in order to see what possible anchorages there were and, so far as he could in the brief time at his disposal, to assist the fleet by digging wells, and doing what could be done to provide markets and shelter for the ships.

There was nothing of any kind to be had in the whole southern strip of Gedrosia, so he sent Thoas, son of Man-drodorus, down to the sea with a party of mounted troops to find out if there was any sort of shelter for ships there-abouts, or any fresh water near the coast, or anything else which might be of use to the fleet. Thoas brought back a report that he had found a few fishermen on the beach living in stifling huts built of shells and roofed with the backbones of fish; they made do with very little fresh water, getting what they could by scraping away the shingle, and even this little was brackish.[42]

At last Alexander reached a part of Gedrosia where provisions were more or less plentiful. He had what he was able to obtain distributed among the baggage-trains, put his personal seal upon it, and gave orders that it should be taken down to the coast; but during the stage of his march which brought him nearest to the sea, the men, including the guards, in spite of the fact that the provisions were officially sealed, took them for their own purposes and shared them out among those of their fel-lows who were suffering most acutely from hunger. So great was their distress that the future prospect of Alex-ander's anger and the chance of punishment was, not un-reasonably, of less concern to them than the opportunity of averting the death which stared them in the face. As it happened, Alexander pardoned them when he realized

42. These were the Ichthyophagi, or Fish-Eaters. They are des-cribed in more detail by Arrian in the *Indica* (chapter 29). cf. Strabo 15.2.2; Diodorus 17.105.3–5; Curtius 9.10.8–10; Plutarch, *Alexan-der* 66.6.

the severity of the need which induced them to disobey his orders.

To provision the troops who would be sailing with the fleet, Alexander by scouring the country got together what he could, and sent Cretheus of Callatis[43] to see to its safe delivery; the natives, too, were ordered to bring to the coast from the inland districts as much ground grain as they could, together with a supply of dates and sheep for the army to purchase. Telephus, one of the Companions, was sent to another place with a small supply of flour.

The next objective was the capital town of Gedrosia, situated in a district named Pura.[44] The march thither from Oria occupied in all sixty days. Most historians of Alexander's campaigns have stated that the sufferings of his men on that march were out of all proportion greater than anything they had had to endure in Asia. Alexander did not choose that route because he was unaware of the the difficulties it would involve (Nearchus is our one authority for this); he chose it because, apart from Semiramis on her retreat from India, no one, to his knowledge, had ever before succeeded in bringing an army safely through. Even Semiramis, according to local tradition, got through with no more than twenty survivors, and Cyrus, son of Cambyses, with only seven – for it is a fact that Cyrus came here with the intention of invading India, but found the going so bad and the country so wild and barren that he lost nearly all his men before he could do so. Alexander heard these old stories; they inspired him to go one better than Cyrus and Semiramis, and that was

43. A town in Thrace on the Black Sea, founded by colonists from Miletus.

44. Bampur, situated on the river of the same name, near the Carmanian border. The date was probably late November 325.

the reason, combined with the hope of being able to keep contact with the fleet and procure supplies for it, why, according to Nearchus, he marched by that route.[45]

The result was disastrous:[46] the blazing heat and the lack of water caused innumerable casualties, especially among the animals, most of which died of thirst or from the effects of the deep, burning, sunbaked sand. Sometimes they met with lofty hills of sand – loose, deep sand, into which they sank as if it were mud or untrodden snow; sometimes, climbing or descending, the mules and horses suffered even greater distress from the uneven and treacherous surface of the track. Not the least hardship was the varying length of the marches, as the fact that they never knew when they would find water made regular, normal marches impossible. It was not so bad when they found water in the morning after covering the requisite distance during the night; but when there was still further to go, and they found themselves plodding on and on as the day advanced, the double distress of heat and raging thirst was almost intolerable.

45. Compare Alexander's rivalry with Hercules and Perseus as a motive for his expedition to Siwah (p. 151). Arrian (*Indica* 9) remarks that the Indians denied that anyone (except Hercules and Dionysus) invaded India before Alexander; cf. Strabo 15.1.6.

46. We may safely reject Plutarch's statement (*Alexander* 66.4) that Alexander had 120,000 infantry and 15,000 cavalry with him, of whom less than a quarter survived. Nearchus (Arrian, *Indica* 19.5) says, more credibly, that Alexander had 120,000 fighting men at the start of the voyage down the Hydaspes. From this figure we must deduct casualties sustained in India, the troops sent back with Craterus, and those left behind in India and with Leonnatus among the Oreitae. Modern estimates range from 8–10 thousand (Tarn, *Alexander* 1.107) – surely far too low a figure – to 60–70 thousand (H. Strasburger, *Hermes* 1952, 486ff.). In any case, we do not know what proportion of the troops or of those who accompanied the army survived.

Casualties among the animals were very numerous; indeed, most of them perished. Often they were killed deliberately by the men, who used to put their heads together and agree to butcher the mules and horses, whenever supplies gave out, and then eat their flesh and pretend they had died of thirst or exhaustion. As every man was involved, and the general distress was so great, there was no one to bring actual evidence of this crime, though Alexander himself was not unaware of what was going on; he realized, however, that the only way to deal with the situation was to feign ignorance, which would be better than to let the men feel that he connived at their breach of discipline. It was, moreover, no easy task, when men were sick or fell exhausted in their tracks, to get them along with the rest; for there were no transport animals left and even the wagons were being continually broken up as it became more and more impossible to drag them through the deep sand. In the earlier stages of the march they had often been prevented for this reason from taking the shortest route and compelled to seek a longer one which was more practicable for the teams. So there was nothing for it but to leave the sick by the way, and any man rendered incapable by exhaustion or thirst or sunstroke. No one could give them a helping hand; no one could stay behind to ease their sufferings, for the essential thing was to get on with all possible speed, and the effort to save the army as a whole inevitably took precedence over the suffering of individual men. Most of the marching was at night, and many men would fall asleep in their tracks; the few who had strength left to do so followed the army when they woke up again, and got safe through; but the greater number perished – poor castaways in the ocean of sand.

There was yet another disaster, perhaps the worst for

all concerned, men, horses, and mules. In Gedrosia, as in India, it rains heavily during the monsoon; the rain falls not on the plains but on the mountains, the summits of which arrest the clouds carried thither by the wind and cause them to condense in rain. It so happened that the army bivouacked by a small stream, for the sake of the water it afforded, and about the second watch of the night it was suddenly swollen by rain. The actual rain was falling far away out of sight, but the stream nevertheless grew into such a torrent that it drowned most of the camp-followers' women and children and swept away the royal tent with everything it contained, and all the surviving animals, while the troops themselves barely managed to escape, saving nothing but their weapons – and not even all of those. Another trouble was, that when plenty of water happened to be found after a hot and thirsty march, most of the men drank so immoderately that the result was fatal to them, and for this reason Alexander usually made his halts a couple of miles or so from water, to stop his men from flinging themselves indiscriminately upon it to their own destruction and that of their beasts, and to prevent those who had least self-control from plunging right into the spring or stream, or whatever it was, and so spoiling the water for the others.

At this point in my story I must not leave unrecorded one of the finest things Alexander ever did. Where it actually took place is uncertain: perhaps here, perhaps, as some historians have declared, in the country of the Parapamisadae some time previously.[47] The army was crossing a desert of sand; the sun was already blazing down upon them, but they were struggling on under the necessity of reaching water, which was still far away. Alexander, like

47. Plutarch (*Alexander* 42.7) says it occurred during the pursuit of Darius, Curtius (7.5.10) in Sogdiana near the R. Oxus.

everyone else, was tormented by thirst, but he was none the less marching on foot at the head of his men. It was all he could do to keep going, but he did so, and the result (as always) was that the men were the better able to endure their misery when they saw that it was equally shared. As they toiled on, a party of light infantry which had gone off looking for water found some – just a wretched little trickle collected in a shallow gully. They scooped up with difficulty what they could and hurried back, with their priceless treasure, to Alexander; then, just before they reached him, they tipped the water into a helmet and gave it to him. Alexander, with a word of thanks for the gift, took the helmet and, in full view of his troops, poured the water on the ground. So extraordinary was the effect of this action that the water wasted by Alexander was as good as a drink for every man in the army. I cannot praise this act too highly; it was a proof, if anything was, not only of his power of endurance, but also of his genius for leadership.

To add to their difficulties, the time came when the guides admitted that they no longer knew the way; all the marks, they declared, had been obliterated by the blown and drifting sand. There was nothing in the vast and featureless desert to determine what course they should take – no trees, as elsewhere, by the roadside, no hills of solid earth rising from the sand. Moreover, the guides had never practised the art of finding their direction by the stars at night and by the sun in the day-time, as sailors do – the Phoenicians setting their course by the Little Bear, the rest of us by the Great Bear.[48] Alexander, accordingly, took the matter into his own hands; feeling that the route

48. The Little Bear contains the Pole Star; the Great Bear is Charles' Wain or The Plough, from which the Pole Star may be found.

should be more towards the left, he rode ahead with a small party of mounted men. The horses soon began to succumb to the heat, so he left most of his party behind and rode off with only five men. At last they found the sea, and scraping away the shingle on the beach came upon fresh, clear water. The whole army soon followed, and for seven days marched along the coast, getting its water from the beach. Finally the guides once more recognized their whereabouts, and a course was set for the interior again.

At the capital city of Gedrosia the troops were given a rest. Alexander, finding that Apollophanes, the governor, had failed to carry out any of his instructions, dismissed him and appointed Thoas in his place.[49] Thoas subsequently died and was succeeded by Sibyrtius, who had recently been made governor of Carmania, where, on being given control of both Arachotia and Gedrosia, he was succeeded by Tlepolemus, son of Pythophanes.

Alexander was already on his way to Carmania when a report reached him of the death of Philip, governor of India: the mercenaries had hatched a plot to assassinate him, and his Macedonian guards had executed the assassins, some caught red-handed, others after subsequent arrest. Alexander accordingly sent written orders to Eudamus and Taxiles in India to take charge of the territory formerly administered by Philip until he sent out a new governor.[50]

After his arrival in Carmania, he was rejoined by

49. Apollophanes had been killed soon after Alexander's departure in a great battle against the Oreitae (Arrian, *Indica* 23.5). His instructions presumably were to forward supplies for Alexander's troops.

50. This had not been done at the time of Alexander's death, some eighteen months later.

Craterus with the troops under his command, and the elephants. Craterus also brought Ordanes with him, under arrest for disaffection and trouble-making. A number of other officers and officials here presented themselves: Stasanor, governor of Aria and Zarangia; Pharismanes, son of Phrataphernes, governor of Parthia and Hyrcania; and the officers left with Parmenio in command of the troops in Media, Cleander, Sitalces, and Heracon, with most of their men.[51] Both the natives and the army had brought a number of charges against Sitalces and Cleander, alleging that they had plundered temples, disturbed ancient tombs, and committed other crimes of a violent and tyrannical nature against the people of the province. Immediately he received the report, Alexander had both officers executed, as an example to other government officials of whatever rank, who would thenceforth realize that if they were guilty of similar irregularities they would suffer the same punishment. If there was one thing more than another which conduced to orderliness and obedience among the numerous and widely separated peoples which found themselves, either by conquest or alliance, under Alexander's sway, it was this: that under his empire no sort of oppression by local government officials was ever permitted.[52] The other officer, Heracon, was cleared for the time being; but soon afterwards some people at Susa had him convicted of robbing the temple there, and he, too, was executed.

Stasanor and Phrataphernes, on learning that Alexander

51. Curtius (10.1.1) adds Agathon. He says that all four were put in chains and 600 of their followers executed. Despite Curtius' silence about their fate it is likely that all four were executed.

For the full story of the 'reign of terror' among Alexander's satraps at this time see E. Badian, *JHS* 1961, 16ff.

52. This is not borne out by Alexander's letter to Cleomenes (p. 389).

was marching to Gedrosia, correctly foresaw the difficulties he would encounter in the desert, and had brought with them, in consequence, a number of draught-animals, including camels; their arrival was certainly fortunate, and the camels and mules were a most timely addition; in due proportion to their number Alexander distributed them among his forces – among the officers individually, and so many to each squadron, company, and platoon.[53]

Certain writers[54] have told the improbable story that Alexander made a progress through Carmania in a sort of double-sized chariot, specially constructed, in which he reclined with his intimate friends, listening to the music of flutes, while the troops accompanied him making merry as on holiday and with garlands on their heads, and that the people of the country, all along the route of the procession, had provided food and every imaginable luxury for their delectation. All this is supposed to have been Alexander's notion of imitating the Dionysiac Revels, or triumphal marches, in accordance with the legend that Dionysus, after his conquest of India, traversed the greater part of Asia with this sort of pomp and ceremony – *Thriambus* (or Triumph) was one of the titles of Dionysus, and the same word *thriambi* – triumphs – was used to describe his ceremonial procession after victories in war. There is no mention of this either in Ptolemy, son of Lagus, or in Aristobulus, or indeed in any other writer whom one might consider to give reliable evidence in such matters. In any case, there is the story; I do not

53. According to Diodorus (17.105.7) and Curtius (9.10.17) Alexander had sent instructions to Phrataphernes and Stasanor to supply provisions. Phrataphernes is probably a slip for Pharismanes; there is no mention of the arrival of Phrataphernes.

54. See the elaborate descriptions in Curtius (9.10.24ff.) and Plutarch (*Alexander* 67) and cf. Diodorus 17.106.1. The story may possibly be connected with the festival mentioned below.

believe it – and that is all I propose to say. I do, however, put on record (on Aristobulus' authority) that while he was in Carmania, Alexander offered sacrifice in gratitude to heaven for his conquest of India and the escape of his army from the desert of Gedrosia, and that he held a festival with public competitions in athletics and the arts. He promoted Peucestas to be a member of his Personal Guard – he had already decided to make him governor of Persia, but in view of the special service he had rendered in the battle with the Mallians, he wanted him to enjoy this mark of honour and confidence before taking over his governorship. Up to that time Alexander's Personal Guards were seven in number: Leonnatus son of Anteas, Hephaestion son of Amyntor, Lysimachus son of Aga-thocles, Aristonus son of Pisaeus (all four from Pella); Perdiccas son of Orontes, from Orestis; Ptolemy son of Lagus and Peitho son of Crateuas from Eordaea. Now there was an eighth – Peucestas, the man who held his shield over Alexander's prostrate body.

Meanwhile Nearchus had completed his voyage along the coasts of the Orians, Gedrosians, and Ichthyophagi, and arrived at the inhabited parts of the Carmanian sea-board. From there he made his way inland with a few companions and gave Alexander his report of the ocean voyage.[55] Alexander sent him back to the fleet with orders to continue his voyage as far as Susia and the mouths of the Tigris. I propose to give a detailed account of his voyage from the Indus to the mouth of the Tigris in the Persian Gulf in a separate volume, basing it on Nearchus' own story; this book, like the present one, will be a Greek

55. Arrian gives a graphic description of Nearchus' meeting with Alexander at Harmozeia (Hormuz) in the *Indica* (chapters 33–6). Diodorus (17.106) says that they met in a seaside town called Salmus.

history written in Alexander's honour. It will be a work for some future date, when I am in a proper mood, and the spirit moves me to embark upon it.[56]

Alexander now ordered Hephaestion to proceed to Persia with the elephants, the baggage-train, and the greater part of the army. His instructions were to take the coastal route, because it was now winter[57] and he would find in the coastal regions of Persia both warm weather and an abundance of supplies. At the same time he moved forward himself with the most mobile infantry units, the Companion cavalry, and some regiments of archers, along the road to Pasargadae. Stasanor he sent home.[58] Arrived at the Persian frontier, he found that Phrasaortes, the governor, had died while the Indian campaign was still going on; the reins of government were in the hands of Orxines, who had not, indeed, been regularly appointed, but considered himself, in the absence of any other governor, a proper person to serve Alexander by keeping Persian affairs running smoothly.[59] At Pasargadae, Alexander was visited by Atropates, governor of Media; he brought with him a Mede named Baryaxes, whom he had arrested for wearing his cap upright in the royal fashion and proclaiming himself King of the Medes and Persians. With him, also under arrest, were his associates in the attempted *coup*. They were all executed.

Aristobulus relates that Alexander found the tomb of Cyrus, son of Cambyses, broken into and robbed, and that this act of profanation caused him much distress.[60]

56. This is the *Indica*, chapters 18–43.

57. It was now early December in the year 325.

58. To Aria.

59. He traced his descent from Cyrus (Curtius 10.1.22).

60. The tomb is now known as the Tomb of the Mother of Solomon. It is frequently reproduced, e.g. by Jean-Louis Huot, *Persia* (London, 1965), plate 68 (in colour).

The tomb was in the royal park at Pasargadae; a grove of
various sorts of trees had been planted round it; there
were streams of running water and a meadow with lush
grass. The base of the monument was rectangular, built
of stone slabs cut square, and on top was a roofed chamber, also built of stone, with access through a door so narrow that only one man at a time – and a little one at that –
could manage, with great difficulty, painfully to squeeze
himself through. Inside the chamber there was a golden
coffin containing Cyrus' body, and a great divan with feet
of hammered gold, spread with covers of some thick,
brightly-coloured material, with a Babylonian rug on top.
Tunics and *candyes* – or Median jackets – of Babylonian
workmanship were laid out on the divan, and (Aristobulus says) Median trousers, various robes dyed in ame-
thyst, purple, and many other colours, necklaces, scimi-
tars, and inlaid earrings of gold and precious stones. A
table stood by it, and in the middle of it lay the coffin
which held Cyrus' body. Within the enclosure, by the
way which led up to the tomb, a small building had been
constructed for the Magi who guarded it, a duty which
had been handed down from father to son ever since the
time of Cyrus' son, Cambyses.[61] They had a grant from
the King of a sheep a day, with an allowance of meal
and wine, and one horse a month to sacrifice to Cyrus.
There was an inscription on the tomb in Persian, signifying: 'O man, I am Cyrus son of Cambyses, who founded
the empire of Persia and ruled over Asia. Do not grudge
me my monument.'

Alexander had always intended, after his conquest of

61. The Magi were a Median priestly class, taken over by the
conquering Persians. Besides the duty of guarding Cyrus' tomb,
they were interpreters of dreams and when a Persian wished to
sacrifice, he had to employ a Magus. See Herodotus 1.120.132.

Persia, to visit the tomb of Cyrus; and now, when he did
so, he found that all it contained except the divan and the
coffin had been removed. Even the royal remains had not
escaped desecration, for the thieves had taken the lid from
the coffin and thrown out the body; from the coffin itself
they had chipped or broken various bits in an attempt to
reduce its weight sufficiently to enable them to get it
away. However, they were unsuccessful and went off
without it.

Aristobulus tells us that he himself received orders from
Alexander to put the monument into a state of thorough
repair: he was to restore to the coffin what was still preserved of the body and replace the lid; to put right all
damage to the coffin itself, fit the divan with new strap-
ping, and to replace with exact replicas of the originals
every single object with which it had previously been
adorned; and, finally, to do away with the door into the
chamber by building it in with stone, covered by a coat
of plaster, on which was to be set the royal seal. Alexander had the Magi who guarded the monument arrested
and put to the torture, hoping to extort from them the
names of the culprits; but even under torture they were
silent, neither confessing their own guilt nor accusing
anybody else; so, as they could not be convicted of any
sort of complicity in the crime, Alexander released them.

He then went to the palace of the Persian kings, which
on a previous occasion he had set on fire, as I have already
related.[62] I remarked, when I mentioned this act, that I
could not commend it, and Alexander himself regretted
it when he saw the place for the second time.

As for Orxines, who took charge of Persian affairs after
Phrasaortes' death, a number of damaging stories were
told about him by the Persians, and he was convicted of

62. i.e. Persepolis; see p. 179.

robbing temples and royal tombs and of illegally putting many Persians to death. He was accordingly hanged by Alexander's agents.[63] Peucestas, of Alexander's Personal Guard, was appointed governor, in recognition of his exceptional loyalty on all occasions – and especially on the occasion of his heroic act during the fight with the Mallians, when at the risk of his own life he helped to save Alexander. Apart from this, he was also a suitable Person for the post, as he liked Oriental ways. He showed this clearly enough immediately he was appointed, being the only Macedonian to adopt the Median dress; he also learned the Persian language, and in all other ways took to living as the Persians lived. Alexander thoroughly approved of this conduct, and the Persians themselves were gratified to find that he preferred their manner of life to that of his own country.[64]

63. Curtius (10.1.22–38) has a different story. According to him Orxines was guiltless and his death was brought about by Alexander's eunuch favourite, Bagoas, who poisoned Alexander's mind against him and bribed accusers to supply false testimony. E. Badian (*CQ* 1958, 147 ff.) argues in favour of this version.

64. The Macedonians, however, resented Peucestas' growing orientalism (p. 356).

BOOK SEVEN

On reaching Pasargadae and Persepolis, Alexander had a sudden impulse to sail down the Euphrates and Tigris into the Persian Gulf; he had already seen something of the mouths of the Indus and of the waters beyond them, and now he wished to do the same with the Tigris and Euphrates. We find in some writers[1] the statement that he intended to sail right round Arabia, Ethiopia, and Libya, pressing forward past the Nomads beyond Mount Atlas to Gadeira, and so into the Mediterranean; thus, had he added Libya and Carthage to his conquests, he could with full justification have claimed the title of King of All Asia, unlike the Median and Persian kings, who, ruling as they did only a fraction of that continent, could not properly call themselves Great Kings at all. Some authorities say that he proposed subsequently to sail into the Black Sea and on to Scythian territory by the Sea of Azov; others, that he meant to make for Sicily and southern Italy to check the Romans, whose reputation, being greatly on the increase, was already causing him concern.

Personally I have no data from which to infer precisely what Alexander had in mind, and I do not care to make guesses; one thing, however, I feel I can say without fear of contradiction, and that is that his plans, whatever they

1. See Curtius 10.1.17–19 and Plutarch, *Alexander* 68.1. Among the plans (*Hypomnemata*) left behind at Alexander's death was one for an expedition against Carthage, North Africa, Spain, and the coast of Italy to Sicily (Diodorus 18.4.4). For a discussion of the genuineness of these plans see E. Badian, *Harvard Studies in Classical Philology* 1968, 183ff., who cites the earlier literature. Asia here, as often, includes Africa.

were, had no lack of grandeur or ambition: he would never have remained idle in the enjoyment of any of his conquests, even had he extended his empire from Asia to Europe and from Europe to the British Isles.[2] On the contrary, he would have continued to seek beyond them for unknown lands, as it was ever his nature, if he had no rival, to strive to better his own best.

I have always liked the story[3] of the Indian sages, some of whom Alexander chanced to come upon out of doors in a meadow, where they used to meet to discuss philosophy. On the appearance of Alexander and his army, these venerable men stamped with their feet and gave no other sign of interest. Alexander asked them through interpreters what they meant by this odd behaviour, and they replied: 'King Alexander, every man can possess only so much of the earth's surface as this we are standing on. You are but human like the rest of us, save that you are always busy and up to no good, travelling so many miles from your home, a nuisance to yourself and to others. Ah well! You will soon be dead, and then you will own just as much of this earth as will suffice to bury you.' Alexander expressed his approval of these sage words; but in point of fact his conduct was always the exact opposite of what he then professed to admire. On another occasion he is said to have expressed surprise at a remark made by Diogenes of Sinope: he was marching somewhere in the Isthmus with a contingent of Guards and infantry Companions, and chancing to see Diogenes lying in the sun, he stopped and asked him if there was anything he wanted.

'Nothing,' replied the philosopher; 'though I should

2. See Arrian's remarks on p. 213.

3. A somewhat similar story is told of Calanus (below) by Plutarch, *Alexander* 65.6.

be grateful if you and your friends would move to one side, and not keep the sun off me.'[4]

One must admit, then, that Alexander was not wholly a stranger to the loftier flights of philosophy; but the fact remains that he was, to an extraordinary degree, the slave of ambition. In Taxila, once, he met some members of the Indian sect of Wise Men whose practice it is to go naked, and he so much admired their powers of endurance that the fancy took him to have one of them in his personal train.[5] The oldest man among them, whose name was Dandamis (the others were his pupils), refused either to join Alexander himself or to permit any of his pupils to do so. 'If you, my lord,' he is said to have replied, 'are the son of God, why – so am I. I want nothing from you, for what I have suffices. I perceive, moreover, that the men you lead get no good from their world-wide wandering over land and sea, and that of their many journeyings there is no end. I desire nothing that you can give me; I fear no exclusion from any blessings which may perhaps be yours. India, with the fruits of her soil in due season, is enough for me while I live; and when I die, I shall be rid of my poor body – my unseemly housemate.' These words convinced Alexander that Dandamis was, in a true sense, a free man; so he made no attempt to compel him.[6]

4. Diogenes was the famous Cynic, who spent most of his life in exile at Athens. Although he could have met Alexander at Corinth in 336, this anecdote, like others in which the philosopher always bests the king, is probably fictitious. In Plutarch (*Alexander* 14) and other writers – no fewer than 22 references to the incident are known – the king remarks 'If I were not Alexander, I should be Diogenes'.

5. Arrian seems to refer to Aristobulus' account given by Strabo (15.1.61).

6. Strabo (15.1.63–5) preserves a fuller version of the account of Onesicritus who was sent to visit the Gymnosophists, as the Greeks

On the other hand, another of these Indian teachers, a man named Calanus, did yield to Alexander's persuasion; this man, according to Megasthenes' account, was declared by his fellow teachers to be a slave to fleshly lusts, an accusation due, no doubt, to the fact that he chose to renounce the bliss of their own asceticism and to serve another master instead of God.[7]

I have mentioned this because no history of Alexander would be complete without the story of Calanus. In India Calanus had never been ill, but when he was living in Persia all strength ultimately left his body.[8] In spite of his enfeebled state he refused to submit to an invalid regimen, and told Alexander that he was content to die as he was, which would be preferable to enduring the misery of being forced to alter his way of life. Alexander, at some length, tried to talk him out of his obstinacy, but to no purpose; then, convinced that if he were any further opposed he would find one means or another of making away with himself, he yielded to his request, and gave instructions for the building of a funeral pyre under the supervision of Ptolemy, son of Lagus, of the Personal Guard. Some say Calanus was escorted to the pyre by a solemn procession – horses, men, soldiers in armour, and people carrying all kinds of precious oils and spices to throw upon the flames; other accounts mention drinking-

called them. His account of their doctrines, however, is 'good Cynic doctrine'. (T. S. Brown, *Onesicritus* 45.)

7. Plutarch (*Alexander* 65.5-6) says that the philosopher's name was Sphines, but the Greeks called him Calanus because, instead of using the Greek word of greeting 'Chaire', he used the Indian word 'Cale'.

8. According to Strabo (15.1.68) his death occurred at Pasargadae, but Diodorus (17.107.1) locates it on the borders of Persia and Susiane. The story had a great vogue in antiquity; see M. Hadas, *Hellenistic Culture*, 178ff.

cups of silver and gold and kingly robes. He was too ill
to walk, and a horse was provided for him; but he was
incapable of mounting it, and had to be carried on a litter,
upon which he lay with his head wreathed with garlands
in the Indian fashion, and singing Indian songs, which
his countrymen declare were hymns of praise to their
gods.[9] The horse he was to have ridden was of the royal
breed of Nesaea,[10] and before he mounted the pyre he gave
it to Lysimachus, one of his pupils in philosophy, and
distributed among other pupils and friends the drinking-
cups and draperies which Alexander had ordered to be
burnt in his honour upon the pyre.

At last he mounted the pyre and with due ceremony
laid himself down. All the troops were watching. Alexander could not but feel that there was a sort of indelicacy
in witnessing such a spectacle – the man, after all, had
been his friend; everyone else, however, felt nothing but
astonishment to see Calanus give not the smallest sign of
shrinking from the flames.[11] We read in Nearchus' account
of this incident that at the moment the fire was kindled
there was, by Alexander's orders, an impressive salute:
the bugles sounded, the troops with one accord roared
out their battle-cry, and the elephants joined in with their
shrill war-trumpetings.

This story and others to a similar effect have been
recorded by good authorities; they are not without value
to anyone who cares for evidence of the unconquerable
resolution of the human spirit in carrying a chosen course
of action through to the end.

About this time Alexander sent out Atropates to his
province. He had himself gone on to Susa, where he had

9. cf. Arrian, *Indica* 10.   10. See below, p. 369.
11. See Plutarch, *Alexander* 69.8, and Strabo 15.1.68. Chares and
Onesicritus, however, stated that he hurled himself into the fire.

Abulites arrested and put to death for abusing his office as governor. Abulites' son Oxathres shared the same fate.[12] In the various countries subdued by Alexander there had been a great many irregularities on the part of government officials, acts of violence against individuals, and robbing of temples and tombs. The reason is not far to seek, for Alexander had been away for a very long time in India, and nobody really felt he was ever likely to return from the innumerable hostile nations of the East – not to mention the elephants! – but would find a grave somewhere beyond the Indus, Hydaspes, Acesines, and Hyphasis. Again, the disasters in the Gedrosian desert were a further encouragement to the governors of these more westerly parts to shrug off the idea of his ever getting safely home. None the less, it must be admitted that, by all accounts, Alexander at this period had become readier to accept as wholly reliable the charges which were made to him against officials, and to inflict severe punishment even for minor offences, in the belief that the sort of attitude which allowed an official to commit some petty irregularity might also lead him to serious crime.[13]

Here at Susa he held wedding ceremonies for his Companions; he also took a wife himself – Barsine,[14] Darius' eldest daughter, and, according to Aristobulus, another as well, namely Parysatis, the youngest daughter of Ochus.[15] He had already married Roxane, daughter of

12. Atropates was governor of Media. Abulites and Oxathres governed Susiane and Paraetacene respectively (pp. 174, 180). According to Plutarch (*Alexander* 68.7) the king ran Oxathres through with a *sarissa*, or pike.

13. cf. Curtius 10.1.39 ff. On the executions of governors at this time see E. Badian, *JHS* 1961, 16 ff.

14. This is her official name, but she is generally called Stateira.

15. Thus linking himself with both branches of the Persian royal family. Artaxerxes III Ochus ruled Persia from 359 to 338 B.C.

Oxyartes of Bactria. To Hephaestion he gave Drypetis, another of Darius' daughters and sister of his own wife Barsine, as he wanted to be uncle to Hephaestion's children; to Craterus he gave Amastrine, daughter of Darius' brother Oxyatres, and to Perdiccas a daughter of Atropates, governor of Media. The bride of Ptolemy (of the Guard) was Artacama, daughter of Artabazus, and Eumenes, the King's secretary, had her sister Artonis; Nearchus was given the daughter of Barsine and Mentor, Seleucus the daughter of Spitamenes of Bactria. Similarly, the other officers – to the number of eighty all told[16] – were given as brides young women of the noblest Persian and Median blood. The marriage ceremonies were in the Persian fashion: chairs were set for the bridegrooms in order of precedence, and when healths had been drunk the brides entered and sat down by their bridegrooms, who took them by the hand and kissed them. The King, who was married just as the others were, and in the same place, was the first to perform the ceremony – Alexander was always capable of putting himself on a footing of equality and comradeship with his subordinates, and everyone felt that this act of his was the best proof of his ability to do so. After the ceremony all the men took their wives home, and for every one of them Alexander provided a dowry. There proved to be over 10,000 other Macedonians who had married Asian women; Alexander had them all registered, and every man of them received a wedding gift.

This also seemed a fitting occasion to clear off the men's debts, and Alexander ordered a detailed schedule to be

16. Chares, the Royal Chamberlain, who described the festivities in detail, gives 92 as the number of bridegrooms; see Athenaeus 12.538b–539a.

For Alexander's purpose see Wilcken, *Alexander* 208.

prepared, with a promise of settlement. At first only a few entered their names, suspecting that the order might be a scheme of Alexander's for detecting the spendthrifts who had failed to make do with their army pay. Alexander was annoyed when he learned that most of the men were refusing to enter their names and concealing their possession of covenants to pay, and told them in no uncertain terms what he thought of their suspicions; a King, he declared, is in duty bound to speak nothing but the truth to his subjects, who, in their turn, have no right to suppose that he ever does otherwise. He had tables set up in the army quarters, with money on them, and instructed the clerks in charge to pay off the debts of every man who produced an I.O.U. without even registering their names. After that the troops could not but believe in Alexander's good faith, and they were even more grateful for the concealment of their names than for having their debts paid. This gift to his men is said to have amounted to 20,000 talents.[17]

He also made a number of other money awards for distinguished conduct in the field, or in recognition of a man's reputation for good service generally. A special decoration consisting of a gold crown was granted to certain officers for conspicuous bravery: the recipients were Peucestas – for saving the King's life; Leonnatus – also for saving the King's life, for hard service in India, for his victory in Oria, for facing and defeating in battle, with the forces left under his command, the rebellious Oreitae and their neighbours, and his satisfactory settlement of affairs in general in Oria;[18] Nearchus (now also arrived

17. cf. Diodorus 17.109.1–2; Curtius 10.2.9–11; Plutarch, *Alexander* 70.3. Plutarch and Curtius both give a figure of 9,870 talents, while Diodorus says 'a little less than 10,000'.

18. See Arrian, *Indica* 23.5; Curtius 9.10.19.

at Susa) for his voyage from India along the coasts of the
Indian ocean; Onesicritus, master of the royal galley; and,
finally, Hephaestion and the other members of the Personal Guard.

Here in Susa, Alexander received the various officials
in charge of affairs in the newly built towns and the governors of the territories he had previously overrun. They
brought with them some 30,000 young fellows, all boys
of the same age, all wearing the Macedonian battle-dress
and trained on Macedonian lines.[19] Alexander called them
his *Epigoni* – 'inheritors' – and it is said that their coming
caused much bad feeling among the Macedonians, who
felt it was an indication of his many efforts to lessen his
dependence for the future upon his own countrymen. Already the sight of Alexander in Median clothes had caused
them no little distress, and most of them had found the
Persian marriage ceremonies by no means to their taste –
even some of the actual participants had objected to the
foreign form of the ceremony, in spite of the fact that they
were highly honoured by being, for the occasion, on a
footing of equality with the King. They resented, too,
the growing orientalism of Peucestas, Governor of Persia,
who, to Alexander's evident satisfaction, had adopted the
Persian language and dress, just as they resented the inclusion of foreign mounted troops in the regiments of the
Companions.[20] Bactrians, Sogdians, Arachotians; Zaran-
gians, Arians, Parthians, and the so-called Euacae from
Persia were all introduced into the crack Macedonian
cavalry regiments, provided they had some outstanding

19. Curtius (8.5.1) dates the formation of this force to 327; so
probably Plutarch (*Alexander* 47.6). Diodorus (17.108) appears to
place it after the mutiny at the Hyphasis.

20. On the remainder of this paragraph see Appendix A, pp.
401–2.

personal recommendation, such as good looks, or whatever it might be. Besides this, a fifth mounted regiment was formed; it did not consist entirely of oriental troops, but the total cavalry strength was increased and a certain number of foreign troops were posted to it.[21] Foreign officers were also posted to the special squadron – Cophen son of Artabazus, Hydarnes and Artiboles sons of Mazaeus, Sisines and Phradasmenes sons of Phrataphernes, the satrap of Parthia and Hyrcania, Histanes son of Oxyartes and brother of Alexander's wife Roxane, Autobares and his brother Mithrobaeus. The command over them was given to Hystaspes, a Bactrian, and the orientals were all equipped with the Macedonian spear in place of their native javelin. All this was a cause of deep resentment to the Macedonians, who could not but feel that Alexander's whole outlook was becoming tainted with orientalism, and that he no longer cared for his own people or his own native ways.

Hephaestion now received orders to move down to the Persian Gulf with more than half the total number of infantry battalions. The fleet had already come up the Gulf to the territory near Susa, and Alexander embarked for a voyage down the Eulaeus[22] to the sea. He took with him the Guards, the special squadron and a few other

21. A slight emendation of the text (see E. Badian, *JHS* 1965, 161) would read 'it consisted almost entirely of oriental troops, for when the total cavalry strength was increased foreign troops were added'.

22. After joining the R. Coprates it was known as the Pasitigris, which in Alexander's day flowed into the Persian Gulf. Nearchus had sailed up the Pasitigris to the neighbourhood of Susa; see Arrian, *Indica* 42.

The Pasitigris now enters the Shatt-el-Arab, as the combined stream of the Euphrates and Tigris is known. In ancient times these two rivers entered the Persian Gulf by separate mouths, as Arrian's narrative shows.

Companions. He left most of his ships, including all
which were in need of repair, just inside the mouth of the
river, and went on with the fastest he had along the sea-
coast from the Eulaeus to the mouths of the Tigris; the
rest of the fleet returned up the Eulaeus to the canal which
joins it with the Tigris, and passed through.

The Tigris and Euphrates, as everybody knows, en-
close a portion of Syria called, for that reason, Mesopotamia by the people who live there. The Tigris flows
through much lower-lying country than the Euphrates;
it receives the water from a number of cuts from the
Euphrates and also from many tributary streams, and
consequently increases in volume until, by the time it
reaches the Persian Gulf, none of its water having been
drawn off for purposes of irrigation, it is a river of considerable size and at no point fordable. The river, indeed,
cannot be used for irrigation of the surrounding country
at all; for such cuts or canals as there are, connecting it
with other rivers, flow into, not from it, as the land on
both banks is above the level of the stream. The Euphrates, on the contrary, runs through higher country, and
throughout its course flows flush and full; consequently
at many points the water is led off through cuttings, some
of them permanent and a regular source of supply to the
natives on either side; others are dug to provide water for
the land during a temporary shortage.[23] There is little rain
in this part of the world, so this is a necessary procedure.
For these reasons the Euphrates becomes, near its mouth,
a more or less shallow swamp.

Alexander sailed off-shore along the stretch of coast
between the Eulaeus and the Tigris, and then proceeded

23. cf. Strabo 16.1.9–10; Herodotus 1.193. Strabo (16.1.11) describes, on the authority of Aristobulus, how Alexander improved
the irrigation of the region.

up the Tigris to the place where Hephaestion and the whole army were encamped. From there he went further up the river to Opis, a town on its bank. During the passage up-stream he had the weirs demolished, thus restoring the river to the same continuous level throughout;[24] the weirs had been constructed by the Persians to prevent a victorious naval force from coming up the river to invade their country – a remarkable piece of engineering for a non-maritime people. Their existence, at frequent intervals, made the passage up-river a very awkward business. Alexander declared that no power which enjoyed military supremacy would ever bother with such contrivances; in his own case a safeguard of that sort was pointless and irrelevant; and indeed, the very ease with which he destroyed these works which the Persians had laboured so hard to complete was sufficient proof that they were not worth much.

At Opis he summoned an assembly of his Macedonian troops and announced the discharge from the army of all men unfit through age or disablement for further service; these he proposed to send home, and promised to give them on their departure enough to make their friends and relatives envy them and to fire their countrymen with eagerness to play a part in similar perilous adventures in the future. Doubtless he meant to gratify them by what he said.

Unfortunately, however, the men already felt that he had come to undervalue their services and to think them quite useless as a fighting force; so, naturally enough, they resented his remarks as merely another instance of the many things which, throughout the campaign, he had done to hurt their feelings, such as his adoption of Persian dress, the issue of Macedonian equipment to the Oriental 'Epigoni', and the inclusion of foreign troops in

24. cf. Strabo 16.1.9.

units of the Companions. The result was that they did not receive the speech in respectful silence, but, unable to restrain themselves, called for the discharge of every man in the army, adding, in bitter jest, that on his next campaign he could take his father with him – meaning, presumably, the god Ammon.

Alexander was furious. He had grown by that time quicker to take offence, and the Oriental subservience to which he had become accustomed had greatly changed his old open-hearted manner towards his own countrymen. He leapt from the platform with the officers who attended him, and pointing with his finger to the ringleaders of the mutiny, ordered the guards to arrest them. There were thirteen of them, and they were all marched off to execution.[25] A horrified silence ensued, and Alexander stepped once again on to the rostrum and addressed his troops in these words: 'My countrymen, you are sick for home – so be it! I shall make no attempt to check your longing to return. Go whither you will; I shall not hinder you. But, if go you must, there is one thing I would have you understand – what I have done for you, and in what coin you will have repaid me.

'First I will speak of my father Philip, as it is my duty to do. Philip found you a tribe of impoverished vagabonds, most of you dressed in skins, feeding a few sheep on the hills and fighting, feebly enough, to keep them from your neighbours – Thracians and Triballians and Illyrians. He gave you cloaks to wear instead of skins; he brought you down from the hills into the plains; he taught you to fight on equal terms with the enemy on your borders, till you

25. Curtius (10.2.12–30) and Diodorus (17.109), who place the arrest after Alexander's speech, say that Alexander seized the ringleaders (13 also in Curtius) with his own hands. On the mutiny cf. Plutarch, *Alexander* 71.

knew that your safety lay not, as once, in your mountain strongholds, but in your own valour. He made you city-dwellers; he brought you law; he civilized you. He rescued you from subjection and slavery, and made you masters of the wild tribes who harried and plundered you; he annexed the greater part of Thrace, and by seizing the best places on the coast opened your country to trade, and enabled you to work your mines without fear of attack.[26] Thessaly, so long your bugbear and your dread, he subjected to your rule, and by humbling the Phocians he made the narrow and difficult path into Greece a broad and easy road.[27] The men of Athens and Thebes, who for years had kept watching for their moment to strike us down, he brought so low – and by this time I myself was working at my father's side[28] that they who once exacted from us either our money or our obedience,[29] now, in their turn, looked to us as the means of their salvation. Passing into the Peloponnese, he settled everything there to his satisfaction, and when he was made supreme commander of all the rest of Greece for the war against Persia, he claimed the glory of it not for himself alone, but for the Macedonian people.[30]

'These services which my father rendered you are, indeed, intrinsically great; yet they are small compared with

26. The gold and silver mines at Mt Pangaeum near Philippi are said to have brought Philip more than 1,000 talents a year (Diodorus 16.8.6).

27. In 346 B.C.

28. He refers principally, no doubt, to his part in the battle of Chaeroneia in 338; see Plutarch, *Alexander* 9.2–4; Diodorus 16.86.

29. Demosthenes (On *Halonnesus* 12) refers to a time when the Macedonians paid tribute to Athens. The Thebans under Pelopidas had settled Macedonian affairs in 368. Philip spent the years 368–365 as a hostage in Thebes.

30. On The events after Chaeroneia see Wilcken, *Alexander* 41ff.

my own. I inherited from him a handful of gold and silver
cups, coin in the treasury worth less than sixty talents and
over eight times that amount of debts incurred by him;[31]
yet to add to this burden I borrowed a further sum of
eight hundred talents, and, marching out from a country
too poor to maintain you decently, laid open for you at a
blow, and in spite of Persia's naval supremacy, the gates
of the Hellespont. My cavalry crushed the satraps of
Darius, and I added all Ionia and Aeolia, the two Phrygias
and Lydia to your empire. Miletus I reduced by siege; the
other towns all yielded of their own free will – I took them
and gave them you for your profit and enjoyment. The
wealth of Egypt and Cyrene, which I shed no blood to
win, now flows into your hands; Palestine and the plains
of Syria and the Land between the Rivers are now your
property; Babylon and Bactria and Susa are yours; you are
masters of the gold of Lydia, the treasures of Persia, the
wealth of India – yes, and of the sea beyond India, too. You
are my captains, my generals, my governors of provinces.

'From all this which I have laboured to win for you,
what is left for myself except the purple and this crown?
I keep nothing for my own; no one can point to treasure
of mine apart from all this which you yourselves either
possess, or have in safe keeping for your future use. Indeed, what reason have I to keep anything, as I eat the
same food and take the same sleep as you do? Ah, but
there are epicures among you who, I fancy, eat more
luxuriously than I; and this I know, that I wake earlier
than you – and watch, that you may sleep.[32]

31. See Curtius 10.2.24; cf. Plutarch, *Alexander* 15.2. For a discussion of Alexander's finances see A. R. Bellinger, *Essays on the Coinage
of Alexander the Great* (New York, 1963) 35ff.

32. For the luxury of Alexander's followers see Plutarch, *Alexander* 42; Athenaeus 12.539ff.; Aelian, *Varia Historia* 9.3.

'Perhaps you will say that, in my position as your commander, I had none of the labours and distress which you had to endure to win for me what I have won. But does any man among you honestly feel that he has suffered more for me than I have suffered for him? Come now – if you are wounded, strip and show your wounds, and I will show mine. There is no part of my body but my back which has not a scar; not a weapon a man may grasp or fling the mark of which I do not carry upon me. I have sword-cuts from close fight; arrows have pierced me, missiles from catapults bruised my flesh; again and again I have been struck by stones or clubs – and all for your sakes: for your glory and your gain.[33] Over every land and sea, across river, mountain, and plain I led you to the world's end, a victorious army. I married as you married, and many of you will have children related by blood to my own. Some of you have owed money – I have paid your debts, never troubling to inquire how they were incurred, and in spite of the fact that you earn good pay and grow rich from the sack of cities. To most of you I have given a circlet of gold as a memorial for ever and ever of your courage and of my regard.[34] And what of those who have died in battle? Their death was noble, their burial illustrious; almost all are commemorated at home by statues of bronze; their parents are held in honour, with all dues of money or service remitted,[35] for under my leadership not a man among you has ever fallen with his back to the enemy.

33. Plutarch lists Alexander's wounds in *Moralia* 327a-b and 341a-c.

34. Surely an exaggeration. We hear only of the ceremony at Susa (p. 355).

35. See above, p. 75. But only the 25 Companions killed at the Granicus appear, then at least, to have been honoured by statues. Plutarch (*Alexander* 71.9) says that Alexander granted pensions to the children of those killed on the expedition.

'And now it was in my mind to dismiss any man no longer fit for active service – all such should return home to be envied and admired. But you all wish to leave me. Go then! And when you reach home, tell them that Alexander your King, who vanquished Persians and Medes and Bactrians and Sacae; who crushed the Uxii, the Arachotians, and the Drangae, and added to his empire Parthia, the Chorasmian waste, and Hyrcania to the Caspian Sea; who crossed the Caucasus beyond the Caspian Gates, and Oxus and Tanais and the Indus, which none but Dionysus had crossed before him, and Hydaspes and Acesines and Hydraotes – yes, and Hyphasis too, had you not feared to follow; who by both mouths of the Indus burst into the Great Sea beyond, and traversed the desert of Gedrosia, untrodden before by any army; who made Carmania his own, as his troops swept by, and the country of the Oreitans; who was brought back by you to Susa, when his ships had sailed the ocean from India to Persia – tell them, I say, that you deserted him and left him to the mercy of barbarian men, whom you yourselves had conquered. Such news will indeed assure you praise upon earth and reward in heaven. Out of my sight!'

As he ended, Alexander sprang from the rostrum and hurried into the palace. All that day he neither ate nor washed nor permitted any of his friends to see him. On the following day too he remained closely confined. On the third day he sent for the Persian officers who were in the highest favour and divided among them the command of the various units of the army. Only those whom he designated his kinsmen were now permitted to give him the customary kiss.[36]

36 . 'Kinsman' was an honorific title bestowed by the Persian king on leading Persians. Curtius (3.3.14) puts their number at 15,000. For the customary kiss see p. 222 n. 31.

On the Macedonians the immediate effect of Alexander's speech was profound. They stood in silence in front of the rostrum. Nobody made a move to follow the King except his closest attendants and the members of his personal guard; the rest, helpless to speak or act, yet unwilling to go away, remained rooted to the spot. But when they were told about the Persians and Medes – how command was being given to Persian officers, foreign troops drafted into Macedonian units, a Persian Corps of Guards called by a Macedonian name, Persian infantry units given the coveted title of Companions, Persian Silver Shields[37] and Persian mounted Companions, including even a new Royal Squadron, in process of formation – they could contain themselves no longer. Every man of them hurried to the palace; in sign of supplication they flung their arms on the ground before the doors and stood there calling and begging for admission. They offered to give up the ringleaders of the mutiny and those who had led the cry against the King, and swore they would not stir from the spot day or night unless Alexander took pity on them.

Alexander, the moment he heard of this change of heart, hastened out to meet them, and he was so touched by their grovelling repentance and their bitter lamentations that the tears came into his eyes. While they continued to beg for his pity, he stepped forward as if to speak, but was anticipated by one Callines, an officer of the Companions, distinguished both by age and rank. 'My lord,' he cried, 'what hurts us is that you have made Persians your kinsmen – Persians are called "Alexander's kinsmen" – Persians kiss you. But no Macedonian has yet had a taste of this honour.'

37. This is a later name for the Guards (*Hypaspists*). Diodorus (17.57.2) uses it of the Guards at Gaugamela. See Tarn, *Alexander* 2.151–2.

'Every man of you,' Alexander replied, 'I regard as my kinsman, and from now on that is what I shall call you.'

Thereupon Callines came up to him and kissed him, and all the others who wished to do so kissed him too. Then they picked up their weapons and returned to their quarters singing the song of victory at the top of their voices.

To mark the restoration of harmony, Alexander offered sacrifice to the gods he was accustomed to honour, and gave a public banquet which he himself attended, sitting among the Macedonians, all of whom were present.[38] Next them the Persians had their places, and next to the Persians distinguished foreigners of other nations; Alexander and his friends dipped their wine from the same bowl and poured the same libations, following the lead of the Greek seers and the Magi. The chief object of his prayers was that Persians and Macedonians might rule together in harmony as an imperial power. It is said that 9,000 people attended the banquet; they unanimously drank the same toast, and followed it by the paean of victory.[39]

After this all Macedonians – about 10,000 all told – who were too old for service or in any way unfit, got their discharge at their own request.[40] They were given their pay not only up to date, but also for the time they would take on the homeward journey. In addition to their pay they

38. An evident exaggeration, unless only officers are meant.

39. This banquet was held to celebrate the reconciliation between Alexander and his Macedonians and (hopefully) between them and the Persians. E. Badian (*Historia* 1958, 428ff.) has finally demolished Tarn's idea (lastly *Alexander* 2.434ff.) that Alexander prayed for the 'Unity of Mankind'.

For the singing of a paean after a banquet see Xenophon, *Symposium* 2.2.1.

40. As Alexander had intended all along; see p. 359.

each received a gratuity of one talent. Some of the men had children by Asian women, and it was Alexander's orders that these should be left behind to avoid the trouble among their families at home, which might be caused by the introduction of half-caste children; he promised to have them brought up on Macedonian lines, with particular attention to their military training, and added that when they grew up he would himself bring them back to Macedonia and hand them over to their fathers. It was a somewhat vague and unsatisfactory promise; he did, however, give the clearest proof of how warmly he felt for them, and of how much he would miss them when they had gone, by his decision to entrust them on their journey to the leadership and protection of Craterus, the most loyal of his officers and a man he loved as dearly as his own life.[41] When he said good-bye to them, his eyes and the eyes of every man among them were wet with tears.

Craterus' instructions were to take them home and, on arrival there, to assume control of Macedonia, Thrace, and Thessaly and assure the freedom of Greece.[42] Antipater received orders to bring out fresh drafts to replace the men sent home; Polysperchon was sent with Craterus as his second in command – Craterus was in poor health, and thus Alexander ensured that if anything happened to him during the journey the men should have someone to take charge of them.[43]

41. See Diodorus 17.114.1; Plutarch, *Alexander* 47.9–10; cf. Curtius 6.8.2. Craterus is said (Plutarch, *Eumenes* 6.3) to have been a favourite with the Macedonians because of his opposition to Alexander's orientalism.

42. i.e. he was to replace Antipater as Alexander's deputy as Hegemon of the Corinthian League.

43. By the time of Alexander's death, some 9 months later, Craterus had not progressed beyond Cilicia.

There are always plausible and malicious people ready
to start whispering campaigns about Court secrets – and
the more secret the better they like it – and to put the worst
possible interpretations upon what appear to most of us
perfectly straightforward actions. So it was in this matter
of Alexander and Antipater.[44] The rumour was, that
Alexander was beginning to be influenced by his mother's
calumnious statements about Antipater, and for that
reason wished to get him out of the country. It may well
be, however, that his recall was in no way meant to dis-
credit him, but was merely to prevent the quarrel between
him and Olympias from reaching a point beyond Alexander's power to heal. Both of them were constantly
writing to Alexander; Antipater's letters were full of the
Queen's headstrong character and violent temper and her
determination (most unsuitable for Alexander's mother)
to have a finger in every pie – indeed, the stories of her
behaviour gave rise to a much-quoted remark of Alexander's, to the effect that she was charging him a high
price for his nine months' lodging in her womb. Olympias, for her part, continually complained that Antipater's
position and the respect to which it entitled him made him
insufferably arrogant; he no longer remembered, she
wrote, who had put him where he was, but claimed absolute pre-eminence among his fellow countrymen and the
rest of Greece. It cannot be denied that the stories which
tended to blacken Antipater's good name did seem to gain
more and more influence over Alexander, for such things
would naturally alarm anyone in his position; neverthe-

44. For the hostility of Antipater and Olympias see Diodorus
17.118.1, Plutarch, *Alexander* 40.11–13; cf. Curtius 10.10.14. The
relations between Alexander and Antipater are discussed by E.
Badian, *JHS* 1961, 36ff., and G. T. Griffith, *Proceedings of the African
Classical Associations* 1965, 12ff.

less we hear of nothing he either did or said, which would
serve as ground for the conclusion that he did not continue to regard Antipater as highly as ever.*

... Eumenes was ready for a reconciliation, and this
argument was enough to induce Hephaestion, though
against his will, to make up the quarrel.[45]

It was in the course of this journey[46] that Alexander is
said to have seen the plain called the plain of Nesaea
where the royal mares were pastured. Herodotus tells us
that the mares were always known as Nesaean. There
were once about 150,000 of them, but when Alexander
saw them there were not more than 50,000, as most of
them had been stolen.[47]

There is a story that while Alexander was there, Atropates, the governor of Media, sent him a hundred women,
who he declared were Amazons. They were equipped like
cavalrymen, but carried axes instead of spears and light
targes instead of the ordinary cavalry shield. According to
some writers, their right breasts were smaller than their
left, and were bared in battle. Alexander sent the women
away to avoid trouble; for they might well have met with
unseemly treatment from the troops, Macedonian or
foreign. However, he told them to inform their Queen
that he would visit her one day and get her with child.[48]
This story is not to be found in Aristobulus or Ptolemy,

* A page has been lost here.

45. cf. Plutarch, *Eumenes* 2.

46. From Opis to Ecbatana (Hamadan).

47. For the Nesaean horses see Herodotus 7.40.2; Strabo 11.13.7.
Diodorus (17.110.6) gives slightly different figures; formerly
160,000 mares, now 60,000.

48. Many writers related a visit by the Amazon Queen to Alexander in Hyrcania or near the Jaxartes; cf. Diodorus 17.77.1, Curtius 6.5.24–32, who call her Thalestris. Plutarch (*Alexander* 46)
gives a long list of writers who accepted or rejected the story.

or, indeed, in any other reliable writer; personally I doubt
if the Amazons still existed at that date – indeed Xenophon, writing before Alexander's time, never mentions
them, though he has references to Phasians and Colchians
and other barbarian peoples which the Greeks encountered on either side of Trapezus, where they would have
certainly found Amazons had there still been any.[49] I cannot, however, bring myself to believe that this race of
women, whose praises have been sung so often by the
most reputable writers, never existed at all:[50] there is the
tradition, for instance, that Heracles was sent to them and
brought back to Greece a girdle belonging to their Queen
Hippolyte; and that Theseus and his Athenians were the
first to defeat them in battle and prevent their invasion of
Europe.[51] There is a picture, too, by Cimon of the battle
between the Amazons and the Athenians, just as there is
of the battle between the Athenians and Persians.[52] Herodotus, moreover, has frequently referred to these women,[53]
and all Athenians who have pronounced eulogies on those
who fell in war have made particular mention of the fight
with the Amazons.[54] If Atropates really did present some
female cavalry troopers to Alexander, I should imagine

49. Xenophon mentions the equipment of the Amazons in the
Anabasis (4.4.16), but does not imply that he had seen any.

50. No ancient writer doubted that the Amazons had existed in
the past, not even the sceptical Strabo (11.5.3).

51. See Plutarch, *Theseus* 27.

52. The second battle referred to is the B. of Marathon in 490.
Both pictures were painted by Micon, who 'flourished' about 460,
and were displayed in the Stoa Poikile at Athens. See Pausanias
1.15, 8.11; cf. Aristophanes, *Lysistrata* 678. We should probably
read 'Micon' instead of 'Cimon', although the mistake may be
Arrian's.

53. cf. Herodotus 4.110–17; 9.27.

54. See Lysias, *Epitaphios* 1; Isocrates, *Panegyricus* 19; Plato,
Menexenus 239B.

they must have been women, of some nationality or other, who had been taught to ride and equipped in the traditional Amazon style.

At Ecbatana, Alexander offered sacrifice, as it was his custom to do to celebrate a happy occasion. He also held a festival with literary and athletic contests, and drank deep with his closest friends. About this time Hephaestion fell sick. On the seventh day of his illness it so happened that there was a big crowd at the stadium to watch the boys' races, which were then taking place. During the races a message was brought to Alexander that Hephaestion's condition was serious; he hurried away, but his friend was dead before he could reach him.[55]

The accounts of Alexander's grief at this loss are many and various. All writers have agreed that it was great, but personal prejudice, for or against both Hephaestion and Alexander himself, has coloured the accounts of how he expressed it. Many writers have told us of things which were beyond all bounds of propriety; those friendly to him apparently wishing us to believe that whatever he said or did in his grief for this friend, whom he loved better than all the world, could but enhance his glory; his critics, on the other hand, indicating that such excesses were discreditable, and unfitting not only for a great potentate like Alexander, but for any King. We are told, for instance, that he flung himself on the body of his friend and lay there nearly all day long in tears, and refused to be parted from him until he was dragged away by force by his Companions; and again, that he lay stretched upon the corpse all day and the whole night too. Some have said that he had Glaucias, the doctor, hanged for giving the wrong medicine; others, because he had seen Hephaestion drinking too much and had made no attempt

55. cf. Plutarch, *Alexander* 72.1; Diodorus 17.110.7–8.

to stop him.⁵⁶ I do not, however, think it unlikely that
Alexander cut his hair short in mourning for his friend,
for he might well have done so, if only in emulation of
Achilles, whose rival he had always felt himself to be,
ever since he was a boy.⁵⁷ Then there is the story – to me
quite incredible – that he personally drove for a short
distance the funeral carriage with Hephaestion's body in
it; and, again, that he ordered the shrine of Asclepius in
Ecbatana to be razed to the ground – a thing one might
have expected from an Oriental despot, but utterly un-
characteristic of Alexander. Indeed, it reminds one of the
absurd story of Xerxes, who, with his reckless disregard
of what men hold sacred, 'punished' the Hellespont by
pretending to bind it with chains.⁵⁸ Another story, to me
a not wholly improbable one, is that on the road to Babylon Alexander was met by a number of deputations from
Greece, with some representatives from Epidaurus
among them.⁵⁹ Alexander granted the Epidaurians' requests, and gave them something to take home and dedicate as an offering to Asclepius in his shrine. 'And yet,' he
said, 'Asclepius has not treated me kindly; for he did not
save the friend I valued as my own life.'

Most authorities have said that he ordered sacrifice to
be always offered to Hephaestion as a demi-god, and some
declare that he sent to inquire of Ammon if he would permit sacrifice to be offered to him as a god; but Ammon
refused.⁶⁰

56. See Plutarch, loc. cit.

57. For Alexander's emulation of Achilles, and for his relations
with Hephaestion see p. 67 above. For Achilles' grief at the death
of Patroclus see Homer, *Iliad* 23.141, 152.

58. See Herodotus 7.35.

59. Epidaurus in the Argolid is the chief seat of the worship of
Asclepius.

60. On p. 389 Arrian states this as a fact.

All the accounts, however, agree in telling us that for two whole days after Hephaestion's death Alexander tasted no food and paid no attention in any way to his bodily needs, but lay on his bed now crying lamentably, now in the silence of grief. He had a funeral pyre prepared in Babylon at a cost of 10,000 talents – or more, if we can believe some accounts[61] – and ordained a period of mourning throughout the East.[62] Many of the Companions, out of respect for Alexander, dedicated themselves and their arms to the dead man, a gesture initiated by Eumenes, who, as I mentioned just now, had quarrelled with him.[63] His object, no doubt, was to prevent Alexander from thinking that he was glad to have him gone. Alexander made no fresh appointment to the command of the Companion cavalry; he wished Hephaestion's name to be preserved always in connexion with it, so Hephaestion's Regiment it continued to be called, and Hephaestion's image continued to be carried before it. Alexander held Funeral Games in his honour, with contests in literature and athletics; the festival was far more splendid than ever before both in the number of competitors and in the money spent upon it. In all 3,000 men competed in the various events – and these same men took part soon afterwards in the Games at Alexander's own funeral.

Alexander's distress was long drawn out; but at last he began to get over it, and the proffered consolation of his friends to have more effect. Once he was himself again, he undertook an expedition against the Cossaeans. These

61. Plutarch also says 10,000 talents, but Diodorus has 12,000. For a detailed description of the 'pyre' see Diodorus 17.115. Plutarch calls it a 'tomb', and it was evidently designed as a monument to Hephaestion; see Wilcken, *Alexander* 234–6.

62. cf. Diodorus 17.114.4–5; Plutarch, *Alexander* 72.3; 75.3; *Eumenes* 2; *Pelopidas* 34.2; Aelian, *Varia Historia* 7–8.

63. See p. 369. The account of their quarrel is lost.

people, neighbours of the Uxians, were a warlike tribe of mountaineers, living in village strongholds high in the hills; on the approach of an enemy, their practice was to abandon their positions, either all together or in small parties as occasion offered, and slip away, thus frustrating any attempt by an organized force to get at them; then, when the enemy was gone, they would return to their normal life of brigandage. Alexander, however, destroyed them. It was winter when he made his raid, but Alexander was never held up by either bad weather or bad country – and the same may be said of Ptolemy, son of Lagus, who was in command of part of the army on this expedition. Alexander, indeed, once he was embarked upon any of his enterprises, never found anything to stop him from carrying it through.[64]

On the way back to Babylon he was met by representatives from Libya, who with congratulatory speeches offered him a crown in recognition of his sovereignty over Asia; Bruttian, Lucanian, and Etruscan envoys also arrived on the same mission from Italy. It is said that Carthage, too, sent a delegation at that time, and that others came from the Ethiopians and European Scythians – not to mention Celts and Iberians – all to ask for Alexander's friendship.[65] It was the first time that Greeks and Macedonians had ever heard the names of these peoples or set eyes upon their unfamiliar dress and equipment. We are told that they even appealed to Alexander to arbitrate in their domestic quarrels, with the result that then,

64. The campaign lasted 40 days. Plutarch (*Alexander* 72.4) says the Cossaeans were massacred – 'an offering' to the dead Hephaestion. However, in the *Indica* (40.6–8) Arrian says that Alexander founded cities to encourage the Cossaeans to adopt a settled and peaceful existence; cf. Diodorus 17.111.6.

65. Diodorus (17.113.1–2) gives a similar, but not identical, list.

if ever, both he and his friends felt that he was indeed master of the world. Two of the writers on Alexander's career, Aristus and Asclepiades,[66] declare that Rome sent him a delegation, and that when he met the delegates and observed the proud freedom of their bearing, their obvious devotion to duty and order, and had learned the nature of their political principles, he prophesied something, at least, of the future greatness of their country. I record the story, which may or may not be true; but the fact remains that no Roman has ever made any reference to this delegation, any more than the two writers on Alexander who are my principal authorities, Aristobulus and Ptolemy, son of Lagus. Moreover, it would have been out of character for the republican Romans, who enjoyed at that date entirely free institutions, to send a delegation to a foreign King, especially at such a distance from their own country, when they had nothing either to fear or to gain from him, and were of all people in the world the most violently averse to Kings, the very word being anathema to them.

After these events Alexander sent Heracleides, son of Argaeus, with a party of shipwrights to Hyrcania with orders to fell timber in the hills and build warships, some decked, some undecked, on the Greek model. The reason for this order was the fancy which had taken him to extend his geographical knowledge by the exploration of the Caspian (or Hyrcanian) Sea; he wished to determine what other sea it was connected with – whether it joined the Black Sea, or whether it was merely a gulf of the great Indian Ocean to the eastward. The Persian – or Red Sea,

66. Their works are not extant. Aristus, of Salamis in Cyprus, described Cyrus' tomb (Strabo 15.3–8), and may be identical with the favourite of Antiochus II. Cleitarchus (in Pliny, *Natural History* 3.57) also said that the Romans sent an embassy.

as it is sometimes called – he had proved to be a gulf of the ocean, and it might, he thought, turn out to be the same with the Caspian.[67] The limits – or origins – of the Caspian had never yet been discovered, in spite of the fact that its shores are inhabited by a considerable number of peoples and navigable rivers flow into it: from Bactria, for instance, the Oxus, the greatest river of Asia outside India, runs into it, and also the Jaxartes after following its course through Scythia, and, as is generally supposed, the Araxes after passing through Armenia.[68] Apart from these three great rivers, there are also many tributaries which join them, and thus discharge their waters, too, into the Caspian; some of these were discovered by Alexander's armies, others, of course, are far to the north in the wholly unknown country of the Nomad Scythians.

On his march to Babylon, Alexander, after crossing the Tigris, was met by some Wise Men of the Chaldaeans,[69] who drew him aside and begged him to go no further, because their god Bel had foretold that if he entered the city at that time it would prove fatal to him. Alexander replied by quoting to them the line of Euripides:

'Prophets are best who make the truest guess.'[70]

'My lord,' said the Chaldaeans, 'look not to the West; do not march westward with your army; but turn about and go eastward.' But this was not easy for Alexander to do, as the country to the east was impracticable for troops.

67. For this view of the Caspian see p. 262, n. 14. Alexander doubtless had been told by Aristotle that the Caspian was not a Gulf, but the discovery of the Persian Gulf had led him to doubt this.

68. On this passage, which goes back ultimately to Aristotle, see Tarn, *Alexander* 2.11.

69. The priests of Bel (Marduk).

70. From a lost tragedy. It is often quoted without mention of author, but Plutarch (*Moralia* 432c) also assigns it to Euripides.

The truth was that fate was leading him to the spot where it was already written that he should die.

Who knows? Perhaps it was better for him to make his end while his fame was unimpaired and the world most grieved for his loss, and before he was overtaken by the ill fortune which, at one time or another, is the lot of all men. That, doubtless, was why Solon advised Croesus to 'look to the end' of a life, however long, and never to say that a man is happy till that end had come.[71] Even in Alexander's case, Hephaestion's death had been no small calamity, and I believe he would rather have been the first to go than live to suffer that pain, like Achilles, who surely would rather have died before Patroclus than have lived to avenge his death.

Alexander had some suspicion that the Chaldaeans' attempt to prevent him from marching to Babylon on that occasion was not, in fact, based upon a prophecy of impending disaster at all; on the contrary, its object, he felt, might well be to secure their own advantage. In Babylon stood the great temple of Bel, a huge edifice of baked bricks, set in bitumen. Like the other shrines in the city, it had been destroyed by Xerxes on his return from Greece and Alexander had proposed to restore it.[72] According to some accounts, he intended to rebuild upon the original foundations, and for that reason the Babylonians had had instructions to clear the site. Others say he intended a still larger building than the old one. The workmen, however, once he was out of the way, dawdled over their job, so he

71. See Herodotus 1.32; cf. Plutarch, *Solon* 27.

72. cf. Strabo 16.1.5. Herodotus (1.181) describes the temple, and says that it existed till his time (see How and Wells' note on the passage).

For Alexander's order for its restoration see p. 173. Diodorus (17.112.2) oddly says that the priests told Alexander that he could escape the danger by rebuilding the temple.

proposed to set all his own troops to work upon it. Now a great deal of land and considerable treasure had been devoted by the Assyrian kings to the god Bel, and from this the temple, in the old days, used to be maintained and the sacrifices offered to the god. But at the time of which I am speaking the Chaldaeans themselves had the disposal of the god's property, as there was nothing upon which the income could be spent. For these reasons it had occurred to Alexander that they might not want him to enter the city, lest the rebuilding of the temple might be rapidly completed and they, in consequence, lose the benefit of the money. Nevertheless, Aristobulus tells us that Alexander, so far as changing his direction was concerned, was ready to yield to their wishes; on the first day he halted his men on the Euphrates, and on the next advanced, keeping the river on his right hand, with the intention of first passing the western section of the city and then wheeling to the eastward. But it turned out that by this route the going was too bad for the army to get through, as anyone approaching the west side of the city and then turning east is bound to get bogged down in swampy land. The result was that Alexander disobeyed the divine command – half deliberately, and half because he could not help it.

In Aristobulus' account we find the following story about Apollodorus of Amphipolis. Apollodorus, one of the Companions and closely associated with Alexander, was in command of the force which had been left with Mazaeus, the governor of Babylon.[73] After Alexander's return from India, he had not been long in his company before he observed the severity with which he was punishing the various provincial governors. He accordingly wrote a letter to his brother Peithagoras, a seer who prac-

73. See p. 173. For the story see also Plutarch, *Alexander* 73.3–5; Appian, *Civil Wars* 2.639ff.

tised divination by the entrails of animals offered for sacrifice, asking him to use his art to foretell whether or not any danger threatened himself. Peithagoras asked in reply who was the principal cause of the foreboding which made him desire the service of divination, and he wrote another letter in which he said that it was the King and Hephaestion. Peithagoras then proceeded to offer sacrifice, first to secure a prophecy in the case of Hephaestion; and, as no lobe could be found on the victim's liver, he sent a sealed message to Apollodorus in Ecbatana, assuring him that Hephaestion would soon be out of their way and that there was, therefore, nothing to fear from him. Aristobulus declares that Apollodorus received this communication the day before Hephaestion's death. Peithagoras then offered a second sacrifice, this time for information about Alexander; once again the victim's liver had no lobe, and Peithagoras wrote another letter to his brother in similar terms to the first. Apollodorus made no attempt at concealment, but told Alexander what the letter contained, in the belief that he would be doing him a good turn if he warned him to be on his guard against impending danger. Alexander thanked him, and on his arrival at Babylon asked Peithagoras the nature of the warning sign which had induced him to write to his brother as he did.

'The victim's liver,' was the answer, 'had no lobe.'

'What,' Alexander asked, 'does that sign portend?'

'Something,' Peithagoras replied, 'of the utmost gravity.'[74]

Far from being angry with Peithagoras, Alexander treated him with all the more consideration for having told him the truth without concealment.

This story Aristobulus declares he heard from Peithagoras' own lips. He adds, moreover, that Peithagoras, on

74. See Cicero, *On Divination* 1.119, 2.32.

a later occasion, practised his art of divination to foretell the fates of Perdiccas and Antigonus; in each case the same warning sign appeared, and in each case the warning proved true; for Perdiccas was killed in his campaign against Ptolemy, and Antigonus was killed in the battle of Ipsus against Seleucus and Lysimachus.[75]

There is a similar story of Calanus, the Indian Wise Man.[76] According to this, on the way to the pyre where he was to meet his death he made his farewells to Alexander's personal friends, but refused to speak any word of the sort to Alexander himself, saying that he would give him his greetings when they met in Babylon. At the time nobody paid much attention to this incident; but when, later on, Alexander died in Babylon, all who had been present on the occasion remembered what Calanus had said, and realized that his words were inspired by some mysterious foreknowledge of Alexander's death.

In Babylon, Alexander was visited by delegations from Greece, for purposes which have not been recorded; most of them, I fancy, were to offer him the victor's crown and congratulate him on his many successes, especially his triumphant campaign in India, and to express their pleasure in his safe return.[77] We are told that he received the envoys graciously and paid them all the honours due

75. Perdiccas was murdered by his own troops at Memphis in 321 (Diodorus 18.36). The B. of Ipsus in Phrygia was fought in the summer of 301.

76. See Plutarch, *Alexander* 69.7; Cicero, *On Divination* 1.47.

77. As it was now spring 323, it would seem rather late for the Greek states to be sending congratulations for this. Diodorus (17. 113.3–4) reports envoys from the Greeks (among others) at this time for a variety of purposes, including the presentation of arguments against receiving back their exiles, as Alexander had ordered. For this order see Diodorus 18.8.2ff. (cf. 17.109.1), Curtius 10.2.4; cf. Tod, nos. 201, 202.

to their position before dismissing them; he also entrusted to their care the statues, images, and other votive offerings which Xerxes had taken from Greece and brought either to Babylon or Pasargadae or Susa or any other Asian city, and this was the means by which the bronze statues of Harmodius and Aristogeiton and the Celcaean Artemis were restored to Athens.[78]

Aristobulus writes that the fleet was in Babylon when Alexander arrived there. Nearchus' squadron had sailed up the Euphrates from the Persian Gulf, the others – two Phoenician quinqueremes, three quadriremes, twelve triremes, and about thirty light galleys – had come over from the Phoenician coast; they had been taken to pieces and transported overland to Thapsacus on the Euphrates, where they were re-assembled and sailed down the river to Babylon. Apparently Alexander was having a new flotilla built as well, and for this purpose was felling the cypresses in Babylonia; cypress being the only sort of timber of which there is an abundance in Assyrian territory, which is otherwise badly off for ship-building material.[79] Man-power and crews for the new vessels were supplied by shell-divers and others whose work was connected with the sea, from Phoenicia and the neighbouring seaboard. He also by dredging operations began the construction of a harbour at Babylon, large enough for 1,000 warships to lie in, and equipped with yards. Miccalus of Clazomenae was sent to Phoenicia and Syria with a sum of 500 talents to hire or purchase more men familiar with ships and the sea. The fact is, Alexander had ideas of settling the seaboard of the Persian Gulf and the off-shore islands; for he fancied it might become as prosperous a country as Phoenicia. The naval preparations

78. See pages 174 n. 39 and 218 n. 25.
79. Arrian's authority here is Aristobulus; see Strabo 16.1.11.

were directed against the Arabs of the coast,[80] ostensibly
because they were the only people in that part of the
country who had sent no delegation to wait upon him, or
shown their respect by any other normal act of courtesy;
actually, however, the reason for the preparations was, in
my opinion, Alexander's insatiable thirst for extending his
possessions.[81]

Report has it that Alexander had heard that the Arabs
worshipped only two gods, Uranus and Dionysus, the
former because he is seen to contain within himself not
only the stars but the sun too, the greatest and clearest
source of blessing to mankind in all their affairs, and the
latter, Dionysus, because of the fame of his journey to
India.[82] Alexander accordingly felt it would not be beyond
his merits to be regarded by the Arabs as a third god, in
view of the fact that his achievements surpassed those of
Dionysus; or at least he would deserve this honour if he
conquered the Arabs and allowed them, as he had allowed
the Indians, to retain their ancient institutions.[83] Moreover, the wealth of their country was an additional incite-
ment – the cassia in the oases, the trees which bore fran-
kincense and myrrh, the shrubs which yielded cinnamon,
the meadows where nard grew wild: of all this report had
told him. Arabia, too, was a large country, its coast (it
was said) no less in extent than the coast of India; many
islands lay off it, and there were harbours everywhere fit

80. An emendation of the manuscript's reading 'against the
majority of the Arabs'.

81. Strabo (16.1.11) gives Aristobulus as his authority for the
statements that the Arabs had not sent a delegation and that
Alexander 'was reaching out to become lord of all'. Arrian evidently adopts this view of Alexander; see p. 213 n. 19.

82. See Herodotus 3.8. (with How and Wells' note).

83. Despite the words 'report has it', Aristobulus is again
Arrian's authority. (Strabo, loc. cit.)

for his fleet to ride in and to provide sites for new settlements likely to grow to great wealth and prosperity.

He was further informed of the existence of two islands off the mouth of the Euphrates. One of them lay fairly close, at a distance of, perhaps, fifteen miles from that point on the shore where the river joins the sea. This, the smaller of the two, was densely wooded, and contained a temple of Artemis the regular service of which was performed by the islanders themselves. Deer and wild goats found pasture there, and as they were held sacred to the goddess it was unlawful to hunt them except for the purpose of sacrifice. For this reason only was the ban upon taking them removed. Aristobulus tells us that Alexander decreed that this island should be called Icarus after the Aegean island of that name,[84] upon which the legendary Icarus, son of Daedalus, fell when the wax melted with which his wings were fastened – it melted, the story goes, because he disobeyed his father and, instead of flying low, soared aloft in his folly until the heat of the sun softened the wax, and falling to his death he bequeathed his name to the isle of Icarus and the Icarian Sea.

The second of the two islands, called Tylus,[85] lay off the mouth of the Euphrates at about the distance a running ship can cover in a day and a night. It was of some size, most of it neither wild nor wooded, but fit to produce all sorts of cultivated crops in their proper seasons.

Some of this information Alexander got from Archias, who was sent out in a galley to reconnoitre the coast for the proposed expedition against the Arabs. Archias reached Tylus, but did not venture beyond; Androsthenes,

84. One of the Sporades, west of Samos, now called Nikaria. For the story of Daedalus and Icarus see Ovid, *Metamorphoses* 2.21–96.

85. The modern Bahrein.

who went in command of another galley, got further,
sailing round a part of the Arabian peninsula,[86] and
Hiero, the shipmaster from Soli, made greater progress
than either. Alexander put him in charge of a third galley
and gave him instructions to circumnavigate the whole
peninsula as far as the Egyptian town of Heröopolis on
the Red Sea. But even he found his courage fail him,
though he had sailed round the greater part of the Arabian
coast; he turned back, and stated in his report to Alexander that the peninsula was of immense size, nearly as
big as India, and that a great headland ran far out into the
ocean.[87] This headland had, indeed, been sighted at no
great distance by Nearchus' men on their voyage from
India, before they altered course for the Persian Gulf, and
they were on the point of crossing over to it, as Onesicritus the pilot advised them to do; Nearchus, however,
says in his account of the voyage[88] that he refused his permission, as after completing his survey of the coast of the
Persian Gulf he would have to report to Alexander on the
object of the voyage, and that object was not to explore
the ocean, but to examine the coast and collect information about the coastal peoples and how they lived, the
fertility or otherwise of the various districts, and the
places where anchorages and fresh water were to be
found. And this, he adds, was what enabled Alexander's
navy to come through in safety; it would have been quite
useless to take it across to the desert coast of Arabia, for that
is said to have been the reason for Hiero's turning back.

While the new warships were under construction and

86. The report of his voyage was used by Theophrastus in his
botanical works.

87. This is Ras Mussandam (Maketa), which Nearchus had
sighted from Hormuz.

88. Arrian, *Indica* 32.

the work of dredging the harbour proceeded, Alexander sailed from Babylon down the Euphrates to the river known as Pallacopas, about 100 miles down-stream from the city. The Pallacopas is not actually a river rising from an independent source, but a canal leading off from the Euphrates.[89] Now the Euphrates, which rises in the mountains of Armenia, is in winter a shallowish river and runs well within its banks, but in spring, and especially round about the summer solstice, its volume is greatly increased by the melting of the snow in the Armenian mountains, so that the water, rising above the level of its banks, floods the neighbouring Assyrian plains. At least, this flooding would inevitably occur were it not for the cutting by which its waters are diverted along the Palla-copas into the marshes and lakes which continue from that point almost into Arabia, and passing thence over a vast area of swampy land, finally reach the sea by a num-ber of ill-defined channels.

In autumn, after the snows have melted, the level of the Euphrates drops, yet even so much of its water continues to find its way along the canal into the lakes; thus, unless the canal were closed by a sluice, to block the entrance of the river-water and allow it to flow along its proper channel, it would, at this season of the year, empty the Euphrates completely, and so prevent the irrigation of the Assyrian plains. The construction of such a sluice was undertaken by the governor of Babylonia; it proved a tremendous task and the result was unsuccessful, as the soil at that point is mostly soft, wet clay which is easily penetrated by the water of the river. Consequently it was no easy matter to keep it from percolating into the canal, though for three months over 10,000 Assyrian workmen were kept on the job.

89. It entered the Persian Gulf near Teredon.

When these facts came to Alexander's knowledge, he was anxious to do something to improve Assyria's prospects. Accordingly, he proposed to construct a really efficient sluice at the junction of the canal and the river; however, at a spot some four miles lower down he observed that the soil was of a harder and stonier nature, and it occurred to him that if a new cutting were carried from that point into the Pallacopas canal, the problem might be better solved, for the water would be unable to penetrate the hard, impermeable ground, and could easily be shut off by the sluice at the proper times.

This, then, was the project which took Alexander to the Pallacopas, and down the canal to the lakes in the direction of Arabia.[90] Happening to observe a good site, he built and fortified a new town and settled some of the Greek mercenaries in it, making up the numbers with volunteers and men who were either incapacitated or too old for active service.[91]

It now seemed that he had proved the Chaldaeans' prophecy to be nonsense. They had foretold disaster in Babylon; none had occurred. He had marched safely out of the city before any mischance could catch him. Accordingly, with renewed confidence he sailed again for the lakes, proceeding to the southward. Some of his ships went astray among the narrow channels through the lakes and swamps, and he had to send them a pilot to get them back into the main stream.

The greater number of the tombs of the Assyrian kings were built in the lakes and marshland, and the story goes that Alexander, while his vessel with himself at the helm

90. cf. Strabo 16.1.9–11.

91. About a year earlier (April/May 324) he had founded an Alexandria (the later Charax) between the mouths of the Tigris and the Eulaeus; see Pliny, *Natural History* 6.138.

was passing through, was wearing a sun hat, bound with the diadem or band, signifying royalty. Suddenly a strong gust of wind blew the hat off, which fell into the water, but the light band went flying away and caught on a reed in a reed-bed near one of the ancient royal tombs. This in itself was a presage, but there was more to come: one of the sailors[92] swam off after the hat-band and, finding when he had taken it off the reed that he could not bring it back in his hands without wetting it as he swam, he bound it round his head. Most historians state that Alexander gave the man a talent by way of reward for his willing service, and then had him beheaded in obedience to the prophecy which warned him not to leave untouched the head which had worn the diadem. Aristobulus, however, though he confirms the gift of money, says that the punishment for putting on the band was only a flogging. He adds that the man concerned was one of the Phoenician sailors. Some writers say it was Seleucus, and declare that the incident portended Alexander's death and Seleucus' inheritance of his vast empire – and Seleucus was, in actual fact, the greatest king among Alexander's successors. There can, I think, be no two opinions about this: he had the royallest mind of them all, and, after Alexander himself, ruled over the greatest extent of territory.[93]

Returning to Babylon Alexander found Peucestas back from Persia with 20,000 Persian troops; the force also included a considerable number of Cossaean and Tapurian fighting men, as it was generally supposed that of all Persia's neighbours these peoples produced the best soldiers. Here too he was joined by Philoxenus with troops from Caria, by Menander from Lydia and by

92. 'One of the oarsmen' in the version given by Diodorus (17. 116.5–7). He says nothing of the man's fate.
93. See p. 272 n. 25.

Menidas with the cavalry which had been serving under his command.[94] Successive delegations from Greece also presented themselves, and the delegates, wearing ceremonial wreaths, solemnly approached Alexander and placed golden chaplets on his head, as if their coming were a ritual in honour of a god. But, for all that, his end was near.[95]

He took this opportunity of thanking the Persian troops for their loyalty and obedience to Peucestas, and of congratulating Peucestas himself on his orderly and successful government. The Persians were then enrolled in the various Macedonian units, so that the 'decad' – or section – now consisted of a Macedonian leader, two of his compatriots, one of them a 'double-pay' man, the other a 'ten-stater' man (so called from the pay he received, which was less than that of the 'double-pay' soldiers but more than that of the ordinary rank and file), twelve Persians, and, last, another Macedonian 'ten-stater'.[96] Four Macedonians, that is – the section-leader and three others on extra pay – and twelve Persians. The Macedonians wore native equipment; the Persians were armed either with bows or light javelins.

94. He is last mentioned in the winter of 328/7, when he was sent from Nautaca to Macedonia to bring reinforcements (p. 232).

95. The important point is that the delegates wore ceremonial wreaths. This shows that they were *theoroi*, sacred envoys, and that their states acknowledged Alexander's divinity. Plutarch (*Moralia* 219e) and Aelian (*Varia Historia* 2.19) mention a request by Alexander himself that he be recognized as a god. On this disputed question see J. P. V. D. Balsdon, *Historia* 1950, 383ff. and, better, Wilcken, *Alexander* 209–15.

96. It seems probable that the staters were silver staters, equivalent to the Athenian tetradrachm, and that the 'ten-stater' man received 40 drachmae per month. The 'double-pay' man perhaps received 60 drachmae and the ordinary infantryman 30 per month. A fragmentary inscription (Tod no. 183) fixes the daily rate of pay for a *Hypaspist* in the expeditionary force at 1 drachma.

Fleet exercises were constantly held at this time. There was much rivalry between the trireme crews, besides the few quadriremes which were on the river, what with frequent rowing races and trials of skill for the ships' masters, and prizes for the winners.

Some time before this Alexander had sent special envoys to the shrine of Ammon to inquire what honours he might with propriety pay to the dead Hephaestion. The envoys now returned with the news that Ammon permitted sacrifice to be offered him as to a 'hero' or demigod. Alexander was much pleased, and from that day forward saw that his friend was honoured with a hero's rites.[97]

About this time he wrote a letter to Cleomenes, an official with a bad criminal record in Egypt.[98] In so far as this letter showed his love for Hephaestion, a love which persisted even beyond the grave, I can find no fault with it; but there were other things in it which, I think, were highly reprehensible. The letter contained instructions for the erection of a shrine in Hephaestion's honour in the city of Alexandria, and another on the island of Pharos, where the lighthouse is, both to be of great size and built regardless of expense.[99] Cleomenes was to see to it that

97. For the dispatch of envoys see p. 372. Plutarch (*Alexander* 72.2) agrees with Arrian. Diodorus (17.115.6), however, states that Ammon replied that Hephaestion should be honoured as a god.

98. For Cleomenes' original appointment see pp. 154–5. He had now secured recognition from Alexander as governor (satrap) of Egypt. He had aggravated the famine in Greece (330–26) by monopolizing the export of corn from Egypt and selling it at high prices, and had extorted a large amount of treasure from the priests (Pseudo-Aristotle, *Oeconomica* 2.33; Pseudo-Demosthenes 56.7ff.). Cleomenes was put to death by Ptolemy, who obtained Egypt in the division of provinces after Alexander's death.

99. Pharos lay about a mile off-shore, twenty miles west of the Nile delta. Alexander joined it to the mainland by a mole, thus

the shrines were named after Hephaestion and that all
mercantile contracts should bear his name. So far, so
good – except that too much feeling was wasted upon
matters of too little importance. It is what followed that
I cannot approve. 'If,' the letter went on, 'I find that
everything connected with Hephaestion's shrines in
Egypt is in proper order, I will grant you free pardon for
your former crimes, and henceforward you will suffer no
punishment at my hands for anything you may do, however heinous.' A remark of this kind, in a letter from a
great king to the governor of a large and populous country
– and a scoundrel at that – is, to my mind, shocking.[100]

Alexander's end was now rapidly approaching. Another
portent of what was so soon to come is mentioned by
Aristobulus: while the King was engaged in incorporat-
ing in the various Macedonian units the troops which had
come from Persia with Peucestas and from the coast with
Philoxenus and Menander, he happened to feel thirsty,
and getting up from where he was sitting moved away
and left the royal throne empty. On either side of the
throne stood couches with silver feet, on which his attendants had been sitting, but they had got up and gone away
with the King, and only the guard of eunuchs was left
standing round the throne. Now some fellow or other –
some say a prisoner under open arrest[101] – seeing the
throne and the couches unoccupied, made his way up
through the eunuchs and sat down on the throne. The
eunuchs, according to some Persian custom, did not turn

---

forming the two harbours of Alexandria. The lighthouse was built
by Ptolemy II. See Strabo's description of the city 17.1.6–10.

100. For the genuineness of this letter see *CQ* 1953, 157ff.

101. Plutarch (*Alexander* 73) says the man was a Messenian named
Dionysius. Both he and Diodorus (17.116) says he was a bound
prisoner, whose bonds were loosed 'spontaneously' or by Sarapis
(see p. 393).

him off, but began to tear their clothes and beat their breasts and faces as if something dreadful had happened. Alexander was at once told, and ordered the man to be put to the torture in an endeavour to find out if what he had done was part of a prearranged plot. However, all they could get out of him was, that he acted as he did merely upon impulse.[102] This served to strengthen the seers' forebodings of disaster.

A few days later Alexander was sitting at dinner with his friends and drinking far into the night. He had previously celebrated the customary sacrificial rites with a view to his success,[103] adding certain other offerings in obedience to his seers' advice, and had also, we are told, distributed wine and sacrificial victims among the various units and sections of the army. According to some accounts, when he wished to leave his friends at their drinking and retire to his bedroom, he happened to meet Medius, who at that time was the Companion most closely in his confidence, and Medius asked him to come and continue drinking at his own table, adding that the party would be a merry one.[104]

The royal Diaries[105] confirm the fact that he drank with Medius after his first carouse. Then (they continue) he left

102. Plutarch and Diodorus say he was put to death as a scape-goat.

103. In the forthcoming Arabian expedition.

104. cf. Plutarch, *Alexander* 75.4, Diodorus, 17.117.1.

105. Plutarch (*Alexander* 76) also gives a version of the royal Diary, which he claims is largely verbatim. It differs only in a few details. Aelian (*Varia Historia* 3.23) has a third version which he attributes to Eumenes, who kept the Diary. It bears little resemblance to the other two.

On the question of whether this Diary is an authentic record of Alexander's last days see L. Pearson, *Historia* 3 (1954/55), 429ff., and A. E. Samuel, *Historia* 1965, 1ff.

the table, bathed, and went to sleep, after which he supped
with Medius and again set to drinking; continuing till late
at night. Then, once more, he took a bath, ate a little, and
went straight to sleep, with the fever already on him.

Next day he was carried out on his bed to perform his
daily religious duties as usual, and after the ceremony lay
in the men's quarters till dark. He continued to issue
orders to his officers, instructing those who were to march
by land to be ready to start in three days and those who
were going with himself by sea to sail one day later.[106]
From there he was carried on his bed to the river, and
crossed in a boat to the park on the further side, where he
took another bath and rested. Next day he bathed again
and offered sacrifice as usual, after which he went to lie
down in his room, where he chatted to Medius and gave
orders for his officers to report to him early next morning.
Then he took a little food, returned to his room, and lay
all night in a fever. The following morning he bathed and
offered sacrifice, and then issued to Nearchus and the
other officers detailed instructions about the voyage, now
due to start in two days' time. Next day he bathed again,
went through his regular religious duties, and was afterwards in constant fever. None the less he sent for his staff
as usual and gave them further instructions on their preparations for sailing. In the evening, after another bath,
his condition was grave, and the following morning he
was moved to the building near the swimming-pool. He
offered sacrifice, and, in spite of his increasing weakness,
sent for his senior officers and repeated his orders for the
expedition. The day after that he just managed to have
himself carried to his place of prayer, and after the ceremony still continued, in spite of his weakness, to issue
instructions to his staff. Another day passed. Now very

106. On the Arabian expedition.

seriously ill, he still refused to neglect his religious duties; he gave orders, however, that his senior officers should wait in the court, and the battalion and company commanders outside his door. Then, his condition already desperate, he was moved from the park back to the palace. He recognized his officers when they entered his room but could no longer speak to them. From that moment until the end he uttered no word. That night and the following day, and for the next twenty-four hours, he remained in a high fever.

These details are all to be found in the Diaries. It is further recorded in these documents that the soldiers were passionately eager to see him; some hoped for a sight of him while he was still alive; others wished to see his body, for a report had gone round that he was already dead, and they suspected, I fancy, that his death was being concealed by his guards. But nothing could keep them from a sight of him, and the motive in almost every heart was grief and a sort of helpless bewilderment at the thought of losing their king. Lying speechless as the men filed by, he yet struggled to raise his head, and in his eyes there was a look of recognition for each individual as he passed. The Diaries say that Peitho, Attalus, Demophon, and Peucestas, together with Cleomenes, Menidas, and Seleucus,[107] spent the night in the temple of Serapis[108]

107. Demophon and Cleomenes were Greek seers, the remainder distinguished Macedonians, Attalus being a battalion-commander and Perdiccas' brother-in-law.

108. It is usually held that Sarapis (or Serapis) was a creation of Ptolemy I and that the god called Serapis here must have been a god with a similar name or possessing a similar function, e.g. Bel (Marduk). On Sarapis see W. W. Tarn and G. T. Griffith, *Hellenistic Civilisation* (3rd edn), 356. C. B. Welles (*Historia* 1962 283ff.) however, argues that Alexander found a cult of Sarapis already existing in Egypt and carried it to the East with him.

and asked the God if it would be better for Alexander to be carried into the temple himself, in order to pray there and perhaps recover; but the God forbade it, and declared it would be better for him if he stayed where he was. The God's command was made public, and soon afterwards Alexander died – this, after all, being the 'better' thing.

The accounts of both Ptolemy and Aristobulus end at this point. Other writers have added that the high officers most closely in his confidence asked him to name his successor, and that Alexander's reply was 'the best man'.[109] There is also a story that he went on to say that he knew very well there would be funeral 'games' in good earnest after he was dead.

I am aware that much else has been written about Alexander's death: for instance, that Antipater sent him some medicine which had been tampered with and that he took it, with fatal results.[110] Aristotle is supposed to have made up this drug, because he was already afraid of Alexander on account of Callisthenes' death, and Antipater's son Cassander is said to have brought it. Some accounts declare that he brought it in a mule's hoof,[111] and that it was given Alexander by Cassander's younger brother Iollas, who was his cup-bearer and had been hurt by him in some way shortly before his death; others state that Medius, who

109. This may equally well be rendered 'the strongest'. See Diodorus (17.117.4–5) and Curtius (10.5.4–5), who relate that he handed his ring to Perdiccas.

110. See Diodorus 17.118; Curtius 10.10. 14ff; Plutarch, *Alexander* 77.2ff.

111. Nothing else could contain the poison. This was often said to be water from the R. Styx, which rose near Nonacris in the north of Arcadia; see, e.g., Pliny, *Natural History* 30.149; Pausanias 8.17.6.

The story that Alexander was poisoned is not generally believed. See, however, R. D. Milns, *Alexander the Great* (London, 1968) 255–8, who suggests that the poison was a low-level dose of strychnine.

was Iollas' lover, had a hand in it, and support that view by the fact that it was Medius who invited Alexander to the drinking-party – he felt a sharp pain after draining the cup, and left the party in consequence of it.[112] One writer has even had the face to declare that when he knew his death was imminent he went out with the intention of throwing himself into the Euphrates, in order to disappear without trace and make it easier for posterity to believe that one of the gods was his father and he had gone away to join them. His wife Roxane, this writer continues, happened to see him as he left the building, and stopped him, whereupon he gave a great cry and bitterly reproached her for grudging him the eternal fame of divine birth. I do not wish to appear ignorant of these stories; but stories they are – I put them down as such and do not expect them to be believed.

Alexander died in the 114th Olympiad, in the archonship of Hegesias at Athens.[113] He lived, as Aristobulus tells us, thirty-two years and eight months, and reigned twelve years and eight months.[114] He had great personal beauty, invincible power of endurance, and a keen intellect; he was brave and adventurous, strict in the observance of his religious duties, and hungry for fame. Most temperate in the pleasures of the body, his passion was for glory only, and in that he was insatiable. He had an uncanny instinct for the right course in a difficult and

112. For the 'cup of Hercules' see Diodorus 17.117.1–2 (with Welles's note in the Loeb edition). The story is explicitly denied by Plutarch (*Alexander* 75.5).

113. His death is now known to have occurred on 10 June 323 B.C.

114. More probably, he was nearly 33 – Plutarch (*Alexander* 3.5.) dates his birth to about 20 July 356 – and reigned about 13 years. For the date of his accession – probably June 336 – see Welles's note on Diodorus 17.117.5.

complex situation, and was most happy in his deductions
from observed facts. In arming and equipping troops and in
his military dispositions he was always masterly. Noble
indeed was his power of inspiring his men, of filling them
with confidence, and, in the moment of danger, of sweeping away their fear by the spectacle of his own fearlessness.
When risks had to be taken, he took them with the utmost boldness, and his ability to seize the moment for a
swift blow, before his enemy had any suspicion of what
was coming, was beyond praise. No cheat or liar ever
caught him off his guard, and both his word and his bond
were inviolable. Spending but little on his own pleasures,
he poured out his money without stint for the benefit of
his friends.[115]

Doubtless, in the passion of the moment Alexander
sometimes erred; it is true he took some steps towards the
pomp and arrogance of the Asiatic kings: but I, at least,
cannot feel that such errors were very heinous, if the circumstances are taken fairly into consideration. For, after
all, he was young; the chain of his successes was unbroken, and, like all kings, past, present, and to come, he
was surrounded by courtiers who spoke to please, regardless of what evil their words might do. On the other hand,
I do indeed know that Alexander, of all the monarchs of
old, was the only one who had the nobility of heart to be
sorry for his mistakes. Most people, if they know they
have done wrong, foolishly suppose they can conceal
their error by defending it, and finding a justification for
it; but in my belief there is only one medicine for an evil
deed, and that is for the guilty man to admit his guilt and
show that he is sorry for it. Such an admission will make
the consequences easier for the victim to bear, and the
guilty man himself, by plainly showing his distress at

115. For examples see Plutarch, *Alexander* 39.

former transgressions, will find good grounds of hope for avoiding similar transgressions in the future.

Nor do I think that Alexander's claim to a divine origin was a very serious fault – in any case, it may well have been a mere device to magnify his consequence in the eyes of his subjects.[116] In point of fact I account him as great a king as Minos or Aeacus or Rhadamanthus, whose claims to be sons of Zeus were not felt by the men of old to be in any way dangerously arrogant; and the same may be said of Theseus' claim to be the son of Poseidon and Ion's to be son of Apollo. Surely, too, his adoption of Persian dress was, like his claim to divine birth, a matter of policy: by it he hoped to bring the Eastern nations to feel that they had a king who was not wholly a foreigner, and to indicate to his own countrymen his desire to move away from the harsh traditional arrogance of Macedonia. That was also, no doubt, the reason why he included a proportion of Persian troops (the so-called 'Golden Apples', for instance) in Macedonian units, and made Persian noblemen officers in his crack native regiments. As for his reputed heavy drinking, Aristobulus declares that his drinking bouts were prolonged not for their own sake – for he was never, in fact, a heavy drinker – but simply because he enjoyed the companionship of his friends.[117]

Anyone who belittles Alexander has no right to do so on the evidence only of what merits censure in him; he must base his criticism on a comprehensive view of his whole life and career. But let such a person, if blackguard

116. Plutarch (*Alexander* 28.6) attributes the same motive to Alexander in his claim to be son of Zeus. See, however, *CQ* 1953, 151 ff. for the significance of Alexander's letter to the Athenians quoted by Plutarch in the same chapter.

117. Arrian has earlier (p. 214) remarked on Alexander's 'barbaric' drinking.

Alexander he must, first compare himself with the object of his abuse: himself, so mean and obscure, and, confronting him, the great King with his unparalleled worldly success, the undisputed monarch of two continents, who spread the power of his name over all the earth. Will he dare to abuse him then, when he knows his own littleness and the triviality of his own pursuits, which, even so, prove too much for his ability?

It is my belief that there was in those days no nation, no city, no single individual beyond the reach of Alexander's name; never in all the world was there another like him, and therefore I cannot but feel that some power more than human was concerned in his birth; indications of this were, moreover, said to be provided at the time of his death by oracles; many people saw visions and had prophetic dreams;[118] and there is the further evidence of the extraordinary way in which he is held, as no mere man could be, in honour and remembrance. Even today, when so many years have passed, there have been oracles, all tending to his glory, delivered to the people of Macedon.

In the course of this book I have, admittedly, found fault with some of the things which Alexander did, but of the man himself I am not ashamed to express ungrudging admiration. Where I have criticized unfavourably, I have done so because I wished to tell the truth as I saw it, and to enable my readers to profit thereby. Such was the motive which led me to embark upon this History: and I, too, have had God's help in my work.

118. See the stories told by Plutarch (*Alexander* 2).

The Change to Regiments (Hipparchies) in the Companion Cavalry

Arrian says nothing of this change, which has to be deduced from his narrative. The earliest mention of 'regiments', apart from one instance in the first year of the campaign (1.24.3), occurs in the autumn of 329, when Ptolemy is sent with a force including 'three regiments of Companions' to arrest Bessus (3.29.7). Later in the same year in a great battle against the Scythians we again hear of regiments of the Companions (4.4.6–7). However, in his valuable article on 'Alexander's Macedonian Cavalry' Professor Brunt has suggested that Arrian uses the term 'regiment' anachronistically, since at this time Hephaestion and Black Cleitus shared the command of the Companions and 'it is obvious that so long as there were only one or two "hipparchs" the term "hipparchy" was inappropriate for each of the eight units in which the Companions were still formed'.[1] He suggests that the change took place after the murder of Cleitus late in 328, and was indeed a consequence of it, since Alexander considered it dangerous to entrust so large and important a body of cavalry to a single commander who might resent, as Cleitus had done, his adoption of Persian dress and Persian court practice. This is an attractive suggestion. Unfortunately, a close examination of Arrian's narrative of the Scythian battle demonstrates, in my opinion beyond doubt, that the 'regiments' were already in existence in 329, well before Cleitus' death. In this battle Alexander first launched against the Scythians 'a regiment (hipparchy) of mercenary cavalry and the four squadrons (ilai) of Lancers', and later he ordered to charge them 'three regiments of Companions and all the mounted javelin-men', while he himself charged at full speed 'with his squadrons in column'. This is a careful and detailed description, evidently

1. *JHS* 83 (1963), 27–46. The quotation occurs on page 29.

based on Ptolemy, and it is inconceivable that Arrian confused 'squadrons' and 'regiments'.[2] In fact, we do not know
when the change took place. The last mention of the Royal
squadron occurs late in 331 at the Persian Gates (3.18.5), in
conjunction with the obscure term 'tetrarchy' for a body of
cavalry. Later, first in 327 (4.24.1), we hear of a bodyguard
(*agema*), evidently the same unit as the former Royal squadron.

More important than the date at which regiments were
introduced is the question of their composition, particularly
if, as it seems reasonable to assume, the squadrons remained
at roughly their former strength. For the regiments were
larger units containing two or more squadrons, and it seems
impossible that the heavy Macedonian cavalry can have
provided enough men to fill all the squadrons. It is not disputed that the Companions numbered 1,800 at the start of the
expedition, that a draft of 300 joined Alexander at Gordium
early in 333, and a further 500 soon after Gaugamela late in 331.
Professor Brunt, however, deduces from Polybius (12.19.2)
that 500 more Macedonian cavalry reached Alexander before
the battle of Issus, and regards as probable the arrival of an
additional 500 in 328/7, about the time when the hipparchies
were constituted. In both cases he is mistaken. What Polybius
says is that, according to Callisthenes, 800 cavalry *from Macedonia* reached Alexander before he entered Cilicia, and, as
Callisthenes is calculating the maximum number of cavalry
that Alexander can have had in the battle of Issus, it is clear
that he did not record the arrival of any cavalry except these
800. We may safely conclude that they were the cavalry which
Arrian (1.29.4) records as having joined Alexander at Gordium, 300 Macedonians, 200 Thessalians, and 150 from Elis.
The remaining 150 Arrian omits to mention, perhaps because
they were mercenaries. Brunt considers that Sir William Tarn
has probably shown 'that a seventh infantry battalion was
formed from new Macedonian troops, which Sopolis, Epocillus and Menidas were sent from Nautaca to bring to him

2. As G. T. Griffith has emphasized in 'A Note on the Hipparchies of Alexander' in *JHS* 83 (1963), 68–74, at page 71.

(Arrian 4.18.3).' But Arrian does not mention the arrival of any Macedonian troops after this date and the mission may have been cancelled. Moreover, Professor R. D. Milns has demonstrated[3] that the seventh infantry battalion, which Tarn considers *must* be part of 'the army from Macedonia' that the officers were sent to bring to Alexander, was in existence early in 330. We must conclude, then, that the total of Macedonian heavy cavalry available to Alexander at the end of 331 was 2,600 less losses, which we can only conjecture. Let us say 2,500. Surely more cavalry was required to make up the new regiments. If the 'Scouts' or 'Lancers' were Macedonians, it is reasonable to suggest, as Brunt does, that they might have been incorporated in the Companions. But, as we have seen from Arrian (4.4.6–7), they existed, unless Arrian is utterly mistaken, as a separate unit at a time when the regiments had already been formed.

But if the 'Scouts' were not incorporated in the regiments, what cavalry was? Much the most probable solution, it seems to me, is that put forward by G. T. Griffith who suggests that it was the Western Iranian cavalry. As he points out, it is difficult to believe that if Alexander had units of Bactrian and Sogdian cavalry by the end of 328 (4.17.3), at a time when fighting was still going on in this region, he had not called upon the excellent cavalry of Western and Central Iran. Yet it is not until 324 that we hear of this cavalry in Alexander's army, when it is described as 'integrated' into the Companion cavalry. In this passage (7.6.2–5) Arrian lists the various grievances – the arrival of the 30,000 young Persians, the marriages at Susa, the 'orientalism' of Peucestas, Alexander's Median dress – which later led the Macedonians to mutiny at Opis. Professor Brunt has shown that these grievances are of recent origin, and it would seem to follow that their resentment at the 'integration' of Eastern cavalry into the Companions and the enrolment of certain distinguished Persians into the Guard (agema) was also recent. However, immediately

3. In *Greek, Roman and Byzantine Studies* 7(1966), 159–166.

before the mutiny Arrian recapitulates (more briefly) the Macedonian grievances (7.8.2.) 'During this whole campaign', he writes, 'the Macedonians had been vexed by the importation of foreign cavalry into the ranks of the Companions'. 'This whole campaign' must refer to the Indian campaign (or, assuming rhetorical exaggeration, to the entire expedition), certainly not to the period after his return from the East. If, then, Mr Griffith is correct in distinguishing between 'integration' and 'importation' into the Companions, we see two successive stages of the policy which he pursued in general towards the Persians, a policy which finds its clearest expression in his prayer at Opis for 'harmony and fellowship in the empire between Macedonians and Persians'. If he is not correct in making this distinction, and if the two passages in Arrian are 'doublets', as Professor Badian has argued,[4] then it seems probable that, while the final reorganization of the Companions was recent, the grievance felt by the Macedonians at the introduction of Iranians extended several years into the past. This is certainly true of their resentment of Alexander's adoption of Oriental dress.

4. In *JHS* 85 (1965), 160–61.

The Chronology of the Expedition

Arrian dates by the Attic months a number of events, such as
the end of the siege of Tyre, and frequently refers to the
seasons at which Alexander leaves or arrives at a town or district. Exact dating of events is not possible, but with the help
of information provided by other writers, particularly the
geographer Strabo, a reasonably satisfactory chronology can
be reconstructed. References to Arrian and other authorities
are given in brackets.

334	Spring	Invasion of Asia	(1.11.3)
334/3	Winter	Alexander at Gordium	(1.29.3)
333	?Spring	Departure from Gordium	(2.4.1)
	November	Battle of Issus	(2.11.10)
332	Jan.–August	Siege of Tyre	(2.24.6; Plutarch, *Alexander* 24.5)
	Sept.–Oct.	Siege of Gaza	(Diodorus 17.48.7)
	Nov. 14	Alexander enthroned as Pharaoh at Memphis.	
332/1	Winter	Expedition to Siwah	(3.3.4)
331	April 7	Foundation of Alexandria	(Pseudo-Callis-thenes 1.32)*
	Late Spring	Departure from Egypt	(3.6.1)

* The foundation of Alexandria is usually put before the visit to
Siwah on the authority of Arrian. See, however, C. B. Welles in
Historia 1962, 276ff.

331	Sept. 20/21	Eclipse of the moon before Gaugamela.	(3.7.6)
	Oct. 1	Battle of Gaugamela	(Plutarch, *Alexander* 31.8)
330	Jan.–May	Stay at Persepolis	(Plutarch, *Alexander* 37.6)
	Mid May	Burning of the palace	(Curtius 5.6.12)†
	July	Death of Darius III	(3.22.2)
329	Spring	Alexander reaches Hindu Kush.	(Strabo 15.2.10; cf. Arrian 3.28.4)
	Midsummer	Battle against Scythians north of R. Jaxartes.	(4.4.8)
329/8	Midwinter	Alexander at Zariaspa (Bactra)	(4.7.1)
328	?Spring	Advance to R. Oxus	(4.15.7)
328/7	Winter	Alexander at Nautaca	(4.18.2)
327	Beginning of Spring	Attack on Sogdian Rock	(4.18.4)
	End of Spring	Departure from Bactria	(4.22.3)
326	May	Battle of R. Hydaspes	(5.19.3)
326	November	Start of voyage down Hydaspes	(Strabo 15.1.17)
325	July	Arrival at Pattala	(Strabo 15.1.17)
	End August	Alexander leaves Pattala	(6.21.2)
	Sept. 20/21	Nearchus leaves Pattala	(*Indica* 21.1)

† According to Curtius (5.6.12), the burning took place after an expedition against the Mardi which began about April 6 (about the evening setting of the Pleiades) and lasted for 30 days.

325/4	Winter	Alexander in Carmania	(6.28.7)
324	Spring	Alexander arrives at Susa	
324/3	Winter	Campaign against Cossaeans	(7.15.3)
323	Spring	Return to Babylon	(7.15.4)
	June 10	Death of Alexander	(Pseudo-Callisthenes 3.55; Babylonian text).‡

‡ See D. M. Lewis in the *Classical Review* 1969, p. 272, on the reading of Pseudo-Callisthenes.

Bibliography

Comprehensive bibliographies of work on Alexander can be found in the sixth volume of the *Cambridge Ancient History* (1926), G. Glotz and R. Cohen, *Histoire grecque*, Vol. IV, Part I, *Alexandre et le démembrement de son empire* (Paris, 1938), and H. Bengtson, *Griechische Geschichte* (2nd edn, Munich, 1960). Eugene Borza appends a select list of modern books and articles to his reissue of Ulrich Wilcken's *Alexander the Great* (below). The most important contributions of the years 1940 to 1950 are reviewed by R. Andreotti in 'Il problema di Alessandro Magno nella storiografia dell' ultimo decennio' (*Historia*, I, 1950, 583–600), while G. Walser provides an excellent summary of recent Alexander scholarship in 'Zur neuren Forschung über Alexander den Grossen' (1956), reprinted in *Alexander the Great: the Main Problems*, ed. G. T. Griffith (Heffer, 1966). E. Badian's 'Alexander the Great, 1948–67' in *Classical World* 65 (1971) 37ff., 77ff. (now published separately) is an invaluable account of recent work on Alexander. A more comprehensive survey, extending over almost a century, is given by J. Seibert, *Alexander der Grosse* (Darmstadt, 1972).

I give here a selection only of the most important recent writings on Alexander, mainly in English. Those reprinted in *Alexander the Great: the Main Problems* are marked with an asterisk.

GENERAL WORKS ON ALEXANDER

A. R. Burn, *Alexander the Great and the Hellenistic World* (2nd edn, Macmillan, 1962). An excellent introduction.

P. Cloché, *Alexandre le Grand et les essais de fusion entre l'Occident gréco-macédonien et l'Orient* (Neuchâtel, 1953).

Peter Green, *Alexander the Great*, Weidenfeld & Nicolson, 1970 is superbly illustrated and stimulating.

R. D. Milns, *Alexander the Great* (Hale, 1968). An up-to-date account for the general reader.

C. B. Welles, *Alexander and the Hellenistic World* (1970). and the four classics:

G. Radet, *Alexandre le Grand* (6th edn, Paris 1950). Relies excessively on the 'vulgate', but probably undervalued today.

F. Schachermeyr, *Alexander der Grosse, Ingenium und Macht* (Wien, 1949). A brutal Alexander bent on world conquest.

Sir William Tarn, *Alexander the Great*, 2 vols. I. Narrative II. Sources and studies (Cambridge University Press, 1948). An idealized Alexander, which has stimulated much recent work on Alexander, often in disagreement.

Ulrich Wilcken, *Alexander the Great*, trans. G. C. Richards (London, 1932). This, the most sensible modern biography, has been reissued (New York 1967) with valuable notes and an excellent 'Introduction to Alexander Studies', by Eugene Borza.

MACEDONIA, GREECE, AND THE EARLY ALEXANDER

E. Badian, 'The Death of Philip', *Phoenix*, 1963, 244–50.

A. B. Bosworth, 'Philip II and Upper Macedonia', *Classical Quarterly*, 1971, 93–105.

V. Ehrenberg, *Alexander and the Greeks* (Oxford University Press, 1938).

G. T. Griffith, 'The Macedonian Background', *Greece and Rome*, 1965, 125–39.

J. R. Hamilton, 'Alexander's Early Life', *Greece and Rome*, 1965, 117–24.

N. G. L. Hammond, *A History of Greece* (2nd ed., Oxford University Press, 1967).

F. Mitchel, 'Athens in the Age of Alexander', *Greece and Rome*, 1965, 189–204.

T. T. B. Ryder, *Koine Eirene* (Oxford University Press, 1965).

PERSIA AND THE EAST

H. Bengtson, *Persia and the Greeks* (Minerva, 1969).

A. K. Narain, 'Alexander and India', *Greece and Rome*, 1965, 155–65.

A. T. Olmstead, *History of the Persian Empire* (Chicago, 1948).
Sir Aurel Stein, *On Alexander's Track to the Indus* (London, 1929).

MILITARY OPERATIONS

Sir Frank Adcock, *The Greek and Macedonian Art of War* (Berkeley, 1957).

E. Badian, 'Agis III', *Hermes*, 1967, 170–92.

A. R. Burn, 'Notes on Alexander's Campaigns', *JHS*, 1952, 84–91.

A. R. Burn, 'The Generalship of Alexander', *Greece and Rome*, 1965, 140–54.

G. T. Griffith, 'Alexander's Generalship at Gaugamela', *JHS*, 1947, 77–89.

J. R. Hamilton, 'The Cavalry Battle at the Hydaspes', *JHS*, 1956, 26–31.

ADMINISTRATION OF THE EMPIRE

E. Badian, 'Harpalus', *JHS*, 1961, 16–43.

E. Badian, 'The Administration of the Empire', *Greece and Rome*, 1965, 166–82.

E. Badian, 'Alexander the Great and the Greeks of Asia', *Ancient Society and Institutions. Studies Presented to Victor Ehrenberg* (Oxford University Press, 1966), 37–69.

G. T. Griffith, 'Alexander the Great and an experiment in government', *Proceedings of the Cambridge Philological Society*, 1964, 23–39.

RELIGION

*J. P. V. D. Balsdon, 'The "Divinity" of Alexander', *Historia*, 1950, 363–88.

E. A. Fredricksmeyer, 'Alexander, Midas and the Oracle at Gordium', *Classical Philology*, 1961, 160–68.

*J. R. Hamilton, 'Alexander and his "so-called" Father', *Classical Quarterly*, 1953, 151–7.

E. G. Hogarth, 'The Deification of Alexander the Great', *English Historical Review*, 1887, 317–29.

H. W. Parke, *The Oracles of Zeus* (Blackwell, 1967).

ALEXANDER'S INTENTIONS

*E. Badian, 'Alexander The Great and The Unity of Mankind', *Historia*, 1958, 425–44.

E. Badian, 'A King's Notebooks', *Harvard Studies in Classical Philology*, 1968, 183–204.

P. A. Brunt, 'The Aims of Alexander', *Greece and Rome*, 1965, 20–215.

*C. A. Robinson, 'The Extraordinary Ideas of Alexander the Great', *American Historical Review*, 1957, 326–44.

*F. Schachermeyr, 'Die letzten Pläne Alexanders des Grossen' *Jahreshefte des österreichischen archaeologischen Instituts*, 1954, 118–40.

R. Andreotti, 'Die Weltmonarchie Alexanders des Grossen in Überlieferung und geschichtlicher Wirklichkeit', *Saeculum*, 1957, 120–66. With extensive bibliography.

ALEXANDER AND THE HELLENISTIC WORLD

M. I. Rostovtzeff, *The Social and Economic History of the Hellenistic World*, 3 vols. (Oxford University Press, 1941).

Sir William Tarn, *The Greeks in Bactria and India*, 2nd edn (Cambridge University Press, 1951).

Sir William Tarn and G. T. Griffith, *Hellenistic Civilization*, 3rd edn (Arnold, 1952).

C. B. Welles, 'Alexander's Historical Achievement', *Greece and Rome*, 1965, 216–28.

Sir Mortimer Wheeler, *Flames over Persepolis* (London, 1968).

ALEXANDER'S RELATIONS WITH THE MACEDONIANS

E. Badian, 'The Death of Philotas', *Transactions of the American Philological Association*, 1960.

*E. Badian, 'Harpalus', *JHS*, 1961, 16–43.

A. B. Bosworth, 'The Death of Alexander the Great', *Classical Quarterly*, 1971, 112–36.

*T. S. Brown, 'Callisthenes and Alexander', *American Journal of Philology*, 1949, 225–48.

G. T. Griffith, 'Alexander and Antipater in 323 B.C.', *Proceedings of the African Classical Associations*, 1965, 12–17.

Ramón I. Harris, 'The Dilemma of Alexander The Great', *Proceedings of the African Classical Associations*, 1968, 46–54. A psychological study.

ART AND COINAGE

A. R. Bellinger, *Essays on the coinage of Alexander the Great* (Thompson, New York, 1963). Might have come under 'Administration'.

M. Bieber, *Alexander the Great in Greek and Roman Art* (Zeno, Chicago, 1964).

M. Bieber, 'A Portrait of Alexander', *Greece and Rome*, 1965, 183–8. Essentially a summary of the foregoing.

S. Perlman, 'The Coins of Philip II and Alexander the Great and their Pan-hellenic Propaganda', *Numismatic Chronicle*, 1965, 57–67.

ADDENDA

I take the opportunity of this (1976) reprint to add a few general works on Alexander. Interested readers will find in them references to much of the extensive recent periodical literature.

Robin Lane Fox, *Alexander the Great* (London, 1973).

Peter Green, *Alexander of Macedon* (Penguin Books). A revised and enlarged version, with an extensive bibliography, of his *Alexander the Great*.

J. R. Hamilton, *Alexander the Great* (Hutchinson University Library, 1973).

Fritz Schachermeyr, *Alexander der Grosse: Das Problem Seiner Persönlichkeit und Seiner Wirkens* (Wien, 1973). A greatly expanded version of his 1949 book, with additional annotation, appendices, and excellent illustrations.

Sources

ARRIAN

An important event is the reissue of A. G. Roos' Teubner text of Arrian's works, I. The *Anabasis*. II. Scripta Minora (1968), to which Gerhard Wirth has contributed some 50 pages of *Addenda et corrigenda*, as well as substantial bibliographies and, in the case of the *Anabasis*, a list of translations. All of these, unfortunately, are out of print, with the exception of E. I. Robson's Loeb edition based on the antiquated Didot text of 1846 which contains many inaccuracies, some of them important, in the translation. E. J. Chinnock's reliable version (London, Hodder and Stoughton, 1884 and 1893 (with the *Indica*)) is sometimes available second-hand. The only book entirely devoted to Arrian is A. B. Breebaart's *Enige historiografische aspecten van Arrianus' Anabasis Alexandri* (Leiden, 1960) in Dutch with a brief summary in English, although H. Montgomery includes a chapter on Arrian's narrative technique in his *Gedanke und Tat* (Lund, 1965).

The following articles are important:

E. Badian, 'The Eunuch Bagoas', *Classical Quarterly*, 1958, 144–57.

G. W. Bowersock, 'A New Inscription of Arrian', *Greek, Roman and Byzantine Studies*, 1967, 279–80.

P. A. Brunt, 'Persian Accounts of Alexander's Campaigns', *Classical Quarterly*, 1962, 141–55. Brief but perceptive remarks on Arrian's method.

P. A. Stadter, 'Flavius Arrianus: The New Xenophon', *Greek, Roman and Byzantine Studies*, 1967, 155–61.

G. Wirth, 'Anmerkungen zur Arrianbiographie', *Historia*, 1964, 209–45. Deals mainly with the chronology of Arrian's works.

OTHER EXTANT SOURCES

(A list of translations is given in the Introduction, p. 19, n. 6).

DIODORUS

C. B. Welles's edition of Books XVI. 66–XVII in the Loeb series (vol. 8) contains, apart from the fine translation, useful notes on the subject-matter and a discussion of Diodorus' sources.

> E. N. Borza, 'Cleitarchus and Diodorus' Account of Alexander', *Proceedings of The African Classical Associations*, 1968, 25–46, doubts whether Cleitarchus was a major source for Diodorus' 17th Book.

CURTIUS

E. I. McQueen provides a general account in *Latin Biography* (ed. T. A. Dorey, London 1967). Curtius' date has been the subject of much discussion, little of it in English. See especially the following:

> H. U. Instinsky, 'Zur Kontroverse um die Datierung des Curtius Rufus', *Hermes*, 1962, 379–83 (Vespasian).
> D. Korzeniewski, *Dei Zeit des Q. Curtius Rufus*, Diss., (Cologne, 1959) (Augustus).
> G. V. Sumner, 'Curtius Rufus and the *Historiae Alexandri*', *Australasian Universities Modern Language Association*, 1961, 30–39. (Claudius).

PLUTARCH

Konrat Zieglers' excellent Teubner text of the *Alexander* is now available in a revised edition (vol. II.2 of the *Parallel Lives*, 1968).

J. R. Hamilton, *Plutarch Alexander: A Commentary* (Oxford University Press, 1969) discusses most of the historical problems. The introduction contains chapters on Plutarch's life and background, the speeches *de Alexandri fortuna*, the *Parallel Lives*, and the sources and value of the *Alexander*.

R. H. Barrow, *Plutarch and his Times* (Chatto & Windus, 1967) is a good general introduction to Plutarch.

A. J. Gossage contributes a chapter on Plutarch to *Latin Biography* (ed. T. A. Dorey, Routledge, 1967).

P. A. Stadter, *Plutarch's Historical Methods* (Cambridge, Mass., 1965) shows that Plutarch had read the authors he cites.

A. E. Wardman, 'Plutarch and Alexander', *Classical Quarterly*, 1955, 96–107, analyses the *Life* and the speeches *de Alexandri fortuna*.

PRIMARY SOURCES

C. A. Robinson translates the fragments of the Alexander historians in vol. I, Part II of his *History of Alexander the Great* (Providence, R. I. 1953). The texts are collected in F. Jacoby, *Die Fragmente der griechischen Historiker*, IIB, Nos. 117–53, with commentary in IID (Berlin, 1927, 1930).

Lionel Pearson, *The Lost Histories of Alexander the Great* (American Philological Association, 1960) is indispensable. It discusses the six major primary sources at length and is admirably documented. For some valid criticisms see E. Badian, *Gnomon* 1961, 660 ff.

T. S. Brown, *Onesicritus* (Berkeley, 1949) is the only full-scale study of any of these authors. It also treats Nearchus in some detail.

The veracity of *Ptolemy* has been the subject of articles by C. B. Welles, 'The Reliability of Ptolemy as an Historian', *Miscellanea ... A. Rostagni* (Turin, 1963), 101–16, and 'The discovery of Sarapis and the foundation of Alexandria', *Historia*, 1962, 271–98.

R. M. Errington, 'Bias in Ptolemy's History of Alexander', *Classical Quarterly*, 1969, 233–42.

Aristobulus is dealt with by G. Wirth in the course of his 'Anmerkungen zur Arrianbiographie', *Historia*, 1964, pp. 213ff.

*The career of *Callisthenes* and the circumstances of his death have been studied by T. S. Brown, 'Callisthenes and Alexander', *American Journal of Philology*, 1949, 225–48.

T. S. Brown has also discussed the fragments of *Cleitarchus* in 'Clitarchus', *American Journal of Philology*, 1950, 134–55. On the date of Cleitarchus see the following articles:

E. Badian, 'The Date of Clitarchus', *Proceedings of the African Classical Associations*, 1965, 5–11.

J. R. Hamilton, 'Cleitarchus and Aristobulus', *Historia*, 1961, 448–59.

and the Appendix to:

F. Schachermeyr, *Alexander in Babylon* (Wien, 1970).

ALEXANDER'S DIARY (JOURNAL) AND LETTERS

*Lionel Pearson, 'The Diary and Letters of Alexander the Great', *Historia*, 1954/5, 429–55, considers both diary and letters Hellenistic forgeries.

A. E. Samuel, 'Alexander's Royal Journals', *Historia*, 1965, 1–12, argues that the diary (as quoted by Arrian and Plutarch) is a Babylonian chronicle.

A. B. Bosworth, 'The Death of Alexander the Great: Rumour and Propaganda', *Classical Quarterly*, 1971, 112–36, suggests that the diary was 'an original propaganda document' perhaps composed by Eumenes.

J. R. Hamilton, 'The Letters in Plutarch's *Alexander*', *Proceedings of the African Classical Associations*, 1961, 9–20, finds a number of the letters probably genuine.

ADDENDUM

The most important recent article on Arrian is A. B. Bosworth, 'Arrian's Literary Development', *Classical Quarterly*, 1972, 163–85. He argues that Arrian wrote *The Campaigns of Alexander* before beginning his civil and military career, perhaps soon after 115 A.D.

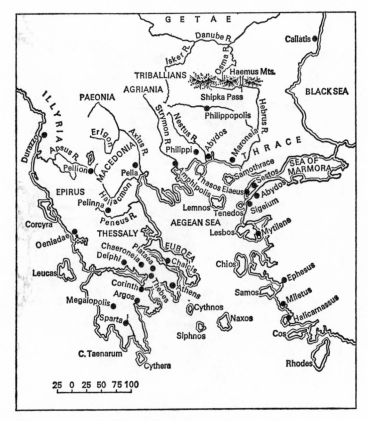

Greece

Alexander's Empire

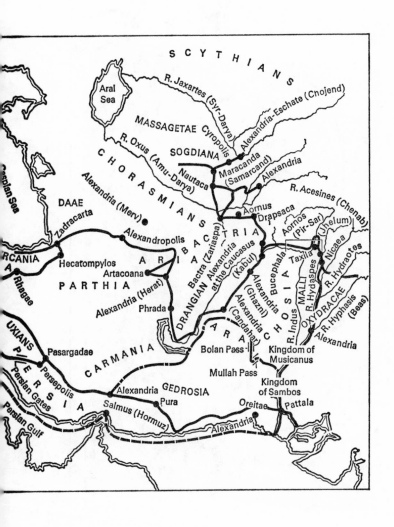

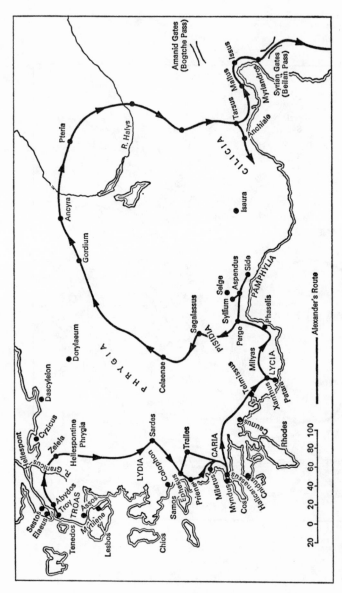

Asia Minor

Index